THE TRINITY AND THE VINDICATION OF CHRISTIAN PARADOX

The Trinity and the Vindication of Christian Paradox

An Interpretation and Refinement of the Theological Apologetic of Cornelius Van Til

B. A. BOSSERMAN

Foreword by
K. SCOTT OLIPHINT

PICKWICK *Publications* • Eugene, Oregon

THE TRINITY AND THE VINDICATION OF CHRISTIAN PARADOX
An Interpretation and Refinement of the Theological Apologetic of Cornelius Van Til

Pickwick Publications
An Imprint of Wipf and Stock Publishers
199 W. 8th Ave., Suite 3
Eugene, OR 97401

www.wipfandstock.com

ISBN 13: 978-1-49822-650-9

Cataloguing-in-Publication Data

Bosserman, B. A.

The Trinity and the vindication of Christian paradox : an interpretation and refinement of the theological apologetic of Cornelius Van Til / B. A. Bosserman, with a foreword by K. Scott Oliphint

xxiv + 268 p. ; 23 cm. Includes bibliographical references.

ISBN 13: 978-1-49822-650-9

1. Van Til, Cornelius, 1895–1987. 2. Apologetics. 3. Trinity. 4. Christianity—Philosophy. I. Oliphint, K. Scott. II. Title.

BX9225.V37 B788 2014

To Thomas George Bossserman
Who taught me to love the biblical Scriptures
The Triune God from whom they came
And to whom they bear witness

Contents

Illustrations and Tables

Foreword

As one who has labored for decades to understand, articulate, and *re*-articulate Cornelius Van Til's Reformed approach to the discipline of apologetics, I have normally been aware of other scholars in the field whose concerns have been coincident with mine. One day, I received an email from Brant Bosserman, with his doctoral dissertation attached, from which this work is taken. I had never heard of Dr. Bosserman, so my instinct was to do (unfortunately) what I do with virtually all emails of this nature—consign it to the digital trash bin. I rarely have time to read what is required of me, much less what comes to me "out of the blue." But, since this work was focused on Van Til's thought, I decided that I should at least skim it.

My attempt to skim Dr. Bosserman's dissertation turned to serious and concentrated reading. I read every page, some more than once. By the time I had finished this work, I recognized that Dr. Bosserman had successfully focused his energies on a topic that is not only central to the Christian faith, but that is central to all of Van Til's thought. I set this work aside and thought, "Why hasn't this been done before?"

There are a number of responses to that question. One response would be that, though Van Til's apologetic method has its genesis in an affirmation of the ontological Trinity, many of the criticisms of Van Til's thought have, historically, focused on other things. For example, there has been, and continues to be, serious misunderstandings about what, exactly, Van Til means by the notion of "presupposition." There have been those who have seen Van Til's rejection of the standard formulations of the "theistic proofs" as a concession to fideism. There have been, in other words, pressing matters of clarity that needed, and still need, to be addressed. Whatever the reasons, however, the topic that is given its due herein is not by any means tangential to Van Til's thinking; it is the warp and woof of everything that he believed, taught and wrote.

Without question, the most radical, revolutionary, requisite and Reformed aspect of the apologetic set forth by Van Til was his insistence that one's defense of Christianity must begin with the ontological Trinity. No apologist prior to him had argued such a thing, in part because it meant that the discipline of apologetics must self-consciously begin with Scripture. So, says Van Til:

> [A] consistently Christian method of apologetic argument, in agreement with its own basic conception of the starting point, must be by presupposition. To argue by presupposition is to indicate what are the epistemological and metaphysical principles that underlie and control one's method. The Reformed apologist will frankly admit that his own methodology presupposes the truth of Christian theism. Basic to all the doctrines of Christian theism is that of the self-contained God, or, if we wish, that of the ontological trinity. It is this notion of the ontological trinity that ultimately controls a truly Christian methodology. Based upon this notion of the ontological trinity and consistent with it, is the concept of the counsel of God according to which all things in the created world are regulated.[1]

Everything that Van Til wrote and taught has its center in the distinctly Christian, biblical truth of God's Triunity. The fact that God is One in Three must take its rightful place in the theology of any Christian, and especially any Reformed Christian. Not only so, but as goes one's theology, so ought to go one's apologetic; a Trinitarian theology demands a Trinitarian apologetic as well.

But, in spite of Van Til's consistent emphasis throughout his career and his writings, the fact of God's Triunity has not yet ascended to its rightful place, especially in the area of a Christian defense of the faith, and the theology that must undergird that defense. Generally speaking, when mention is made of Van Til's emphasis on the Trinity, the discussion usually turns to the philosophical problem of the "one and the many." Aside from that, little is said, and even less is elaborated.

One can peruse the books and writings of authors who follow in Van Til's line (including mine!) and there will not be a primary and focused articulation of the Trinity, and the implications of that doctrine, in virtually any of them. There is "honorable mention" made in most works, and some have wanted to move *from* that doctrine *to* possible implications, but none of us has, in my opinion, drawn out the deep and rich entailments that a rich, robust, Reformed doctrine of the Trinity requires for the way that we

1. DF4, 121–22.

think about the world, about our theology, and about apologetics. This is not as it should be.

We owe Dr. Bosserman a debt of deep gratitude for mounting the difficulties of Van Til's Trinitarian thought, grabbing the reins, spurring it in the side, and moving it forward, as he guides us through the trail of the rich and radical contours that have otherwise been lying pent up and dormant, virtually hidden from view.

With the pathway now clearer because of Dr. Bosserman's work, those of us who seek to follow in Van Til's line can better recognize its direction, as well as its boundaries. There will be more brush to clear along the way; a work of this depth and breadth is bound to have a few briars and brambles still remaining in the path. But the Trinitarian trail, mapped out by Van Til, has now been extensively trod. Its end has not been reached, and we may want to sidestep it in places in order to mark off a better side-path, but wisdom points to the trail Dr. Bosserman has blazed as the best place to begin.

K. Scott Oliphint
Professor of Apologetics and Systematic Theology,
Westminster Theological Seminary

Acknowledgments

This is based on a thesis originally submitted to the University of Bangor for the award of Doctor of Philosophy in 2011. Many individuals are deserving of thanks for aiding me to complete that initial project. I wish to thank first of all Dr. Keith Warrington, and especially Professor Julian Ward for their invaluable critique, guidance, and encouragement in the production of the present manuscript. I also thank my father and mother, Tom and Marilyn Bosserman, and sister and brother in-law, Noelle and Jon Baylor for their regular prayer, support, and interest in this project; my brother Dustin Bosserman for thoroughly editing this thesis and engaging its main ideas, despite his fundamental disagreement with Christian theism; and the many theologians who have contributed to Van Til scholarship—James N. Anderson, John M. Frame, K. Scott Oliphint, Vern S. Poythress, Ralph Allan Smith, and Lane G. Tipton—whose influence, although from a distance in the initial production of my thesis, is thoroughly reflected in this manuscript. A special thanks to K. Scott Oliphint, James Anderson, Ralph Alan Smith, and my examiner Daniel J. Hill for their willingness to read my manuscript, and to offer insights as to how I might modify and/or better develop my main arguments. Second only to the Lord Himself, the author is thankful to his children Nicea, Chalcedon, and Augustine, and most of all to his wife Heather Bosserman for the many sacrifices that they have made on account of this project, and their unceasing faith that the Lord would bring it to completion.

Introduction

Christian thinkers throughout the ages have felt the burden to guard and develop what often seem to be three competing ideals—the systematic harmony of Christian doctrine (Luke 24:44), the novelty of certain paradoxical doctrines (John 6:52–60), and the possibility of a robust Christian apologetic (Acts 17:31). All too often, however, brilliant theologians have hardily embraced two out of the three above-mentioned aims, only to be frustrated by the third. For example, those who have proven to be capable defenders and organizers of Christian theology have at times betrayed embarrassment about apparently contradictory doctrines such as the Trinity, the dual nature of Christ, the compatibility of divine sovereignty and human responsibility, etc. Among those who resist the temptation of heretical resolutions to such paradoxes, a common strategy is to settle with an unhappy compromise between an apologetic where the distinctive Christian doctrines play no significant role, and a class of "supernatural" mysteries that admit for no rational proof. Other theologians have reveled in the mysterious truths of Christianity and set them up as the centerpieces of the Christian system, but flatly disparaged the responsibility to produce a compelling defense of Christianity. And still a third group has taken advantage of theological paradoxes as apologetic tools that possess an inherent capacity to illuminate the absurdity of the human situation, but only so long as we resist the temptation to capture their essential significance as parts of a static system.

Against the backdrop of the historical tension between theological system, paradox, and apologetics, Dr. Cornelius Van Til stands out as anomalous, if only for the harmony between the three ideals that he aspired to engender. Although he spent the bulk of his career occupying the chair of apologetics at Westminster seminary, Van Til's students have long recognized his profundity as a theologian and Christian philosopher. A military general devotes himself to assessing the strategic advantages of his own position and the weaknesses of his opponent's. Likewise, Van Til was preoccupied both with the nature of the Reformed theological system, and the details of secular philosophies. Van Til's novel conclusion was that certain theological paradoxes, such as the doctrine of the ontological Trinity are essential to the coherence of Christian theology, and to the potency and validity of a Christian apologetic. His proposed "Copernican shift" involved the claim that genuine knowledge must revolve around the Triune God—the ideal of unity in difference—and His revelation concerning the proper aims and boundaries of human comprehension. To be specific, Van Til held that nothing about reality can be known truly, except as it is understood as an expression of God's eternal plan for the cosmos, and unless it is appreciated as accessible to the human mind through the mediation of the Triune God, the very archetype of harmony in difference. The proof for this Christian position turns on the impossibility of its pagan and secular alternatives, which cannot scale the enduring one-many problem of philosophy. So long as the unbeliever carries on as if his principles are able to govern facts; as if his intellect makes contact with reality; as if there is a proper and productive order for society, etc., he betrays his dependence on the Triune God. For, the history of philosophy has only confirmed man's[2] incapacity to transcend himself, and directly confirm that reality is marked by (much less headed for more profound degrees of) the sort of harmony that is generally conducive to human life and reasoning. Only the God Who embodies perfect unity and difference in Himself, and exhaustively sustains the creation as His analogue can authoritatively instill, and further, justify human confidence about such matters. Although the Trinity is unmistakably paradoxical, renewed acquaintance with Him through the saving work of the Father, the Son, and the Holy Spirit is the precondition of knowledge. Counterintuitive as it may be, genuine coherence in theology (and every realm of inquiry), a valid and compelling apologetic, and honor for Christian paradox can only be upheld if the three are allowed to qualify and interpenetrate one another.

If nothing else Van Til's vigorous claims have caught the attention of other Christian thinkers. And yet, Van Til's ambiguities, sparsely developed inferences, and wandering writing style have led many readers to applaud his spirit but to reject his more ostentatious claims. Still others simply deride his project as basically confused. Arguably, the basic difficulty with Van Til's theological-apologetic is that the alleged "harmony" between systematic knowledge, apologetics, and paradox appears to devolve into a procedure

2. In agreement with a handful of contemporary Christian and secular philosophers, the present author is convinced that when referring to persons without regard for their sex, it is preferable to use masculine nouns and pronouns rather than feminine nouns and pronouns, or both together. Cf. Bonjour and Sosa, *Epistemic Justification*, 11 n. 5; Frame, *The Doctrine of the Knowledge of God*, xvi–xvii.

of: (a) relying on the laws of logic when convenient (in apologetic critiques); (b) setting logic aside when inconvenient (with respect to Christian paradox); (c) somehow using the doctrine of the Trinity as a license, and the biblical Scriptures as a guide for when to carry out (a) or (b); and then (d) designating (a), (b), and (c) a "systematic method." Supposing that such a representation were accurate, Van Til's "systematic" reasoning would be nothing more than a haphazard procedure that fails to foster, and even militates against any sort of logical coherence. It would not at all be clear how or why the Christian apologist's demand for logical consistency from his opponents, alongside his own insistence on the right to appeal to mystery could not be mimicked by advocates of any worldview. And, far from honoring the profundity of the doctrine of the Trinity and safeguarding Christian paradox, it would make the Trinity into a ground for breaking Christ's command to treat others as we would hope to be treated (Matt 7:12).

Given not only how widespread, but also how grave the above interpretation of Van Til happens to be, the present author aims to inject clarity into the situation by identifying Van Til's genuine triumphs and his relative failures, and then offering a rectification of the latter. In order to accomplish these ends the argument passes through four stages. The first part begins with a thoroughgoing examination of the three schools of thought which were the most influential on Van Til, namely Old Princeton Seminary (ch. 1), Old Amsterdam Seminary (ch. 2), and absolute idealist philosophy (ch. 3). Identification of the guiding presuppositions and collective aims of each school, as well as an explanation of their theological and philosophical terminology is essential to developing an accurate understanding of Van Til's position. Even more pertinent is an understanding of how Van Til believed he was able to preserve the great theological and philosophical insights of his forbearers, while overcoming their latent tendencies toward rationalism and irrationalism. Thus, even at the stage of historical analysis, it is necessary to register Van Til's main critiques of each school.

The second part contains a systematic statement of Van Til's Trinitarian apologetic (ch. 4), epistemology (ch. 5 and 6), and theology (ch. 7). The chief insight offered by Van Til pertains to how the doctrine of the Trinity supplies a personalist solution to the ever-reoccurring one-many problem of philosophy. Properly speaking, the one-many problem pertains to how universals may overlap with historical particulars. But, in its broadest import, the one-many problem lies at the base of questions concerning how subjects may intelligibly relate to objects; governments and citizens may live together harmoniously; ethical norms may be relevant to diverse situations; etc. The Trinity solves the problem, not as a theoretical explanation for how universal principles and ideas control matters of fact, but as a personal

Authority Who is a perfect harmony of unity and diversity in Himself, and thus uniquely qualified to guide man in developing an analogous harmony in his own life and thought. Apologetically, the Trinitarian perspective carries with it an illuminating diagnosis of sinful thinking as the self-defeating attempt to treat principles found in creation, rather than the Creator, as the ultimate sources of unity and/or diversity in reality. In terms of systematic theology, the doctrine of the Trinity proves to foster the sort of coherence between Christian doctrines after which unbelievers may only grope. And epistemologically, a Trinitarian theology implies a theory of knowledge where a given human perspective is true only if it reflects the mind of God, and justified only if that man's mind has been reoriented to God through the saving work and revelation of Jesus Christ and the Holy Spirit. The genius of Van Til's position consists in the fact that the epistemology derived from the Triune God and His Word, requires a uniquely Christian interpretation of the laws of logic that renders Christian paradoxes true, and exposes non-Christian perspectives as genuine contradictions. Those who accept the biblical distinction between two fundamentally different sorts of beings—the Creator and his creation—ought to be keen to the fact that the laws of identity and contradiction do not apply to everything in the same fashion, such that all things are self-identical, and incompatible with certain other things, in the same way. The only course for determining, for example, whether perfect deity and perfect humanity may exist together in the single person of Christ is by discerning whether such a doctrine is possible or necessary within the boundaries of a concrete, systematic worldview. To be specific, Christian paradoxes are vindicated as true by virtue of the fact that (a) their supposedly conflicting elements or "poles" imply one another in a discernible fashion when set in the light of the Christian system; and (b) the paradox, in return, enhances the internal coherence of the Christian system. Nevertheless, these doctrines rightfully retain the epithet "paradox" because they never cease to challenge our day-to-day applications of certain concepts, and squarely conflict with the (widely accepted) logic that would exalt our mundane notions of identify and contradiction as standards by which we may judge God. Finally, all opposition to the Christian system and its mode of reasoning may be rejected as resting on a genuine self-contradiction, namely, that of attempting to level rational arguments against the Creator when one's godless (Trinity-less) presuppositions undermine the very possibility of rational discourse.

Having provisionally vindicated the heart of Van Til's system we return, in the third part, to the negative caricature of his position in order to discover its source, and in order to identify the extent of its validity (ch. 8). We validate the charge not only that Van Til's better insights are obscured by his failure to develop their implications in a focused manner, but that the same oversights have actually had an adverse effect on the feasibility of his fundamental claims. Chiefly, Van Til fails to employ his own logic of implication to the extent of proving that the oneness and threeness, as opposed to mere many-ness of God mutually imply one another, and are equally indispensable to the harmony of created reality. As a result, an arbitrary element appears to infiltrate the heart of the Christian system in such a way that it is difficult to distinguish it from the irrationalism of those secular systems of thought that Van Til critiques so relentlessly. Furthermore, despite the brilliant developments supplied by several schools of thought that were inspired by, or preoccupied with similar concerns as Van Til, each one falls short of clarifying and expounding his concept of a "Christian" logic of implication, much less drawing out the import of a specifically *Tri*nitarian worldview.

Finally, in the fourth part the present author offers his own positive exposition of the Christian system according to a refined application of Van Til's method of implication. A detailed application of this method brings to light the manner in which (a) the poles of Christian paradoxes logically imply one another, and the Christian system as a whole; (b) non-Christian paradoxes and systems of thought represent genuinely self-defeating contradictions; and (c) how the above-mentioned procedure is the exclusive property of Trinitarian Christianity. The Trinity is the first among the Christian paradoxes that are vindicated in the manner described (ch. 9). The argument turns on the scriptural-covenantal observation that God's self-definition need not only exist through personal distinctions (so that God is *multi*-personal), but that every personal distinction in the Godhead must be facilitated by, and appear within the overarching context of a third, and only a third person. For, if the number of divine persons were decreased to two, then the relationship between those two persons would have to appear within an impersonalist void, since there is no third, divine and personal context to be found. If the number of divine persons were multiplied beyond three, then the relationship between any two divine persons would have to be facilitated by an additional "group" of divine persons (which is not, properly speaking, a "person"). Each individual person of the Trinity would fail to comprehend the entire divine life in and by Himself, and that which comprehended the whole of the Godhead and his self-relationship would not be a person, but an impersonal dynamic. Hence, in the Christian system, where God is a personal Absolute, it can be concluded that the oneness and threeness of God mutually necessitate one another. Utilizing a similar methodology, the apparently conflicting poles of eight additional paradoxes of the Reformed faith are proven to imply one another, and once combined, to form a coherent system together. These paradoxes include, (1) the order and equality of divine persons; (2) the simplicity and multiplicity of the divine attributes; (3) divine immutability and temporal creation; (4) the finitude and complexity of creation; (5) the analogical and objective character of human knowledge; (6) the sovereignty of God and the freedom of man; (7) the original goodness of man and his capacity for sin; and (8) the sinlessness and genuine humanity of Jesus Christ (ch. 10–12). Finally, the argument supports the Van Tillian emphases that have been cultivated by the schools of thought described in Part III.

At the conclusion of our study we obtain a robust Trinitarian worldview the likes of which has seldom been seen. Apologists throughout the ages have offered proofs for the existence of God. A few among them have aimed at proving that God must be Triune. An even smaller group of Van Tillian presuppositionalists have argued that a personal God, who is fundamentally one and many, is the precondition of all rational discourse, and the primary object of a transcendental proof. But, the present volume is unique in its aim to demonstrate that only the specifically tri-personal God, who has reconciled men to himself in the work of the Father, the Son, and the Holy Spirit, can be regarded as the transcendental condition of intelligible existence. Indeed, the development of a coherent theology, of a definitive apologetic, and of a logic that consistently embraces theological paradox and excludes contradictions is proven to hinge on acknowledging the Triune God from the outset, and allowing Him to set all things in their proper light.

Abbreviations

C67	*The Confession of 1967: Its Theological Background and Ecumenical Significance*
CA	*Christian Apologetics*
CB	*Christianity and Barthianism*
CFC	*The Case for Calvinism*
CG	*Common Grace and the Gospel*
CC	*Christianity in Conflict*
CI	*Christianity and Idealism*
CIM	*Christianity in Modern Theology*
CJ	*Christ and the Jews*
CTE	*Christian Theistic Ethics (In Defense of the Faith, Vol. 3)*
CTEV	*Christian Theistic Evidences (In Defense of the Faith, Vol. 6)*
CTK	*A Christian Theory of Knowledge*
DF3	*The Defense of the Faith*, 3rd ed.
DF4	*The Defense of the Faith*, 4th ed.
FCE	*Foundations of Christian Education: An Address to Christian Teachers*
GD	*The Great Debate Today*
GH	*The God of Hope: Sermons and Addresses*
IST	*An Introduction to Systematic Theology (In Defense of the Faith, Vol. 5)*
JA	*Jerusalem and Athens*
NH	*The New Hermeneutic*

NM	*The New Modernism*
PA	*Paul at Athens*
PDS	*The Protestant Doctrine of Scripture (In Defense of the Faith, Vol. 1)*
PR	*Psychology of Religion (In Defense of the Faith, Vol. 4)*
RP	*The Reformed Pastor and Modern Thought*
SCE	*A Survey of Christian Epistemology (In Defense of the Faith, Vol. 2)*
SG	*Sovereignty of Grace: An Appraisal of G. C. Berkouwer's View of Dordt*
TJD	*The Theology of James Daane*
WI	*Why I Believe in God*
WCV	*The Works of Cornelius Van Til (CD-Rom, version 1.0)*
WTJ	*Westminster Theological Journal*

PART I

The Origins of Van Til's Theological Apologetic

In itself, the task of identifying those schools of thought which inspired Cornelius Van Til's apologetic system is hardly a difficult or even a novel endeavor. Several Van Til students and expositors have made such identifications,[1] and their accounts differ hardly at all from the one Van Til himself gave on multiple occasions. As it stands, there is no doubt that Van Til was indebted to (1) "Old Princeton" Seminary and to (2) the Free University of Amsterdam for shaping and solidifying his Reformed theological commitments.[2] And, many of his epistemological insights were positively or negatively inspired by (3) absolute and personal idealist philosophers.[3] When boiled down to their lowest common denominators a most unusual combination appears, with Calvin as the most significant theological influence, and Hegel as the underlying philosophical influence on Van Til.

Accompanying the well-established account of the origins of Van Til's position, is the regular interpretation of Van Til's own project as an attempt to "reform" Christian apologetics, by combining and morphing certain theological, epistemological, and apologetic insights taken from each of the above-mentioned schools. First, Old Princeton stood upon Calvin's

1. Bahnsen, *Van Til's Apologetic*, 596–612; Frame, *Van Til*, 19–37; Muether, *Van Til*, 21–63; MacLeod, "Amsterdam, Old Princeton, and Cornelius Van Til," 261–82; McConnel, "The Influence of Idealism," 557–88.

2. DF4, 345–82; SCE; 198–99; IST, 21–61; CG, 14–64.

3. Borrowing a phrase directly from the British idealist. Bernard Bosanquet, Van Til declares that a "method of implication" is that which "a Christian would be naturally bound to use." SCE, 6–7.

doctrines of natural revelation and man's innate sense of deity, as they constructed a robust apologetic for the Christian Faith. Second, Amsterdam, on the other hand, emphasized Calvin's doctrine of total depravity, and developed the view that unregenerate reasoning must be antithetical to Christian thinking at virtually every point, with the result that it is largely futile to attempt to develop a Christian apologetic. And third, British-American idealism championed the Hegelian doctrine that a single all-encompassing system, dubbed the "Absolute" is the precondition for all rational discourse. On their view, even those philosophers who doubt, deny, or fall short of a vision of the Absolute, can be proven to unwittingly rely upon it. In this way, opposing philosophies are disproven by way of a "transcendental"[4] argument to the effect that they presuppose the sort of all-encompassing rational system which they claim to deny. When all three basic convictions are combined and allowed to qualify one another, they form an apologetic that is uniquely consistent with the essence of Reformed theology. The Christian apologist must presuppose the truth of the Reformed theological system solely on the authority of the Triune God. He must reject any positive demonstration that might appeal to illusive "neutral" premises shared by believers and unbelievers alike. And yet, the apologist may escape the pitfalls of fideism by demonstrating that non-Christians must, in the development and articulation of their views unwittingly presuppose many things (the reliability of his senses, the possibility of predication, etc.) which only the Triune God of Scripture can account for. Hence, the Christian system of truth can be established by way of an indirect proof along the lines developed by absolute idealists.

Given the above-mentioned consensus, a fresh inquiry into the origins and implications of Van Til's theological-apologetic system may appear superfluous. However, the general accuracy of the established account does not negate the fact that it often overlooks one of the most interesting and complicated features of Van Til's project. For, in addition to identifying an apologetic method that is worthy of the Christian system of truth, Van Til was equally committed to developing a position that thrived on the distinctive paradoxes of the Christian Faith. Hence, a thorough analysis of Van Til's appropriation of Princeton, Amsterdam, and absolute idealist philosophy must take into account not only their beliefs about Christian theology and apologetics, but also their distinctive beliefs about paradox. As it stands,

4. A "transcendental" argument aims to prove that a given something is the precondition for reason and/or rational discourse with the result that whether one directly affirms or denies its bearing, he must indirectly affirm it. For a discussion of transcendental argumentation with respect to Kant, see 1.3.1; to Hegel, see 3.2.1; and to Van Til, see 4.2–3.

even a meager acquaintance with the three schools in view shows that paradox figures quite centrally. As thoroughly orthodox bastions of Reformed theology, Princeton and Amsterdam were zealous to defend theological mysteries such as the Trinity, the Incarnation, the compatibility of divine sovereignty and human responsibility, etc. And if Hegel's philosophy is commonly known for anything, it is for its highly paradoxical inferences, and mysterious doctrine of the absolute. However, what critics have questioned in their own way is whether any one of these three schools succeeded in developing a coherent combination of system, apologetics, and paradox.

It is the present author's contention that the genius of Van Til's project can best be understood as an attempt to overcome the conflict between apologetics, system, and paradox in the three above-mentioned schools by qualifying their chief doctrines with insights taken from the other two. Hence, the argument below is marked by three fivefold investigations of each school's system of thought, apologetic method, and notion of paradox, as well as Van Til's positive appropriation, and negative critique of each. Surely the *prima facie* enigma of Van Til's positive project is how he could hope to render the ideals of theological "system" and rational proof *consistent* with paradoxes that are by definition apparently contradictory, and *inconsistent* in themselves. Given, however, that Part I must focus on how Van Til took issue in various ways with each school, it contains a greater discussion of his critiques than of his positive insights. In fact, the reader will find a running, and relatively chronological critique of Western philosophy that extends through Van Til's negative assessment of each school. And yet, statements of Van Til's positive system are unavoidable since his transcendental critiques of unbelieving and less consistently Christian systems presuppose the Christian system in a more pure form.

Although this anticipatory summary simplifies matters somewhat, the critiques yet to be leveled against each individual school can be divided into two different sorts: those which turn on the school's own inconsistency; and those which are inspired by the other two camps (see fig. 1). Princeton for example is inconsistent for (1) embracing God's status as the sovereign governor of history, but denying that he is necessarily the governing premise of healthy reasoning. If they had ingested Amsterdam's insight that (2) a non-Christian use of logic must undermine Christian paradox, and the absolute idealist demonstration that (3) common sense shrouds the truth, they would have been well on their way to understanding that a sovereign Trinity must also be the presupposition of all rational discourse. Amsterdam on the other hand correctly holds to an antithesis between Christian and non-Christian thought, but (5) inconsistently so. For, it is precisely because Christian thought differs so radically from that of unbelievers that it alone is self-consistent. (Exposition of this sweeping claim must be left for its proper place.[5]) Had they taken seriously Princeton's critique that (4) fideism is characteristic of non-Christian worldviews, and (6) the absolute idealist insight that an absolute Trinity must function as the self-consistent context and ground of every inconsistent belief system, they would have come very close to the sort of theological-apologetic proposed by Van Til. And finally, the absolute idealist school was (9) inconsistently transcendental in their methodology. Although they were able to effectively expose the self-defeating character of prior systems of philosophy, they really had no self-consistent doctrine of the Absolute which they could set forth as the precondition of intelligibility. Had the absolute idealists begun their labors with (8) an orthodox doctrine of the Trinity, and had they (7) denied that the temporal universe is essential to the self-development of the eternal God, then, in addition to embracing Christian orthodoxy, they would have been ripe to develop an absolutely compelling apologetic.

Source of Critique / Object Of Critique	Princeton	Amsterdam	Absolute Idealism
Princeton	**(1)** Inconsistent with a sovereign Trinity	**(2)** Undermines Christian paradox	**(3)** Failure to be critical of common sense
Amsterdam	**(4)** Fideism characteristic of irrationalism	**(5)** Inconsistent with doctrine of antithesis	**(6)** Failure to exploit the apologetic value of the Trinity
Absolute Idealism	**(7)** Renders God finite and undermines his sovereignty	**(8)** Failure to presuppose the Trinity	**(9)** Inconsistently transcendental

Figure 1: Sources and Objects of Critique

5. See 4.1–4.

1

Old Princeton

1.1 INTRODUCTION

Van Til imbibed Reformed Christianity at virtually every stage of his development.[1] Although he was born in Holland, Van Til's family immigrated to the United States in 1905 in pursuit of religious freedom amidst a national controversy between the liberal and conservative branches of the Dutch Reformed Church. He would go on to attend Calvin Preparatory School, College, and Seminary (1921). Instructors the likes of Louis Berkhof exposed Van Til to the teachings of Abraham Kuyper and Herman Bavinck, the great neo-Calvinist theologians. However, after only one year at Calvin Seminary, Van Til transferred to Princeton Seminary, where the theological legacy of Charles Hodge and B. B. Warfield remained significant. In contrast to the Dutch neo-Calvinists, William Brenton Green would introduce Van Til to the robust "evidentialist" apologetic method once championed by Hodge.[2] Nevertheless, the influence of Dutch Reformed Christianity continued to exert itself even at Princeton. In addition to welcoming many Dutch Reformed students,[3] the Scottish Presbyterians at Princeton recognized the prominent Dutch Theologians as comrades worthy of contributing to their own *Princeton Theological Review*. In fact, the Dutch theologian Geerhardus Vos, who had been offered the chair of Old Testament at the Free University of Amsterdam, elected instead to accept a faculty position at Princeton. Moreover, Dutch theologians including Kuyper, Bavinck, and Valentine

1. Muether, *Van Til*, 21–39.
2. White, *Van Til*, 57.
3. Muether, *Van Til*, 51

Hepp were invited to deliver the "Stone" lectures at Princeton in 1898, in 1909, and in 1930 respectively.[4]

Given his academic pedigree, it can hardly be surprising to find Van Til, as early as his Th.M. thesis "Reformed Epistemology," citing the theology of Calvin as mediated by Princeton and Amsterdam theologians as foundational to his thinking.[5] Reformed Christianity is to a considerable degree a single fundamental influence on the thinking of Van Til, as both schools led him to believe that Calvinism represented "Christianity come to its own."[6] And although significant differences between them must be explored below, Princeton and Amsterdam together impressed upon Van Til an appreciation for at least five central Reformed doctrines—Trinity,[7] covenant, redemptive history,[8] *sola scriptura*, and divine sovereignty (especially in affecting salvation)—that would figure heavily in Van Til's interpretation of the Christian system.

1.2 THE OLD PRINCETON PERSPECTIVE

Since its formation in 1812 under Archibald Alexander, Princeton Seminary was committed to providing a rational defense of the Christian Faith.[9] The method of defense would rely on the axioms of Scottish Common Sense Realism.[10] Thomas Reid (1710–96), the champion of the Common Sense Philosophy, emphasized that certain basic principles concerning the validity of human perception, rational inference, and moral intuition are recognized by all sane men and require no demonstration, being as they

4. These lectures are the basis for Kuyper's, *Lectures on Calvinism*; Bavinck's *The Philosophy of Revelation*; and Hepp's *Calvinism and the Philosophy of Nature*.

5. Van Til, "Reformed Epistemology," NP. Cf. SCE, 198–99.

6. CA, 86–9, 124. cf. CTE, 6; RP, 31; CTK, introduction. This phrase was inspired by B. B. Warfield's explanation that "Calvinism conceives of itself as simply the more pure theism, religion, evangelicalism, superseding as such the less pure." Warfield, "Calvinism," *Works*, 5:356.

7. That refinement of the doctrine of the Trinity was one of the major interests of Calvin and of the subsequent Reformers, has been argued in great detail by Richard Muller. Muller, *Post-Reformation Reformed Dogmatics*, 4:151–67.

8. Geerhardus Vos must be given special credit for cultivating Van Til's appreciation for historically mediated knowledge over against the Greek ideal of timeless truth.

9. "It [the seminary] is to form men for the Gospel ministry, who shall truly believe, and cordially love, and therefore endeavor to propagate and defend . . . the Christian system of religious belief." Archibald Alexander, quoted in Cannata, "History of Apologetics," 58–59.

10. Noll, *Princeton*, 31–33.

are "the foundation of all reasoning and of all science."[11] Virtually universal consent to the reliability of our senses, the reality of causation in nature, and other beliefs, confirms, though it cannot be taken to prove, their truth.[12] John Witherspoon, the Scottish President of Princeton College in 1768, disseminated the common sense philosophy to his pupils of whom Archibald Alexander was one. In turn, Alexander was involved in the Christian conversion of one of the greatest Princeton Divines, Charles Hodge.[13]

1.2.1 Classical-Evidentialist Apologetics

Charles Hodge expressed his commitment to the basic tenets of the Common Sense philosophy in the opening chapters of his *Systematic Theology*.[14] Hodge distinguishes what he calls the "inductive" method in theology from that of theological rationalism and mysticism.[15] The former involves drawing one's theology from the facts of Scripture and the latter involves forming one's theology introspectively.[16] As with the practitioner of any science, the theologian must embrace three fundamental axioms concerning the reliability of his "sense perceptions . . . mental operations . . . [and] those truths which are not learned from experience, but which are given in the constitution of our nature."[17] With additional data supplied by sane and reputable men, the human intellect must be trusted in its ability to organize the facts into a coherent system or account, whether the matter is historical, geological, biological, legal, etc. What distinguishes the theologian's task is that he must commit himself to organizing and systematizing the facts recorded in Scripture.[18] Before the theologian can execute his task, the apologist must first demonstrate, among other things, that the Bible is all that it purports to be—true and of divine authority. By designating man as the image of God, Scripture itself would seem to warrant the sort of apologetic efforts involved in establishing its own divinity.[19] Man knows *a priori* that if Scripture is in fact the Word of God it cannot teach certain things—the self-contradictory, the immoral, that which conflicts with truths evident from the

11. Copleston, *History*, 5:368.
12. Ibid., 5:371.
13. Cannata, "History of Apologetics," 58, 62.
14. Noll, *Princeton*, 32.
15. Ibid., 1:3–17.
16. Hodge, *Systematic*, 1:13–15
17. Ibid., 1:9.
18. Ibid., 1:15–7.
19. Ibid., 1:15, 49–53.

constitution of man, nor that which would conflict with truths discovered in other realms.[20] In addition to manifesting consistency both with itself and with reality, the Bible must enjoy the support of positive evidence for its reliability.[21]

In developing a positive apologetic which lays a foundation for the theological science, the Princeton Divines were at odds with the Dutch Calvinists who preferred a modest and primarily defensive apologetic. Benjamin Breckenridge Warfield, who took up the chair of theology at Princeton in 1892, followed Hodge in defending the typical Princeton view.[22] He identified at least five matters that the apologist must establish through reasoned argumentation and appeal to evidence, prior to the execution of the theological task. These include the existence of God, man's capacity for religion, God's involvement in human history, Christianity's divine origins, and the reliability of Scripture.[23] Van Til's apologetics professor William Brenton Green, his theology professor C. Wistar Hodge, and contemporaries such as Floyd E. Hamilton, devoutly carried on the Old Princeton apologetic tradition.[24] In his six-part series, "The Metaphysics of Christian Apologetics," Green offered proofs of the reality of the external world, the dualistic (spirit-body) composition of man, the reality of self-governing persons distinct from the material universe, the objectivity of man's moral duty, the immortality of the soul, and the reality of the supernatural.[25] In stacking one independent proof upon another in order to lay a foundation for the theological science, Warfield and Green exemplify what Van Til called a "block-house" apologetic.[26]

In executing the apologetic tasks of proving God's existence, and man's capacity for religion, Hodge and Warfield believed themselves to be in line with Calvin. In his thorough analysis of "Calvin's Doctrine of the Knowledge of God," Warfield observes that, for Calvin, man cannot contemplate his own existence or that of the universe without immediately arriving at a sense of his Creator. "The knowledge of God is given in the very same act by which we know self . . . as dependent, derived, imperfect, and responsible

20. Reason is, to use Hodge's phrase, the "*judicium contradictionis*." Ibid., 1:52–53.

21. Ibid., 1:53. cf. Green, "Function of Reason," 498–500.

22. Warfield, "Apologetics," 9:5–6. Cf. Warfield, "Idea of Systematic Theology," *Works*, 9:74.

23. Warfield, "Apologetics," 9:13.

24. For Van Til's response to these men see DF4, 368ff.

25. Green, "Metaphysics of Apologetics I–VI."

26. CA, 136–59.

being[s]."[27] Up to this stage, Warfield's thinking follows Calvin's. But Calvin goes on to mark the fact that while God's revelation of Himself in man and in the universe is both ubiquitous and clear in its implications,[28] original sin has left men with an inborn desire to pervert that revelation, and deny God His due honor. Because of this, Calvin emphasized the importance of special revelation over natural revelation, because only the former can overcome man's perverse interpretation of himself and reality.[29] Warfield did not take Calvin's emphasis on special revelation (or his silence with respect to theistic proofs) to indicate a disapproval of apologetics. Instead, Warfield explained that Calvin was so "dominated . . . by practical interests" in man's need for religion and absolution from guilt, that he preferred to advance straightway to the gospel and its theological correlates.[30] Warfield's reading of Calvin was not without precedent. Francis Turretin, the third generation presbyter of Geneva, embraced the classical theistic proofs as in line with Calvin's doctrine of natural revelation.[31]

The Princeton theologians recognized that the cosmological and teleological proofs, as classically constructed by Thomas Aquinas rested upon common sense premises regarding the reality of causation, man's ability to detect order in the world, the impossibility of an infinite regress of causes, etc. Hodge dismisses as contrary to reason Hume's objection to the cosmological proof that the principle of causation has no basis in experience. He is equally intolerant of Kant's contention that organizing categories such as causation only apply to the universe as it appears, and not to the universe as it really exists. In Hodge's estimation, both Hume's denial and Kant's limitation of the principle of causation are self-defeating, because they undermine the basic convictions of human reason, which in turn calls into question any rational argumentation in their favor.[32] Hodge and Warfield place the great-

27. Warfield, "Calvin's Doctrine of the Knowledge of God," *Works*, 5:31.

28. Ibid., 5:33–46. cf. Calvin, *Institutes*, 1:5.

29. Hodge, *Systematic*, 1:191–203; Calvin, *Institutes*, 1:1–3. Warfield summarizes the main elements of Calvin's doctrine of the knowledge of God and of the noetic effects of sin, "these include the postulation of an innate knowledge of God in man, quickened and developed by a very rich manifestation of God in nature and providence, which, however, fails of its proper effect because of man's corruption in sin; so that an objective revelation of God, embodied in the Scriptures, was rendered necessary, and, as well a subjective operation of the Spirit on the heart enabling sinful man to receive this revelation." Warfield, "Calvin's Doctrine of the Knowledge of God," *Works*, 5:31; cf. 5:43.

30. Ibid., 5:41–42.

31. Turretin, *Institutes*, 1:169–80.

32. Hodge, *Systematic*, 1:212–15, 228–30. Hodge's reaction to Hume echoes that of Thomas Reid, who understood Hume's *Treatise on Human Nature* to be a "*reduction ad absurdum* of skepticism." Copleston, *History*, 5:365.

est stock in the anthropological/moral proof for God, which turns on the claim that man's sense of morality and guilt is only explicable if he is in fact accountable to a personal Creator. The moral proof serves double duty in both establishing the existence of God and proving His personal interest in human affairs as a lawgiver/judge. It also implies man's capacity for an ethical and religious relationship to God.[33] Thus, in his critique of *Some Dogmas of Religion* by atheist John McTaggart, Warfield largely bypasses McTaggart's involved metaphysical critiques of a transcendent deity. For, metaphysical speculation cannot compete with the fact that the simplest and most natural explanation for the widespread belief in the supernatural and for man's sense of moral guilt is that a transcendent Judge directly impresses Himself on the human conscience.[34]

Alongside of their defense of theism and of man's religious nature, Hodge, Warfield, and Green were equally committed to disproving atheism in its materialist and pantheist forms. As the argument goes, both philosophies blatantly conflict with the demands of common sense. The materialist reduction of reality to its "material" component, is at odds with man's intuition that he is a "spiritual" and subjective "self." "If," reasons Hodge, "consciousness is to be trusted in reporting the testimony of the senses" concerning natural processes, "why is it not to be trusted when it reports the facts of our interior life?"[35] Warfield echoes Hodge's point in his evaluation that Darwin's lapse from Christianity (though he remained a theist of sorts) was birthed out of a refusal to heed his natural and "inextinguishable conviction" that there exists a personal God.[36] (With regard to Darwinism, Warfield thought that although it might be reconcilable with Scripture, it lacked sufficient evidence. Hodge and Green were generally more critical of the theory.[37]) Pantheists err in the other direction, reducing reality to one substance on the basis of mystical speculation, while disregarding the testimony of the senses.[38] Theoretical proofs for the unreality of distinct individuals and substances are overturned by the indispensability of such distinctions in day-to-day living. The pantheist even cuts off his ability to

33. Hodge, *Systematic*, 1:233–40.

34. Warfield, Review of *Some Dogmas of Religion*, *Works*, 10:149–50. Warfield is aware that certain world religions such as Buddhism are properly atheistic, but even Buddhism has a strong moral element, and various permutations of the religion acknowledge the need for a transcendent and enlightened class of beings.

35. Hodge, *Systematic*, 1:277; cf. Green, "Metaphysics of Apologetics II," 262–88.

36. Warfield, "Darwin's Argument," *Shorter Writings*, 2:141.

37. Hodge, *Systematic*, 1:12–41; Green, "Another Criticism of Evolution," 537–61.

38. Hodge, *Systematic*, 1:332. "Nescience" or the lack of knowledge, "is the alternative to realism" argues Green. Green, "Metaphysics of Apologetics I," 81.

appeal to religious authorities, since acknowledgement of such *external* authorities undermines his fundamental contention that all men are identical with the divine being and should enjoy immediate access to the truth.[39] In addition to their distinctive shortcomings, materialism and pantheism suffer in common from several others. For example, neither view can be squared with man's intuition that he is a free agent.[40] And they either deny outright the reality of objective ethical standards[41] or assert the mystical identification of good and evil, which no sane man can concede.[42]

When it comes to establishing Christianity's divine origins and the reliability of Scripture the apologetic task comes closer to the theological task. The biblical Scriptures themselves bear the marks of a trustworthy and even supernatural witness. These marks include: the theological agreement between books that were written by authors who were widely separated in time and location; the record of prophecies that have been fulfilled; the evident sanity and profound moral wisdom of the biblical authors; their historical reliability; the wealth and antiquity of biblical manuscripts which confirm the reliability of its transmission, etc.[43] Considerations such as these provide rational men with every reason to believe the biblical record of Jesus' miraculous ministry and resurrection, and to assent to the supernatural origins of Christianity. Other compelling evidences are so tied to specific doctrines, that they are most appropriately discussed by the systematic theologian. For example, Hodge derives support for the doctrine that man is a combination of soul and body from the prevalence of anthropological dualism across all cultures.[44] Likewise, the doctrine that man fell from an original state of innocence is confirmed by "the traditions of all nations" which "treat of a golden age from which men have fallen."[45] But, the bond between a compelling apologetic and a precise theology is the most evident with respect to those doctrines which afford immediate experiential proof. Inspired by Romans 5:1, Warfield argues that a believer's overwhelming

39. Warfield, "Latest Phase of Historical Rationalism," *Works*, 9:617. Hodge also points out that alleged mystical revelations frequently yield contradictory conclusions. Hodge, *Systematic*, 1:101–3.

40. Ibid. 1:278, 333.

41. Ibid., 1:278–80.

42. Ibid., 1:233.

43. Ibid., 1:37–38. The *Presbyterian and Reformed Journal*, and the *Princeton Theological Review* by which it was replaced, teem with defenses of the authenticity and reliability of the Bible.

44. Hodge, *Systematic*, 2:44, 378.

45. Ibid., 2:93.

sense of "peace with God," confirms the power and reality of justification by faith in Christ.[46]

Finally, the theologian himself is the most equipped to engage in "polemics," that is, apologetics directed to defending the faith against heretical perversions.[47] Thus, the Princeton theologians offered unrelenting exegetical defenses of Nicene Christology against the Arianism;[48] Augustinian soteriology against the Pelagianism;[49] particular redemption against various forms of universalism;[50] etc. However, even in polemical contexts, the Princeton school continued to rely on the indubitable axioms of common sense. In his refutation of Albrecht Ritschl's perfectionism[51] and rationalism, Warfield is interested to demonstrate that Ritschl's views are illogical, as well as unbiblical. Ritschl's doctrine that man's appetite for sin originates from the nurture of a corrupt society is doubly refuted by the testimony of Genesis 3, and by the fact that it involves a "hysteron-proteron" (the fallacy of putting the cart before the horse). Common sense leads us to the conclusion that some original set of humans must have birthed every perverted culture to follow, without themselves having had any prior culture to blame for their moral failures.[52]

1.2.2 Theological Paradox

In addition to building on Calvin in the areas of natural revelation and apologetics, the Princeton theologians shared Calvin's unabashed trust in Scripture, and the divine paradoxes that it discloses. Hodge argues that it is

46. Warfield, "Argument from Experience," *Shorter Writings*, 2:142–51. cf. Hodge, *Systematic*, 1:39.

47. Warfield, "Apologetics," 9:11.

48. Hodge, *Systematic*, 1:448–521, 2:378–454; Warfield, "Tertullian and the Beginnings of the Doctrine of the Trinity," *Works*, 4:3–109; Warfield, "The Biblical Doctrine of the Trinity," *Works* 2:133–72; Warfield, "The Person of Christ," *Works*, 2:175–209.

49. Hodge, *Systematic*, 2:331–53, 675–732; Warfield, "Augustine and the Pelagian Controversy," *Works*, 4:289–412.

50. Hodge, *Systematic*, 2:544–62; Warfield, *Plan of Salvation*, 69–86.

51. "Perfectionism," in this context, refers to a theological stance that reduces the Christian Faith to a pursuit of moral perfection.

52. Warfield, "Ritschl the Rationalist," *Works*, 7:1–52. Working as he is with Post-Kantian categories, Ritschl would of course deny that human society must have been birthed from an original pair of humans. One idealist in the Kantian tradition, Johann Gottleib Fichte (see 2.1) had explicitly argued that a pre-temporal transcendent subject has eternally posited for itself a society of finite persons through which its freedom can be realized. Fichte also viewed society as a corrupting influence, and an ethical hurdle above which finite individuals must rise.

perfectly in keeping with common sense to admit the truth of things which we do not understand: "Men know unspeakably more than they understand. We know that plants grow; that the will controls our voluntary muscles; that Jesus Christ is God and man in two distinct natures, and one Person; but here as everywhere we are surrounded by the incomprehensible. We can rationally believe that a thing is without knowing how or why it is."[53] With respect to God, man ought to be particularly comfortable with partial, analogical, and anthropomorphic knowledge, seeing as he cannot even form a mental image of the divine essence (cf. Exod 20:4; Deut 4:9–20; 5:8; 1 Tim 1:17).[54] Moreover, comprehension involves knowing an object's essence, attributes, internal relations, and external relations to all other things, and certainly man cannot hope to attain such an exhaustive understanding of God.[55] Thus, God is "above reason" in the sense that His being and activity are *quantitatively* too immense for men to comprehend. But God is not, as Green explains, "above reason" in the sense that his nature is qualitatively different "from what reason can apprehend."[56] We may formulate a true and accurate conception of God and rest assured that whatever "the thought (or idea) of God" entails, it certainly "involves no contradiction," for a contradiction involves something which we "cannot think."[57]

Significant for our present purposes is the fact that several of the theological mysteries identified by Hodge and his successors may easily be construed as contradictions. And yet, they generally opt to designate such doctrines "mysteries" rather than "paradoxes" as if any flirtation with the latter concept would invite the charge of irrationality. For example, Hodge grants that the nature of the union between body and soul is "mysterious . . . [for] we do not know how the body acts on the mind or the mind acts on the body."[58] And yet, in most instances reason would dictate that two fundamentally different substances must either be united as members of some third thing which contains them both, or fail to be a unity in an essential, non-accidental sense. But, Hodge refuses to postulate the existence of any third substance, on the basis that Scripture will not admit for a trichotomous anthropology. Yet, he maintains that body and soul somehow form an intimate unity. The biblical doctrine of the unity and diversity of the human race presents comparable problems. Hodge rejects both the Platonic

53. Hodge, *Systematic*, 1:50.
54. Ibid., 1:337–39; 3:290.
55. Ibid., 1:337.
56. Green, "Function of Reason," 486–87.
57. Hodge, 1:336–37
58. Hodge, *Systematic*, 2:44

doctrine that "humanity" is a single spiritual substance that divides itself in the conception of every new person (traducianism), and the atomistic doctrine that each human soul is created immediately and individually by God (creationism). And yet, Hodge makes no attempt to resolve the dilemma of humanity's unity and diversity. Instead, he advises a humble biblicism: "It does not become us to be wise above that which is written. We may confess that generation, the production of a new individual of the human race, is an inscrutable mystery."[59] Hodge's own reserved conclusion is that Scripture is best understood as "denying the creation of the soul *ex nihilo* . . . without insisting on an identical essence in all human beings."[60] Yet, it would seem overly charitable to characterize a doctrine that conflicts with the law of excluded middle as a "mystery." To deny both that every soul is created anew, and that each soul is composed of one identical substance, begs the question as to what is the actual material source of each new soul? Normally, one would conclude that humanity is either fundamentally "one" so that each person is a member of a common substance (realism), or it is fundamentally "many," and "humanity" is a synthetic term used to identify fundamentally distinct individuals (nominalism). Apart from some kind of an explanation, to affirm the real, as opposed to nominal unity of the human race, and to deny the implication that men are parts of one identical substance strikes one as a contradiction.

The doctrine of the Incarnation/dual nature of Christ involves a difficulty similar to that posed by man's dualistic constitution. However, the paradox of the Incarnation is enhanced by the fact that the single person of Christ must simultaneously enjoy everything pertaining to deity, including omniscience, and everything belonging to humanity, including limited knowledge. With respect to the apparently contradictory, the notion that the same person both is and is not omniscient must be ranked quite high. However, Hodge and Warfield avoid the language of paradox, and simply designate the doctrine of the Incarnation an inscrutable "mystery."[61] The mysteries associated with the Incarnation even spill into the Reformed doctrine of the Lord's Supper, which asserts that although Christ is not physically present in the bread and wine, his finite humanity is personally present through the omnipresent divine person with whom it is united. In the face of the paradox that a spatially limited human nature could somehow share in the divine attribute of omnipresence, Hodge writes, "If anyone asks, How the humanity of Christ, his body and soul in heaven, can sympathize

59. Ibid., 2:73.

60. Ibid., 2:73.

61. Ibid., 2:378. Cf. B. B. Warfield, "Real Problem of Inspiration," *Works*, 1:226.

[through personal communion] with his people on earth? the answer is, that it is in personal union with the Logos. If this answer be deemed insufficient, then the questioner may be asked, How the dust of which the human body is formed can sympathize with the immortal spirit with which it is united? Whether the mystery of this human sympathy of Christ can be explained or not, it remains a fact both of Scripture and of experience."[62]

Other doctrines such as that of creation out of nothing (*ex nihilo*) present significant problems in light of Parmenides' ancient dictum (based on the law of identity) that out of nothing, nothing comes (*ex nihilo, nihil fit*). If Christians contend that creation is indeed materially distinct from the Creator, then that which exists must have somehow sprung "from" its very opposite, namely non-existence.[63] Even if we grant that God has somehow accomplished the intuitively impossible in creation, the further notion that He superintends all that which comes to pass (Isa 45:7–8) would seem to conflict with the biblical teaching that God is not the author of evil/sin (Jas 1:13; 1 John 1:5), and that men are morally responsible for disobeying God (1 Sam 15:35; Acts 7:51). The Princeton theologians argue that although it may be beyond our comprehension *how*, Scripture requires us to believe *that* human freedom and evil are compatible with divine sovereignty.[64] Yet, for many, to assert both that God has determined that evil should come to pass, and that God is inculpable for its existence is tantamount to a self-contradiction. A similar paradox is involved in the biblical doctrine of inspiration, which asserts that the personality, style, and volition of the human authors are evident in Scripture, even though God has determined exactly what they wrote. In describing the process of inspiration the Princeton divines gravitate toward the language of "mystery" over that of "paradox," or apparent contradiction.[65]

Finally, we may take special note of how the Princeton theologians faithfully exposit the Christian paradox *par excellence*, the doctrine of the

62. Hodge, *Systematic*, 3:639. Despite Hodge's plea for mystery with respect to the Reformed doctrine of the Lord's Supper, Hodge assesses the Lutheran doctrine as marked by true "inconsistencies" and "impossibilities" since it ascribes omnipresence to Jesus humanity directly (as opposed to through the mediation of the divine logos). Ibid., 2:414–15.

63. Hodge argues that Parmenides' law may be taken to mean that everything owes its constitution to something else—"no effect can be without a cause." In this respect, the biblical doctrine presents no problems because it asserts that God is the prime cause of the universe. However, if Parmenides should be taken to mean, as he almost certainly does, that matter cannot be created, then argues Hodge, the law set forth is not self-evident. Ibid., 1:562–63.

64. Ibid., 2:563–64.

65. Warfield, "Real Problem of Inspiration," *Works*, 1:226.

ontological Trinity. To begin, Hodge explains that the Trinity resists rational explanation because it is, "out of analogy with all other objects of human knowledge."[66] Hodge's refusal to develop a speculative proof or to discuss analogies for the Trinity (e.g., Augustine's analogy of mind, understanding, and love/will) is in accord with Calvin's strictly exegetical treatment.[67] Warfield devotes his scholarly acumen to demonstrating that Calvin's tact, far from representing a step backward uniquely secured the equality of the three divine persons, earning him a place among alongside of Tertullian and Augustine as one of the greatest theologians of the Trinity.[68]

Warfield explains that while many of the theologians since the Council of Nicea had granted that the Son is co-eternal with the Father, those theologians had typically speculated that it was due to "a perpetual communication of the divine essence from the Father as the *fons deitatis* [fountain of deity] to the Son."[69] Such a view betrays inspiration from Plato, who hypothesized that a secondary personal deity must exist alongside the eternal principle of the "Good," as a mediator between the transcendent Reason and the unruly cosmos.[70] To many, a semi-Platonic Christology appeared to comport with the biblical doctrine of the eternal generation of the Son (cf. John 5:26). But, more importantly, such a Christology seemed to soften the apparent contradiction involved in describing God as both "one" and "three" by clarifying that the oneness of God is logically prior to His multiplicity. In this case, the oneness and threeness may be equally eternal, without being equally essential to the divine nature, since the second and third persons of the Trinity are derivative from the Father. In contrast, Calvin appeals to Scripture alone in support of the view that the Son and the Spirit enjoy the divine attribute of aseity, or self-existence just as well as the Father.[71] Calvin argues that the name "Jehovah" borne by the Son and the Spirit (Acts 2:21; 4:10–12; Judg 3:10) is expressive of self-existence (Exod 3:14).[72] To suggest that the deity of the Son and the Spirit is derivative from the Father must "logically . . . make them creatures of the Father's power, if not of His will;

66. Hodge, *Systematic*, 1:443.

67. Warfield, "Calvin's Doctrine of the Trinity," *Works*, 5:250–51.

68. Ibid., 5:224, cf. 5:189.

69. Ibid., 5:260.

70. On the strongest interpretation, Plato's god is a secondary being in relation to the eternal forms as they are united by the supreme form, the "Good." Copleston, *History*, 1:190–93.

71. This doctrine became known as the "autotheotes," or the "God-in-himself-ness" of the second and third persons of the Trinity. Warfield, "Calvin's Doctrine of the Trinity," *Works*, 5:233.

72. Ibid., 5:239.

by which their true deity is destroyed."[73] Calvin affirms the eternal generation of the Son and the eternal procession of the Spirit, but he insists that they refer to personal, rather than ontological relations.[74] In other words, the Father is the source, the Son is the content, and the Spirit is the power of an eternal *agenda*, not of the divine substance. The offense of Calvin's position, as it was vehemently exploited by his Catholic contemporary Robert Bellarmine, was the unremitting paradox which it fosters.[75] If the single divine nature is identical with three *equally self-existent* persons, then God must be essentially "one" and "three," rather than essentially "unitary" (and only derivatively "tertiary"). Supposing that Calvin could not remain content with such a paradoxical position, his opponents hoped to push him to consistency in the direction either of Sabellianism or of Tri-theism.[76] If the three divine persons are equally self-existent without an ontological order between them, then they must either be one and the same person, or three different deities. Yet, Calvin repudiated both extremes, designing his doctrine to instigate "in his readers a sense of the mystery of the divine mode of existence" that speculative doctrines diminished.[77]

Despite his rejection of a speculative foundation for the Trinity, Calvin observed that the biblical doctrine receives subjective confirmation in the assurance of salvation that arises from knowing that the "Redeeming Christ and the Sanctifying Spirit are each divine persons."[78] Furthermore,

73. Ibid., 5:272.

74. Ibid., 5:228.

75. Warfield records Bellarmine's judgment that Calvin's doctrine is "repugnant to Scripture, the definitions of the councils, the teaching of the Fathers, and reason itself, and as well to Calvin's own opinions [expressed elsewhere]." Ibid., 5:255.

76. Contemporary theologian Cornelius Plantinga has identified modalism as a valid logical conclusion that may be drawn from premises such as those held by Calvin, but as an invalid exegetical conclusion. Cornelius Plantinga Jr., "Threeness/Oneness Problem," 48–50. Plantinga's own solution involves beginning with the threefold personality of God, and offering the concepts of the family or the "body" of Christ as the best conceptual analogues to the kind of "oneness" enjoyed by God. However, when it comes to explaining what the Scriptures mean by asserting the oneness of God, Plantinga's solution is undeniably foreign to Calvin's thought, if Warfield's account is valid. Plantinga accepts, and Calvin rejects, as viable, the views that God's oneness may be identified with (1) the Father as the fount of deity; (2) a generic "essence" shared by each person; or (3) the collective unity of the three persons. Ibid., 47. Warfield, on the other hand, represents Calvin as denying the first and the second points outright, and insisting, contrary to the second view, and in favor of paradox, that the notion of tri-personality enters into the very essence of God just as well as the notion of oneness does.

77. Warfield, "Calvin's Doctrine of the Trinity," *Works*, 5:189

78. Ibid., 5:195.

those who know God through Christ and the Spirit have concrete insight into the interpersonal nature of the divine life. In contrast, generic forms of monotheism terminate in an ineffable god for whom we can form no idea of his ontological character, so that in speaking of god, "there is nothing but the bare and empty name of God . . . floating in our brain."[79] Semi-Platonic Christologies are prone to the same error when they argue that a nameless, indefinable, and strictly unitary divine nature is logically prior to God's inter-Trinitarian communion. For this reason, Calvin insists that tri-personality must enter "into the very idea of God," if we are to have true conception of Him.[80]

1.2.3 Theological System

Princeton's combination of an apologetic stance which refutes competing worldviews by exposing their self-contradictory claims, while defending a theological system that is replete with its own mysteries, may itself seem paradoxical. However, Hodge and Warfield identified two distinguishing characteristics of mysteries/paradoxes, over against contradictions: (a) mysteries are established directly from the facts of human experience or indirectly from trustworthy authorities;[81] and (b) mysteries support one another as members of a common system. The first criterion is the more important of the two, and is alone necessary to establish a supposed contradiction as merely apparent. In fact, although a paradoxical doctrine may be coherent with the Christian system, it must be rejected if it falls short of the first criterion. For example, one might suppose that it is coherent with the doctrine of the Trinity to posit a substantial unity between the distinct members of the human race. Yet, Hodge reasons to the contrary. Not only is such a view lacking in biblical support, but "it is clearly taught in Scripture and universally believed in the Church that the persons of the Trinity are one God in an infinitely higher sense than that in which all men are one man."[82]

Virtually all of the paradoxes common to the Reformed theological system can be justified by the twofold criteria mentioned above. In accordance with the first criterion, man discerns immediately that he is composed of body and spirit, even though he cannot comprehend the mystery of their union. Significantly, man's innate awareness of his dual nature is a sufficient ground for supposing that the apparent contradiction involved in

79. Ibid. 5:190; cf. Calvin, *Institutes*, 1:13:2.

80. Warfield, "Calvin's Doctrine of the Trinity," *Works*, 5:191.

81. Hodge, *Systematic*, 1:40.

82. Ibid., 2:58.

their unity is indeed *merely* apparent. In agreement with the second criterion, the biblical doctrine that man is composed of two distinct substances with diverse and even contrary attributes (e.g., materiality and spirituality) coheres with the biblical doctrine of Christ's dual nature, which requires an analogous type of union.[83] Likewise, although it is impossible to explain how a spirit operates through a physical body such a doctrine coheres quite well with the biblical teaching that a spiritual God is the first cause and Creator of the material universe.[84] Other theological paradoxes might not be validated by man's reflection on of his own constitution, but on the basis of multiple truths established independently of one another. Convinced of the validity of theistic proofs, alongside of the empirical reality of evil, Hodge concludes, "Sin is, and God is; therefore the occurrence of sin must be consistent with his nature."[85] Moreover, although it is impossible to appreciate exactly how God remains blameless for ordaining evil to come to pass, the existence of a perfect deity is justly inferred from man's immediate sense of absolute moral standards (the moral proof).

Many Christian paradoxes are confirmed by indirect evidence contained in the testimony of Scripture. As we have seen, the Princeton theologians believed that with the use of several compelling evidences, they could establish both the trustworthy character of the apostles, and the supernatural origins of their ministry. Thus, should Scriptural writings of the Apostles yield paradoxical doctrines those doctrines must be embraced as true. Thus, Hodge argues that divine foreordination must be compatible with the existence of evil and human responsibility, because in Scripture God both "predestined" the crucifixion of Christ and chastised His crucifiers as morally reprehensible (Acts 2:23).[86] In light of the biblical testimony that "The Scripture cannot be broken" (John 5:35) there is good reason to suppose that apparent inconsistencies within the Bible, and conflicts between its teaching and extra-biblical sciences (e.g., archeology) must be resolvable, even if solutions have yet to be found.[87] Finally, the most cherished paradoxes of the Christian Faith are based almost exclusively on Scripture. These include the Trinity, the Incarnation, the dual authorship of Scripture, the personal presence of Christ in the Supper, etc. Nevertheless, we have observed that Hodge/Warfield believed that the doctrine of the Trinity receives experiential confirmation in its ability to secure a believer's assurance of salvation.

83. Ibid., 2:378–80, 391, 395.

84. Ibid., 1:562.

85. Ibid., 1:548.

86. Ibid., 1:547.

87. Ibid., 1:170.

Moreover, the doctrine of the ontological Trinity is foundational for the doctrines of the Incarnation, justification, inspiration, etc.

In keeping with their refusal to extricate paradox from the Christian system and their candid admission that they could not (presently) resolve every apparent inconsistency in Scripture, the Princeton theologians argued for the *probability*, rather than for the *conclusive demonstrability* of the Christian faith. There is an obvious tension in claiming that the biblical authors have well-established reputations as honest, trustworthy, and sane men on the one hand, but were teachers of incomprehensible doctrines on the other. The Princeton response to this predicament is the same as that of non-Reformed apologists such as Thomas Aquinas and Bishop Joseph Butler: the rational support for Christianity outweighs the evidence against it, making it, at best, highly probable.[88] Warfield asks rhetorically, "Who doubts that the doctrines of the Trinity and of the Incarnation present difficulties to a rational construction?"[89] But, he responds that "because of the weight of the evidence" confirming the biblical testimony, these doctrines must be true.[90] In a passage that could have appeared in Butler's *Analogy of Religion*, Hodge explains, "The universe teems with evidences of design, so manifold, so diverse, so wonderful, as to overwhelm the mind with the conviction that it has had an intelligent author. Yet here and there isolated cases of monstrosity appear. It is irrational, because we cannot account for these cases, to deny that the universe is the product of intelligence. So the Christian need not renounce his faith in the plenary inspiration of the Bible, although there may be some things about it in its present state which he cannot account for."[91]

In contrast to the passing observations mentioned above, the first and only contributor to the *Princeton Theological Review* to give a clear and systematic expression to a strategy for dealing with paradox was Charles Hodge's Nephew, William Henry Hodge (1838–1919). Both in his article "The Infinite, Contradictory, and Faith," and in his full length volume *Intuitive Perception*, W. H. Hodge defends a novel philosophical realism that

88. Butler, *Analogy*, 33ff, 331ff.

89. Warfield, "Real Problem of Inspiration," *Works*, 1:215.

90. Ibid., 1:218.

91. Hodge, *Systematic*, 179; Butler reasons, "Hence, namely from analogical reasoning, Origen has with singular sagacity observed, that 'he who believes the Scripture to have proceeded from Him who is the Author of Nature, may well expect to find the same sort of difficulties in it as are found in the constitution of nature.' And in a like way of reflection it may be added, that he who denies the Scriptures to have been from God, upon account of these difficulties, may, for the very same reason, deny the world to have been formed of him." Butler, *Analogy*, 37.

involves the contention that "Upon proper testimony men do and should believe much that is *to them* contradictory, ever bearing in mind that that which is a real contradiction cannot be true."[92] Reviewers like James Orr questioned the faithfulness of the younger Hodge's philosophy to the views of his uncle, as well as his philosophy's feasibility on its own terms.[93] Yet, the basic method of dealing with theological paradox is certainly true to Old Princeton. The younger Hodge explains that although the biblical doctrines of the Trinity and the Incarnation are "contradictions to the human mind," they must be self-consistent if we encounter "rational proofs that the Bible is the Word of God."[94] "Once convinced that" Scripture is the Word of God we must "accept without question all its mysteries."[95] His point is that only God could definitively declare that apparent contradictions are, in fact, only apparent, and once He has so declared, the matter is settled beyond all doubt.[96] In keeping with his forbearers, the younger Hodge cites intuition, theistic proofs, the biblical Scriptures, and the miracle of the Incarnation as conclusive proofs that God exists, and has so spoken to man. But in order to evade any doubt about Scripture's veracity and/or the acceptability of Christian paradox, the younger Hodge advanced an unpalatable (because extreme) common sense doctrine, that the testimony of man's senses and intuitions are strictly infallible.[97] Hence, beyond its philosophical difficulties, Hodge's doctrine proved inconsistent with the Reformed doctrine of Total Depravity.[98]

1.3 VAN TIL'S CRITIQUE OF OLD PRINCETON

Van Til's critique of Old Princeton makes an appearance in most of his major books and syllabi.[99] His critique centers on Princeton's advocacy of a common sense philosophy. First, the Hegelians showed that the Scottish and Kantian philosophies (both of which attempted to preserve the reliability of common sense against the onslaught of skepticism) carried the seeds of their own destruction. For, both viewed ultimate reality as consisting of a myriad of chance related particulars, which cannot be justifiably

92. Hodge, "Infinite, Contradictory, and Faith," 592; cf. Hodge, *Intuitive Perception*.

93. Orr, "A Thoroughgoing Realist," 409–10.

94. Hodge, "Infinite, Contradictory, and Faith," 595.

95. Ibid., 595.

96. Ibid., 596–597.

97. Ibid., 592.

98. Minton, Review of *Intuitive Perception*, 320.

99. DF4, 345–69; CA, 100–109; CTK, 229–72; SCE, 186–93; IST, 31–42.

known to exist in a fashion that is conducive to basic human enterprises. The more overt "modern forms of irrationalism," are but the "children and grandchildren" of common sense philosophies.[100] Second, common sense coupled with natural theology proved to undermine distinctive Reformed doctrines such as divine sovereignty, and total depravity. And third, the Princeton school was mistaken to hold that the fallen intellect could judge the evidence for Christianity with equity, much less affirm the veracity of Scripture in the face of paradox prior to repentance.

1.3.1 Modern Philosophy and the Inadequacy of Common Sense[101]

Over time, the rationalist project initiated by René Descartes proved to undermine its own most foundational claim: unaided reason can grasp the fundamental nature of reality. This was because the leading lights of the movement had advanced the most fantastic and disparate conclusions among themselves.[102] However, Van Til observes that both the British empiricists, and the later, more practically minded philosophers (pragmatists), were in basic agreement with Descartes over Calvin, that man could make a great deal of sense of the world, without considering his relationship to the Creator from the outset.[103] The empiricists simply preferred probabilistic reasoning that was grounded in fact, over deductive introspection. And many Christian apologists, including the Princeton Divines, were largely persuaded by men like Joseph Butler that the Christian Faith could be proven by the strong analogy between its teaching and the design that was evident in nature.[104] However, David Hume made it quite clear that left to its own devices pure inductive reasoning posed its own insurmountable problems. Not only is it impossible to calculate probability against the backdrop of a potentially infinite universe,[105] but the concept most pertinent to

100. IST, 35; cf. SCE, 184ff.

101. The argument below is generally representative of Van Til. Cf. SCE, 103–15.

102. An overt example pertains to the basic nature of reality. Descartes held that it was dualistic, Spinoza monistic, and Leibniz pluralistic. Ibid., 103–6.

103. Ibid., 103–4; cf. PDS, 14–15; CTK, 152, 298, 337; CC, 225, 264.

104. Butler, *Analogy*, 38ff. cf. CTEV, 2–5.

105. Hume, *Treaties*, 89; CTEV, 25. Many evidentialist apologists do not appear to have grasped the gravity of Hume's point. For example, Daniel P. Fuller admits that the conclusions of Warfield's apologetic may, though probably will not prove false in the future. Daniel P. Fuller, "Warfield's view of Faith and History," 75–83. But, as W. T. Jones explains, "It is important to see that it is not merely a matter of not being certain" whether an alleged probable belief will prove true, "It is much worse than this . . . we

science (causation) simply cannot be construed as the product of inductive reasoning. Before one can infer that causation is a real principle from repeated observations of cause-effect relationships, he must already construe himself as standing in a cause-effect relationship to reality where general patterns in the latter give rise to general ideas in the former. But, Hume argues, if anything is clear it is that "The same principle cannot be both the cause and effect of another."[106]

To the dead ends reached by rationalism and empiricism in their pure forms, the two great champions of common sense did not respond by grounding their thinking on the Christian Faith.[107] Thomas Reid and Immanuel Kant, each, in his own way, took his stand on the presupposition that knowledge is the possession of mankind. From this self-assured vantage point, each philosopher worked his way backward to develop systematic insights that undergird the conviction of the common man.[108]

Thomas Reid's common sense philosophy bears a great affinity with modern empiricism, and it represents something quite close to the philosophical niche of the Princeton school. As we have seen, Princeton latched on to the common sense notion that by virtue of his natural constitution, man is able to develop accurate sense perceptions, as well as immediate intuitions concerning, ethical norms, mathematical principles, laws of logic, the existence of God, etc. That certain beliefs are so widely held is strong proof that they are self-evident, and the burden of proof is on any theory that would deny them.[109] Reid takes the fact that the empiricists were driven to skepticism as evidence that they must have gone astray in their reasoning.[110] He locates their root error in the assumption that, between a perceiving subject and a particular object, there must be a mental image, or idea. On this view, one will be left with the dilemma of explaining how his perceptions of causation were themselves caused.[111] As an alternative, Reid advances the view that, in perceiving, man beholds external objects directly.

have no rational basis for thinking" that any hypothesis will probably prove correct in the future. Jones, *History*, 3:321.

106. Hume, *Treatise*, 72; cf. CTEV, 20.

107. Although Hume went on to articulate a practical philosophy of his own, Van Til estimates that "the skepticism of Hume is the best reduction to absurdity of the position that takes its start from the human individual." SCE, 105.

108. Van Til regards the turn toward practical philosophy as a tacit admission that the basic questions of existence cannot be answered. CC, 22, 33–34.

109. Similar claims were made by the Princeton Apologists. Recall, 1.2.1. Green, "Metaphysics of Apologetics IV," 493. Cf. Van Til, DF4, 355.

110. Reid, *Inquiry*, v.

111. Copleston, *History*, 5:365–67.

In this case, man's belief in causation is due to his immediate acquaintance with innumerable causal relationships, and not somehow the cause of itself.

Despite what may appear to be clear advantages in Reid's approach, Van Til discerns that the common sense philosophy not only fails to take seriously, but also becomes the unsuspecting victim of, an equally basic "common folly."[112] To begin with, both Reid and Princeton agreed that folly, just as well as sense, is all too common. Reid recollects that he once embraced Locke's doctrine of ideas as self-evident.[113] Hodge marvels that even though it offends man's natural sense of individuality, "pantheism has so extensively prevailed in every age and in every part of the world."[114] In order to explain these oddities, the advocates of common sense must locate the major source of error within one's reasoning and interpretive process.[115] And yet, the common man has always embraced speculations, superstitions, and religious dogmas as lenses through which to interpret the facts of his day-to-day experience. It is difficult to imagine an adult observing a sunset without immediately inferring multiple conclusions, both consciously and unconsciously, about its meaning and significance in terms of a specific language, a set of cultural beliefs, a set of aesthetic beliefs, and ultimately,

112. Van Til accredits "common folly" to original sin. IST, 38–39.

113. Copleston records Reid's admission, in a letter to Hume, that Locke's "system appears to me not only coherent in all its parts, but likewise justly deduced from principles commonly received among philosophers: principles which I never thought of calling in question, until the conclusions you draw from them in the *Treatise of Human Nature* made me suspect them." Copleston, *History*, 5:365. A more recently, and indeed more famous example is Gottlob Frege's supposedly self-evident principle that for each property there is a set which contains every object which bears that property. After proceeding with such a premise for many years, Bertrand Russell left him "thunderstruck" by showing that his principle leads to a self-contradiction in the case of the property of "being a set that does not contain itself." Such a set both must and must not contain itself, and therefore it cannot be true that for every property there is a set of objects which bears that property. And so, what was thought of as a self-evident truth was proven to be false. See Russell, *Philosophical Development*, 76–83.

114. Hodge, *Systematic*, 332. At other points, Hodge notes that the supposedly indefensible polytheistic view has enjoyed pervasive boons. Ibid., 243.

115. Hodge assures his readers that when "the mind is left undisturbed, and allowed to act according to its own laws, men, in the great majority of cases, think alike on all the great questions about which philosophers are divided. It is only when they stir up the placid lake, and attempt to sound its depths, to analyze its waters, to determine the laws of its currents, and to ascertain its contents, that they see and think so differently." Hodge, *Systematic*, 2:279. And Reid prefaces his inquiry into the human mind saying, "Conjectures and theories are the creatures of men, and will always be found very unlike the creatures of God. If we would know the works of God, we must consult them with attention and humility without daring to add anything of ours to what they declare. A just interpretation of nature is the only sound and orthodox philosophy: whatever we add of our own, is apocryphal, and of no authority." Reid, *Inquiry*, 3–4.

some view of reality as a whole.[116] The history of philosophy, not to mention the pervasive phenomenon of war, attests to the fact that common assent to ethical principles in the abstract (e.g., murder is evil) has not at all detracted from the fact that men attach to those principles fundamentally different interpretations regarding their nature, origins, and purpose.[117] As F. H. Bradley quips—"metaphysics is the finding of bad reasons for what we believe upon instinct, but to find these reasons is no less an instinct."[118] Importantly, the common sense school is no exception. By driving a wedge between the relatively pristine testimony of the senses and man's broken interpretation of them, Reid and his school engage in a bit of speculation that does violence to the widespread convictions of the vulgar (e.g., that their religious philosophies are reliable in their unique details), with the result that the common sense philosophy is dubious by its own standard.[119]

Along the same lines, Van Til delights in demonstrating that those philosophies which are supposed to be based on the modest testimony of the intellect, senses, or both (e.g., the common sense philosophy) are always in fact married to an equally basic, and indeed highly speculative metaphysic.[120] Stated simply, Van Til's case turns on the point that "self-evident" truths are always, in fact "chance-evident" in the sense that they

116. In recent times, Willard Quine has emphasized the point that not even the meaning of logical concepts is self-evident. Not only are attempts to define tautological and analytic judgments reliant on an undefined notion of "synonymy," but also, there are a host of judgments for which it is ambiguous as to whether they may pass as "analytic." For example, Quine confesses, "I do not know whether the statement, 'Everything green is extended' is analytic. . . . The trouble is not with 'green' or 'extended,' but with 'analytic.'" The seemingly unanswerable question raised by Quine is whether the quality of extension is logically, or accidentally married to our notion of green. Quine, *Logical Point of View*, 32. The upshot of Quine's discussion are the conclusions that (a) synthetic considerations enter into what we call analytic judgments; and (b) logicians must bow to the pragmatist insight that the meaning of central logical concepts is determined by their concrete linguistic uses, and not vice versa. Ibid., 46.

117. CTE, 126–37; SCE, 190–91; IST, 39, 90–91.

118. Bradley, *Appearance*, xiv.

119. Thus, Van Til critiqued Reid and his school, saying "We should, however, be on our guard not to make too much of the distinction between unconscious or pre-conscious and self-conscious action. Scottish Realism (as also Hepp) and the theology based upon it, has made too much of this distinction. It has often spoken as though intuition were something quite different from and something more elemental than ratiocination. This, we believe, is not the case. . . . In itself, however, reasoning is nothing but self-conscious intuition, and intuition is nothing but unconscious reasoning." IST, 90; cf. SCE, 132, 138.

120. Van Til repeats with approval Bernard Bosanquet's criticism of Bertrand Russell's common sense philosophy—"The hunt for the psychologically primitive is the root of all evil." SCE, 138.

imply a pluralist and indeed indeterminist metaphysic. If one's perception of a sunset, belief that circles cannot be squares, and conviction that one should not bear false testimony, are, each of them, clear solely with respect to themselves then their meaning cannot be fundamentally altered when combined or separated. They must be viewed as accidentally related, atomic truths. Implicitly, then, the common sense philosopher embraces a view of ultimate reality as a sphere of chance[121] within which any number of empirical, rational, and ethical truths are allowed to exist in relative indifference toward one another.[122] Reid, of course, regarded the law of contradiction as setting a negative limit on how all true intuitions may relate to one another (e.g., in a non-contradictory manner).[123] But, like Aristotle, he concedes that the strictures of a timeless logic must be limited by an opposing sphere of chance—x cannot be not-x, *at the same time*—if it is to be understood properly.[124] And, in so doing, they betray their conviction that there is but one *basically relevant* belief that colors all others, namely that atomic truths appear in their full significance within a realm pure contingency, as opposed to mutual necessity.[125] Problematically, a universe that is to any

121. Although Reid believed in God, God certainly was not his ultimate organizing principle since for him the truths of ethics, logic, perception, were clear without any reference to God. In this way, Reid is basically subject to the same evaluation Van Til gave of modern agnostics, "they have, as a matter of fact, said that all the facts . . . are able to get along without God. They think they have said nothing about ultimate matters, while as a matter of fact they have in effect said everything that could be said about them, and, we believe, more beside. They have tried to be so modest that they did not dare to make a positive statement about anything ultimate, while they have made a universal negative statement about the most ultimate consideration that faces man." SCE, 212.

122. The incisive reader will be aware that what we have just articulated is a version of Hegel's argument that the naïve belief in discrete objects of knowledge implies its opposite: non-being or pure chance. See 3.2.1. Van Til makes the same point when he denies that there can be two ultimately independent beings. Either the one must rule over the other, or the two must owe their *relative* independence to a supervening context, or dialectic. SCE, 16.

123. Reid's conviction that the principles of common sense must be consistent with one another is implicit in his claim that "what is manifestly contrary to them [the principles of common sense], is what we call absurd." Reid, *Inquiry*, 52.

124. Aristotle qualified the law of contradiction in this way because he understood, all too well, Parmenides' point that a strictly *self*-evident truth must be an individual, all-encompassing truth that resists multiplicity. CTK, 171. Similar conclusions reached by Baruch Spinoza issued the same warning against exclusive reliance on logic. SCE, 106.

125. With respect to Russell's common sense philosophy, Bosanquet reflects the sentiments of absolute idealism in noting that "*a priorism*," or the belief that logical laws possess a self-evident character that goes unaffected by temporal reality, actually fosters relativism. For, such a belief divorces reason from the concrete universe, and

measure marked by unadulterated chance gives us every reason to doubt our senses regardless of how regularly men may assent to their testimony.[126] Finally, in light of the fact that common sense philosophers implicitly wed an all-encompassing metaphysical story to every truth claim, one is left with the question of why one should embrace their relatively short and unilluminating story over those which account for why/how the common man may rest assured that his empirical judgments are reliable?[127] It is because Kant attempted just this sort of explanation that he towered above Reid as the true protector of the common man,[128] and, in Van Til's estimation, set himself apart as worthy of immeasurably more interaction and critique.[129]

Kant's critical philosophy begins, not unlike Reid's, with the assumption that an ordinary man's day-to-day vantage point is reliable.[130] Such an ordinary man is capable of making sense of himself and of the world autonomously, or without any prior reference to a divine authority. The difference, however, is that Kant is aware of his responsibility to explain how the dictates of reason and the otherwise random facts of experience can coexist without compromising each other. Even more, Kant sought to delineate precise boundaries between those judgments that can be construed as "knowledge" and those speculative doctrines, which are objects of a rational "faith."

---

necessarily consigns the happenings of the latter to irrational forces. Bosanquet explains, that the common sense "view implies a sharp distinction between real and ideal. . . . Apriorism, indeed, as a mere necessity of our mental process, is rejected (rightly in my judgment) as a form of relativism." Bosanquet, *Implication*, 145–46; Hegel, *Logic*, §142–59; SCE, 138.

126. "It is by means of universal timeless principles of logic that the natural man must, on his assumptions, seek to make intelligible assertions about the world of reality or chance. But this cannot be done without falling into self-contradiction. About chance, no manner of assertion can be made. In its very idea it is irrational. . . . Realizing this dilemma, many modern philosophers have argued that any intellectual system of interpretation is therefore no more than a perspective." DF3, 127; cf. RP, 29.

127. In evaluating that the "love of simplicity, of reducing things to a few principles, hath produced many a false system,'" and chiding Descartes on the basis that "his system is built upon one axiom," Reid seems unwilling to consider that assent to a gamut of independent axioms, betrays that his thought is ultimately governed by but one: reality is fundamentally a multiplicity. Reid, *Inquiry*, 461.

128. Van Til regards Kant as "undoubtedly correct" in holding (against realists like Reid) that "the mind of man and the facts of the universe should never have been separated." SCE, 108.

129. Van Til makes greater reference to Immanuel Kant than any other philosopher. CTE, 242ff.

130. CTE, 227; cf. Ameriks, *Kant and the Fate of Autonomy*, 55ff.

Kant's key insight was that the modern ideal of human autonomy[131] must be construed more radically than it had before, as indicating that man actually imposes a spatio-temporal form and logical relationships—of quantity, quality, relation, and modality—onto the objects of experience.[132] With this unique blend, or better yet, alternative, to rationalism and empiricism Kant believed that he stood in a position to solve the basic problems of philosophy, and to dispel common errors. On this view, the realm of pure contingency can supply us with any number of unforeseen characteristics (colors, scents, atomic structures, etc.) and natural processes (condensation, photosynthesis, etc.),[133] without calling into question the belief that facts must be characterized by regular cause-effect relationships. For, as soon as that thing which occasions our empirical knowledge (a noumenon) is apprehended by the human mind it is immediately characterized by certain

131. Taking his cues from the Kant scholar/translator extraordinaire, Normal Kemp Smith, Van Til explains how Kant sought to save science and morality by positing the primacy of unadulterated contingency—"Norman Kemp Smith tells us that Kant was the first to take time seriously. That is to say, he openly disclaimed the possibility of the direct identification of rationality with changing factuality. Any such direct effort Kant spoke of as dogmatic thought. And dogmatic thought, whether of the rationalist or of the empiricist school, he argued, always runs into the same blind alley. It never can make contact between abstract thought and abstract brute fact. Therefore no form of dogmatic thinking can account for scientific knowledge. And no form of dogmatic thought can account for the significance of moral and spiritual reality as it is based on human freedom and autonomy. On the dogmatic view man would actually have to be in possession of exhaustive knowledge to be able to say that he knew anything. And how can man know the changing realities of space and time by means of exhaustive conceptualization? Again, if man knew everything, then on the dogmatic view, he himself as an individual would be swallowed up in the network of his conceptual relations. He would no longer be free. What then was the answer? How was science to be saved? And how was freedom, and with it morality, to be saved? Kant discovered the answer to both questions at once. In fact the two questions involve one another and require a single answer. The answer for Kant lies in the idea of the utter self-sufficiency or freedom of human personality. Science is to be saved by assuming that man's free theoretical thought is the source of the order found in it." CTE, 244.

132. Kant identifies twelve categories in all, three under each of the four headings mentioned in the text. The three categories of quantity are unity, plurality, and totality; the three categories of quality are reality, negation, limitation; the three categories of relation are substance and accident, causality and dependence, reciprocity between agent and patient; and the three categories of modality are possibility-impossibility, existence-non-existence, necessity and contingency. Kant, *Critique of Pure Reason*, A67–114/B92–116. Thus, in the judgment "all men are rational" the quantity is universal/total (all); the quality is that of reality/affirmation (are); the relation is that of a substance and accident (between men and rationality); and the modality is aimed at asserting a necessary as opposed to contingent relationship between the subject and predicate (men necessarily exude rational qualities).

133. Ibid. A376–80.

logical categories and thus rendered a scientific object (a phenomenon).[134] Unlike the common sense philosophers, Kant held that perception and ratiocination must be equally ultimate.[135] This is not because man consciously shapes empirical objects, but because a pre-reflective transcendental subject at work within man so constitutes the universe. Notably, Kant has a ready response to the skeptic who might deride his transcendental idealism as doubtful. In Kant's estimation, only the man who treats his logical categories as universally applicable in his day-to-day life could intelligently navigate his way through the world and thoughtfully construct an argument against his theory. But because Kant believed that only his theory could establish the universal authority the categories, one must presuppose something akin to his position before one can deny it.[136] Kant identifies this mode of argument as "transcendental" because it proves that the categories of understanding preside "over" all of experience, by showing that they make possible their own discovery, as well as any attempt at their denial.[137] In this case, whether we *directly affirm* or *directly deny* the applicability of the categories of understanding to empirical reality, we always *indirectly affirm* them.

By defining empirical knowledge as that which is initiated by definite experiences but formed by the intellect, Kant could draw a clear line between empirical knowledge and those beliefs which are speculative, but ethically/

134. NM, 14–8. Van Til's reading of Kant is in line with the widely held "two-world" interpretation of Kant as later defended by P. F. Strawson and Paul Guyer. However, another school contends that Kant's distinction between phenomena and noumena must not be taken to imply that, in the act of perceiving, the transcendental subject imposes a rational form onto an *ultimately independent* object. Instead, the thing-in-itself (noumenon) is nothing but a perception that one envisages abstractly and hypothetically, *as if* it enjoyed independent existence prior to its constitution as a phenomenon. Allision, *Kant's Transcendental Idealism,* 3, 16, 42, etc. Van Til would have been acquainted with this reading of Kant through the writings of various idealists. E.g., Pringle-Pattison, *Scottish Philosophy*, 130–32. Insofar as this interpretation places Kant in greater continuity with the German idealists that followed him, Van Til's critique of the latter (see 3.3) will serve double duty in also undermining the fundamental claims of an idealist Kant.

135. In Kant's famous words, "Thoughts without content are empty, intuitions without concepts are blind. It is just as necessary to make the mind's concepts sensible (i.e., to add an object to them in intuition) as it is to make its intuitions understandable (i.e., to bring them under concepts)." Kant, *Critique of Pure Reason*, A75/B51.

136. Ibid., A737/B765. Kant's transcendental argument is valuable for the sort of skeptic who doubts that he is *justified* in counting his beliefs as knowledge, but not for the extreme sort of skeptic who doubts that anything like truth exists. Walker, "Kant and Transcendental Arguments," 238–68; cf. Mourad, *Transcendental Arguments*, 10.

137. For Kant, each of the categories is a presupposition (*grundsatz*) that "has the special property that it first makes possible its ground of proof, namely experience, and must always be presupposed in this." Kant, *Critique of Pure Reason*, A737/B765.

practically necessary to embrace. To begin, the belief that man himself is a transcendental subject (i.e., the transcendental unity of apperception) who resides above the scientific realm of cause and effect cannot be reduced to empirical "knowledge," because, by definition, the transcendental subject never appears in nature. On the one hand, Kant's theory clarifies why men normally develop notions of an immortal soul, a universe, and of God. Each one is a hypothetical, but never scientifically verifiable apex to his three categories of relation—the soul is an immutable substance that underlies every accident; the universe is the sum total of conditions underlying every cause-effect relationship; and God is the lone necessary being Who resides above every mutually exclusive and mutually dependent relationship.[138] On the other hand, each member of a pair of metaphysical arguments for and against the human soul (not to mention a spatio-temporal limit to the universe, uncaused causes, and a necessary being) is just as demonstrative (and undemonstrative) as is the other member of the pair. And this indicates that those rational categories which characterize the scientific realm (nature) cannot yield true and dependable knowledge when divorced from the apprehension of concrete objects, as the rationalist philosophers supposed.[139] The natural question, then, is on what grounds the rational man can embrace certain religious/metaphysical beliefs? The answer, for Kant, is that man's ineradicable sense of right and wrong and ideal of final justice requires that he postulate the existence of the soul, the existence of God, and the reality of a final judgment.[140] And yet, man must confess that these ideas are practically necessary "beliefs," and not scientifically verifiable "knowledge." The truths of ethics and religion may never infringe on scientific pursuits, and the scientist can never prove or disprove God. Hence, by beginning with the utter autonomy of the human subject Kant believed that he could both save science from skepticism and save faith from the speculative philosopher.[141]

The philosophical world was initially mesmerized by the manifold benefits that Kant's philosophy seemed to procure. But it would not last. The great German Idealist philosophers detected fatal problems left by Kant, which Van Til was equally pleased to seize upon. First, Kant's philosophy asserted a deeply ambiguous relationship between the subject of knowledge and the nebulous thing-in-itself (noumenon) that occasions empirical experience. How is it that man may enjoy dependable "knowledge" of

138. Ibid., A323/B380. The three categories of relation are that of (a) substance and accident, (b) cause and effect, and (c) a community of mutually exclusive possibilities.

139. Ibid., A405–643/B432–670. Cf. CTE, 223–24.

140. Kant, *The Critique of Practical Reason*, 125. cf. CTE, 233–36.

141. "Whatever sort of God may remain, on Kant's view he is not the supreme interpretive category of human experience." SCE, 109.

phenomena, when they are produced by an interaction between noumenal realities (the subject and the thing-in-itself), the properties of which evade our understanding?[142] On the face of it, to assert that metaphysical knowledge is impossible would seem to require a rather extensive knowledge of what extrasensory reality is and is not capable of.[143] In order to speak of the thing-in-itself as "occasioning" or "causing"[144] empirical intuitions Kant would have to abandon his claim that the rational categories are inapplicable to the noumenal realm.[145] Van Til also points out that when Kant rejects the traditional theistic proofs because they make unwarranted claims about noumenal reality, he implicitly advances his own claim about noumenal reality—it cannot accurately reveal itself through phenomena.[146] How could Kant prove that the unknowable something that occasions our empirical knowledge cannot intrude upon the natural realm and produce miracles that exceed scientific explanation, or imbue man with occult modes of knowledge?[147] If the noumenal realm itself evades our knowledge, but gives

142. Pringle-Pattison takes note of the odd conclusion of the Kantian philosophy: the stronger term "knowledge" is reserved for the phenomenal realm, while the softer term "belief" is reserved for that noumenal realm on which the phenomenal realm must be thought of as resting. Pringle-Pattison, *The Idea of God*, 49–50.

143. SCE, 110. Michael Forester describes Kant as holding to an ironic sort of "dogmatic skepticism," where he claims to know that men cannot know any number of things about the noumenal realm. Forester, *Hegel and Skepticism*, 34. Kant was no doubt a target of Bradley's aphorism, "The man who is ready to prove that metaphysical knowledge is wholly impossible has no right here to any answer. . . . He is a brother metaphysician with a rival theory of first principles. And this is so plain that I must excuse myself from dwelling on the point." Bradley, *Appearance*, 1–2.

144. Kant defines a noumenon as "an object in itself, but only as a transcendental object, which is the cause of appearance (thus not itself the appearance)." Kant, *Critique of Pure Reason*, A288/B344.

145. Karl Ameriks defends Kant against the charge of inconsistency on the basis that Kant's arguments "exclude only certain specific kinds of claims to theoretical knowledge of things in themselves, namely, about their spatio-temporality." Ameriks, *Kant and the Fate of Autonomy*, 118; cf. 126ff; Guyer, "Thought and Being," 189. But even with this qualification, it is quite difficult to construe how Kant's positive description of noumena as occasioning sensible cognition can be squared with his claim that "the pure concepts of the understanding" which include causation, "can never be of transcendental, but always only of empirical use, and that the principles of pure understanding can be related to the objects of the senses . . . but never to things in general." Kant, *Critique of Pure Reason*, A246/B303. The rhetorical force of Kant's antinomy of pure reason is that rational categories such as cause-effect go astray when they are extended to matters that lie beyond the empirical sphere.

146. Using the term "univocal" to describe claims of direct knowledge about supersensible reality, Van Til alleges "Kant has slain univocal arguments for the existence of God by a univocal argument against such arguments." SCE, 111.

147. Ibid., 110. Kant admits that the Swedenborgian doctrines of telepathy and

rise to phenomena, Kant would have to admit that there is no prima facie reason why the categories with which man currently organizes the universe may not, at some point, change.[148] So long as Kant's position embraces a realm of unadulterated chance at the perimeter of our conceptual universe, it compromises the force of Kant's "transcendental" proof. Such uncertainties cannot be the precondition of rational discourse,[149] much less disbar supernatural phenomena or inexplicable intrusions into the natural universe.

The second major critique pertains to Kant's transcendental subject. Despite their widely different conclusions, Van Til and Hegel are agreed that the only sort of subject who can guarantee that the universe will not infringe on its rational freedom, is one who supplies both the form and the content, both the rational and the contingent element to external reality.[150] That Kant, even with his high doctrine of human autonomy, fell short of this goal is evident from the fact that he retained several dichotomies: subject/object, noumena/phenomena, freedom/nature, practical reason/pure reason. As a result, Kant was forced to deny that man could positively define his transcendental "self" through his historical development.[151] But a truly free and truly self-assured subject must be capable of identifying itself with its concrete history, precisely because both the normalcy and the novelty of the latter are expressions of the rational freedom inherent in the former. Kant's piecemeal deduction of the rational categories one by one, as opposed to charting their dialectical development from one another

---

intuitive knowledge of the future cannot be regarded as contradictory on his position. He chides such esoteric doctrines as "groundless," but it is quite clear that Kant is simply echoing the common conviction that such phenomena are fictitious, rather than proving that they have not on any anomalous occasion occurred. Kant, *Critique of Pure Reason*, A223/B270, A770/B798.

148. SCE, 109–15; CC, 33–34; CTE, 156–57. cf. Walker, "Kant and Transcendental Arguments," 259 cf. 254. Guyer believes that Kant's response to this sort of critique would be that: (a) such uncertainties are "the inevitable price to pay" if we are to be able to transcendentally deduce the categories, and (b) "there is no [better] alternative" to such a program. Guyer, "Thought and Being," 204–5.

149. Van Til explains, "There is on Kant's view no guarantee of any actual unity in science and philosophy any more than in theology. On this view contingency is ultimate. It is meaningless to speak of imposing the formalizing activity of the universal mind of man, itself the product of chance, on a bottomless shoreless ocean of chance." CTE, 250.

150. The relative superiority of Hegel over his predecessors consists in the fact that "he has included in rationality that which Leibniz took for granted as being inherently alien to it, namely, pure contingency itself." NM, 51.

151. In Van Til's estimation, Kant's identification of man with a pre-empirical subject leaves him with the daunting question "How then can the individual thinker think himself? He cannot. If he thinks, he *is not* the individual that thinks. If he *is* an individual, he does not think." CTE, 244.

within an all-encompassing mind/spirit (*geist*), betrays the fact that his "subject" was but a formal principle of unity which owes its self-expression to a contrasting principle of chance.[152] Hegel and his school go on to develop an absolute system where the empirical, ethical, political, aesthetic, and religious domains are proven to develop out of one another through an organic process.[153] For our present purposes, we need only observe how that philosophical current, which once asserted the self-sufficiency of the common man, and the dependability of his common sense, has given birth, and naturally so, to that Hegelian system, which is arguably one of the most speculative, counterintuitive philosophies of all time.

1.3.2 The Princeton Apologetic Undermines Reformed Theology

One of the upshots of the previous discussion is the insight that every philosophy allows a particular metaphysical vision to color every other judgment and inference. This point is directly related to Van Til's contention that, in so far as it is based on a common sense philosophy, the Princeton apologetic is incompatible with high doctrines of divine sovereignty and total depravity. First, the common sense notion that there is a multiplicity of *self*-evident truths carried with it the ironic conclusion that there is no single principle that binds them all together, except chance. Not only is pure contingency inconsonant with divine sovereignty, but it supplies us with every reason to doubt that universals and particulars, laws and facts, subjects and objects are, or will continue to be intelligibly related. Thus, Van Til insists that we must not speak of a set of independent self-evident truths, but of God-evident truths that are properly known and organized only in light of God and His specially revealed redemptive-historical plan.[154] In this

152. Hegel praises Kant for testing "the value of the categories employed in metaphysic," even though he fails to "inquire into the exact relation they bear to one another; but considers them as affected by the contrast between subjective and objective." Hegel, *Logic*, §40.

153. "To be sure, Hegel was in many respects more consistent than Kant. He saw and enunciated clearly that if man can have knowledge of any one fact he must have knowledge of all facts, inasmuch as all facts are interrelated. Of course, Hegel did not mean that any one human being or for that matter that all human beings together do know all things or can know all things comprehensively. Yet, it is in consonance with his most fundamental contention that, in principle, mankind must be able to know all things to know any one thing. . . . He saw clearly that Kant's creativity theory of thought demanded a more consistent application than Kant himself had given it. . . . If anything, Hegel developed still more than Kant the idea that the a priori and the a posteriori should never be separated." SCE, 114. Cf. NM, 47–52.

154. Van Til's denial that truth and meaning are ever *self*-evident as opposed to

case, knowledge of God cannot be construed as standing in need of theistic proofs, nor can God be the object of but one true belief among many others. If either situation were the case, it would reduce God to a mere member of man's actual or conceptual universe rather than acknowledge His actual prerogative as its transcendent Creator and Governor (see fig. 2).[155] Nevertheless, the classical proofs for God can be rectified if they are developed "analogically." The apologist must begin with facts and principles that he regards to be creations of God, which stand in need of interpretation with special revelation from God. From this theistic vantage point he may draw any number of inferences about the created sphere, including the conclusion that the universe could not exist as it does were it not created by an uncaused cause, a wise designer, a moral law-giver, an artistic genius, etc.[156] But, in this case, the apologist advances from a basic knowledge of God as the Creator to ever more refined visions of Him. God will not be mistaken for a logically possible, or highly probable being, but instead, He will be regarded as the very ground of reasoning since the only working conception of logical "possibility has its source in God" (see fig. 3)[157]

---

context-evident, and thus *God*-evident manifests itself in the following critique: "In the case of Scottish realism, there is to say the least, an undue emphasis given to the attempt to establish a realism or independence of the object over the subject," for "whatever we may find to be 'psychologically primitive,' as long as it seeks objectivity by a direct contact with the universe without an equally and more fundamental contact with God, it is thoroughly antitheistic." SCE, 132, 138.

155. Van Til regularly charges that the theistic proofs as normally understood demonstrate the existence of a finite god. IST, 56–61, 198; CTEV, 27–32, 47–48, 68; CG, 191; DF3, 142, 208; CA, 98.

156. CGG, 49–50; IST, 56, 198; DF4, 196–99.

157. SCE, 190; cf. IST, 38–41. Van Til distinguished his vision of a consistently Reformed epistemology from the Scholastic alternative thus, "Aquinas sought to show the unbeliever that the Christian story is in accord with logic and in accord with fact. Calvin sought to show that "logic" and "fact" have meaning only in terms of the Christian 'story.'" Van Til, "Calvin as Controversialist," WCV, NP.

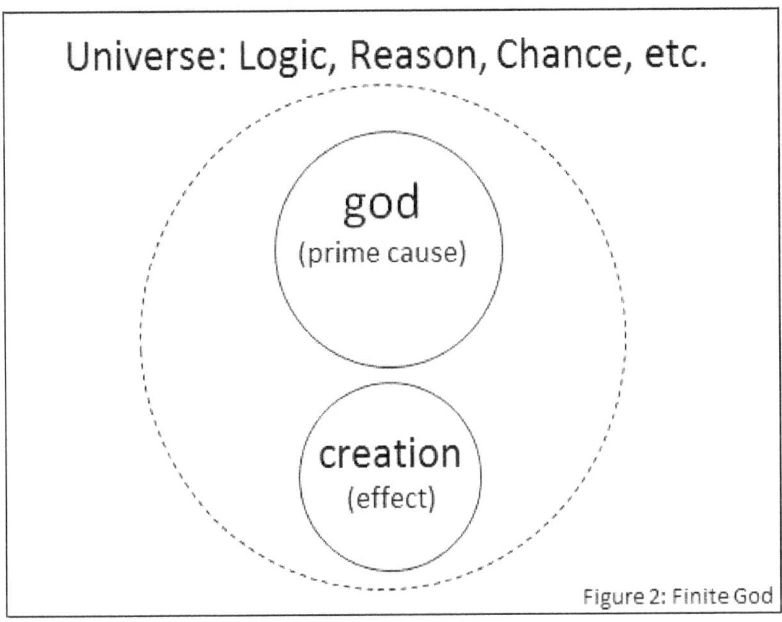

Figure 2: Finite God

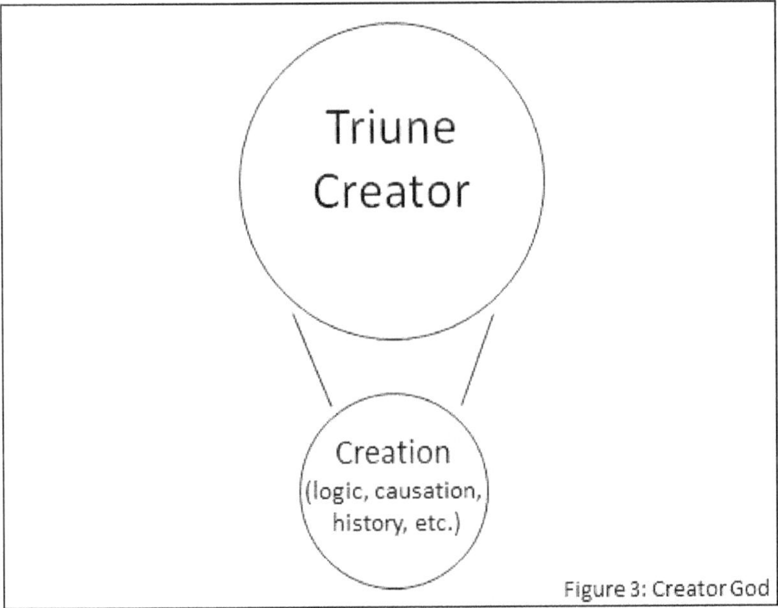

Figure 3: Creator God

Van Til's view, that our laws of thought can only function properly when set within a theistic context, comports rather well with Calvin's contention that true knowledge of man is always married to true knowledge of God. On such a scenario, it is also quite clear why sinful suppression of theistic knowledge would have such dire effects on man's knowledge in every other realm. However, if logic represents a set of principles, the meaning of which are self-evident and rightly apprehended by fallen man, then depravity is *not* total or all-encompassing. For, the interpretation of at least some features of the image of God in man (i.e., his reasoning power) is entirely untainted by man's unrelenting war to suppress the revelation of God from within and without. It would seem to follow that man is in some measure autonomous and capable of making sense of the world apart from divine guidance. For, man's reflection on his own laws of thought (i.e., logic) would not turn him immediately to contemplate how they are qualified by their status as divine images (as Calvin suggested that they must). Arguably then, the Princeton apologetic undermines Princeton's very own traditional Reformed doctrines of God, sovereignty, man, and sin. Nevertheless, at their best, the Princeton theologians do faithfully develop Paul's doctrine that men must be "renewed to a true knowledge" of all things by the work of Christ and the Holy Spirit (Col 3:10; Eph 4:23).[158] Van Til simply hopes to bring the Princeton apologetic into conformity with its own better insights on Pauline theology.

1.3.3 Theological Paradoxes Conflict with Common Sense

Finally, Van Til exposes Princeton's naivety in failing to appreciate that non-Christian presuppositions necessarily alter the implications and force of logic in a manner that renders certain Christian paradoxes unacceptable and flatly self-contradictory. Working on the presupposition that reason and reality are identical, Baruch Spinoza was driven, by a rigorous application of logic, to a monism that would render a biblical Creator-creature distinction wholly impossible. Kant's presuppositions led him to the conclusion that logical contradictions (antinomies) always result whenever we attempt to prove or disprove the existence of certain metaphysical concepts—God, a self-complete universe, etc. Furthermore, evolutionary naturalism renders logic subject to radical revision, as the human intellect constantly adapts

158. Van Til cites Hodge's exposition of Col 3:10 in his commentary on Colossians as standing in line with a presuppositional apologetic. CTK, 295; cf. DF3, 202. Even in his systematic theology, Hodge states clearly that the Scriptural teaching must be allowed to stand in judgment of philosophical theories (such as the realist doctrine of universals), rather than be shaped by them. Hodge, *Systematic*, 2:226–27. However, Hodge does not seem to take seriously the fact that the common sense philosophy to which he gives credence stands in need of scriptural assessment just as well.

to changes in its environment. According to these presuppositions, then, it is impossible to say with finality that any doctrine constitutes a logical certainty or a logical impossibility; except, perhaps, the doctrine of a self-complete God Who is impervious to development. Employing similar critiques, secular philosophers have also discarded as self-contradictory the doctrines of divine sovereignty, the inspiration of the Bible, etc.[159]

Some may be tempted to respond that in each of the above instances, Christian theology is only rendered self-contradictory when considered in the light of highly-developed and far-from-self-evident presuppositions about reality. However, the situation for Christian advocates of common sense is much bleaker than that. As we have seen, there is a long list of biblical doctrines that strike even the common man as obviously at odds with themselves. The tension between Princeton's commitments to common sense alongside of biblical paradox is evident in Princeton's distinction between "impossibility" and "incomprehensibility." Allegedly, the former refers to that which transgresses the laws of logic, while the latter refers to that which is infinitely and painfully complex. Hodge offers examples of the strictly impossible, explaining that "We cannot think of a round square, *or that a part is equal to the whole*."[160] But, ironically, the Christian doctrine of the Trinity, which Hodge and Warfield faithfully expound, involves the explicit claim that each of the *members* of the godhead is equal to the *whole* divine Being. Of course, Hodge's denial that the "part" may equal the "whole" implicitly concerns spatial objects, while God is spiritual. But this distinction only raises the question of how the demands of logic differ in their application to the spatio-temporal universe versus the transcendent Creator. An explanation of how the demands of logic take on a unique significance with respect to God requires an involved metaphysic that is far from self-evident. Thus, the Princeton apologetic strategy of indirectly vindicating the mysteries of Christianity by defending the trustworthy and reliable character of their source (the biblical texts and authors) will prove impotent to the masses who do not share Christian metaphysical presuppositions from the outset.[161] Hume taught that it is always more rational to disbelieve than to believe in miracles, because they are by definition improbable aberra-

159. IST, 37; SCE, 188–90.

160. Emphasis mine. Hodge, *Systematic*, 336–37.

161. Thus, Van Til qualifies Hodge's claim that the revelation of God cannot contradict "'any of the laws of belief which he has impressed on our nature'" noting that it is "true for the theist," who presupposes the created character of the laws governing his finite thinking, and thus expects that the revelation of God's nature will present him with surprises, "but not [true] for the antitheist," who invests his laws of thought with absolute authority. SCE, 191.

tions from the normal course of events. An even stronger case could be made for rejecting "paradoxes" which are by definition apparent and unresolved aberrations from the normal demands of logic. Hence, the committed advocate of common sense may only embrace biblical paradox—the Trinity, the Incarnation, the compatibility of divine sovereignty and human responsibility,[162] the notion that a self-complete God may receive glory from a finite creation,[163] etc.—*in spite* of his most basic commitments.

1.4 Van Til's Appropriation of Princeton

Having taken note of Van Til's critique of Old Princeton theology and apologetics we may very briefly identify those elements of their position that he embraced, and which drove his criticisms of the Amsterdam and absolute idealist schools. First, whatever disagreements he had concerning methodology, Van Til agreed with Old Princeton that the Christian apologist can develop an objectively valid argument for the Christian Faith, definitively vindicating it against heretical and pagan alternatives. Van Til's respect for his forbearers in the Faith is obvious from the fact that he consciously and avowedly modeled his career after the example of J. Gresham Machen, a devout evidentialist. Van Til's concerted critique of Karl Barth, *Christianity and Barthianism* was intended to function as something of a sequel to Machen's *Christianity and Liberalism*. Second, although he rejected the apologetic value of "common sense," he believed that the image of God in man is inextricable, and that it furnishes "common ground" between believers and unbelievers. This common ground consists of the fact that unbelievers are (a) created images of God, who (b) know that God exists, and (c) cannot wholly eradicate their confidence that the universe has been tailored by God to be enjoyed and manipulated by man. However, because fallen man naturally and immediate distorts his confidence (accrediting it to some self-evident characteristic of the universe, or a groundless psychological disposition) the aforementioned common ground cannot supply the apologist with a set of premises on which he and the unbeliever are mutually agreed. Van Til's objectively valid proof for God turns on the fact that the unbeliever's day-to-day orientation toward life is unjustified on his professed philosophy (non-Christianity), and indirectly confirms his reliance on God as the precondition of intelligible existence. Third, Van Til frequently acknowledges

162. DF3, 44–46.

163. Drawing on the image of a full bucket that will not admit for any addition of water, Van Til calls the paradox of God's reception of glory the "full bucket" problem. Ibid., 45; CG, 10, 27; IST, 40.

his debt to the Princeton Theologians for faithfully expounding and defending the paradoxes of the Christian Faith, especially Calvin's doctrine of the ontological Trinity. Still more, Van Til's preference to speak of the Triune God as both "one person" and "three persons" actually has antecedents in Hodge and Warfield.[164] As we will see, Van Til believed that only a doctrine of the Trinity that expressly affirms the ontological equality of the three persons can be the specially revealed solution to the greatest problems of philosophy, and the solely-fitting presupposition of a coherent worldview (see chs. 4–5).

164. IST, 299.

2

Old Amsterdam

2.1 OLD AMSTERDAM PERSPECTIVE

The once committed advocate of Modern Liberal Theology, Abraham Kuyper founded the Free University of Amsterdam in 1880, after having converted to the orthodox Reformed faith that was the historic status quo in Holland.[1] Controversy swelled as the national church increasingly capitulated to the influence of modern thought leading some Dutchmen to secede in pursuit of traditional expressions of the Reformed faith. Others, including Kuyper, insisted on reasserting Reformed principles in the political sphere that would both protect the purity of Reformed practice and worship from the state, and ensure religious freedom to the adherents of other schools of thought.[2] Having both held and observed the conflicting interpretations of life and politics developed by the adherents of different belief systems, Kuyper naturally took an interest in Kant's critical investigation of the human subject, and his attempt to identify the difference between knowledge, belief, and mere opinion. Unlike the Princeton theologians who had little to no affection for Kant, Kuyper held that "However much Kant and his contemporaries and followers intended to injure the Christian religion," they must be praised for "investigating the human subject" and its proper orientation to the manifold of objects.[3] Kuyper and his associates Herman

1. Hendrik de Vries, "Biographical Note," iv.
2. Meuther, *Van Til*, 21–28.
3. Kuyper, *Encyclopedia*, 300; cf. 49.

Bavinck and Valentine Hepp took very seriously the task of theological prolegomena, whereby one explains how and on what basis man is able to obtain legitimate theological knowledge. Already, we have alluded to the fact that the Amsterdam school generally rejected natural theology and apologetics in favor of a fideistic stance. And yet, in subordinating reason to revelation, the Amsterdam theologians did not capitulate to agnosticism, mysticism, or to a careless indifferentism toward systematic theology as William Brenton Green supposed a fideist must.[4] Instead, they went on to develop a full-orbed Christian worldview abounding with impressive insights on how biblical presuppositions must shape one's understanding of the natural sciences, law, politics, art, and culture.[5]

In order to appreciate Amsterdam's counterintuitive combination of a faith-based starting point and a subsequent rigorous and systematic development of the sciences,[6] a word must be said about post-Kantian developments in philosophy. Above we saw that Kant's philosophy seemed to leave nature and freedom, as well as science and ethics, at odds with one another. Empirically, man must conceive of himself as a causally determined phenomenon, confined to a natural universe where metaphysical and theological claims can never be elevated to the status of knowledge. But practically, man must conceive of himself as utterly autonomous and under the deepest compulsion to believe in God as the transcendent Judge Who finally rewards righteous conduct with eternal blessing. Hence, many perceived that unless philosophy is to succumb to the irrationalist conclusion that reason is inherently at odds with itself, either scientific or practical reason must be subordinated to the other.[7] Those who granted primacy to the objective deterministic realm held that although a distinction appears to exist between man and nature as we know it, we must look to the latter if we are to discover the principles which bind them together. But others, such as Johann Gottleib Fichte granted priority to ethics, and held that man must live *as if* a universal "subject" or "ego" is the ultimate ground of reality. Fichte frankly acknowledged that the transcendental subject cannot be proven to exist via

4. Green, "Function of Reason," 481–86.

5. Even an evidentialist the likes of B. B. Warfield revered Kuyper and his school for their commitment to reforming every discipline in light of Christ. Warfield, Introductory Note to *Encyclopedia*, in *Shorter Writings*, 1:447.

6. Following Dutch-German practice, we use "science" (*wissenschaft/wetenschap*) to refer to every legitimate field of inquiry, and not simply the hard, measurable sciences as in the English use of the term. See Kuyper, *Encyclopedia*, 16–28.

7. Frederick Beiser explains, "the main problem for philosophers after Kant, then, was to find some means of uniting Kant's disastrous dichotomies." Beiser, "Hegel and the Problem of Metaphysics," 11.

deductive or inductive reasoning. Such would implicitly involve granting primacy to logical categories and the principles of science. As with man's sense of morality, the transcendental subject may only be felt and intuited when in the midst of self-reflection one senses that the active "self" that beholds the objective and individual "self" is distinct from and prior to the latter. Although men who are ethically inclined will sense that positing the primacy of the transcendental subject over the objective realm is essential to preserving human freedom, nothing can detract from the radical decision that men must make between subjecting nature to freedom, or freedom to nature. Once one has decided in favor of the former, Fichte believes that he will embrace the speculative conclusion that the transcendental ego has spontaneously produced finite egos (humanity) and non-egos (nature), in order that it may forever pursue its own ethical freedom from the latter through the former. In other words, man's mission is to forever harness his natural desires and overcome the obstacles and challenges posed by the external world in order that the self-directing freedom of the transcendental subject may be realized in ever increasing measure.[8] Fichte went on to envelop the natural sciences, politics, and religion into his ethical doctrine of the transcendental subject.

2.1.1 Theological Encyclopedia

Kuyper's indebtedness to Fichte in his *Encyclopedia of Sacred Theology* is at times expressly acknowledged. To begin, the project of "encyclopedia" is not merely one of cataloguing distinct objects of knowledge, but of ascertaining (1) how the various objects relate to one another; (2) how man's mental faculties complement one another, and are fine-tuned to their object; and (3) the nature of the "knowledge" that results from the organic relationship between (1) and (2).[9] Kant paved the way for encyclopedia in the above sense, but "the victory of the organic idea" over an atomistic science "was first manifested in the writings of Fichte."[10] Expectedly then, Fichte furnishes us with a valuable list of insights. He was correct over against the naturalists in holding that the subjective life of man—"the image of God" (Gen 1:26)—furnishes a higher, more ultimate perspective on reality than the objective world.[11] Likewise, the spiritual sciences themselves ought to

8. Copleston, *History*, 7:61.

9. Kuyper, *Encyclopedia*, 66.

10. Ibid., 12.

11. Kuper declares that although the "idealism of Fichte in its own onesidedness may have outrun itself, you nevertheless cease to be man when the reality of spiritual

be geared toward the collective human subject/ego, as embodied first in Adam and second in Christ.[12] Last, "The line from Kant to Fichte" must be accredited with birthing the insight that every science begins with a faith-based certainty (Heb 11:1) that perceptions and intuitions are reliable.[13] Nevertheless, Fichte's ethical idealism is deficient in its failure to recognize: (1) that the human subject has been fractured into two groups: the fallen and the regenerate; and (2) that divine revelation represents a third object of knowledge—alongside of man and nature—that furnishes the only absolute perspective on reality.[14]

Were it not for the Fall, Kuyper is willing to concede that something very close to Fichte's subjectivism would have served as the natural and legitimate mode of reasoning. Originally, Adam was created with an innate trust that nature, man himself, and divine revelation were each distinct and legitimate objects of knowledge. Nature supplies man with innumerable perceptions of basic essences—of plants, animals, colors, emotions, societies, etc.[15] Man understands his intellect to be a "micro-cosmos," after the image of God's mind, that is prepared not only to receive external impressions, but to actively interrelate and organize them with the use of reason, the very divine Logos within him.[16] As God's vicegerent over the creation, man is able to actively investigate and even to manipulate nature, his body, his soul, and social life in pursuit of his divinely disclosed ends.[17] Knowledge of God, on the other hand differs from that of other realities in the twofold respect that it is both utterly dependent on God's revelation, and necessarily indirect. First, God is not a passive object of study, but the person Who actively creates our capacity to know Him. In this case, natural revelation could not enhance man's ability to know God in the least had God not first implanted the supposition in man that creation facilitates our knowledge of the divine nature.[18] Once God has revealed Himself, man lacks any standard by which to judge God's claims, or any means to transcend his finitude in order to pursue new avenues of theological

---

things is not more certain to you than what by investigation you know of plants and animals." Kuyper, *Encyclopedia*, 25; cf. 21, 48–49.

12. Ibid., 26–27, 64, 113.

13. Ibid., 41.

14. Kuyper, *Encyclopedia*, 69; Bavinck, *Philosophy of Revelation*, 29–52.

15. Kuyper, *Encyclopedia*, 22–3

16. Ibid., 19; cf. 107.

17. Ibid., 80–1.

18. Ibid., 97–8.

knowledge.[19] Second, any predicate that man might assign to God must first be found in a finite creation that cannot be directly identified with God. Only God possesses "archetypal" and immediate knowledge of Himself, while man's theological knowledge is necessarily "ectypal" and indirect.[20] Hence, the proper object of the theological science is not God in Himself, but God's free (though still certainly truthful) disclosure of Himself in revelation.[21] Kuyper supposes that, originally, God would have incrementally communicated various truths about his nature and will directly unto the human subject. In a manner comparable to that envisaged by Fichte, man in his innocence would have developed a flawless encyclopedia by internal guidance alone.[22] His limited perspective would have naturally blossomed into an "organic knowledge of the whole cosmos,"[23] that inter-related five basic objects: God, man (psychic, somatic, social), and nature (see fig. 4).

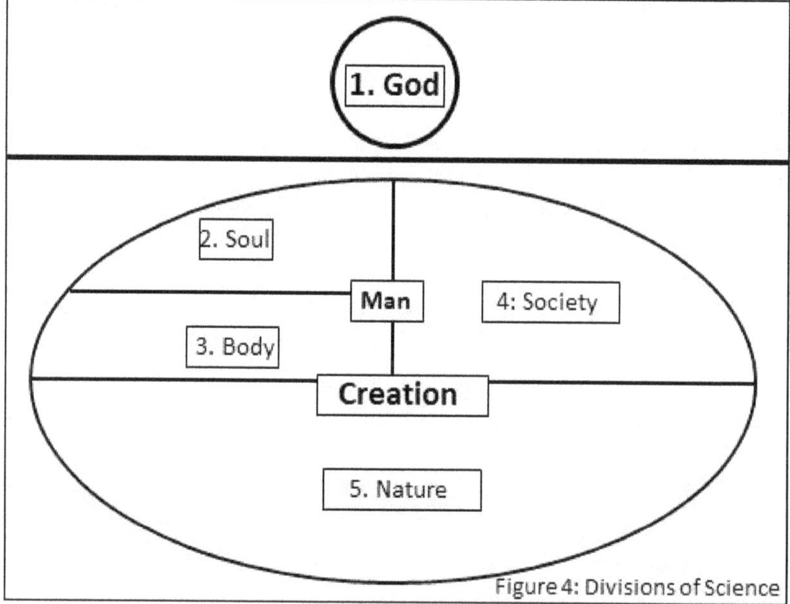

Figure 4: Divisions of Science

19. Ibid., 96–100.

20. Ibid., 81, 96–117.

21. Kuyper stressed that the biblical authors did not base their insights on a theological examination of prior revelation, but were directly granted inspired interpretations that could only be supernaturally mediated. Ibid., 116, 192. Van Til and Geerhardus Vos differ with Kuyper on this ponit, in holding that inspiration need not be opposed to active theological reflection, with the result that the biblical authors (e.g., Paul) may well be identified as theologians. Gaffin, "Geerhardus Vos and the Interpretation of Paul," 228–44.

22. Ibid., 20–28, 111.

23. Ibid., 20.

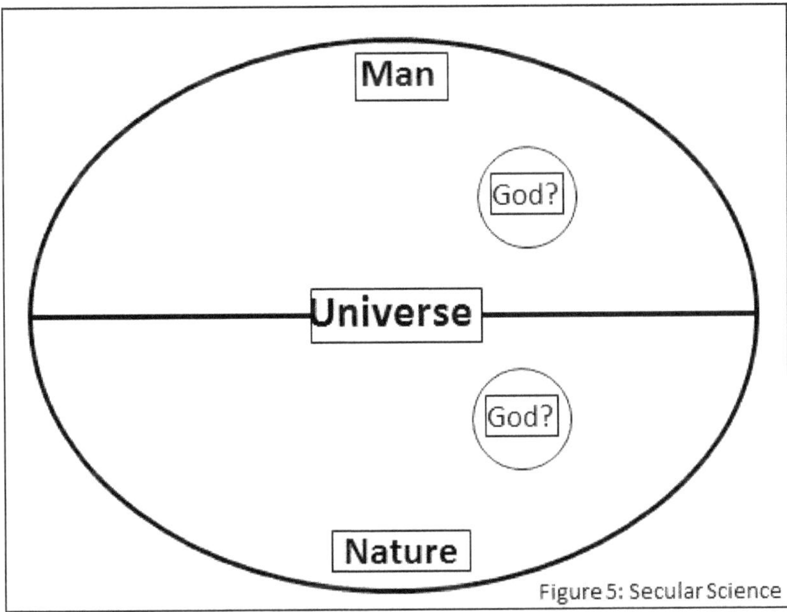

Figure 5: Secular Science

Adam's distrust of God's word in eating from the Tree of Good and Evil disrupted fatally the objective and subjective harmony of the created universe. As the covenantal representative of the collective human ego, Adam's faithless disposition toward God passed to every subsequent person in such a way that fallen men suppose their falleness to be perfectly normal.[24] By the same right, the objects of a fallen science are not only incomplete, excluding God, but broken and disorderly because of the unremitting wrath of God. Whereas the original human subject could trust himself, the myriad of baseless opinions entertained by fallen humanity, not to mention the ethical strife between individuals and societies has led many to skepticism that consensus, much less objective truth is attainable.[25] And yet, common grace has enabled humanity at large to retain its capacity for logical reasoning,[26] and even a muddled sense of deity.[27] Because men are still rational and religious, but lack a disposition of faith in God's revelation, secular thinkers and societies are prone to either (1) acknowledging God as a truly transcendent but frightening and unpredictable force (Acts 17:23);[28] or (2) reducing God

24. Ibid., 83.

25. Kuyper, *Encyclopedia*, 28.

26. Ibid.

27. Ibid., 16. Cf. Bavinck, *Philosophy of Revelation*, 1–28; Bavinck, *Certainty of Faith* , 31–50.

28. Kuyper, *Encyclopedia*, 110.

to a member, or to the whole, of the objective or subjective spheres. The latter disposition lies at the base of polytheism, pantheism, natural theologies which make God into a moral enforcer of *self-existent* ethical axioms (Kant, Fichte), and natural theologies which allow for a divine organizer of an otherwise unruly, and equally eternal cosmos (Plato, Aristotle).[29] In every case, God is reduced to a finite being who is subordinate to the basic principles of ethics and nature (see fig. 5), and beset by an equally original and pervasive principle of disorder.

The gospel contains the basic message of God's program for overcoming the disharmony and confusion that has infected creation. Because human reason has been hopelessly impaired by man's lack of immediate communion with God, man must be confronted with an objective portrait of the true ideal of human thought and life from without. Thus, reconciliation with God cannot possibly be accomplished apart from the Incarnation of the Son of God, the divine "Logos."[30] Christ's perfect submission to the Father, even unto death, is the embodiment of true wisdom (1 Cor 1:30) which perfectly heeds God's direction. Christ's example is a corrective to fallen reasoning, not because fallen men lack any sense of logic, but because they are given to grossly mistaken premises about themselves and their own authority.[31] But, Christ's work was not merely a matter of revelation. He also had to serve as a substitute for the first Adam (i.e., all of humanity), offering God perfect obedience and bearing the requisite penalty for mankind, in order to satiate the divinely wrath and confusion poured out on creation. But, only those members of the fallen race who are regenerated by the Holy Spirit and incorporated into the body of Christ, the new collective "ego," enjoy reconciliation with the Father and a renewed perspective on reality.[32]

The saving work of God simultaneously "breaks humanity in two and repeals the unity of the human consciousness."[33] The two types of men—the fallen and the regenerate—may agree on basic matters (e.g., measurement and counting), but their interpretations of the facts diverge indefinitely. Believers submit to Christ's revelation contained in Scripture and interpret all of creation as if it were in an abnormal state. Unbelievers suppose that disorder and death are necessary moments of evolutionary development.[34]

29. Ibid., 48–49, 82, 112.

30. Ibid., 111–17.

31. Ibid., 115.

32. Bavinck calls explicit attention to the Trinitarian mode of salvation presented here— "It is the Father who, through the Son as Logos, imparts himself to his creatures in the Spirit." Bavinck, *Dogmatics*, 1:214.

33. Kuyper, *Encyclopedia*, 50

34. Hepp, *Calvinism and the Philosophy of Nature*, 202; Bavinck, *Dogmatics*,

Believers demand that civil magistrates submit to God's law. Unbelievers elevate tyrannical leaders and popular consensus to the status of a divine rule.[35] Nothing in the way of reasoned argumentation or empirical evidence can heal this rift, for it is with regard to the very same matters of fact that such conflicting interpretations arise.[36]

2.1.2 Divine Mystery

If Abraham Kuyper was the pioneer of Christian Encyclopedia, Herman Bavinck was the genius to consolidate and apply his theological insights in the construction of a well-rounded and complete *Reformed Dogmatics.* As with Charles Hodge before him, Bavinck's fidelity to Scripture led him to acknowledge that several Christian doctrines represent incomprehensible truths. Bavinck generally supplies the same list of theological paradoxes mentioned with respect to Princeton—"The incarnation, the mystical union, the sacraments, etc."[37] Yet, with their distinctive beliefs about the place of theology among the sciences, the Amsterdam school was uniquely prepared to declare that, "Mystery is the lifeblood of dogmatics."[38] Catholic theologians who begin with "natural" reason are able to make room for theological mystery only by positing a higher, supernatural order of truth that can be anticipated by human reason, but finally lies beyond its fringes. The Princeton theologians took up a similar strategy. Bavinck, on the other hand, argues that every science deals with matters that reside beyond our full comprehension. The offense of divine mystery is due, not to its other worldly quality (after all, the theologian only deals with this-worldly revelation), but to man's fallen distrust of God.[39]

In laying down incomprehensible doctrines, God does not and cannot violate His own eternal Logos by requiring men to believe genuine contradictions. Acquaintance, knowledge, and comprehension are different matters, pertaining, respectively, to "that," "what," and "how" a thing happens

2:511–29.

35. Kuyper, *Encyclopedia*, 86; Kuyper, *Lectures on Calvinism*, 78–109.

36. David Lee Ratzsch observes that for Kuyper, "What causes the split is that believers and unbelievers differ in the data of their consciousness," the one being disposed to trust in the revelation of God, and the other not. Ratzsch "Abraham Kuyper's Philosophy of Science," 288, 300.

37. Bavinck, *Dogmatics*, 1:620.

38. Ibid., 2:29.

39. Ibid., 1:616–21.

to be.[40] With regard to "incomprehensible" doctrines men must have a valid foundation for believing *that* they are (e.g., experience, intuition, revelation, etc.), and be able to form an intelligible idea of *what* they are and imply, although they cannot conceive of *how* they exist as they do. Complex objects are comprehensible because their manner of being can be analyzed into more simple members and processes. The basic parts on the other hand are incomprehensible insofar as their essence cannot be analyzed further.[41] Theological mysteries offend us, and even appear to violate the law of contradiction, because secular men refuse to acknowledge theology as a distinct science with its own special ground of knowledge in revelation. As a result, they demand that the Christian theologian explain the irreducible facts of theology—the Trinity, the Incarnation, etc.—in terms supplied by the objective and subjective spheres of human existence. However, the regenerate man is perfectly comfortable, and in fact joyful, to declare that the nature and activity of a truly transcendent Creator God must be distinct from the elements and processes of nature and human existence.[42]

With the above account in mind, we may note that in identifying mystery as the life of dogmatics, Bavinck is not simply calling attention to the wonder that it excites within believers, but to the fact that our knowledge and communion with God is mysterious. Nowhere is this more evident than in Bavinck's discussion of divine incomprehensibility. Due to the ineradicable sense of deity in man, philosophers have long grappled with the intuition that beneath all things there resides an "unknowable abyss" upon which the known universe surfs. Plato, Aristotle, and Plotinus have in various manners and degrees identified this "unknown" as a static "one" over against the "many" moments/object of time, as an "All" in contrast to every finite fact and particular idea.[43] Beginning with the same sense of an unknowable "one," the Christian theologian nevertheless parts ways with the secular philosopher when he trusts the biblical revelation that the all-encompassing Absolute is also a person. Expectedly, secular philosophers such as Fichte denounce as self-contradictory the notion that a limitless Absolute could be a definite person, since definition implies limitation. Ludwig Feuerbach held that any concrete description of God must be a mere projection of human categories, a god made in the image of man.[44] However, in addition

40. Ibid., 1:619.

41. Kuyper, *Encyclopedia*, 16–19, 23.

42. Bavinck cites Tertullian with approval, "It is believable because it is absurd . . . certain because it is impossible." Bavinck, *Dogmatics*, 1:620.

43. Bavinck, *Dogmatics*, 2:30

44. Ibid., 2:43, 46. Cf. Kuyper, *Encyclopedia*, 48–49.

to retorting that an impersonal God is still, as such, meagerly defined, the Christian theologian frankly takes his stand on the mystery of revelation as pre-eminently displayed in the Incarnation. In the Incarnation, flesh does not take on deity, nor do human categories envelop the divine Being, but the Creator God declares that He has somehow vested finite reality with the capacity to reflect His nature.[45] Hence, God, the mysterious "one" discloses something of His nature in the paradox of revelation, and through that paradox He actively sustains a believer's ongoing relationship to Himself.

2.1.3 Supportive Apologetics

The Amsterdam school retained a small place for apologetics. Kuyper grants the systematic theologian the polemical task of refuting heretical doctrines from Scripture. On another level, the Christian philosopher must labor to demonstrate that Christianity fosters a degree of coherence between all of the sciences that is at best unsuccessfully mimicked by pagan theologies and secular philosophies.[46] Negatively, Kuyper, Bavinck, and the later Valentine Hepp denounced the modern trend toward materialism as inadequate for making sense of the human person, or for supplying particularly enlightening conception of nature.[47] With respect to Schelling and Hegel's pantheistic cosmogonies, Bavinck evaluates that they are "obscure," "unprovable," and subject to "open contradiction."[48] Likewise, in maintaining that physical objects can explain metaphysical realities (laws, forces, etc.) materialists land themselves "in an antinomy that has not yet been resolved by anybody."[49] Positively, Bavinck even grants that historical evidences, fulfilled prophecy,[50] and even the classical arguments for God "though weak as proofs," are nevertheless "strong as testimonies" to those who have experienced regenera-

45. Bavinck, *Dogmatics*, 2:49; cf. 1:344, 380. In contrast to Kant, Bavinck and Kuyper believe on the basis of revelation that it is possible to enjoy substantial knowledge of the noumenal realm. MacLeod, "Amsterdam, Old Princeton, and Cornelius Van Til," 265.

46. Kuyper, *Encyclopedia*, 121–24; 271. It is precisely this purely negative apologetic, without any positive demonstration of the faith that leads Warfield to criticize Kuyper's position as demanding that Christianity remains for the Amsterdam Theologians nothing more than a "great assumption." Warfield, Introduction to Beattie's *Apologetic*, *Shorter Writings*, 2:96.

47. Bavinck, *Dogmatics*, 1:219–22; Hepp, *Calvinism and the Philosophy of Nature*, 97–182.

48. Bavinck, *Dogmatics*, 2:413.

49. Ibid., 2:414–15.

50. Bavinck makes note of the fact that Jesus Himself on occasion calls us to believe on the basis of His works (John 10:38). Bavinck, *Certainty of Faith*, 57–60.

tion.[51] And yet, Kuyper ultimately cautions his readers against supposing that the grand coherence of Christianity as set over against the deficiencies of non-Christian thought can be taken as a definitive proof for the former. The unbeliever could well contend that human thought was never intended to rise above a fragmented perspective on the universe. Or, better yet, he could simply set his hopes on the future discovery of a coherent naturalistic account of things. In either case, the relative incoherence of secular worldviews does not imply that they need to be reworked according to Christian presuppositions, any more than "the coincidences of the facts, that one of your children is lost and that I have found a lost child" implies "that the child I have found is your child."[52]

2.2 VAN TIL'S CRITIQUE OF AMSTERDAM

Van Til often levels his cases against Amsterdam and Old Princeton together.[53] Such a procedure not only helps call attention to their differing interpretation of Calvin, but to their ironic agreement in embracing non-Christian versions of rationalism and irrationalism. We have already taken note of how the common sense underlying Princeton's classical apologetic method actually gave substantial footing to irrationalism. In the present context, we begin by taking note of how a fideistic trust in Christian presuppositions involves a lack of appreciation for how Christianity *differs* from non-Christian system of thought. This point precipitates Van Til's second critique that Amsterdam's irrationalism comes alongside of an equally basic rationalism that allows for "self-evident" truths in certain areas. Again, the self-defeating tendency to correlate rationalism and irrationalism is germane to the secular systems of Greek, Scholastic, and Modern philosophy. Third, Van Til contends that the Amsterdam's aversion to apologetics could have been corrected by embracing the Triune God as the solution to the basic philosophical problem of relating unity to diversity.

2.2.1 Amsterdam Apologetic Inconsistent with Antithesis

On the face of it, Kuyper's doctrine of antithesis would seem to undergird his depreciation of apologetics. If the Christian views non-Christian

51. Bavinck, *Dogmatics*, 2:91.

52. Ibid., 161.

53. DF4, 345–83; IST, 31–61.

attempts to construct a coherent worldview as fundamentally misguided,[54] and vice versa, then it would seem that there is no common ground between the two that would allow either camp to convince the other of their position. However, Van Til contends that those who "withdraw from all intellectual argument . . . have virtually admitted the validity of the argument against Christianity."[55] This is not simply because in withdrawing from offensive apologetics, fideists allow unbelievers to presume that their case against Christianity is valid. Instead, it is because one of the primary ways in which the Christian Faith differs from its secular competitors is in its exclusive capacity for objective demonstration. If Christian and non-Christian systems of thought were equally indemonstrable they would actually be the same, that is, *not in antithesis* in one of the most important respects. Yet, Scripture supplies a doctrine of antithesis that secures the possibility of an objective proof of Christianity. First, the Bible presents man as morally culpable for failing to serve God because knowledge of His existence and His ethical demands is inescapable. Man's problem is that he suppresses his knowledge of the truth (Rom 1:18ff).[56] Second, the Scriptures present non-believing worldviews as self-defeating (Prov 8:36; Jer 2:13, 19; Matt 16:25; 1 Cor 1:20–25). In this case, the apologist does not need any neutral point of contact to begin his apologetic. Instead, he may reason from the impossibility of non-Christian systems to the validity of Christianity.

2.2.2 Fideism Characteristic of Non-Christian Irrationalism and Rationalism

Van Til's second critique is based on the observation that Amsterdam theologians succumbed to rationalist and irrationalist tendencies that are common to secular thought. In this respect, the Amsterdam school flirts with the basic contradiction that has hampered secular philosophical programs throughout the ages.[57] Philosophers have oscillated between a view of reality as a unified system, and a view of reality as open-ended and receptive to a multitude of unforeseen facts, moments, and events. At base, the conflict

54. "As soon as the thinker of palingenesis (regeneration) has come to that point in the road where the thinker of naturalism parts company with him, the latter's science is no longer anything to the former but 'science falsely so called." Kuyper, *Encyclopedia*, 61.

55. CTEV, 34.

56. For Van Til's understanding of several key texts concerning the ubiquity of divine revelation see his pamphlet, PA.

57. For Van Til's concept of contradiction, see 6.3.

is between a view of the universe as "one" or "many." Yet, the question spans into virtually every realm of philosophy, appearing in the dichotomies between eternity and time, idealism and realism, determinism and freedom, etc. Several philosophers have decidedly embraced one principle over the other, but most have felt the need to do justice to both unity and diversity. On the one hand, human thought must refer to self-evident, immutable ideas if it is to be true and reliable. On the other hand, human reasoning must acknowledge that reality is marked by a principle of novelty and unpredictability that resists rational penetration.

Although it may initially seem impractical, the "one and many" question has vast implications. The epistemological problem regarding whether our sense perceptions correspond to external reality, is ultimately one of how we may be certain that our rational categories (the one) do justice to the spatio-temporal objects (the many) they supposedly represent.[58] A similar, metaphysical question is whether the future must be consistent with the past, such that there is a discernible unity of development (the one) that binds together the diverse moments of time (the many).[59] When one ponders whether moral absolutes exist, he is asking whether there are unchangeable ethical standards (the one), which are equally authoritative in all situations (the many). Identification of the proper social dynamic between governments, religious bodies, families, and their individual members rests upon our ability to determine whether the needs of the group (the one) sufficiently represent the needs of each individual (the many), or whether one takes precedence over the other.[60] In the event that the "one" does not perfectly overlap with the "many," how do we know that they can overlap at all? If, for example, we concede that our ideas (the one) cannot perfectly represent concrete objects (the many) as they really are, then it would seem that our ideas might consistently miss something detrimental or, worse yet, might lack correspondence with reality altogether.[61] Likewise, if we allow that moral laws only apply to some, or even to most situations, how can we determine when or if they ever apply? On the other hand, if the "one" does exhaustively represent the "many," has not the "many" been swallowed

58. This Van Til designates the "Subject-Object" relation. SCE, 217.

59. Ibid., 217.

60. Although Van Til does not expound on the dynamic between the "one and many" in social spheres he applauded the efforts of R. J. Rushdoony in this area. Van Til, "Response to Rushdoony," 339–48. Cf. Rushdoony, *One and Many*.

61. If even the slightest bit of reality evades the comprehension of reason, "There would be an area of reality totally unknown to anyone. And yet this area might have some influence upon the reality that we seem to have knowledge of. Hence, we would not even have knowledge of that which we thought we had knowledge." SCE, 40.

up entirely, so that the "many" is an illusion? If, for example, the past, the present, and the future are not only similar, but exactly the same, have we not done away with time altogether?[62] Or, if the ends of the state are taken to exhaust the ends of each individual citizen, have not the citizens lost their individuality entirely? Can citizens have any individual rights or freedoms to pursue their own course? Furthermore, if eternity or time reigns supreme, how did the illusion of the opposing concept even arise?[63]

In considering the three basic answers to the "one and many" problem, Van Til held that Plato had early on "exhausted the possibilities of all anti-theistic thought, whether ancient or modern" (cf. Eccl 1:9; 2:11–12).[64] First, Plato considered and rejected the view that the "many" spatio-temporal facts might be able to furnish sure and dependable knowledge. Perhaps, he thought, the lone dependable feature of reality is the fact that it is constantly fluctuating, and passing into its opposite. But, a universe which is constantly and unpredictably changing may very well pass into non-existence altogether, in which case every feature of the universe, including change itself would be lost. Second, Plato looked to the "one" for a dependable foundation for knowledge. The world of ideal forms seemed to represent an immutable and harmonious system in which every form—"man," "god," "existence," etc.—could be viewed as subordinate to the one ultimate form of the "good." But upon reflection, one can also form ideas of "falsehood," "change," "evil," etc. that cannot be incorporated into a system of ideas that are chiefly characterized by "goodness." Thus, there would seem to be conflict in the ideal realm just as well as the real.[65] Third, Plato concluded that only those forms which can be harmonized with the "good" are truly ideal, while characteristics like evil, change, and falsehood must be associated with temporal material. Plato was never able to explain how two things as distinct as the real and the ideal could merge or overlap in the universe as we know it. Somehow the universe is conducive to man's knowledge of eternal truths, even though the ultimate nature of reality is beyond all searching out. Although Aristotle would insist on a tighter union between the real

62. NM, 12.

63. Van Til believes that the unanswerable question for all those who grant priority to eternal unity along the lines of Parmenides and Plotinus is, "*Cur Deus Homo*?" or why did the eternal rational principles ever give rise to the illusive temporal universe of which man believes himself to be a part?" SCE, 28, 35.

64. SCE, 38; CTE, 21. For a similar evaluation see Dooyeweerd, *Twilight of Western Thought*, 35ff.

65. "The question was, by what right did the idea of Good rule over all the others? . . . [S]ince it was of the very nature of all ideas to be unchangeable and to oppose their opposites, it would certainly be intolerable to contemplate the Idea of the Good as bringing forth the Idea of the Bad." SCE, 37.

and the ideal where neither can exist apart from the other, he too regarded their union to be fundamentally mysterious.[66] It is not surprising then, that later Greek thinkers (Stoics, Epicureans, etc.) turned their interest to practical matters since the metaphysical difficulty of relating the "one and many," pure rationalism and pure irrationalism proved impossible.

The story of modern philosophy as we have considered it in the previous chapter led to similar conclusions as that of the Greeks. Kant's argument that the natural realm must be characterized by immutable forms and categories even though it rests upon a sea of pure freedom, is in many respects the same as Plato's marriage of eternal forms with temporal material (see fig. 6 and fig. 7). Both allow man to reason like a rationalist, as if he were able to comprehend ideal essences and logical relations, without any regard for the evasive and indefinable "something" that underlies them. On the other hand, both make a concession to irrationalism in their admission that if either the "one" or the "many" has priority over the other, we have no idea how, and if the two are harmonized by some third principle we have no idea what it might be. Most importantly for our purposes, both the Greeks and the Moderns manifest a resolve to press forward in offering what are at best "probable" solutions to practical difficulties, even though their ultimate metaphysical portraits of reality cannot, by their own admission, be definitively proven.[67] Hence, a self-assured sort of fideism is, in many respects, *the* conclusion of Western philosophy.

66. In identifying the union of essence and existence as *the* fundamental "paradox" of reality, Etienne Gilson accurately conveys the conviction of Aquinas and Aristotle. Gilson, "The Spirit of Thomism," 646.

67. Van Til regards the turn toward practical philosophy as a tacit admission that the basic questions of existence cannot be answered. CC, 22, 33–34. Bertrand Russell's qualification of his own philosophy is a prime example—"I do not pretend that the above theory can be proved. What I contend is that, like the theories of physics, it cannot be disproved, and gives an answer to many problems which older theorists have found puzzling. I do not think that any prudent person will claim more than this for any theory." Russell, *My Philosophical Development*, 27.

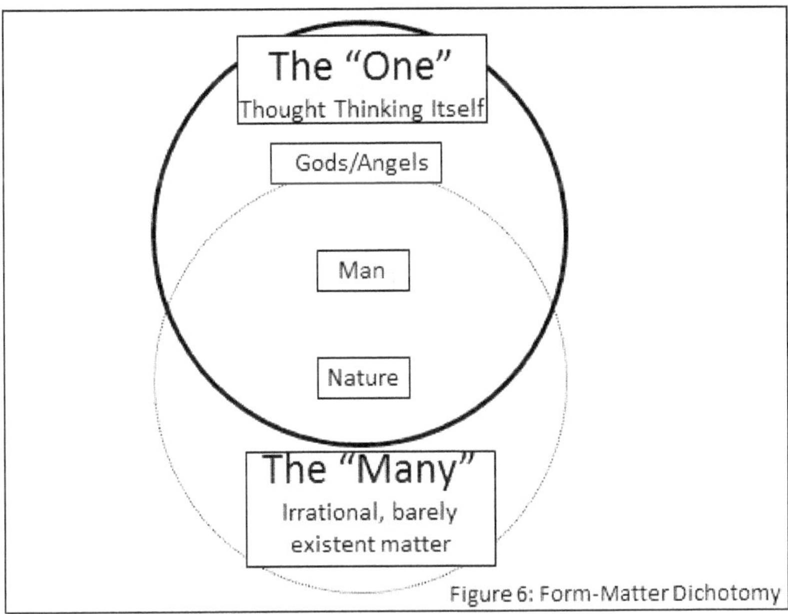

Figure 6: Form-Matter Dichotomy

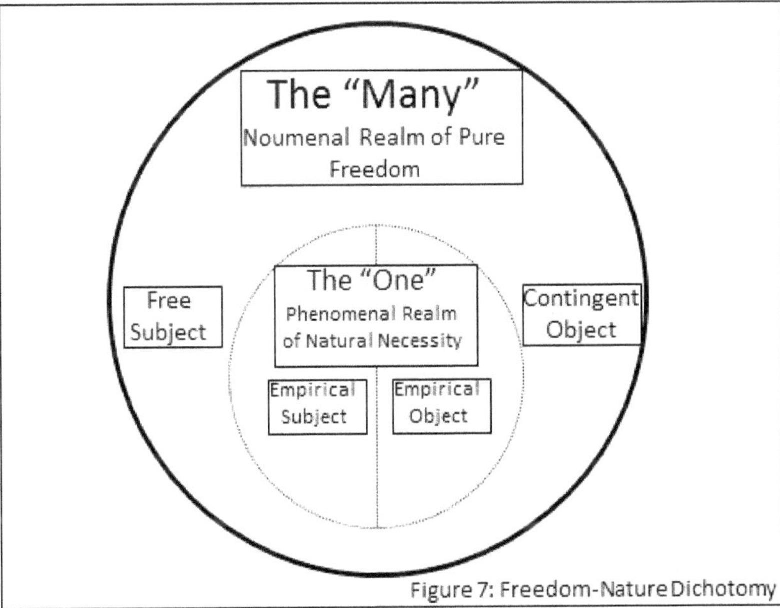

Figure 7: Freedom-Nature Dichotomy

Given his evaluation of secular philosophy, ancient and modern, as at once rationalist and irrationalist, it is not surprising that Van Til would critique the Amsterdam school for imbibing too much Aristotle, and too much Kant. First, Amsterdam's rationalism is evident in Kuyper's contention that man can comprehend logical relations and universal categories, although the individual facts that embody them are strictly unknowable.[68] He also contends that the results of "counting" and "measuring" are self-evident to believers and unbelievers alike, even though they build radically different systems around them.[69] On occasion, Kuyper even speaks of the divine Logos as if it were identical with the human intellect, recalling Plato's association of reason with eternity and God, and flesh with time and chance.[70] And Bavinck explicitly argues for a "moderate realism," after the manner of Aristotle, as a viable alternative to rationalism and empiricism.[71] Second, Amsterdam's irrationalism is evident from the tendency to treat the factual element in the universe as resistant to rational definition. Still more, Bavinck's approval of the idea that whatever binds together the "one and many" must itself reside beyond all, or nearly all positive definition, is to make the irrational just as basic to reality as the rational. Van Til decries Bavinck's contention that the philosophical idea of a universal unknown "became the starting point and fundamental idea of Christianity."[72] Third, given their combination of eternal, self-evident truths with an unpredictable and ultimately indescribable system of reality, it follows that Amsterdam would reject any attempt to definitively prove the Christian Faith. The Christian and the non-Christian reside in a similar position. They both have equal access to neutral tools of reasoning (logic, mathematics, perception, intuition, etc.) with which to construct a view of reality that is practical and useful. But, both are ultimately incapable of vindicating their interpretation of things because reason itself is beset by an equally pervasive "unknown" that will admit of any number of interpretations. Amsterdam's relative depreciation of the theistic proofs as merely supportive of the Christian system is not significantly different from Princeton's insistence that they prove Christianity with high probability.[73] Both schools deny that the Christian worldview represents the only intelligible interpretation of reality, and each, in their own methodologies, succumbs to a rationalist-irrationalist scheme that has so frustrated secular thought.

68. Kuyper, *Encyclopedia*, 16–19, 23. Commenting on this tendency in Kuyper, Van Til states, "All this is still Platonic. It is more than that: it is Kantian." CG, 36–37.

69. Van Til, on the other hand, denied that there is any realm of neutrality. Ibid., 34–63.

70. Ibid. 107.

71. Bavinck, *Dogmatics*, 1:207–33.

72. Ibid., 2:36.

73. In keeping with the rationalist trend, Van Til discerns a growing appreciation for the theistic proofs from Kuyper, to Bavinck, to Hepp. IST, 48–61; CG, 58–64.

2.2.3 Failure to Exploit the Apologetic Import of the Doctrine of the Trinity

The Amsterdam school should have been keenly aware of the radical difference between the mystery involved in the Christian doctrine of the Triune God, and the mystery of the universe as conceived of by Plato.[74] The paradoxical harmony between the "one and many" postulated by the Greeks is admitted to be incomprehensible to man, and to any authority with whom he has personal contact. In contrast, the paradox of unity and diversity within the Godhead is paradoxical to man, and yet perfectly comprehensible to the Triune Creator with whom believers enjoy personal relationship. In one respect, Greek thinkers were correct that man does not know God, for indeed sinners actively suppress their knowledge of the truth (Acts 17: 23; 1 Cor 1:20; Gal 4:8; Eph 4:18; 1 Thess 4:5; 2 Thess 1:8). On the other hand, all men retain an inextricable and robust awareness of their Creator as a longsuffering, righteous, and holy person as they attempt to erase their consciousness of him (Ps 19:1–4; Acts 14:16–17; 17:26–29; Rom 1:18–23).[75] The human tension between relative ignorance and relative knowledge of the truth (created and divine) is not due to the fact that the universe is partly rational and partly irrational. Quite the contrary, the doctrine of the Trinity ought to inform us that both the consistency and the novelty of the universe reflect the ontological harmony of their Creator. The only reason man first thinks himself consigned to a probabilistic, and then to a fideistic interpretation of reality is because he has misconstrued the universe as something less than the creation of the Triune God from the outset. Had Amsterdam taken this point seriously, they would have held that Christianity is certainly true, and demonstrably so, on the basis that the alternative position renders everything uncertain and deprives man of *the right* (though certainly not of the careless resolution) to suppose that predication of any kind is possible.[76]

2.3 Van Til's Appropriation of Amsterdam

As a conclusion to our study and critique of Amsterdam's theology and apologetics, it is necessary to identify those elements that Van Til warmly embraced. First, Van Til forever defended the notion of an antithesis between Christian and non-Christian worldviews that was resultant from

74. SCE, 31–32; CG, 29, 46.

75. Bahnsen's dealing with these two complementary biblical themes is particularly informative. Bahnsen, "Encounter of Jerusalem with Athens," 235–76.

76. For Van Til's positive argument for Trinitarian Theism see 4.2–4.

their opposing epistemological presuppositions. Second, Van Til largely embraced and defended Kuyper's doctrine that believers and unbelievers are able to communicate and even work together because of common grace, whereby God restrains unbelievers from thinking and living in strict accordance with their presuppositions. And third, Van Til acknowledges his debt to the Amsterdam school for the insight that God, nature, and man represent the three fundamental objects of a Christian science. Such a view undergirds the notion that the theological science must rest on the Trinitarian economy between the Father Who serves as the essential foundation, the Son Who penetrates the natural world as the objective foundation, and the Spirit Who penetrates the heart of man as the subjective foundation for theological knowledge.[77]

77. IST, 44, 62–109.

3

Absolute Idealism

3.1 INTRODUCTION

Although Van Til's academic career culminated in a philosophy Ph.D. from Princeton University, his interests in philosophy were first cultivated within what were primarily theological institutions. At Calvin College, Van Til sat under W. Harry Jellema, who had, in turn, studied under the greatest American Idealist philosopher, Josiah Royce. Jellema required that his students read F. H. Bradley's *Appearance and Reality*, quite possibly the most important absolute idealist text produced in English.[1] Kuyper and Bavinck, the well-known heroes of neo-Calvinism evinced the influence of Kant and Fichte and consciously interacted with various absolute idealist doctrines. Although they were not generally fond of Hegelianism, several Princeton professors and contributors to the *Princeton Theological Review*,[2] proved capable of grappling with the absolute idealist philosophy. Van Til was acquainted with C. W. Hodge's interpretation of the failures of Hegelianism as evinced by its division into the warring schools of pantheism, neo-Kantian scientism, and Schopenhauerian pessimism.[3] And yet, others offered a qualified commendation of absolute idealism. E. D. Miller concludes his

1. Frame, *Van Til*, 21.

2. Van Til's list of the 24 most important works on formulating a Christian Epistemology includes 11 articles from either *Presbyterian and Reformed Review* (1890–1902), or its replacement, *Princeton Theological Review* (1903–1929). SCE, 198–99.

3. Hodge, "Recent German Philosophy," 211–27.

critical evaluation of Josiah Royce's philosophy by saying, "we are forced to recognize that, as an ideal of greatness and as an intellectual exhortation to achievement and attainments, Hegel's philosophy is truly great, imposing and inspiring. And to Prof. Royce we are indebted as a defender of the faith, as a brilliant author, and as a great intellectual quickener and educator."[4] Earlier affiliates of Princeton seminary anticipated several of Van Til's most "Hegelian" teachings: e.g., the epistemological import of a personal absolute;[5] the significance of the "one and many" problem;[6] and the benefit of defending Christianity by way of transcendental argument.[7] But ultimately, Van Til's sustained engagement with absolute idealism came at Princeton University via the guidance of the distinguished personalist idealist, A. A. Bowman. Van Til's dissertation, "God and the Absolute" is driven by the attempt to distinguish and, ultimately, to vindicate the Christian God over against the Absolute as defined by Hegel's British disciples.

With a view to appreciating the underlying impetus of a philosophy as complicated as absolute idealism, we begin our account below with its patriarch, Hegel rather than his British innovators. This is because difficult Idealist doctrines often appear to be without any discernible benefit when divorced from the problems posed by Kant's system that Hegel labored to overcome. Nevertheless, the British representatives will come to the forefront when we discuss Van Til's critique of absolute idealism. As we will, see the disharmony among British Idealists calls attention to the ambiguities and inadequacies of the system left by Hegel. The fivefold division of what follows includes a discussion of (a) the nature of the absolute idealist system; (b) the place of paradox; (c) the status of Christianity within absolute idealism; (d) Van Til's critique of absolute idealism; and (e) Van Til's modified[8] appropriation of absolute idealist categories.

4. Miller, "Professor Royce's Idealism," 298.

5. Griffin, "Personality the Supreme Category," 507–23.

6. Bouma, "Hegelianism and Theism," 201–14.

7. Griffin, "Epistemological Argument for Theism," 341–63; Bouma, "Christianity's Finality," 337–54; Orr, *Christian View of God and the World*, 10, 13–14, 114. Notably, Van Til critiques Orr for presenting the logic of history, and its trajectory toward a vindication of Christianity, as if it were self-evident, prior to being interpreted through the lens of special revelation. CTEV, 47–48; cf. Knudson, "Progressive and Regressive Tendencies," 280–83.

8. Van Til's use of absolute idealist concepts and terminology never represents a simple adoption of their ideas. McConnel, "The Influence of Idealism," 557–88.

3.2 ABSOLUTE IDEALIST PERSPECTIVE

3.2.1 Hegel's System

Whatever doubts there may be with respect to the quality and intelligibility of Hegel's philosophy, there can be no disagreement that it is unparalleled in its grandiose ambitions. Van Til's keen interest in absolute idealist philosophy was based on Hegel's refusal to rest content with tenuous dichotomies between the "one and many," and on Hegel's vehement pursuit of a positive and rationally demonstrable portrait of the Absolute reality that harmonizes all things.[9] Hegel appreciated the fact that unresolved dichotomies between universals and particulars, eternity and time, freedom and necessity, subject and object, open the door to a hampering sort of skepticism that undermines man's most basic pursuits. His basic program for overcoming such dichotomies involved rejecting both the rationalist doctrine that the meaning and implications of logical principles and empirical facts are self-evident, as well as the irrationalist doctrine that the temporal course of events is fundamentally chance driven.[10] Instead, he argued that reason and reality are only intelligible (a) through their mutual contrast with one another, and (b) as united by a concrete system which comprehends them both. In this case, the ultimate "one" that comprehends the universe is not a general notion of "being" that can be abstracted from the "many" members, but a concrete universal, or Absolute system, the unity of which is only evident through the diversity of its parts. Since humanity and the social relationships between its members represent the most complex and robust sort of system, the Absolute is most accurately described as an infinite mind/spirit (*geist*) who realizes his autonomous rationality in and through human consciousness. Finally, Hegel believed that his doctrine of the Absolute could be proven with certainty via a transcendental argument to the effect that one cannot employ reason or appeal to facts in defense of a less comprehensive view, for such principles are self-defeating when divorced from their Absolute context.[11]

9. Hegel "saw and enunciated clearly that if man can have knowledge of any one fact, he must have knowledge of all facts, inasmuch as all fact are interrelated." SCE, 114.

10. Absolute idealist Bernard Bosanquet reflects the sentiments of his school in noting that "*a priorism*," or the belief that logical laws possess a self-evident character that goes unaffected by temporal reality, actually fosters relativism. For, such a belief divorces reason from the concrete universe, and necessarily consigns the happenings of the latter to irrational forces. Bosanquet, *Implication*, 145–46.

11. Forester, *Hegel and Skepticism*, 117–26.

Although Hegel labored to solve the all-pervasive "one and many" problem the distinctive features of his program are especially evident when compared and contrasted with two other German Idealists who had labored to overcome the unresolved problems left by Kant, namely Johann Fichte and Friedrich Schelling. We have already alluded to the fact that Hegel wished to construct a rational demonstration for the Absolute, rather than to rest content, as Fichte had, with the subjective intuition, that a universal subject which treats nature as an ethical hurdle is a postulate of moral consciousness. Hegel took sides with his one-time compatriot Friedrich Schelling, who rejected Fichte's deprecation of nature, as a mere negative to mind. More importantly, Hegel followed Schelling in arguing that the apparent dichotomy between subject and object *must* rest upon a more fundamental unity between them. It was Schelling's contention that an ultimate subject-object identity may be transcendentally deduced (in a manner reminiscent of Kant's categories) as the precondition of intelligible experience, including one's doubts and denials of it, for there could be no contact between mind and matter unless they were members of some common substance.[12] Nevertheless, Hegel rejected Schelling's conclusion that the subject-object identity which underlies all things is indefinable. On Hegel's view, the Absolute subject-object identity must itself be identical with the world of dichotomies that rests upon it.[13] To use his favorite analogy, the Absolute is comparable to an organism, say a tree, which is preeminently expressed in its maturity as a fruit bearing plant, but which is equally inseparable from its various stages of development from seedling, to growing limbs, to blooming blossoms, etc.[14] Unlike Fichte's transcendental subject, which is definable but indefensible, and Schelling's subject-object identity, which was defensible but indefinable, Hegel pursued an Absolute that could be both proven and robustly defined, as a universal organism.

Hegel's initial and perhaps most celebrated attempt to expound and defend his doctrine of the Absolute against all known competitors is the *Phenomenology of Spirit*. For Kant, "phenomenology" referred to the study of things as they appear in contrast to how they exist in themselves. But, as we have noted above, Hegel denies the existence of independent things-in-themselves. Thus, his phenomenology catalogs not only the various sorts of phenomena, but the states of consciousness that accompany them, and which even mistake those phenomena for self-intelligible entities. The

12. Beiser, "Hegel and the Problem of Metaphysics," 15–16.

13. As Copleston puts it, "The Absolute is not simply the One. It is the One, but it is also the Many: it is identity-in-difference." Copleston, *History*, 7:193.

14. Hegel, *Philosophy of History*, 18, 78.

ultimate subject-matter of the phenomenology is that all-pervasive Spirit, which progressively comes to self-consciousness in the dynamic between the finite subjects and objects which it posits for itself. The difficult survey of the *Phenomenology of Spirit* that follows is intended to convey three important points. First, supposedly self-intelligible concepts owe their definition in part to their opposites. Second, every opposition between concepts implies a superior notion which harmonizes them. And third, the major dichotomies of Western philosophy are supposed to be overcome in Hegel's vision of the Absolute. Finally, Hegel's phenomenology must not be mistaken as charting the chronological course of development in each person's thinking. His point is to unfold the ideal course of development between the broad forms of consciousness manifested in human history.

At the most rudimentary level of (i) sense certainty,[15] man considers atomic facts, without regard for their general qualities, to be the basic and most immediate objects of knowledge. He, in turn, views himself as an equally empty and indifferent receptacle of those facts. But upon reflection, such a view proves self-defeating. Every attempt to consciously identify a brute fact betrays dependence on universal qualities—e.g., "this is *red*," "here is a *dog*," etc. Even "pointer" words such as "here" and "now," as in "this *here*" betray a dependence on a general notion of "presence." Thus, human consciousness passes to the stage of (ii) perception[16] where rational ideas—of "green," "man," "number," etc.—are held to be the true and immediate objects of knowledge. In this case, the human subject conceives of itself, too, as a universal (a soul), which maintains its essential quality through the many moments of life. But again, upon scrutiny it becomes clear that rational ideas lack definition except as they are unified and contrasted with one another in concrete facts. What could it mean to know "whiteness" apart from an empirical awareness that it is incompatible with "blackness," and yet perfectly capable of union with "sweetness" and "cubeness" in the form of a sugar cube? In this case, universals are not self-defined, but have their definition mediated through factual combinations. Man is led to the frustrating conclusion that universals and particulars are unintelligible and indistinguishable when taken in themselves, and equally impotent to make sense of their dynamic together. Nevertheless, the oscillation between universals and particulars births a higher stage of consciousness associated with the concepts of (iii) force and understanding (*verstehen*).[17] Unlike static particulars and abstract universals, Newtonian "forces" or "laws" are inher-

15. Hegel, *Phenomenology*, §90–110.

16. Ibid., §111–31.

17. Ibid., §132–65.

ently active.[18] Forces seems to solve the "one and many" problem because their immutable inner character (the one) is inseparable from the temporal dynamic between facts and qualities (the many) that they produce. Gravity, for example, is neither a mere idea nor the incidental fact of the falling rock, but a law that is identical with a multitude of phenomena. Supposed self-defined facts and universals can now be construed as moments in the self-expression of forces, which have been artificially abstracted (in thought) from their unity in difference. At this stage, human consciousness is also construed as a force. As Kant taught, the understanding actively contributes a form to its empirical perceptions.

Just as soon as the "one and many" problem is solved by the notion of force, a new dualism arises between subject and object. Upon realizing that he is active in constituting his objects of knowledge, man enters the stage of (iv) self-certainty. At this point, man considers his own rational freedom to be the lone self-intelligible object of knowledge to which he enjoys immediate access, since the forces active beneath his understanding, in nature, are for him empty "things-in-themselves."[19] Withdrawing from practical affairs, man embraces the life of either a philosopher king or a contemplative slave who turns his gaze inward to explore his own unbounded imagination. But in truth, neither the king nor the slave enjoys insight into the character of freedom. A wanton king is enslaved to those industrious servants who have actually taken mastery over nature. Likewise, the withdrawn peasant is enslaved to the lord whose administrative prowess represents a genuine freedom to realize his ends. The contemplative life reduces man to an empty and ineffective "thing-in-itself," not unlike the very sub-phenomenal forces which he contemptuously disregards. Out of this contradiction, man graduates to the stage of (v) reason (*vernunft*), where he realizes that his freedom only shows itself when he actively harnesses the natural world. But again, men go astray first in trying to identify their rational powers with natural processes;[20] second in trying to discover themselves through hedonistic indulgence of their natural pleasures;[21] and third by locating their essence in a natural skill to manipulate nature for the ends of his community (e.g., farming, woodcutting, etc.).[22] In each case, the free subject is reduced to a mere

18. Robert Solomon's discussion of Newton and Kant as the implicit targets of Hegel's argument in this section is instructive. C. Solomon, *Spirit of Hegel*, 363–85.

19. Hegel, *Phenomenology*, §166–230.

20. Hegel titles this sub-stage, "Observing reason." Ibid., §240–346.

21. Hegel titles this sub-stage, "The actualization of rational self-consciousness through its own activity." Ibid., §347–93.

22. Hegel titles this stage, "Individuality which takes itself to be real in and for itself." Ibid., §394–437.

natural law, or "instinct" that does not consciously behold the principle of its own self-direction. Hence, subject and object, freedom and natural necessity are unintelligible in themselves, and equally incapable of illuminating their interaction with one another. From this contradiction, man graduates to the stage of (vi) spirit,[23] where he realizes that true freedom involves suppressing and harnessing his natural desires, in order to heed his ethical responsibility to other men. Not only do ethical imperatives seem to embody the sort of "self-evident" truth that man has been after, but the ethical family unit overcomes the dichotomies between subject and object, freedom and nature. A family consists of persons who are both naturally and ethically related to one another as subjects and objects. A strictly free subject, who is not bound to any object, is an illusion, for all men are naturally bound to an objective family. A strictly natural object that is not bound to any subject is also an illusion, for the natural sphere culminates in man, and exists for his ethical ends.

Unfortunately, the stage of ethical consciousness represents a premature victory. For, sons birthed from the natural ethical order (family) create synthetic social orders (tribes, cities, states) which inevitably present demands on their countrymen that take precedence over the family. But if the highest ethical imperatives are temporally and culturally determined, then, once again, man is left without a self-evident and immutable standard of truth that makes sense of all other things. The contradiction that arises between these two ethical spheres births a higher stage of consciousness, where the conflict between eternal and temporal truths are overcome in the notion of a universal mind whose eternal freedom is identical with a historical process of self-limitation and self-transcendence, in the succession of social orders. The one who understands that each historical state is subordinate to the free self-development of a universal Mind has graduated to the (vii) the religious understanding.[24] The religious consciousness passes through three stages in its attempt to form an idea of Mind/God. First, naturalistic religions look to the most noble and pervasive features of nature as appropriate images for God (light, life, order, etc.). Second, artistic religions portray something of God's ironic and sometimes tragic self-expression in history through theatrical productions. Third, only the Christian religion supplies an image for God that transcends, and even challenges all natural and social forms of existence.[25] In the image of the Trinity, God (the Father) is beheld as both distinct from and identical with objective reality (the Son),

23. Ibid., §438–671.

24. Ibid., §672–787.

25. Ibid., §699–747.

but only through a process where the latter dies and is resurrected anew in ever higher orders of social harmony (the Spirit).[26] Nevertheless, even the Christian religion represents a penultimate stage of consciousness. At the final stage of (viii) absolute knowing[27] man turns from the religious image for God to the reality that it represents. The object of man's reflection is the life of Spirit as it has been manifested in the ideal development of human consciousness, and the product of his reflection is something like Hegel's own *Phenomenology of Spirit*.[28] Hegel's Absolute is this final system within which every lesser idea and philosophy can be organized as moments in Spirit's self-expression.

Although our abstruse survey of Hegel's argument has called attention to many of his chief ideas and emphases, special attention must be given to the "logic" that is supposed to be at work throughout. In contrast to traditional interpretations of logic, Hegel delineates three states of reasoning—Understanding, Dialectic, and Speculation.[29] At the level of "understanding" man supposes that all things are self-identical (X = X) and incompatible with certain contrary qualities (X ≠ ~X). The only sorts of inferences that one may draw from the observation that "an object is blue" are either negative (e.g., "the object is *not orange*"), or of a more general character (e.g., "the object is colored," ". . . is visible"; etc.). Neither inference yields new information about the self-identical character of "blue" or the object that is characterized by it. But Hegel proposes a second, "dialectical" stage of logical reflection that is calculated to undermine the simple self-identity of ideas, and their supposed stark opposition to their contraries. Hegel argues that definition implies limitation not by just anything, but by reference to a specific contrary.[30] That which is "not-light" is not the number "three," but "darkness." Light, then, invites limitation and contrast from a specific opposite that is marked by qualities which are uniquely fit for its own negation. However, meditation on light and darkness reveals that when they

26. Ibid., §748–787. When asked to convey the essence of his system in a single sentence, Hegel offered the quasi-Christian maxim "die to live." Caird, *Hegel*, 44.

27. Ibid., §788–808.

28. The British Idealist, Edward Caird, identifies Hegel's great achievement as the reconciliation of two great concepts: (a) the Greek notion of the organic union of the real and the ideal in the natural universe, and especially in the state; and (b) the allegedly "Protestant" notion, championed in philosophy by Rousseau, Kant, and Fichte, that the human subject possesses a free conscience which it respects above every exterior authority—the state, the church, the university, etc. Caird, *Hegel*, 35–38; cf. 3, 13–44.

29. See Burbridge, "Hegel's Conception of Logic," 86–101.

30. In Caird's words, "Every definite thought, by the fact that it is definite, has a necessary relation to its negative, and cannot be separated from it without losing its meaning." Caird, *Hegel*, 136.

are neatly contrasted, they are, ironically, indistinguishable. For, a blinding undifferentiated light is indistinguishable from pure darkness. Finally, at the speculative stage, the dialectical passage of logical opposites into one another births an awareness of a higher category that recaptures the distinction between the previous two, by placing them in a new context.[31] Light and darkness, for example, must be thoroughly integrated and contrasted in a concrete field of vision that admits for different "tints" and colors.

The threefold movement of reasoning is expressed with the greatest clarity in the earliest stages of Hegel's *Logic*. According to Hegel, the simplest and most universal category is that of (a) being. Most people suppose that they possess an intelligible idea of being, and that they are saying something very important when they assign a given matter the quality of existence. "To be" is quite simply the opposite of (b) "not being." However, upon reflection it becomes clear that when taken alone, being is wholly devoid of meaning. No specific quality may be assigned to it because it is the most general of all qualities. Being is certainly not heavy, wise, handsome, etc. Ironically, then (a') being-in-itself is indistinguishable from its supposed opposite, non-being. On the other hand, (b') non-being must enjoy some sort of ideal existence in order for us to reason about it, and in this respect it is indistinguishable from being, which was initially thought of as the quality of existence deprived of a concrete form. Thus, being and non-being pass over into one another. Fortunately, the disorienting conceptual oscillation between the two categories is overcome by the higher category of (c) becoming. In becoming, an existent present advances into a not-yet-existent future and a not-yet-existent future displaces an existing present. Thus, the category of becoming manages to combine being and non-being, even as it enjoys a unique temporal character not present in the earlier two. But, once again, the whole (α) being-nothing-becoming complex is itself dialectically related to the category of (β) being determinate. Being determinate refers to a stable sort of existence, in which the positive quality of a given reality is appreciated via contrast or limitation supplied by a contiguous opposing reality (e.g., the timberline is limited by the atmosphere). Unlike mere becoming where being and non-being pass into one another, being determinate involves the coexistence of being and nonbeing in two definite realities that owe their positive quality to negation or limitation from the other.

31. In discussing how the category reached through speculation serves as the "negative of the [dialectical] negative," Michael Forester explains that it manages to unify, "a given pair of mutually implying contrary categories by, in a sense, preserving while, in a sense, abolishing them, thereby eliminating their self-contradictoriness, *and being the one known category that does so while remaining closest to them in conceptual content*." Forester, "Hegel's Dialectical Method," 148.

However, in truth, that which is (α') becoming must always enjoy a determinate spatial form and that which is (β') determinate must also be subject to temporal flux. This calls for another speculative movement, wherein the category of (γ) being-for-self, or individuality, is appreciated as affecting a meaningful synthesis of the previous two. Unlike a mere (α') determinate being which owes its definition to a contrasting other, an individual enjoys self-distinction because it refers to a sort of unity that combines a manifold of successive moments and parts—e.g., a single plant joins together several contrasting members. Hence, as it increases in complexity Hegel's logical system manages to envelop the major conceptual categories inherent in the universe (see fig. 8).[32]

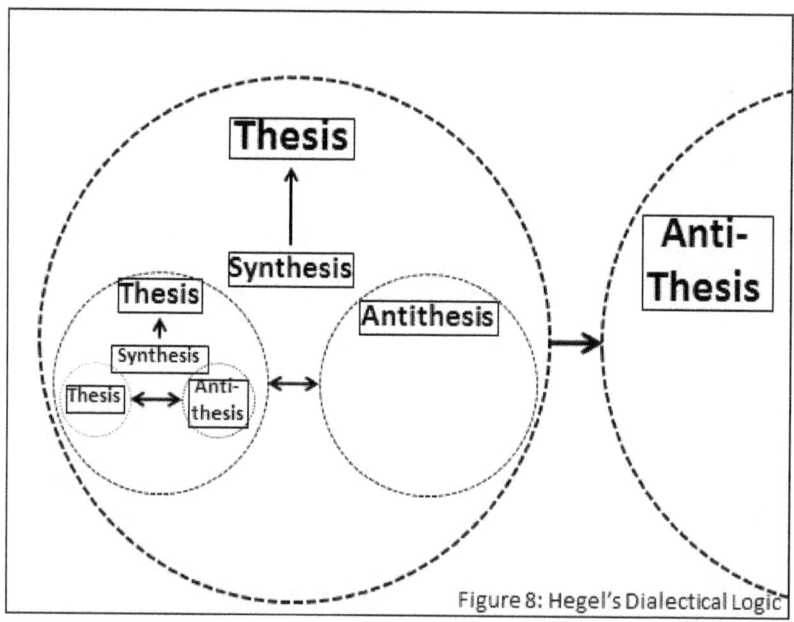

Figure 8: Hegel's Dialectical Logic

Many have mistakenly concluded that dialectical reasoning involves an attempt to deduce every feature of empirical reality from reason alone. But, in fact, its focus is on discovering the *a priori* relationship between those broad *categories* that appear in an *a posteriori* universe.[33] In this case, many events and combinations of qualities will be purely contingent, even though the category of "contingency" occupies a definite place within the logic.[34] The apparent opposition between logic and history, eternity and

32. Hegel, *Logic*, §15.

33. Bradley, *Logic*, 360–61.

34. McTaggart, *Hegelian Dialectic*, §26–66. Cf. Wartenberg, "Hegel's Idealism," 107ff.

time, the one and the many is overcome only when they are understood to be equally indispensable expressions of an Absolute Spirit who is at once free and rational. And, the conclusion that the Absolute actually exists is proven through a series of transcendental arguments to the effect that lesser opposing categories are literally self-defeating when detached from one another and the Absolute System in whom they are harmonized.[35]

3.2.2 The Status of Paradox in Hegel's System

The subtleties and complexities of Hegel's system have left many with the horrifying impression that he meant to affirm the reality of logical contradictions. Hegel's attempt to draw positive conclusions from contradictions within and between categories led Bertrand Russell to accuse him of basic "confusion."[36] Hegel's interpreters have themselves complicated matters by offering an array of solutions to the obvious problem. John McTaggart and Edward Caird held that the Hegelian system makes no room for real contradictions whatsoever, since they simply represent subordinate stages that are ultimately displaced by an absolutely consistent idea[37] Although far less optimistic about our ability to attain a vision of a finally coherent Absolute, F. H. Bradley developed his own semi-Hegelian view that contradictions may arise in reality as it *appears*, but not in ultimate reality itself.[38] Others have held that the Hegelian contradictions represent our own subjective tendency to assign conflicting predicates to the same concepts *at different times*.[39] And yet, the obvious problem with consigning "contradictions" to past stages of the dialectic, to the world as it appears, or to our own subjective inconsistencies, is that Hegel's system purports to overcome the dichotomies between eternity and time, reality and appearance, subjectivity and objectivity, etc. Thus, if contradictions should arise at any point in the way the world appears, or in the manner that man conceives of it, they must, in some novel sense, exist. However, it does not therefore follow that Hegel has committed the unforgivable sin of affirming contradictions of empirical reality or of mental concepts. On the contrary, Hegel intends to acknowledge the relative reality of contradictions only in the life of that Absolute

35. Burbridge, "Hegel's Concept of Logic," 92–93.

36. Russell, *Problems of Philosophy*, 143. Cf. Moore, "The Refutation of Idealism," 24.

37. McTaggart, *Hegelian Dialectic*, §8. Cf. Caird, *Hegel*, 134–50.

38. Bradley, *Appearance*, 1–132.

39. For an explanation of this strategy and a catalog of others, see Forester, "Hegel's Dialectical Method," 141–43.

Spirit which transcends "the essentially oppositional concepts of reality or object, on the one hand, and thought or concept, on the other."[40] And yet, the Absolute Spirit, which is vivified through the "negative moment" of contradiction and spurred on toward a more profound synthesis,[41] somehow resembles mind more than it does reality.

3.2.3 The Place of Christianity in Hegel's System

To Hegel's credit, he was not content to embrace the fundamental doctrines of the Christian Faith as mere objects of belief. He was zealous to communicate that the doctrines of the Trinity, the Incarnation, and the Resurrection were the most profound images of the life of reason. In characterizing his entire philosophy by the maxim "die to live," Hegel seemed to elevate Christ's well known saying (Matt 16:25) to a metaphysical principle.[42] However, because Hegel was overtly hostile to Christianity in his earlier years, and assigned the Christian religion a penultimate place in the life of Spirit, several have understood Hegel's use of Christian concepts as politically motivated, but nevertheless, philosophically expedient.[43] In the *Philosophy of History*, Christianity is several steps removed from the zenith of man's *corporate* consciousness in the nineteenth-century Prussian state.[44] Moreover, Hegel admitted that there is no telling what new horizons the Absolute Spirit might birth in the consciousness of future nations.[45] Hence, whatever affection for Christian images Hegel may have had, he certainly does not regard them as supplying the final diagnosis of the human situation.[46]

3.3 VAN TIL'S CRITIQUE OF ABSOLUTE IDEALISM

The basic critique of absolute idealism developed in Van Til's doctoral thesis "God and the Absolute," reappears in several of his most important works.[47]

40. Ibid., 144.

41. Hegel, *Logic*, §11.

42. Caird, *Hegel*, 212.

43. Solomon, *Spirit of Hegel*, 597–634; Rushdoony, *One and Many*, 306ff.; Magee, *Hegel and the Hermetic Tradition*, 36–50, 61–69.

44. Hegel, *Philosophy of History*, 334–35.

45. Ibid., 86–87.

46. Bernard Bosanquet conveys Hegel's sentiment, "I am very far from believing that philosophy confers the gift of prophecy. . . . Philosophy comes after the fact, and interprets it. It neither preaches nor predicts." Bosanquet, *Value and Destiny*, 291.

47. Oliphint, *Consistency of Van Til's Methodology*, 5.

In disposing of absolute idealism, Van Til believed that he had sufficiently dealt with the best that fallen reason had to offer. Van Til's first critique turns on the observation that the infighting between British Idealists calls attention to the incoherence of Hegel's doctrine of the Absolute, and to its incapacity to serve as the object of a transcendental proof. His second critique turns on the fact that the absolute idealist system will only admit for a finite god. And, his third critique focuses on the absolute idealists' failure to begin their program by submitting to direction from an Absolute Creator.

3.3.1 The Absolute Incompatible with Time

After nearly half a century, Hegel's Idealism began to take root in Great Britain through the influence of T. H. Green, and John and Edward Caird. At the turn of the twentieth century, neo-Hegelianism enjoyed a brief reign as the dominant philosophical persuasion in Britain-America Institutions. In some respects, the British Idealists enhanced Hegel's system by providing it with more lucid definition, by clarifying certain dialectical inferences, and by rejecting dubious steps in his logic. Bernard Bosanquet may be credited with several such advancements. Bosanquet developed a Hegelian sort of logic that he termed "implication,"[48] which was both highly readable and even commonsensical. The reasoning process begins with an initial systematic view of reality, which is then frustrated by an aberrant and unaccounted for matter of fact, but eventually enhanced and expanded by such a challenge into a more robust system. A child with a simple but nevertheless systematic understanding of social customs may reach out for a handshake to a family member at a funeral only to have his offer denied, and met with a hug. This aberration from his expectations will lead him to amend his system, and to develop categories and connections that could not be deduced from his original system alone. For example, in addition to forming a notion of different social contexts, the child will be able to predict that a hug is a more appropriate gesture than a handshake before his brother leaves town, although he has never before experienced such an event.[49] By developing conclusions that exceed the information supplied in his *a priori* and *a posteriori* premises, a "method of implication" differs from "linear" sorts of inferences. Deduction and induction, for example, advance in a

48. Bosanquet, *Implication*, 4

49. Among the more complex examples or reasoning by implication, Bosanquet provides a detailed explanation of how William Harvey developed his monumental theory that capillaries must connect veins and arteries in order to circulate blood, prior to the empirical discovery of capillaries. Ibid., 75–78.

straight line from an established connection between events or qualities to the conclusion that the same sorts of combinations must, or will probably, appear together in the future.[50] Nevertheless, in expounding his method of implication, Bosanquet abandons Hegel's enigmatic claim, that opposites must for a moment appear indistinguishable before a synthesis between them can be affected.

Although Bosanquet held that implication rests on the postulate that reality actually is an all-encompassing system that reason may discover,[51] his doctrine of the Absolute manifests the plaguing tension between eternity and time. Bosanquet's thought tended to diverge in two contradictory directions.[52] On the one hand, Bosanquet understood that if the temporal universe is open to new and unforeseen facts and events, there cannot be a self-complete system of reality that undergirds the reasoning process. For this reason, Bosanquet sometimes speaks of the Absolute as a timeless and divine standard of truth.[53] On the other hand, he was sensitive to the fact that human experience is undeniably marked by the discovery of new and unforeseen facts. Thus, Bosanquet speaks of the Absolute as a mysterious union between God and man, and eternity and time, that resists a finally coherent description. He calls the Absolute a "finite-infinite" being. He designates his own descriptions of the Absolute as "finite illustrations—the only kind at our disposal."[54] For example, he speaks of the relationship between eternity and time as "something which *we might remotely* liken to the difference between . . . a man's mind and that of a lower animal."[55] In cases like this one, Van Til does not object to mystery per se, but to its incompatibility with Bosanquet's rationalist procedure of (a) rejecting as ultimately untrue those philosophies and ideas that cannot be expressed consistently,[56] and (b) refusing to recognize revelation from a transcendent authority above man.[57] By Bosanquet's own standard, if the Absolute cannot be consistently defined, then we have every reason to doubt its existence.[58] If man is the

50. Ibid. 21–30.

51. Bosanquet, *Value and Destiny*, 299, 303.

52. Van Til, "God and the Absolute," 17–18.

53. Bosanquet, *Individuality and Value*, 71–72.

54. Bosanquet, *Value and Destiny*, 299.

55. Emphasis mine. Ibid., 303

56. Van Til, "God and the Absolute," 21.

57. Bosanquet candidly states, "We do not with Theism assume specific and miraculous communications of grace to the finite mind." Bosanquet, *Value and Destiny*, 250.

58. An otherworldly solution to man's dilemmas, "contradicts the basic demands of Idealism that reality be essentially perspicuous to man." Van Til, "God and the Absolute," 21.

highest cognizant expression of the Absolute, then the only possible ground for supposing that there exists an Absolute who finally resolves the conflicts that characterize reality, is that man has come to decipher the nature of that solution. In order to reach a self-consistent notion of the Absolute, such that it might be proffered as the ground of all rational discourse, it would appear that either time or eternity must be sacrificed.

The most famous of the British Idealists, F. H. Bradley, abandoned Hegel and Bosanquet's doctrine that the Absolute envelops time.[59] Bradley, therefore, makes no effort to decipher an ideal order between the categories and forms of temporal existence as Hegel had. They are but self-contradictory *appearances* rather than the one, immutable *reality* upon which all things depend.[60] Nevertheless, Bradley must be given credit for exposing the self-contradictions inherent in finite categories of thought—substance, quality, relation, space, time, motion, change, causation, self, etc.—with greater clarity and brevity than the master himself. The underlying argument in Bradley's negative program is that: (1) qualities are unintelligible in themselves since they owe their definition to a contrasting relationship with other qualities; (2) qualities remain unintelligible when married to external relations, since a contrasting relationship is supposed to be the result of a pre-existing difference between things and not the product of a relationship; and (3) even if relations are taken as independent things which impart a distinct character to the qualities they relate, then relations too would have to be related to the qualities they relate and so on *ad infinitum*.[61] But on this third scenario, relations never get down to the business of relating and defining anything. Hence, relatedness, multiple qualities, substance, attributes, etc., cannot be predicated of reality so long as men allow the law of contradiction to determine what is real. When it comes to the task of positively defining the sort of unitary reality that must exist, Bradley's contribution is meager. Allegedly, the occasional experience of becoming so enraptured with an external object that one loses virtually any awareness that he is distinct from it provides a small window into the nature of the Absolute.[62] Somehow, insists Bradley, the fractured categories which characterize the world of appearance must be transmuted and altered from their present form in the "one"

59. According to Bradley, the temporal universe must not be regarded as real in the Hegelian sense that it positively contributes to the nature of the Absolute. The Absolute is real, and the temporal world muddles and contradicts it. And, "to hold that what contradicts the real must be real" in the same positive sense, "is a logical mistake." Bradley, *Logic*, 142.

60. Bradley, *Appearance*, 11, 144, 551.

61. Ibid., 25–34. Cf. Copleston, *History*, 8:202–6.

62. Bradley, *Appearance*, 144–47.

reality.[63] Hence, if Bradley avoids Bosanquet's mysterious doctrine that time and eternity are on equal footing, he does so by asserting another paradox to the effect that time and multiplicity are "somehow" transformed in the Absolute.[64] But Van Til explains that Bradley, just as much as Bosanquet, has no right to appeal to mystery, since he too exalts human reason as the highest authority in all investigations, and invests it with the right to disregard inconsistent categories as mere appearances.[65] Again, the one who grants that ultimate reality transcends reason must forfeit any certainty that his applications of logic are correct, and with it the claim that an Absolute is the precondition to all rational discourse.[66]

In response to Bradley's relative failure, John McTaggart strove to develop a positive doctrine of the Absolute. Although Bradley was the most penetrating disciple of Hegel,[67] McTaggart believed that the only way to evade his nondescript and mysterious conclusions about reality would be by embracing a pluralistic, rather than a monistic sort of idealism. If reality is a conglomerate of personal members, then the Absolute may be defined as a society, described with ever increasing depth through the exposition of those categories which define their common experience.[68] However, in order to secure reality's capacity for analytic definition, McTaggart was led to the conclusion that certain categories, with an indefinable but clearly identifiable character, must lie at the base of all definition (e.g., reality, existence, truth, quality, relation, etc.).[69] McTaggart believed that he could evade Bradley's conundrum concerning the relationship between qualities and relations. Qualities may very well be intelligible in themselves. And although every relation must itself be related to those qualities it resides between, there is no reason why certain "primary" relations may not stand at the forefront in characterizing the connection between qualities, so that

63. Ibid., 488.

64. Ibid., 131, 140, 204, 349, 488, 499. Equally dissatisfied with Bradley's strict dichotomy between appearance and reality, Bosanquet pointed out that it is schizophrenic to erect a dualism in order to safeguard a metaphysical monism. Bosanquet, *Knowledge and Reality*, 16–26.

65. "One who assumes that the Real is the Rational and at the same time makes man a charter member with 'God' in the Universe cannot, without destroying his basic principle appeal to mystery." Van Til, "God and the Absolute," 17; cf. 12–13; IST, 182, 186–87.

66. Van Til extends the same sort of critique to the early Wittgenstein. CTE, 140; cf. 139–48.

67. McTaggart, *Nature of Existence I*, §51.

68. McTaggart, *Nature of Existence II*, §433.

69. McTaggart, *Nature of Existence I*, §2, 5, 10, 60, 78.

the infinite regress of sub-relations is of no consequence.[70] On the other hand, McTaggart was enough of an absolute idealist to agree that the "real" must be a self-complete system,[71] and to become the chief apologist for the conclusion that open-ended time is an illusion.[72] Allegedly, the only thing that could render a moment "present" as opposed to "past," or "future" would be its simultaneity with an Absolute reference point that is outside of time. And yet, the only way that successive moments could be simultaneous with an external standard but not with each other, is if that standard were to pass over them as a traveling spotlight over a piece of land (see. fig. 9).[73] In this case the Absolute must be subject to time in order to function as that timeless standard by which time is defined. Such is a clear contradiction. The problem, however, is that, having once already admitted that several categories are indefinable but self-evident features of human experience,[74] there does not seem to be any reason why "time" could not, or should not, be added to their number.[75] Once one incorporates the notion of "self-evidence" into his thinking, he certainly cannot argue that the vision of an all-encompassing system is the precondition to rational discourse, for many things are perfectly intelligible in isolation. Hence, McTaggart's philosophy was the last idealist precursor to the pluralistic realism of the early analytics. For Van Til, McTaggart not only showcases the absurdities to which absolute idealism drives itself, but its natural tendency to devolve into an irrationalist philosophy where the indefinable plays a central role.[76]

70. Ibid., §88.

71. Ibid., §9–18. Van Til argues that it is because Reformed Christians recognize that there is a self-complete description of reality in the mind of God, while unbelievers (like McTaggart) do not, only the former may rest assured that their knowledge is true even if finite, and at points paradoxical. Van Til, "God and the Absolute," 27–28.

72. Copleston records the comment of McTaggart's reverent but unconvinced biographer, C. D. Broad, that his opinions with respect to time failed to win him any disciples. Copleston, *History*, 8:246.

73. McTaggart, *Nature of Existence II*, §328.

74. McTaggart, *Nature of Existence I*, §9–18.

75. McTaggart admits that past, present, and future are probably indefinable, but register his own opinion that, "It does not seem to me that we can know, for example, the meaning of pastness, if we do not know the meaning of presentness or futurity." McTaggart, *Nature of Existence II*, §327.

76. Van Til, "God and the Absolute," 27–28; SCE, 138–40, 150, 218–20.

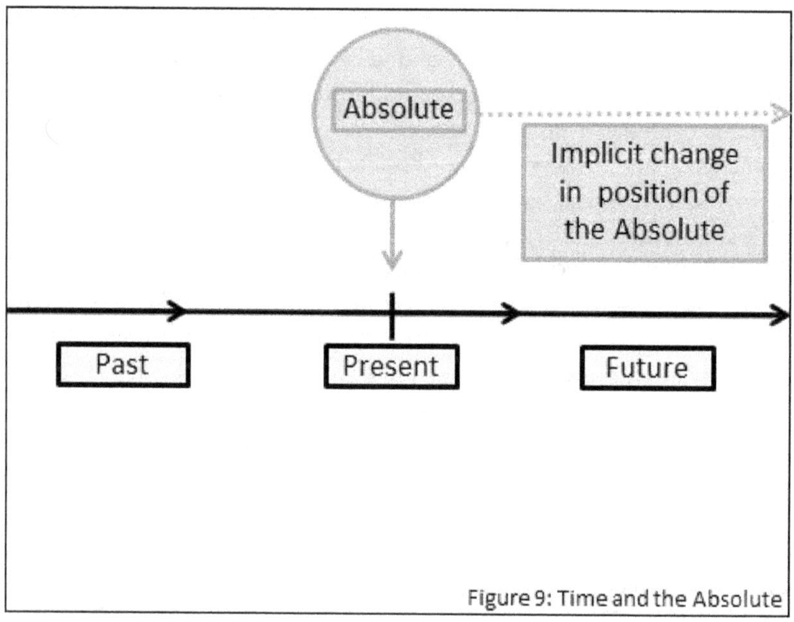

Figure 9: Time and the Absolute

As a philosophical influence on Van Til, Andrew Seth Pringle-Pattison was second only to Bosanquet.[77] Pringle-Pattison was among the first to challenge the widely publicized view of T. H. Green, that Hegelianism represented a personalist philosophy.[78] Hegel had reduced men to "foci" in the self-development of an eternal and impersonal thought-thinking-itself. By granting the slightest upper hand to eternity over the temporal universe, even Bosanquet was prone to depreciating personal-reciprocal relationships as an essential quality of the Absolute. The twofold remedy proposed by Pringle-Pattison was to clearly identify the Absolute as a personal God, and to affirm the essential role that human persons play in contributing to the divine life. Pringle-Pattison's position led naturally to a rejection of creation *ex nihilo*, in favor of a doctrine of eternal revelation whereby God communicates his nature in and through mankind with ever greater clarity.[79] However, by making God's relationship to human individuals essential to His own personal experience and self-expression, Pringle-Pattison was forced to admit a final mystery into his system—"the time-process must

77. Cf. McConnell, "Influence of Idealism," 563–65.

78. Pringle-Pattison, *Hegelianism and Personalism*, 69–82.

79. Pringle-Pattison, *Idea of God*, 308–9.

somehow enter into that [divine] experience" without compromising its all-encompassing character.[80]

In certain respects, Van Til could applaud Pringle-Pattison's critique of classic Hegelianism, and his insistence that reciprocal relationship is an essential quality of personhood.[81] If the God Who governs all things is not personal in the fullest sense, then even finite persons will eventually be reduced to impersonal expressions of natural processes.[82] However, by making man the eternal correlative of God, that is a temporal "many" set against an eternal "one," Pringle-Pattison had effectively elevated man above his creaturely status and demoted God from His position as the self-complete Absolute. Once God is made dependent on an open-ended temporal universe He ceases to be the "presupposition of possible experience," and becomes Himself subject to the ultimately unknown.[83] In this case, the distinctive emphasis of absolute idealism on the necessity of a self-complete standard of truth is finally lost, and the pragmatism of William James and John Dewey must prevail.[84] Arguably, the greatest thinkers of the twentieth century—including the later Wittgenstein and Martin Heidegger—have embraced the essential doctrine of pragmatism, that truth is subjective and unstable.[85]

3.3.2 Finite Deity

Van Til's next critique was anticipated in the previous paragraphs: the absolute idealist system will allow for three different interpretations of God, each of which renders Him a finite deity (see fig. 10).[86] God might be identified with the universe as a whole (god #1); that logical principle which organizes reality (god #2); or a finite but abnormally powerful member of the universe (god #3).[87] In the first case, finitude, ignorance, and evil are natural and

80. Ibid., 363.

81. Van Til was laudatory of this emphasis in Josiah Royce, but critical of his presumption that man must be God's essential interlocutor, through whom God realizes and explains Himself. SCE, 163.

82. SCE, 97.

83. Van Til, "God and the Absolute," 29. "The negative instance," or unforeseen future developments, are "really beyond God, as well as beyond man." CTEV, 46.

84. Van Til, "God and the Absolute," 25; SCE, 137; CTEV, 137.

85. NM, 107–30. A similar thesis is advanced by Richard Rorty. Rorty, "Wittgenstein, Heidegger, and the Reification of Language," 337–57.

86. SCE, 161. cf. Van Til "God and the Absolute," 22–23, 26.

87. Whereas Pringle-Pattison identified God with the Absolute and was led to affirm the Absolute's temporality, Bosanquet affirmed the temporality of God and was led

necessary limits to God's infinitude which is the same as to say that he is not infinite or sovereign at all. In the second case, God is only a "law" insofar as he is dependent on, and limited by, an extra-divine reality. And, in the third case, God is admittedly subject to time. Not one of these portraits of God is compatible with the biblical data, or conducive to an epistemology that can yield certainty.

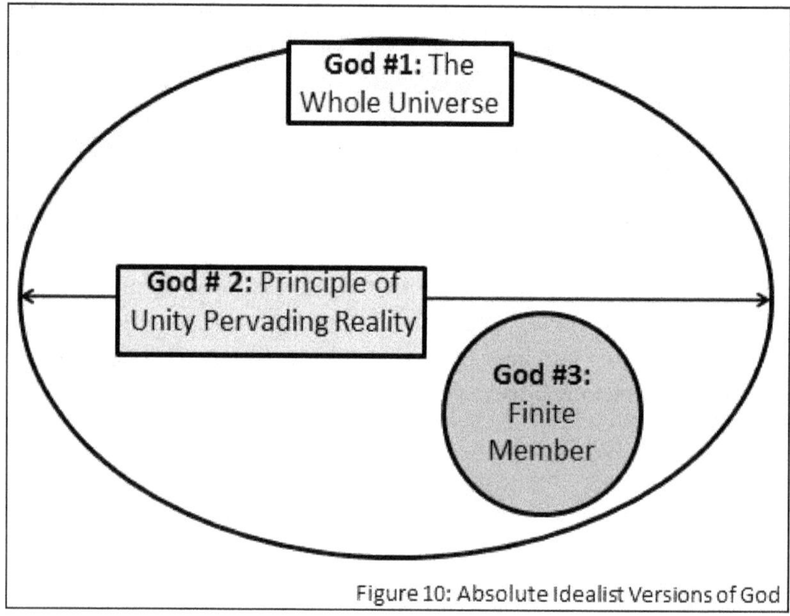

Figure 10: Absolute Idealist Versions of God

3.3.3 Failure to Presuppose the Ontological Trinity

The root error of the absolute idealist project was to entertain and develop a vision of an all-encompassing system of reality without heeding the guidance of their Triune Creator from the outset. Functionally, they treated their own intellects as if they were vested with the basic principles which govern the universe. When man's interpretation of things runs into apparent contradictions (as the absolute idealist project had) he has every reason to believe that the universe is fundamentally at odds with itself. In turn, his belief in an Absolute may at best be counted as a subjective hope.[88] But it cannot possibly be directly defined, or transcendentally proven to exist.[89]

to deny that he was the Absolute. Bosanquet, *Individuality and Value*, 342; idem. *Value and Destiny*, 251, 255.

88. By the designation, "subjective" Van Til means, "any system of thought . . . if it sets up human thought or the human consciousness as the ultimate standard of truth." SCE, 134.

89. Bradley and Bosanquet admit that the incoherence of their competitors' views

For, the Absolute is fraught with the same inconsistencies as those lesser belief systems that it is supposed to rise above. In Van Til's estimation, a Trinitarian worldview is able to deliver where the absolute idealist systems come up dry. This claim turns on the fact that the Triune God represents a self-complete system over and above the temporal universe, and beyond the principles at work in the mind of man. On the one hand, man's failure to comprehend God's systematic plan for reality does not detract in the least from its existence. On the other hand, since the Triune God has freely provided a sufficient portrait of reality for man to carry out his covenantal duties, he may rest assured that he understands reality truly, though not exhaustively. Furthermore, he may rest assured that when he exercises his reasoning powers in submission to God, he will be able to develop an ever more coherent interpretation of things, which reflects all the more the vantage point of God.

3.4 Van Til's Appropriation of Aspects of Absolute Idealism

We may mention three idealist emphases that left a significant impression on Van Til. First, Van Til held that something akin to the transcendental argumentation of absolute idealism represents the lone valid method of theistic proof. The Christian apologist must argue that the Christian system represents the only intelligible interpretation of reality and that all of its secular alternatives borrow principles, not to mention a self-confidence that only the Triune God can justify. Second, despite their heretical formulations of the doctrine of the Trinity, the absolute idealists must be given credit for inspiring Van Til to set up the orthodox Trinity as the true Absolute, and true center of the Christian system. Third, Van Til followed absolute idealists in assigning the highest epistemological import to the happenings of history. Only a sort of logical reflection that is intertwined with historically mediated truths can be squared with the Reformed doctrines of redemptive history and the progressive maturation of humanity in relationship to God.

---

and the *relative* coherence of their own cannot be taken as a definitive proof for the latter. Bradley, *Logic*, 499–500; idem. *Appearance*, 136–37. Cf. Bosanquet, *Essentials of Logic*, 165–66; idem. *Logic*, 2.

PART II

Van Til's Orthodox Trinitarian System

HAVING IDENTIFIED THE THREE primary strands of influence on Van Til, we must turn to the task of accurately conveying how Van Til synthesized elements taken from Princeton, Amsterdam, and Absolute Idealism. Even more to the point, we must take note of how Van Til places the theological paradox of the Trinity at the center of his apologetic, epistemology, and theological system. Below, we begin with a brief review of those doctrines mentioned in Part I, which Van Til sought either to retain or to discard. What follows is a threefold explanation of how the paradox of the ontological Trinity guides an effective apologetic, a dependable theory of knowledge, and a coherent theological system. In many respects, Van Til's project is an expansion on Herman Bavinck's contention that "mystery is the lifeblood of all dogmatics."[1]

In Part I we identified fourteen prominent emphases, doctrines, and/or methods that Van Til sought to retain, and nine that he labored to refute from the schools of Old Princeton, Amsterdam, and Absolute Idealism. Another five were common to both Princeton and Amsterdam (see fig. 11).

When taken together and properly organized, the positive emphases represent the core of Van Til's apologetic, theological system, and epistemology, while the negative emphases represent the basic ideas that he opposed. Van Til's apologetic begins counter-intuitively with the (8, 20) paradox of the ontological Trinity, as the (13) Absolute context and (2, 16) sovereign governor of created reason and reality. The Triune God's distinctive nature, combined with His (1) personal guidance, is the lone dependable solution

1. Bavinck, *Dogmatics*, 2:29; cf. CG, 46.

Positive Points	Negative Points
Reformed: (1) Sola scriptura (2) Divine sovereignty (3) Covenant (4) Redemptive history (5) Trinity in salvation	
Princeton: (6) Objectively valid apologetic proofs (7) Common ground, based on *imago dei* (8) Theological paradox/Calvin's Trinity	**Princeton:** (15) Common sense (16) Inconsistent with divine sovereignty (17) Autonomous reason hostile to paradox
Amsterdam: (9) Presuppositions/Antithesis (10) Common Grace (11) Christian system—God, man, nature	**Amsterdam:** (18) Inconsistent with antithesis (19) Rationalism-Irrationalism (20) Lack of Trinitarian apologetic
Absolute Idealism: (12) Transcendental argumentation (13) Trinitarian Absolute (14) Historically conditioned logic	**Absolute Idealism:** (21) Time-bound absolute/not transcendental (22) Finite deity (23) Failure to presuppose the Trinity

Figure 11: Positive and Negative Emphases in Van Til

to the one-many problem. The Triune God functions as the believer's most basic (9, 23) presupposition, which sets the believer at odds with the unbeliever in his interpretation of all things. Thus, the believer cannot appeal to (15) common sense in order to establish the existence of God. However, the believer has at his disposal an (6) objectively valid (12) transcendental proof, which turns on the observation that the Christian theory of reality (18) differs from its non-Christian alternatives precisely in its exclusive capacity to render reality intelligible. The unbeliever's presuppositions of (19) rationalism and irrationalism, married as they are to a (21) time-bound Absolute, and perhaps, a (22) finite deity, are self-defeating. And yet, the burden that the unbeliever feels, to fashion some system or novel course of action in order to make sense of his condition betrays a perverted awareness of his Triune Creator's covenantal demands. The only reason why the unbeliever manages, even for a time, to evade the dire consequences of his beliefs, is because he dwells in a generous (7) God-governed universe, and is restrained by (10) common grace from wholly suppressing God's internal witness that reality has been crafted for him. The unbeliever's most effective rejoinder is that even if his belief system is broken, (17) theological paradox renders the Christian Faith just as irrational. In response, the believer must first demonstrate that the paradox of the Trinity fosters rather than undermines the coherence of the Christian system (1, 2, 3, 4, 5, etc.), while His redemptive work is the lone remedy to the unbeliever's rebellious condition. Second, the believer must further expound on how a Trinitarian theory of knowledge allows the (11) Christian system to set limitations on the (12) formal laws of logic, but in such a way that there is a clear and consistent rule for distinguishing paradox from genuine, self-defeating contradictions.

4

Transcendental Argument from and for the Trinity

4.1 INTRODUCTION

At the heart of Van Til's apologetic is the claim that the Trinity solves the infamous one-many problem. On Van Til's interpretation, the problem in view is the fruit of *abstract* reasoning. By contrast, the Trinity constitutes ultimate reality as a *concrete* universal, whose mode of self-revelation comes in the form of a direct personal disclosure of His expectations of man, and His plan for history. The Trinity may be described as the *dis*solution to the one-many problem, since he challenges the presupposition that gives birth to it, namely that reality can or should be interpreted in light of abstract principles, ideas, and forces (logic, energy, time, gravity, space, etc.). Stated another way, the Trinity solves the one-many problem by being free from it himself, and then enabling believers to reason concretely on the basis of a systematic interpretation of reality so that they are effectively freed from it as well.

4.2 CALVIN'S DOCTRINE OF THE TRINITY AND THE ONE-MANY PROBLEM

The one-many problem has proven to represent one of the most pervasive quagmires of Western philosophy.[1] At root, the problem concerns whether rational forms (the one) or material particulars (the many) constitute ultimate reality, and if both coexist, how such a dynamic is possible. The same problem proves to lie at the base of a host of difficulties in metaphysics, epistemology, ethics, politics, and religion. In each case, that which is supposed to unify some sphere of reality is an abstract category (dog) which sheds the details of those concrete things which it defines (Rover, Lassie, Spot), while that which accounts for the diversity between particulars is an abstract principle of chance. Problematically, the broadest category with which we define all other things (e.g., being), and the ultimate source of diversity and individuation, both evade the synthetic and analytic sorts of definition that they are supposed to facilitate. That is to say, neither can be grouped into a class of things which possess some common characteristic, and neither can be divided into simpler parts.[2] And yet, without some means of illuminating the abstract "one" and "many" there is no way to determine that they really do or will continue to complement one another, rather than destroy human experience.

In Van Til's estimation, Absolute Idealists were correct to deny that abstract ideas (the one) and/or temporal chance (the many) can adequately illuminate themselves, or the concrete universe. Instead, the concrete system of reality, which is best described as a "Spirit/Mind," is what gives rise to metaphysical abstractions as subordinate moments in its own life of self-development. In this case, the ultimate principle of unity is a systematic "whole" that envelops every particular without shedding its concrete details. The "whole" is also the ultimate source of diversity, as that which creates distinctions within itself in order to more clearly express itself. Thus, the ultimate System/Spirit was described as a "*concrete* universal," and specifically designated the "Absolute." However, Van Til advances the sharp criticism that Absolute Idealists fell short of their own lofty ideal. Upon reflection, an Absolute that synthesizes time and eternity, open-ended development and finality, evades human comprehension. But because man is one with the Absolute, he must either predicate finitude and lack of knowledge to that mind which is supposed to harmonize all things, or regard his own failure to comprehend reality as indicative of the fact that the Absolute has not yet

1. Recall 1.3.1, 2.2.2, and 3.2.1.
2. Cf. Frame, *Van Til*, 63–78; cf. Anderson, "If Knowledge then God," 61–64.

ascended to self-comprehension. In either case, the Absolute is not the sort of all-encompassing mind/system that man needs it to be. Insofar as man elects to view reality as an incomprehensible principle that unifies all things, he has capitulated to an abstract "one." Insofar as he resolves to hope that a more comprehensive vantage point will be birthed in the future which currently evades every mind, he has given precedence to open-ended time, which evades the comprehension of every intellect.

On the presupposition that the Trinity (as articulated by Calvin) exists, Van Til believes that it is quite clear why *He* would not be subject to the one-many problem in its various permutations.[3] Like the Idealist Absolute, the Triune God is a harmony between unity and diversity, but unlike the Idealist Absolute, He is (a) strictly eternal, and (b) exhaustively personal. The first point indicates that the Trinity is not in any measure dependent on an opposing, ever incomplete temporal sphere that would compromise the finality of His knowledge and being. The second point indicates that the Triune God is not married to any sort of unconscious being that would resist, and fail to fully express his own eternal Self-awareness and Self-direction. With these observations in mind, God is justly regarded as at once uni-personal (Exod 20:3; Isa 35:10; 44:24), and tri-personal (Matt 28:19; 2 Cor 13:14).[4] This is not because the unity of the Godhead constitutes a fourth person above the three, but because the three are identical with the one Godhead they share, even as they are eternally distinct. Another way of stating the same mystery is that any two divine persons are exhaustively expressed *within* the context of the third (John 10:37–38; 14:9–11; 1 Cor 12:4–6; Col 2:9) who is the "one" Absolute God.[5] And yet, because the same two persons express themselves *unto* that third personal context, they are also irreducibly three. Calvin's covenant theology comes to the service of

3. Curiously, Norman Geisler and Paul Feinberg deny that the Trinity solves the one-many problem, since the Nicene doctrine of the Trinity states a relationship between one divine *being* and three divine *persons*, while (allegedly) the one-many problem concerned the relationship between different types of being. Geisler and Feinberg, *Introduction to Philosophy*, 174–76. Nevertheless, Van Til has been echoed by Colin Gunton in observing that insofar as the Nicene Doctrine of the Trinity states the relationship between one "universal" (God) and three "particular" persons, it is perfectly relevant to the one-many problem. Gunton, *God, Creation, and the Culture of Modernity*, 129ff.

4. IST, 204; CFC, 82–83. Cf. Tipton, "Function of Perichoresis," 291–94. Cf. Smith, *Paradox*, 52–54; Hodge, *Systematic*, 1:462.

5. Tipton argues that for Van Til, "the sense in which we speak of God as one person involves the interpenetration and coinherence of the persons within the Godhead. This interpenetration is so exhaustive and complete that it is appropriate to refer to Triune God as possessing one will, one mind, and one consciousness. In this sense, then, he is one person." Tipton, "Function of Perichoresis," 297–98.

his Trinitarian doctrine at this point,[6] as it emphasizes the biblical theme that the character of fathers, priests, kings, and most of all, the Christian Savior, is expressed to and through groups which are effectively collective individuals (Rom 5:12–20; cf. Num 14:15; Judg 20:8; 1 Cor 12:12). But, of course, human covenantal relationships are but reflections of the Trinity's transcendent harmony (John 17:20–26)

Ontologically, the "one" God cannot recede into oblivion as an abstract and indistinct universal, for He is concretely and infinitely defined in relationship to the "three" persons. Nor can the "three" degrade into irrational "particulars" that evade definition at some point, for they are exhaustively defined by the one Trinitarian dynamic. Nothing, then, would fall outside of God's personal comprehension, including the relationship between His trifold being and his comprehensive self-knowledge. God would be a self-contained, self-defined, and self-sufficient person.[7] A subject-object dichotomy could never arise for God because each person would at once enjoy exhaustive internal access to those persons to Whom He is externally related. It is equally impossible that the ethical dynamic between the three could come to conflict with the convictions of the individual, for each person's will is an eternal expression of the others'.[8] Furthermore, the Father's eternal relationship to the Son and Spirit could not be due to an unmotivated choice or to a logically determined decision, which would subject him to irrational chance or impersonal principles. Instead, the Father's eternal decision to relate to the other persons as Father must be motivated by the deepest interests of the Son and the Spirit at work within him, right alongside his own pleasure to honor them. Indeed, this multi-personal sort of self-determination is the biblical ideal of freedom (cf. John 4:34; 5:30; 6:38; 14:10; Rom 8:27; Phil 2:12–13).[9] With Calvin, then, we must be forthright in opposing Logos Christologies for which the Father's original decision to generate the Son and to spirate the Spirit was either unmotivated, or logically determined.[10] Generation and procession must be regarded as eternal relationships that reflect the will of all three of the self-existent divine persons. Seizing on

6. SCE, 96ff.

7. "Hence the problem of the one and the many, of the universal and the particular, of being and becoming, of analytic and synthetic reasoning, of the a priori and the a posteriori must be solved by an exclusive reference to the Trinity." SCE, 96; cf. 54; cf. DF4, 48–49; DF3, 181–82, 192; CTEV, 64–65; CG, 7–8; IST, 22–23; CI, 75.

8. CTE, 21.

9. SCE, 68–70; 97–98; CTE, 48–50.

10. Van Til is especially critical of any "Logos" Christology which conceives of the Son as emanating from the Father as a subordinate being or principle. CJ, 4–5; CTK, 143–55; NM, 145–48.

Idealist terminology, and setting it to a uniquely orthodox Christian use, we must insist that the Trinity is an "Absolute Person,"[11] whose eternal motive, standard, and goal of being, is ultimately the Father, the Son, and the Spirit themselves (Rom 11:36).

The man who is in faithful covenant with God is freed from the one-many problem. For, the Trinity can facilitate among men the sort of concrete thinking after which the Absolute Idealists only groped, because He is an Absolute *person* who may verbally disclose a finite, but dependable description of his eternal plan with which his people may organize the facts of nature and, in turn, refine their vision of the whole. Indeed, the consistent believer accepts God's self-attesting revelation at the beginning of his theoretical and practical projects (2 Cor 10:5; Job 28:28; Ps 111:10; Prov 1:7) as the only light in Whom the creation can be understood (Ps 36:9).[12] The believer is grateful for those linguistic categories and logical laws that help him to organize the universe, and he is appreciative for the freshness and novelty of spatio-temporal phenomena. He also knows that language and logic will shed light on nature and history, and that the latter will increasingly add definition to the former, only because they are both expressions of God's eternal wisdom. By the same right, when he is confronted with the several paradoxes involved in explaining how universals and particulars, laws and facts, subjects and objects, and groups and members manage to relate, he takes it as confirmation of his presupposition that the Trinity finally contains and explains creation (Acts 17:28; Heb 1:2–3), and not vice versa. Indeed, both the continuity and discontinuity between his knowledge and that of God, verify his starting belief that he is God's created image.[13] All that the believer needs, in order to be logically consistent in treating an apparent contradiction as an exciting impetus to greater discovery, is personal assurance from God that his revelation-based knowledge is true and sufficient, even though finite.

On this position, logical reasoning is best defined as a procedure of "implication" where the believer (a) looks through the lens of the biblical worldview upon created facts, events, qualities, etc.; (b) discerns how they

11. CTE, 21; DF4, 33.

12. For Van Til the basic contrast between believing and unbelieving thought is that the former unabashedly begins by submitting to the "self-attesting" authority of Christ. Van Til, "My Credo," 3–5; CTK, 15, 25–34, 51; CC, 6–10; GH, 7–9.

13. "If we do place the ontological Trinity at the foundation of all our predication then there is no need to fear any scepticism through the avenue of sense. Sensation does 'deceive us' but so does ratiocination. We have the means for their corruption in both cases. The one without the other is meaningless. Both give us true knowledge on the right presupposition; both lead to scepticism on the wrong presupposition." IST, 66.

are illuminated by the Christian system, and in turn constitute new contributions to it; and (c) develops a fuller portrait of the biblical worldview. Man is never entirely sure how new and unforeseen information will, or even currently does contribute to his vision of the Christian system (Isa 43:19; Jer 31:22). But because he is certain that his basic knowledge is true (John 14:6), he knows that whatever insights the facts may yield, they will only enhance and stretch his categories of thought, rather than overturn them. He may deduce that certain events, phenomena, and ideas are flatly impossible because they contradict essential features of the Christian system (Deut 13:1–5; 1 Cor 14:32–33; 2 Tim 2:13). The important point to grasp, however, is that on a Christian logic, a contradiction in one's beliefs is not an idea or a perspective that violates a formal rule, but an idea that confuses, or resists incorporation into the Christian system. Stated another way, one cannot determine the logical possibility or impossibility of a given idea by isolating it from its Trinitarian context, and measuring it according to abstract principles of identity and contradiction. Ideas that may seem to be free from self-contradiction, and possible when considered in relative isolation (e.g., that we may discover the bones of Jesus Christ; that man may evolve into a sinless being; etc.) are self-contradictions for the Christian, since they contradict the only system of reality that is able to preserve any kind of intelligibility. On the other hand, ideas that appear to be impossible and even logically contradictory when viewed in isolation, are sufficiently intelligible, even to the degree that they can be proven necessary, when viewed from within the Christian system (e.g., resurrection from the dead; Jesus's simultaneous ignorance and omniscience; etc.). The doctrine of the Trinity, despite its apparent contradiction, turns out to be the most logical, and indeed most necessary of all ideas. For, even if we cannot comprehend His nature entirely, we may, and indeed already have, deduced that only such a person can be free from the one-many problem in himself, and as such, be the indispensable authority and reference point for human reasoning.[14]

14. God's status as Triune (and transcending the one-many problem) is an essential credential for an absolute authority. Thus, "The idea of the Scriptures as the [authoritative] Word of God is both the source and the result of knowledge of the self-contained triune God. To appeal to the one without appealing to the other is impossible." GD, 33; cf. IST, 12.

4.3 TRANSCENDENTAL PROOF FOR GOD

From the vantage point of the Christian system, Van Til believes that he is able to diagnose and definitively critique secular thought.[15] To begin, the biblical Scriptures present Adam as having known his Creator immediately upon creation, so that he naturally recognized and obeyed God when he was verbally confronted with the requirements of the covenant (Gen 1:28–31; 2:15–25). With this covenantal vision of reality Adam was able to organize the world around him (Gen 2:18–20). Adam could reason in a systematic fashion where special revelation was allowed to illuminate natural revelation, and vice versa so that he would develop an ever deeper knowledge of reality. In the Fall, Adam and Eve were confronted with the aboriginal invitation to reason in the abstract fashion that has governed secular philosophy ever since. By suggesting that God lied about the fatal penalty that would follow from touching the Tree of Good and Evil, the serpent taught man to reason autonomously, as if divine guidance were inessential and in fact highly questionable. As an alternative to systematic reasoning, the serpent prescribed equal doses of rationalism and irrationalism. Like a rationalist, the serpent told man that by reflecting on his own capacity for selfishness he may deduce that God restricted access to the tree out of greed, and fear that man might become like Him. Like an irrationalist, the serpent presented his position as a hypothesis that could only be confirmed finally through experience.

What is important to appreciate is that when men reject God's special guidance, they must settle for a hypothetical sort of rationalism that is at the mercy of an irrational universe. On the one hand, fallen man is all too aware that he cannot hope to know the universe in exhaustive detail. For this reason, he cannot confidently engage in the sort of systematic reasoning prescribed by the covenant. If knowledge is about relating things to an all-encompassing whole, "all things must be exhaustively known, or nothing can be known,"[16] for it is conceivable that an unforeseen fact might render all that we currently believe patently false (e.g., that we are under the influence of Descartes' evil demon). On the other hand, fallen man recognizes his need for certain immutable reference points if he is to possess knowledge of any kind. Therefore, the sinner turns to "abstractions." Abstract reasoning involves divorcing certain characteristics and features of the creation from their concrete contexts (e.g., being, logic, entropy, evolutionary development, language, etc.), and treating them as if they were

15. Van Til describes the Christian as "presenting to [the unbeliever] the picture of himself as taken through the X-ray machine called the Bible." DF3, 232; cf. CTK, 18.

16. IST, 163.

self-intelligible, immutable principles. Abstractions are supposed to replace God, by sufficiently accounting for the relative normalcy of things. But unlike the divine intellect, which comprehends all things in their infinitesimal and systematic details, abstract principles shed the details of temporal reality, and are supposed to be exhaustively understood solely with reference to themselves. Inevitably, then, such principles will not be able to account for every anomaly, irregularity, or frustrating evil that man encounters in time. However, irrational "chance" can itself be made into a generality or "anti-principle" that accounts for the novelty, change, and diversity of things. In this way, entirely random occurrences (e.g., "brute facts") can exist right alongside of all-encompassing laws.[17] And man can be both a rationalist, who is capable in himself of determining what is possible, as well as an irrationalist, who regards the course of history, and even his own freedom, as ultimately beyond explanation. In place of the Triune person, the unbeliever embraces as his triad of, too often unarticulated, presuppositions: (a) human autonomy, (b) abstract reason, and (c) brute facts.

Far from striking anything like a happy medium between unity and diversity, the fallen man, in his rebellion from God, actually *creates* for himself the one-many problem. To recap the dilemma but one more time: abstract principles and brute facts prove to shed all definition when divorced from a concrete system.[18] And it is beyond comprehension how principles which are themselves vacuous can account for the intelligibility and novelty of the universe.[19] Furthermore, the dialectical conclusion (whether Aristotelian or Hegelian) that logical abstractions and brute facts mutually, and indefinitely, qualify one another is equally inadmissible. For, it leaves man with the unanswerable question as to how he might be certain, or even determine with high probability that the dynamic between logic and time is, or will continue to be conducive to knowledge, a decent quality of life, harmony in society, existential meaning, ethical imperatives, etc. The fallen man rejects from the outset the notion that he is reliant on an absolutely sovereign God, Who harmonizes the created "one" and "many" in His redemptive historical plan. As a result, he is without any dependable standard for supposing that the temporal flux might not swallow up every vestige of intelligibility in the universe, or that logical principles will not bring time to a standstill.[20] The unbeliever cannot justify his belief that when he assigns qualities to

17. DF3, 126–27.

18. Recall 3.2.1.

19. Recall 2.2.2. Cf. CG, 2; DF4, 47–51.

20 Rousas Rushdoony summarized Van Til's apologetic challenge to unbelievers with the phrase "By what standard?" Rushdoony, *By What Standard?*, 100–107.

empirical objects (predication), or asserts an inferential relationship between ideas, that his judgments have any basis in reality.[21] Every attempt to justify them is self-defeating because they represent impersonal solutions to what is at root a personal problem that he has with his Lord and Creator. The unbeliever may for rhetorical purposes embrace the fate of his presuppositions, and profess agnosticism. But, insofar as he gathers that a noncommittal stance is an appropriate response to take given his predicament, he betrays his belief in the objectivity of the very sorts of judgment and inference which he has officially consigned to naught. The unbeliever cannot escape asserting, in practice, that reality is the very sort of place that, in theory, he denies it to be. Hence, to repeat Van Til's conclusion, unbelieving thought is fundamentally self-defeating (Prov 8:36; Jer 2:13, 19; Matt 16:25; 1 Cor 1:20–25).

In light of the despondent conclusion that arises when secular man scrutinizes his own presuppositions, the apologist ought to realize the futility of basing his proofs for Christianity on "common sense." The history of philosophy and the biblical Scriptures converge in their teaching that when man treats himself as an autonomous standard of truth, the stability of "common sense" and even traditional social structures eventually collapse on themselves (Judg 17:6; 21:25; Rom 1:24–27). Instead, the apologist must challenge the unbeliever's triad of presuppositions as a self-defeating effect of rebellion against his Triune Creator. Each argument for Christianity ought to be *ad hominem* in the sense that the apologist caters it to a specific conversation partner, with the aim of exposing his unique version of self-destructive idolatry.[22] One of the rhetorical effects of a faithfully executed apologetic is that the unbeliever proves to indirectly affirm the truth of the Christian worldview as he relies on induction, logic, predication, and other tools to construct a position that so thoroughly undermines them. As a creature made in the image of God, the unbeliever betrays an irrevocable awareness that it is incumbent upon him to justify his beliefs in various ways.[23] But as a rebel against God, he would rather search the universe high and low for a different ground of certainty than his Creator, even if it involves suppressing the basic insight that dependable knowledge

21. "God as self-sufficient, as the One in whom the One and the Many are equally ultimate, is the One in whom the persons of the Trinity are interchangeably exhaustive, is the presupposition for the intelligent use of words with respect to the universe, whether it be trees of the garden or the angels of heaven." IST, 102; SCE, 11.

22 SCE, 205.

23. Even those who prefer irrationalist modes of justification based on the elegance, existential value, or artful style of a given belief system betray a dissatisfaction with "nothing" as the ground of their beliefs.

is the prerequisite, and not simply the result of our rational inquiries. The unbeliever will, of course, vehemently deny that his actions or arguments betray an awareness of God. But the apologist's retort is that the biblical diagnosis of unbelief, and indeed the entire biblical system *must be true* by virtue of the impossibility of the contrary position. As we have seen, as long as the unbeliever fails to harmonize logic and time, he lacks justification for supposing that any inference, act of predication, or even interpretation of his own state of affairs is correct.[24] Nevertheless, the unbeliever's capacity to follow the transcendental proof and its implications reveals that he is not the sort of nescient rock to which his own belief system would reduce him. And since only the Triune God can account for the validity of reason, the Christian apologist is necessarily correct in his evaluation that the unbeliever is culpably reliant on God. Yet, the unbeliever will object again that even if his arguments presuppose the validity of induction, mathematical principles, and any number of other tools, it does not *logically* follow that he consciously or unconsciously knows anything about this Triune God Who allegedly renders them effective. But again, the unbeliever has not appreciated the gravity of his predicament. The one-many problem to which he is subject renders his notion of formal logic unintelligible, and undependable because divorced from a concrete vision of the "whole."[25] When set within the Christian system, which is the only sort of logic that evades the one-many problem, the unbeliever's tools of reasoning certainly do imply an awareness of the Triune Creator (Rom 1:19–24). On the Christian scheme, God's self-revelation is so pervasive within and around man that it is like an oxygenated atmosphere on which man relies at every moment even if he refuses to consciously acknowledge it.[26] Man is confident (whether he claims to be or not) that he is relatively able to navigate his way through the world, only because of an inextricable sense that he and his natural context are the creations of a wise, gracious, longsuffering, and self-sufficient Creator. This natural and immediate inference from man and nature to their Creator only seems dubious to the unbeliever, because he is naturally prone, and

24. "For the only conclusive argument for Christianity is precisely the fact that only upon the presupposition of the truth of its teaching does logic or predication in general touch reality at all." IST, 39.

25. To the extensive degree that the unbeliever does make important discoveries and rational inferences, it is because he is inconsistent with his metaphysical principles. "Non-Christian science has worked with the borrowed capital of Christian theism, and for that reason alone has been able to bring to light much truth." CTEV, 64; cf. 68; IST, 85; CIM, 17.

26. IST, 106.

subsequently nurtured to suppress the knowledge of God by replacing Him with self-defeating abstractions.[27]

Given this subversive and even offensive interpretation of the unbelieving condition, one might ask how Van Til hopes to lure the unbeliever *into* Christianity. But the presuppositional argument turns the question around, and involves asking the unbeliever how he supposes himself able to *get out* from under the biblical interpretation of himself.[28] The "common ground" between the apologist and the unbeliever resides in the fact that the unbeliever is, in spite of his best efforts to deny it, a creature of God whose confidence in reason and the stability of reality is only explicable as the product of divine testimony from within and without.[29] Were it not for the restraining power of God's common grace, the unbeliever's rebellious interpretation of things would swiftly result in death and self-destruction. Likewise, the apologist's only hope that the unbeliever will repent of his sins is based on God's promise that when the gospel is faithfully set against a man's dire predicament, the Spirit will apply unto sinners Christ's atoning work, according to the election of the Father.

Van Til's transcendental argument[30] may be distinguished from the traditional theistic proofs formally,[31] and by virtue of the "absolute probative force" of its conclusion.[32] Unlike arguments that rely on the logical relationship of *implication* (x implies y), arguments based on the relationship of

27. Van Til does not dismiss the apologetic value of observing that there is widespread belief in some sort of god. Van Til is simply careful to add that pagan theologies simultaneously attest to man's sinful tendency to pervert his sense of deity, with the result that we must not build upon them. IST, 108–9; cf. PA, n.p.

28. It is because Van Til offered a positive solution to philosophical problems, and a positive task to develop a Christian philosophy that Hendrik G. Stoker praises Van Til's perspective over that of Herman Dooyweerd, who focused on offering internal critiques of non-Christian philosophies. Hendrik G. Stoker, "Reconnoitering the Theory of Knowledge of Prof. Dr. Cornelius Van Til," in *Jerusalem and Athens*, 36–37.

29 When used as a synonym for "common sense" Van Til opposes the expression "common ground." CB, 280; CG, 49. But he embraces the expression when used to denote the fact that believers and sinners do both dwell in God's universe, and, therefore, do both experience something of his general benevolence. DF4, 14–19.

30. Van Til clearly indicates that his transcendental method is slated to supply the definitive sort of proof after which Kant had unsuccessfully striven. SCE, 110; cf. CTE, 250.

31. Don Collet was the first to identify a formal difference between the logical relationship of "implication" and "presupposition," explaining that they have different truth functions. Collett, "Van Til and Transcendental Argument," 302. Even John Frame, who formerly denied that there was any fundamental difference between the traditional and transcendental proofs for God, was convinced by Collet's article that a genuine difference exists. Frame, "Reply to Don Collet," 307–9.

32. DF4, 198.

presupposition (x presupposes y) are validated by both the affirmation and the denial of the antecedent proposition (x or ~x). For many centuries, philosophers have evaded the theistic proof from contingency—(x) contingent being *implies* (y) a necessary being—by denying that logical categories such as "contingency" apply to reality as it is in itself.[33] Quite obviously, if there is no such thing as a contingent being, then one cannot hope to reason from it to the existence of a necessary being. On the other hand, if one contends that (x) contingency *presupposes* (y) the Triune God, as the very ground of intelligibility, the conclusion is quite different. If the Triune God is the precondition of intelligibility of any kind, then both the affirmation and the denial of contingency (x and ~x) prove the existence of the Triune God, since both betray the attribute of intelligibility. Thus, supposing that Van Til's analysis of the one-many problem is correct, and that a secular solution is not forthcoming, Van Til's conclusion for the existence of God is indeed certain. Van Til's transcendental argument may be succinctly summarized:

(1) Every inference and act of predication presupposes the existence of the absolute and personal harmony of unity and diversity, within the Triune God

(2) Denials that the Trinity exists are acts of predication

Therefore

(3) The Triune God exists[34]

In the execution of his task, the apologist may be understood as critiquing and displacing the unbeliever's metanarrative with the biblical alternative. This point has undoubtedly been missed by many readers of Van Til, because personal histories play little role in his major treatises. However, this is because Van Til focused on telling the tragic story of unbelieving thought on the macro level of Western Philosophy (cf. §21–26, 43–47, and 59–65). In works such as *A Christian Theory of Knowledge*, *A Christian Survey of Epistemology*, and *Christianity in Crisis*, Van Til expounds the church's maturation in appreciating the redemptive-historical system, and in rejecting ahistorical Platonic visions of reality. In *The New Modernism*, *Christianity and Barthianism*, and *The Great Debate Today*, Van Til critiques the Kantian story of reality, especially as it pertains to neo-orthodoxy. Other treatises examine how specific theologians have made dangerous concessions to the unbeliever's metaphysical narrative—e.g., G. C. Berkouwer (*The Sovereignty of Grace*), Edward J. Carnell (*The Case for Calvinism*), and James Daane (*The*

33. This is of course Kant's response to the theistic proofs.

34. James Anderson identifies and defends several versions of this argument as it appears in the Van Til corpus. Anderson, "If Knowledge then God," 61–68.

Theology of James Daane).[35] Yet, the clearest illustration of Van Til's commitment to overturning the secular story can be found in his brief pamphlet *Why I Believe in God*. In this short and subtle case for Christianity, Van Til surveys the various factors that conditioned him to accept Christ, and he interprets them as having been graciously superintended by God. At various points throughout, he takes note of the naturalist/behaviorist interpretation of his Christian conviction as lacking objective validity, because so obviously the product of cultural influences. In his monologue, Van Til refrains from offering a direct refutation of the naturalist position.[36] Van Til seems to hope that his readers will themselves discern how self-defeating and even tragic the non-believing narrative happens to be. Why would man elect to interpret himself in a manner that deprives him of the capacity to develop a true and objective interpretation of reality? Can he not see, or does he not care, that such an interpretation undermines itself? Van Til shamelessly relays the warm assurance he enjoys as he submits to the interpretation of himself and the world supplied by God the Father. Ironically, as the naturalist clumsily attempts to be his own father (Ps 100:3), laying bare his own origins and existential purpose, the self-defeating story he tells himself only confirms the biblical metanarrative and its diagnosis of sin.

4.4 ANSWERS TO OBJECTIONS

4.4.1 Circular Reasoning

The most natural allegation to level against Van Til's apologetic is that it is illogical, as a blatant example of circular reasoning.[37] However, this critique is imperceptive of Van Til's point that self-confirmation is the unique prerogative of, and is indeed something quite different for, the Triune God than it can be for anything else. For example, claims that the laws of logic are evidently true, on the basis of nothing but their own self-testimony, negate themselves. For, the applicability of logic to the spatio-temporal universe cannot be deduced from logical principles alone. And yet, the meaning of the law of contradiction cannot be conceptualized apart from notions of incompatibility and repulsion that are supplied by a number of contrasting principles and spheres (e.g., space, time, facts, qualities, ideas, languages, cultures, feelings, etc.).[38] For this reason, Van Til contends that one must

35. CFC, 24.

36. WI, np.

37. Sproul et. al., *Classical Apologetics*, 323; Geisler, *Apologetics*, 61–62.

38. For an extended critique of the notion of self-evident ideas, recall Van Til's

acknowledge the Triune God Who harmonizes universals and particulars, logic and history, subjects and objects, before he can be justified in believing that any of these pairs overlap at any point. For the same reason, God's Self-testimony in Scripture must be accepted on the basis of His unparalleled authority alone (Heb 6:13; Mark 1:22), since the rest of reality cannot even bear a consistent witness to itself apart from His illumination.[39] At this point, one might object that Scripture depends for its meaning on a host of extra-biblical factors, with the result that its testimony is no more self-evident than that of the laws of logic.[40] But, the point belabored by Van Til is that Scripture, nature, and man are three distinct but complementary forms of divine revelation, so that when they are allowed to qualify one another, they comprise a single self-elucidating Word of God.[41] God's Word in Scripture is not self-confirming in the simple sense that it is followed by the addendum "and this word is trustworthy" (although this appears on occasion—Matt 5:18; John 3:11; Rev 21:5; etc.). Instead, it is self-confirming as a light which so illuminates every other aspect of creation that they respond with their own unique testimonies to God's nature and existence (Ps 36:9). Thus, it is better to speak of the proof for God as an instance of "spiral"[42] reasoning, which begins with God's self-testimony, turns in His light to evaluate other aspects of reality, and finally returns with an ever more refined and confirmed[43] vision of God.[44] In contrast, unbelieving perspectives

critique of common sense, recounted in 1.3.1, and the brief account of Hegel's *Phenomenology of Spirit* in 3.2.1. Or, look ahead to the Van Tillian interpretation of logic in 6.3.1–2.

39. "The only alternative to 'circular reasoning' as engaged in by Christians, no matter on what point they speak, is that of reasoning on the basis of isolated facts and isolated minds, with the result that there is no possibility of reasoning at all." IST, 147.

40. Sproul et. al., *Classical Apologetics*, 212–27. The authors of classical apologetics do not consider the possibility that Scripture and Logic must qualify one another in order for either to function properly. Both are "self-evident" to the believer in the informal sense that they are obviously essential to developing a God-fearing worldview, and to interpreting one another. RP, 87–89; IST, 11. Yet, when the believer says that "'Scripture and reason convince me that this or that is true,' he should mean by this that his reason as it looks at everything in the light of Scripture, has convinced him." IST, 197.

41. Ibid., 62–109.

42. SCE, 12. Cf. Packer, "Biblical Authority," 146.

43. In his discussion of Van Til's use of evidence and the legitimacy of the verifiability principle, Thom Notaro explains that for Van Til, the Christian System "is verifiable" by every forthcoming fact, but is not by any means "falsifiable." Notaro, *Van Til and Evidence*, 76.

44. Van Til explains that the sort of circular reasoning to which he is committed involves the recognition that "The starting-point, the method, and the conclusion are always involved in one another." CA, 30.

lack coherence altogether, since not even the simplest act of predication is justified.

4.4.2 Irrationalism

Due to his contention that human logic is finite, and unfit (apart from divine direction) to determine what is possible for God, some of Van Til's Christian critics have accused him of being obtuse to the possibility that our laws of logic may enter into the very nature of God.[45] However, such a position compromises the Creator-creature distinction by rendering human reason divine, rather than a finite *image* of God's intellect (Gen 1:26–27).[46] Additionally, the identification of logic with God is undermined by the fact that the paradox of the Trinity cannot be logically resolved,[47] and attempts to do so have proven to engulf God in the one-many problem. Gordon Clark's study of the Trinity is a case in point. Clark is led to the conclusion that "God" refers to an abstract genus or "definition," as opposed to a numerically individual substance.[48] His rationale is simple: if God were an individual being, and the Father *is God*, and the Son *is God*, then the heretical conclusion that the Father *is* the Son would follow with necessity. And yet, Clark's position, that God is a genus instead of a being, conflicts with the predominant interpretation of the Christian creeds,[49] fails to take seriously a host of biblical passages where "God" speaks as an individual person (Isa 44:24; 35:10; Exod 20:3), and lends itself to Tri-theism. With respect to the relationship between unity and diversity in the Godhead,

45. Sproul et. al., *Classical Apologetics*, 76, 138ff. Carnell, *Apologetics*, 161–64. Cf. Geisler, *Apologetics*, 61ff;

46. Gordon Clark's paraphrase of John 1:1 is a case in point, "In the beginning was Logic, and Logic was with God, and Logic was God . . . in Logic was life and the life was the light of men." Clark, "Wheaton Lectures," *Works*, 7:58–59. Cf. Nash, *The Word of God and the Mind of Man*, 91–112. Even if Clark's translation were justifiable, one may no more conclude from it that God is identical with the laws of logic *as conceived by man*, than 1 John 4:8—"God is love—allows one to conclude that God is identical with the love shared between a man and a woman. Furthermore, such a view would make for a Greek sort of Pantheism, wherein the divine nature is identical with human reason. IST, 162.

47. In the most thorough catalog to date of attempts to logically resolve the paradoxes of the Trinity and the Incarnation, James N. Anderson has demonstrated that each option is either unorthodox or ineffective. Anderson, *Paradox*, 59.

48. Clark, *Trinity*, 51–53, 86, 95. Cf. Sproul et. al., *Classical Apologetics*, 77.

49. For interpretations of the Nicene terminology as demarking a numerically singular substance shared by the persons of the Trinity, see Anderson, *Paradox*, 16–31; Hodge, *Systematic*, 1:460, 462; Bavinck, *Dogmatics*, 2:170–77; IST, 228–30.

Clark contends that the Father alone is the original fount of deity, while the generation of the Son and procession of the Spirit are the products of the Father's arbitrary, but nevertheless eternal decisions.[50] Because the Son is the divine Logos, it may even be said God is a logical being by virtue of a (logically?) prior free decision.[51] In this way, Clark reduces God to the sort of combination between arbitrary irrationalism and formal rationalism that consistently births skepticism.[52] The God who is an unadulterated, voluntaristic will prior to every personal distinction and rational attribute with which we are acquainted cannot be known in and of himself,[53] nor can he be trusted to not negate his present nature. In contrast to Clark, Van Til argues that it is only when God's personal relations enter into His very essence, in a manner that stretches our normal conception of the law of identity, that He can be known truly, while not exhaustively.[54] Because God is a mysteriously tri-personal individual, believers may rest assured that His decisions are not arbitrary or irrational, but always motivated and guided by three holy and immutable persons.

4.4.3 Incomplete Disjunction

Some have argued that Van Til's proof fails to establish the truth of Christianity, because he has not proven that every alternative to Christianity that has, or ever will be developed must presuppose the Christian system.[55] However, such a point is imperceptive, on two levels. First, Van Til locates the destructive feature of unbelieving thought in its reliance on abstractions, and not on any particular abstraction (idol) that one advocates. In this case, until and unless one is able to demonstrate how fallen man could reason without abstract principles, or solve the "one and many" problem with them, the Christian apologist has every reason to believe that his critique is conclusive. Second, the unbeliever's romantic hope that somehow, some

50. Clark, *Trinity*, 111–13.

51. Clark, *Christian View of Man and Thing*, 268.

52. In contrast to Clark, Van Til contends that believers should never attempt to explain "the Trinity to the satisfaction of the natural man by reducing the objectionable irrational element to his own non-objectionable irrational." IST, 231.

53. Clark forthrightly denies that man can know anything God's mode of knowing. Van Til responds that "if one does not know anything about God's mode of knowing then one can know nothing of God's mode of being," since knowing and being must interpenetrate one another in an absolute being. Ibid., 170.

54. IST, 159–73.

55. Kuyper made this observation (recall 2.1.2). Cf. Montgomery, "Once Upon an A Priori," 388.

way, autonomous man might be able to make sense of the universe apart from God, represents a reliance on the irrationalist notion of open-ended chance that Van Til has already proven self-destructive.[56]

4.4.4 Merely Theistic

Others have argued that a non-Christian deity (Allah in particular) could be hailed as solving the one-many problem in a fashion that transcends human understanding, and as providing man concrete guidance just as well as the Trinity, so that Van Til's proof is effectively robbed of its transcendental force (from the impossibility of every contrary position).[57] This critique is based on a mistaken interpretation of what Van Til means by "mystery." God's Triune mode of being, which places Him above the one-many dilemma, is not mysterious in the sense that it evades all definition and discernible sense. Although paradoxical, it is nevertheless evident that a multi-personal God alone can be self-contained and absolutely authoritative.[58] That is to say, the Christian God does not merely *claim* to speak with absolute authority, but the information which he has disclosed about himself (e.g., that he is Triune) discernibly implies his absolute authority. The contrary must be said for those secular, pagan, and heretical theologies which explicitly deny to their god(s) the status of existing as a personal One and Many. Unitarian theologies, for example, succumb to a stultifying sort of mystery[59] where god is identical with, or subject to, an ineffable void, that renders him incapable of speaking altogether, or of speaking with authority. For, nothing can be accurately predicated of a strictly unitary deity, since the multiplicity involved in predication is at odds with his nature.[60] If such a being were to enjoy negative definition as he exists in contrast to the created sphere, it would only demonstrate his dependence on the temporal universe in order to enjoy the sort of differentiation, purpose, and relationship that he lacks in himself. And, even if such a god were thought of as enjoying internal dis-

56. For a further discussion of the notion of logical possibility see 6.3.2.

57. See Johnson, "Is Cornelius Van Til's Apologetic Method Christian, or Merely Theistic?" 275–86. Cf. Montgomery, "Once Upon an A Priori," 389.

58. GD, 33; IST, 12

59. When Van Til speaks of "mysteries" with respect to unbelieving systems of thought, he has in mind genuine contradictions. See SCE, 31–32, 51, 98; CA, 41. IST, 13 169, 180; CG, 82.

60 The idea at work in Van Til's reasoning at this point is accurately conveyed by Edward Caird when he says that "a thing which has nothing to distinguish it is unthinkable, but equally unthinkable is a thing which is so separated from all other things as to have no community with them." Caird, *Hegel*, 135.

tinctions between principles, faculties, motives, and interests that were distinct from his person, whether as simple "parts," or as a governing "nature," he would be an effect of sub-personal principles (which cannot illuminate themselves). Such a god would not be an absolute authority, or even true deity.[61] Likewise, polytheistic theories undercut the authority of the gods by conceiving of them as subject to an impersonal sphere which facilitates their personal, and often menacing, interactions with one another. As with naturalistic atheism, pagan forms of polytheism fail to posit the existence of an Absolute God who may speak with absolute authority, because literally all things were created, and continue to be upheld by the word of his power (Heb 1:3).

4.4.5 Speculative and Ahistorical

Some have sensed that Van Til's position is overly speculative,[62] and prone to the errors of Hegelianism[63] or Barthianism,[64] such that it undermines redemptive history. For, the very claim that the Trinity is the lone reference point of true knowledge,[65] conflicts with the biblical portrait of men as holding true beliefs long before they became acquainted with God as Father, Son, and Holy Spirit. However, Scripture clearly confirms that the Old Testament saints enjoyed a faint awareness of the divine Christ (John 8:56; Heb 11:26; Col 2:17), and of the operations of His Spirit (1 Cor 10:3–4). In other words, it was possible for the Old Testament saints to know the Trinity truly, even though they did not know of Him exhaustively, or even explicitly. But,

61. Due to the indissoluble relationship between God's authority and his Triune nature, Van Til contends that "Basic to all of the doctrines of Christian theism is that of the self-contained God, or, if we wish, that of the ontological Trinity." CA, 128. Cf. SCE, 5, 94–97.

62. Even sympathetic readers have leveled this charge. Krabbendam, "The Methodological Objective," 125.

63. The earliest barrage of criticism of Van Til leveled by Cecil DeBoer and Jesse DeBoer in the *Calvin Forum*, centered on Van Til's alleged Hegelian rationalism, and the charge has been leveled many times thereafter. See Daane, *A Theology of Grace*, v-ix, 22, 39, 102–105. See also Meuther's account of the controversy. Meuther, *Van Til*, 162–75. Dooyweerd, "Cornelius Van Til and the Transcendental Critique," 81. Pinnock, "The Philosophy of Christian Evidences," 421–25.

64. Traditional Reformed critics of Van Til have taken his emphasis on irresolvable paradox to be a capitulation to a Barthian sort of irrationalism. Sproul et. al., *Classical Apologetics*, 245. Hoeksema, *Clark-Van Til Controversy*, 33–39, 62–67. Barthians, on the other hand, have curiously assessed that Van Til's denunciations of Barth were due to an unreflective aversion to philosophical language, despite Van Til's own liberal use of such language. Richardson, *Reading Karl Barth*, 71.

65. IST, 10.

it is exactly this sort of situation that a fully developed Trinitarian logic is slated to undergird. As God is perfectly unified and diverse, He providentially ensures that significantly different historical vantage points on Him may be logically equivalent, not because they can be deduced from each other, but because they reside on the same trajectory of development, and must attract or repel the same information when presented with it. The mature doctrine of the Trinity is a case in point.[66] As a genuinely new idea, the Trinity forced believers to stretch their understanding of certain concepts (e.g., like "one," "three," "person," etc.) and with them the boundaries of logical possibility. But, in return, the Trinity illuminated many Old Testament passages (e.g., where God's Messenger is identified with God—Gen 16:7–13; 19:24; Exod 3:2ff.), and provided deeper insight into its teaching that God is a *self-sufficient* unity Who is identical with inter-personal attributes (Lev 19:2; Ps 119:15).[67] Once revealed, it was clear that the God Whom the Old Testament saints knew as the absolute personal context and Creator of the universe could never have been anything but Triune. On the other hand, it followed that unitarian theologies are not merely retrogressions, but outright perversions (Prov 30:6; Deut 4:2) of an absolute biblical religion, which never denied, but always anticipated, the revelation of the Trinity.[68]

In maintaining that the Trinity undergirds the possibility of progressive revelation, Van Til stands in sharp disagreement with Hegel's dialectical theory that the eternal God *realizes* Himself in human history. He is also far from Barth's equally dialectical position that God's radical freedom can only be manifested by identifying Himself in facts, texts, and proclamations, the objective content of which hide and obscure Him.[69] For Barth, revelation is not progressive in the sense that it allows man to develop an ever more robust notion of God's nature, but in the sense that God continues to encounter and direct men unto His ends through revelation. Van Til argues that Hegel and Barth's hostility to the traditional notion of progressive revelation is due to their common presumption that God's essential nature can only be manifested and realized through its opposite (time, finitude, etc.), rather than in relationship to the ontological Trinity Himself.[70]

66. IST, 220–21.

67. Cf. Frame, "Divine Aseity and Apologetics," 115–30. Smith, *Eternal Covenant*..

68. CJ, 35.

69. Barth, *Church Dogmatics*, 1.1: 166, 175.

70. Van Til was well aware that Barth explicitly (and frequently) affirms God's *ontological* Tri-unity, but he discerned that Barth's doctrines of revelation and election necessitate the conclusion that God's Tri-unity is the effect, rather than the foundation of his free decision to elect humanity in Christ. Barth scholars have advanced similar theses. For example, Bruce McCormack argues that Barth's "commitments require that

4.4.6 Inconsistent with New Testament Evidentialism

Many have denounced Van Til's apologetic for failing to follow the New Testament example of appealing directly to historical evidences as powerful proofs for the Faith (John 14:11; Acts 17:30–31; 1 Cor 15:1–11).[71] Nevertheless, Van Til's difference with evidentialists pertains to their failure to take seriously fallen man's hostility to the evidence for the resurrection, the veracity of Scripture, etc. Because the message of Christianity is at odds with the unbeliever's basic convictions about reality (1 Cor 2:18) he will either prefer fantastic explanations of Christian evidences (Matt 28:11–15), or he will accept the fact of certain miracles while denying the distinctively Christian interpretation of them (Acts 8:14–24).[72] Thus, appeals to evidence must be married to an attack on the unbeliever's presuppositions.[73] Notably, this holistic approach is what one finds in Scripture (Acts 14:14–19; 17:16–34; 1 Cor 1:18—2:16; 15:3–11).[74]

4.4.7 Transcendental Argument for the Non-Existence of God

A more hostile objection comes from atheist philosopher Michael Martin, who developed an opposing (but inaccurately titled[75]) "transcendental argument for the non-existence of God" (TANG). According to TANG, rational discourse is incompatible with a super-logical God, for such a being could frustrate man's perspective by realizing logical contradictions. Martin himself elects to proceed pragmatically as if the testimony of his

---

we see the triunity of God logically as a function of divine election. . . . In other words, the works of God *ad intra* (the trinitarian processions) find their ground in the *first* of the works of God ad extra (viz. election)." McCormack, "Grace and Being," 103. cf. NM, ix, 145–148; CB, 490.

71. Montgomery, "Once Upon an A Priori," 380–92. Pinnock, "Philosophy of Christian Evidences," 420–22. Canata, "History of Apologetics at Princeton," 57–76. Sproul et al., *Classical Apologetics*, 189–211. McGrath, *Intellectuals Don't Need God*, 217–21.

72. Jeffry Jue has argued that Van Til's doctrine of a suppressed natural knowledge of God is not only anticipated by Calvin, but has particularly strong antecedents in the work the sixteenth-century reformer, Francis Junius. Jue, "Theology Naturalis," 168–89.

73. CTK, 293; cf. IST, 9

74. This Van Til's contention in PA.

75. Michael Butler was the first to point out that in fact, Martin's argument is not "transcendental" at all. Transcendental arguments purport to establish that a given belief is the precondition for valid reasoning, and thus implicitly at work whenever one makes an intelligible claim or inference. But Martin simply undertakes a demonstration that belief in God is potentially hazardous to logic and truth. Butler, "The Great Debate Gets Personal," n.p.

senses and the convictions of reason were sufficiently clear on their own. Evasively, he passes over the question of how he might rest assured that logic applies to the spatio-temporal universe, observing that it "*may be* a pseudoproblem because it is difficult to see how logic could not apply to the world."[76] Apparently, the universe may just happen to be the sort of place that is conducive to human reasoning, and since the alternative scenario is hardly imaginable there is no reason to doubt the former. Martin's informal reasoning overlooks the fact that if the universe were conducive to human reasoning by chance, then it cannot, for that very reason, be conducive to human reasoning in any measure. For, man's beliefs could never be true or justified because the ultimate force by which the rational and the real (the one and many) are related to one another, would itself be a nebulous void of pure chance. That is to say, in the end, there is no rational relationship between the one and many, such that either might be said to justly represent or embody the other. In contrast, the Triune God who comprehends all things with reference to Himself may speak with Absolute authority to the exhaustive interpenetration of the real and the rational within Himself, and an analogous interpenetration in the created sphere. Such a God invites and undergirds logical reasoning about him and the universe so long as it is conducted according to His special guidance. And because he is a perfect unity with his own Word (John 1:1; 10:30) it is impossible that he could mislead his people even unintentionally (1 Cor. 14:33; Titus 1:2; Jas 1:13). In suggesting that if God is all-powerful then he could mislead his people, Martin is utilizing an abstract logic which (a) undercuts itself, and (b) must borrow from Christianity insofar as it is supposed to be applicable to reality in any degree.

4.4.8 Pragmatism

Another objection to Van Til's presuppositionalism is that it is covertly pragmatic. Far from making any headway toward demonstrating that Christianity is objectively true, Van Til has really only proven that Christianity represents a most, or even the most useful and desirable belief system. Yet, again, the objector has lapsed back into the very sort of position that Van Til has proven untenable. If reality were the sort of place where subjective and objective truth could be so disconnected, the objector would have no ground for supposing that his reasoning process advances by objectively valid inferences.[77] Hence, the objection that Van Til's proof is *merely* prag-

76. Emphasis mine. Martin, "Does Logic Presuppose the Existence of God" n.p.

77. Michael Martin argues that "it might be the case that science, logic, and ethics

matic, rather than both useful *and true* is itself incoherent, until and unless the objector can prove that reality is, or even could be, marked by such a dichotomy.[78]

4.4.9 Subjectivism

In the course of his own survey of epistemology, Van Til considers Absolute Idealist, A. E. Taylor's objection that only God knows Himself with certainty, while man's belief in, and interpretation of God can, at best, be highly probable. For, a finite mind cannot comprehend all of the relevant information to any topic, with the result that his vantage point may always be overturned.[79] If this inference were correct, Van Til would be guilty of compromising the Creator-creature distinction by suggesting that man may be absolutely certain that the Triune God exists. But, as Van Til explains, only God enjoys exhaustive knowledge of the universe, with the result that only He can declare whether His people's perspective on reality may be finally falsified, rather than indefinitely refined. Hence, in order to level the claim that divine revelation is necessarily *ambiguous* and *falsifiable* to man, Taylor would need to possess an *unambiguous* and *non-falsifiable* knowledge of what God may and may not accomplish. But this is the very sort of thing that he claims to deny.[80]

4.5 Ambiguity of a Christian Logic

However effective his transcendental critiques and rebuttals may be, many of Van Til's detractors have argued that the force of his argument is vitiated by the fact that his own Christian logic is incomprehensible. It seems that Van Til often vacillates between demanding logical consistency and appealing to mystery whenever it suits him.[81] Even in contexts where Van Til attempts

are impossible and should be rejected" with the result that the transcendental argument for God, "would not establish the truth of the Christian worldview but only the inconsistency of atheists who presuppose science, logic, and objective ethics." Michael Martin, "Does Induction Presume the Existence of God," n.p. Ironically, in drawing such an inference Martin numbers himself among those who fall prey to the transcendental argument for God, since his claim that on a conceivable scenario "ethics . . . *should be* rejected" is self-defeating insofar as it relies upon some concept of human responsibility.

78. Cf. Butler, "The Transcendental Argument for God's Existence," 87–89, 121–23.

79. A. E. Taylor, *The Faith of a Moralist*, 2:207ff.

80. SCE, 172–74. Cf. IST, 136–40.

81. Nash, *The Word of God and the Mind of Man*, 99–101; Robbins, *Cornelius Van*

a direct explanation of his views, one gets hampered down by unnecessary excursions into the errors of unbelieving thought, or the mistakes of his opponents.[82] And his most penetrating insights are scattered here and there throughout his works, and never presented in an orderly fashion.[83] In the hope of rescuing something of the ingenuity of Van Til's system, the next three chapters (5, 6, and 7) provide an explanation of Van Til's: (a) theory of knowledge; (b) conception of a Christian logic; and (c) understanding of how the paradox of the Trinity fosters coherence in the Christian system.

Til The Man and the Myth, 1–7, 22–29; White, *What is Truth?* 57–58.

82. Clark, *Trinity*, 94; Brown, *Philosophy and Christian Faith*, 249.

83. North, *Dominion and Common Grace*, 10. Cf. Frame, *Van Til*, 7; Frame, "Problem of Theological Paradox," 305–10.

5

Trinitarian Theory of Knowledge

5.1 INTRODUCTION

Due to his position that every feature of the universe, including logic, is subject to historical refinement, Van Til has been interpreted as succumbing to the irrationalist zeitgeist of the twentieth century.[1] And yet, Van Til insists that it is also objective and dependable. Fundamental to appreciating Van Til's claims at this point, is his doctrine of analogical knowledge. When knowledge is a matter of reflecting the mind of God, by allowing His special revelation to inform man's interpretation of every other matter, then man may rest assured that his own finite and historical perspective is true. Below, we contrast Van Til's doctrine of analogy with those doctrines of analogy proposed by Thomas Aquinas and Karl Barth, respectively. We then consider how Van Til's doctrine weathers under the general critique of analogy developed by Reformed theologian Gordon Clark. What emerges is a Van Tillian theory of knowledge as (a) Christ-justified, (b) Spirit-motivated belief, that is (c) true, because correspondent with God the Father."[2]

1. Meuther, *Van Til*, 110. Recall 4.4.5.

2. Greg Bahnsen's characterization of knowledge as "*believing* certain propositions . . . that are *true* and for which one has *good evidence*," is helpful. But, replacement of the justification requirement with "good evidence" obscures the fact that knowledge must be based on Christ's redemptive (justificatory) work. Bahnsen, *Van Til*, 180.

5.2 ANALOGICAL CORRESPONDENCE

5.2.1 Thomistic and Barthian Doctrines of Analogy

Despite their radical differences of opinion with respect to the legitimacy of natural theology, Thomas Aquinas and Karl Barth embrace metaphysical schemes that allow human concepts/terms to represent reality in one of three different ways—univocally, equivocally, or analogically. At the beginning of his project, Aquinas adopts Aristotle's metaphysical model of the universe as a combination of eternal rational "forms" and time-bound "material" (hylomorphism). The various forms of existence may be organized on a scale, or as he calls it an "analogy of being" (*analogia entis*) with those that are more rational at the top (man, angels, etc.), and those that are relatively more material/chance-laden at the bottom (animals, rocks, etc.). Barth, on the other hand, adopts a more radical, Kantian sort of dichotomy between a realm of "nature" as that which is law governed, and a transcendent realm of divine "freedom" which is completely beyond "human classification, understanding and description."[3]

For Aquinas, the three different ways in which concepts can represent reality correspond to the three broad sorts of existence: natural essences, bare material, and supernatural beings. First, man enjoys direct insight into the unchanging forms embodied by natural objects (e.g., oak tree, swan, star, etc.) with the result that his ideas are univocal, or identical with them.[4] Second, the material substrate that differentiates one individual from the other members of the same class resists definition, for it is that nebulous something to which every oscillation in attributes attaches itself (e.g., a dog's change in size, location, disposition, etc.). As a result, one is guilty of equivocation or distortion when he represents matter as "heavy," "spatial," or even "actual."[5] Third, if man is to formulate any positive conception of the God who resides above nature, he must limit himself to predicating the highest natural principles and virtues to God (being, love, wisdom, etc.), with the careful recognition that God exceeds even these notions. Such "analogical" predicates are neither univocal nor equivocal with the reality they describe, but in some subtle fashion, "between" the two.[6] Although "analogy" cannot be defined, Aquinas believes that there are several undeniable examples of it. "Wise" is a quality that may characterize a "proverb" and a "man" in

3. Hart, "Revelation,," 38ff. NM, 3; CB, 206; 253ff.; CTK, 192; Dooyeweerd, *Twilight of Western Thought*, 139–40.

4. Aquinas, *Summa Theologica*, , 1a: 85:1.

5. Ibid. 1a: 86:1.

6. Ibid. 1a:13:5. Wippel, "Metaphysics," 91.

two very different but *comparable* ways. By the same right, wisdom ought to be ascribed to God, but with the recognition that it belongs to Him in a unique archetypal fashion. Nevertheless, Gordon Clark follows Duns Scotus in pointing out that Aquinas' doctrine of analogy conflicts with the Aristotelian logic with which he begins, and derives no support from his examples of analogy in nature.[7] To begin, a two-valued logic demands that a given descriptor be either true or false of that to which it is predicated. "Wisdom" can be ascribed to proverbs and men only because it is a more general concept than both, which takes on different accidental qualities when instantiated in each. But Aquinas denies that there is any univocal quality (e.g., being) that resides above God and nature and could facilitate a comparison between the two. Without any unambiguous knowledge of the divine nature, Aquinas has no means to justify his conviction, even if it happened to be true, that our ideas resemble the divine nature in the least degree. All knowledge of God, must then, be negative.

In contrast to Aquinas, Karl Barth labored to preserve the radical dichotomy between God's supernatural freedom and the natural world by making man's knowledge of God wholly dependent on special revelation. On Barth's scheme, secular man carries on under the impression that his perceptions of the natural world and beliefs about history are virtually identical (univocal) with the matters they describe. In fact, the stable and dependable character of secular thought is the prerequisite to the manifestation of God's ineffable freedom in Christ. In Himself, God is "wholly other," and not even relatively similar to any quality or category known to man. All of man's ideas are flatly equivocal of the divine nature.[8] Even God's revelation of Himself through Jesus Christ, the written Word, and preaching must obscure the divine nature, until and unless the Word of God chooses to reveal Himself in them.[9] The only point at which man encounters an analogue of God is in the *event* of faith in Jesus Christ (*analogia fides*).[10] Man's faith in proclaim-

7. Clark, *Christian View of Men and Things*, 311–12; "Wheaton Lectures," *Works*, 7:66–67; Ronald H. Nash, "Gordon Clark's Theory of Knowledge," *Works*, 7:122–24. For Duns Scotus' critique of the Thomistic doctrine of analogy, see Copleston, *History*, 2:505.

8. Hart, *Regarding Karl Barth*, 9.

9. "The thinking of faith will always be a realistic or idealistic thinking, i.e., a thinking that in and of itself is most un-Christian . . . nor can we make our thinking Christian, nor even affirm that it is so in ourselves or others. We can only believe this as God's grace. . . . Hence, believing means either hearing the divine content of God's Word, even though nothing but the secular form is discernible by us or it means hearing the secular form of God's Word even though only its divine content is discernible by us." Barth, *Dogmatics*, I.1, 175–176; cf. 88ff.

10. In the act of faith, "the Word of God *becomes* a human thought" albeit "in

ing the unspeakable—that God is revealed through a natural medium that simultaneously hides Him—is itself an expression of that mysterious sort of freedom involved in the work of Christ. Both Clark and Van Til discern that Barth's doctrine opens the door to skepticism with respect to theological knowledge.[11] Barth candidly admits that every proclamation of Christ is equally capable of revealing and of obscuring the truth about God. The only definitive criterion for determining that a given perspective on God is false is if it sets itself up as a definitive standard by which to judge every other revelation.[12] Of course, this raises the question of whether Barth's claim that faith is an analogue of God is but another provisional perspective on God. If not, then God may be identified with the event of faith, in which case He would lose His radical freedom, and He could be mistaken for a projection of man.[13] If, however, even the analogy of faith represents an amendable attempt at defining God, then one is left without any dependable theological knowledge. In both cases, there is no way to justify the conviction, even if it is true, that man has participated in the Speech of God through faith.

5.2.2 Van Til's Doctrine of Analogical Knowledge

Most secondary discussions of Van Til's doctrine of analogy have correctly contrasted it with the metaphysical assumptions of Thomism and Barthianism,[14] but have fallen short of directly explaining how he avoids their same basic pitfalls. In an endeavor to accomplish both ends, we begin with the observation that Van Til's doctrine of analogy concerns the relationship between *different sorts of minds*—that of God and man—and not between concepts and *different grades of objects*. Just as there are two levels of existence (uncreated and created) there are "two levels of knowledge, the level of God's knowledge which is absolutely comprehensive

infinite dissimilarity and inadequacy" in comparison to its divine prototype." Barth, *Dogmatics*, I.1, 241.

11. Clark, *Barth's Theological Method*, 146–50. Cf. CB, 490.

12. Barth, *Church Dogmatics*, I.1, 164.

13. Interpreted in this way, the divide between Barth and the subjectivist theology of Friedrich Schleiermacher is not nearly as wide as Barth had thought. CB, 415–29, 437.

14. Gilbert B. Weaver, lists three basic differences between Van Til and Aquinas with respect to analogy: (1) Aquinas's *knower* is autonomous, while Van Til's is absolutely dependent upon God; (2) Aquinas's *knower* must begin with experience, while Van Til's must begin with experience interpreted by revelation; and (3) Aquinas posits a scale/analogy of being, while Van Til posits a strict Creator-creature distinction. Weaver, "Man the Analogue of God," 326–27; cf. Frame, *Van Til*, 89–95; Oliphint, *Reformation of Christian Apologetics*, 12–15.

and self-contained and the level of man's knowledge which is not comprehensive but is derivative and re-interpretive."[15] The pertinent question regarding our thought forms is not whether they reflect external objects when taken in isolation, but whether they reflect God's all-encompassing interpretation/plan for that object. After all, no object can convey the whole story about itself. But, supposing that there is a Creator who has foreordained the end from the beginning, it follows that he must possess a complete systematic interpretation of things. Man's interpretations, then, are "analogical" of God's when they reflect, in a finite measure, God's perspective on reality.[16] Capturing the sense of the term "analogy," true beliefs are *like* the divine mind as its finite reflection, and *unlike* the divine mind as quantitatively and qualitatively inferior to God's self-contained perspective. Notably, on Van Til's scenario, all true beliefs are analogical,[17] with the result that the skeptic cannot disparage man's knowledge of God as more ambiguous than his perceptions of other sorts of objects (see fig. 12).[18] In fact, because the knowledge of God is the precondition of true (analogical) knowledge of all other things, it can be said that theological knowledge is the most certain, clear, and well attested of all.

15. IST, 12; cf. CTK, 16.

16. Hence, Van Til often characterized his theory of knowledge by the resolve to "think God's thoughts after him." CA, 77, 80, 131. Cf. IST, 181; CG, 37; DF3, 47–48; CTK, 16.

17. It is a basic error of unbelieving thought to suppose that one's concepts are "exhaustive of the 'essence of the thing' they seek to express. By taking each concept as wholly expressing the essence of a thing, non-Christian thought seeks to express the whole of reality, even of temporal reality, in terms of concepts that are static." CG, 201.

18. Randal Zachman expounds Calvin's doctrine of analogy in very similar terms to that articulated by Van Til. Zachman, *Calvin as Teacher, Pastor, and Theologian*, 209–29.

Knowledge Type / Theologian	Analogical	Univocal	Equivocal
Van Til	God, Man, Nature	--	--
Aquinas	God, Super-nature	Natural Forms	Individuals, matter
Barth	God in Christ/Faith	The Natural Realm	God outside of Christ

Figure 12: Three Views of Analogy

5.2.3 Clark's Critique

At this point, Gordon Clark becomes perhaps even more critical of Van Til than he was of Barth and Aquinas. Far from securing the objectivity of knowledge, Clark alleges that Van Til's position would lead to the deepest skepticism. For, if every proposition pertaining to God and creation were but symbolic, analogous representations of God's conception of them, then there would be no reference point with which man might determine the manner and extent to which they represent the mind of God (or reality) at all.[19] In fact, Van Til, by granting that human knowledge is like and unlike the divine archetype at every point, essentially follows Hegel, in holding that finite vantage points are largely consigned to being both true and false in various degrees. In contrast to Van Til, Clark proposes his own sort of presuppositionalism, where man may know many propositions univocally with God (those provided by Scripture),[20] which allow him to determine the sense in which metaphorical propositions are true, and the measure to which they are false. From this vantage point, Clark insists that if there is

19. Clark's critique of Barth on this point also conveys his concern with Van Til. Clark, *Barth's Theological Method*, 129; cf. White, *What is Truth?*, 57–58.

20. Clark, *Trinity*, 75; cf. Nash, "Clark's Theory of Knowledge," 140.

some quality that differentiates God's knowledge from that of man, then Van Til should straightforwardly identify it.[21]

5.2.4 Analogical Truth

Three considerations effectively deflect Clark's contention that Van Til's position devolves into skepticism. First, the persons of the Trinity are simultaneously like and unlike one another, but their unlikeness does not imply that they are false representatives of one another or of the Godhead at any point. This ought to caution believers against conflating difference with falsity. Second, Van Til agrees with Clark (over Aquinas) that man can only rest assured that analogical knowledge is true if he has some standard that can confirm this belief. However, he denies that this standard can be a set of impersonal qualities/propositions that have identical meaning for God and man. The only way that man's finite knowledge could be univocal with the divine mind is if certain propositions were *self*-evident expressions of a universe that was independent of, and superior to both its divine and human interpreters. However, the only being who resides above man and God alike, and Who may confirm the correspondence of the mind of the former to the mind of the latter, is God Himself, in the second person of the Trinity (1 Tim 2:5). *The* Word of God testifies that finite *words* may reflect the mind of God truly, even though not identically (John 1:18), by utilizing and authenticating them himself (Matt 5:18).[22] Barth, then, is mistaken to suppose that the conceptual contents of written revelation are ever equivocal with the mind of God. Our third consideration against Clark's criticism is that, with Christ's word as a reference point, true and false beliefs can be sharply dis-

21. In what has been called the "Van Til-Clark controversy," Gordon Clark's insistence that human and divine thought/knowledge are univocal at many points sparked significant controversy surrounding his ordination in the Orthodox Presbyterian Church. Although Van Til was not directly involved, a study committee which included many sympathetic to Van Til's theory of analogical knowledge was appointed to investigate the details of Clark's ordination. Indeed, one of the leading voices among the complainants was Van Til's Westminster colleague, John Murray. Without delving too deeply into the controversy and its aftermath, we may note that when Clark later pressed Van Til to explain exactly how the content of God's knowledge differs from man's, Van Til declined any attempt, on the basis that it would involve him in a self-contradiction. Muether, *Van Til*, 100–114. In a related context, Van Til explains that, "this inability to comprehend fully what we ourselves mean by analogical action or by analogical thought, so far from giving us cause for worry, should be to us a sign that we have caught the truly theistic conception of action and thought. Mystery has lost its terror for us as soon as we know that there is no mystery for God." FCE, 86. Cf. IST, 24.

22. "It is the Christ of Scripture who alone can and does tell man what he can know, what he ought to do and what he may hope for in the future." NH, 66. Cf. CFC, 132–35.

tinguished. A true belief corresponds to the mind of God because it is formed in faithful submission to the Word of Christ,[23] while a false belief does not correspond to the mind of God, because it refuses the illumination of Christ.[24] A true belief is coherent because it is informed by that Being Who holds all things together, and a false belief is incoherent because it is ultimately informed by an empty void (see fig. 13).[25] Hence, alluding to 1 Corinthians 10:5, Van Til offers the rather straightforward definition of "analogical" reasoning: "To make every thought captive to the obedience of Christ speaking in Scripture, is to reason *analogically* in the proper sense of the term."[26]

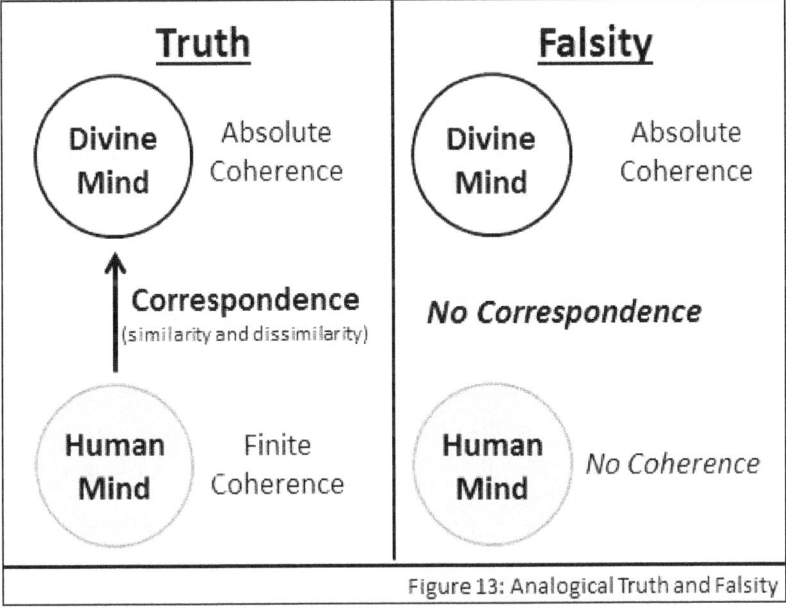

Figure 13: Analogical Truth and Falsity

Given the above portrait of truth, it should be clear that before the Fall, all of Adam's beliefs were true because he allowed natural, anthropological, and special revelation to inform one another.[27] Contrary to Aquinas and Barth, Adam, with a believing mind, could not form false beliefs.[28] This

23. IST, 23; CA, 33; SCE, 1–4.

24. Van Til speaks of the unbeliever's natural knowledge of God as undergoing "continual falsification" as it is suppressed and married to perverse beliefs and perspectives. IST, 197.

25. IST, 104–5. Cf. CFC, 85ff.; GH, 60, 85.

26. SCE, 65.

27. James Emery White mistakenly characterizes Van Til as limiting "true" knowledge to Scriptural propositions. White, *What is Truth?*, 54, 60.

28. Aquinas argues that a finite intellect must be naturally susceptible to forming

claim may seem surprising since Adam undoubtedly could have judged that there was a lake in the distance when, in fact, it was a mirage formed by light refracted off of a sand dune. Yet, on the theory articulated, even though such a belief is relatively imprecise, it is true in the sense that it faithfully conveys the sand dune's God-given capacity for lake-like appearance. Were Adam to discover that the lake was a mirage, it would only compel him to develop a more sophisticated and coherent interpretation of reality. However, it is the *imprecision* of his first belief, and not its unqualified falsity, that would compel him to further exploration. The quibble that imprecise judgments are strictly false is at odds with the prominence of metaphor in Scripture—e.g., "God *is* a consuming fire" (Deut 4:24).[29] The truth of poetry consists in the fact that, although subjective impressions may overlook certain details, they sometimes capture the essence of a matter better than technical descriptions.[30] In fact, a more coherent/objective vision of the truth will enable one to identify more appropriate subjective symbols for it.[31] Van Til's theory of knowledge accords remarkably well with the idea of redemptive-historical development.[32] As each successive covenant furnishes more information about God, it carries with it certain discontinuities in the symbols, sacraments, and laws which define the divine-human relationship (Heb 10:1; cf. Matt 5:17; Gal 3:24–25; Col 2:17). Quantitative differences in information carry with them qualitative differences in man's impression of the said information. And although an economic priority must be given to the new covenant revelation of God in Christ (Heb 1:1–2; Matt 11:11) since the earlier vantage points exist for the latter (Heb 11:39–40), they are all equally true.[33]

---

errant, and thus false impressions. Aquinas, *Summa Theologica*, 1a,17, 3. Barth's notion of creation in Christ involves the idea that creation is justified, and fallen (susceptible to error) from the beginning. Barth, *Dogmatics*, 3.1: 272ff.

29. IST, 154–55; cf. 66–67. Nevertheless, John Frame explains that Van Til did not understand "analogical" to be a synonym for "symbolic" (as opposed to literal speech). Frame, *Van Til*, 94. "Symbolism" involves describing something with reference to an object from which it is different. Analogy involves *knowing* the same object (truly) in different ways, and to different degrees.

30. To be true to Van Til's terminology, he frankly equates "subjectivity" with "falsehood" when it is connected with rebellious fantasies about reality. SCE, 4. But with respect to pre-fall, and redeemed thought Van Til argues that judgments may be "subjective," and yet "true," in the sense that the analogical reasoning which births them is minimal and relatively more intuitive. IST, 90, 27.

31. Ibid., 66–67.

32. In this respect, the influences of Geerhardus Vos' biblical theology and eschatology are evident in Van Til's major works. GD, 170–175. Vos, *Pauline Eschatology*; cf. Vos, *Biblical Theology*.

33. Van Til qualifies his acknowledgement of differences between Old and New Testament ethics thus, "But even this difference is not the same difference that the

Finally, from these observations it should be clear why Van Til never obliged Clark's demand that he identify exactly how divine knowledge differs qualitatively from that of man.[34] One can no more answer this question than a child could explain how his understanding of responsibility will differ as an adult; or an Old Covenant believer could explain how his impression of God would be altered by Christ.[35] Only the greater comprehends how he differs from the lesser. And only God comprehends how His thoughts transcend man's (Isa 55:7–8).

As true beliefs are faithfully receptive to God's revelation, false beliefs are the product of a rebellious desire to suppress, pervert, and replace various features of God's revelation with idolatrous fictions (Ps 14; Rom 3:9–18). Considered in terms of what they actively entertain and profess, unbelieving worldviews are incoherent, self-destructive, and lacking in any true beliefs whatsoever.[36] For Van Til, affirmation of simple mathematical equations (e.g., 3 + 1 = 4), and basic matters of fact (Mount Everest is over 29,000 feet high), are basically false (and frustrating to human enterprise) when the matters involved are not conceived of as creations, which exists as they do, by and for the plan of God. The technological advances of the modern age seem to supply an unshakable argument against the claim that unbelievers lack true and ultimately useful beliefs about physics, chemistry, biology, medicine, etc. Yet, Van Til qualifies his position in three ways that mitigate his claims. First, as represented by Adam, all unbelievers inherit that Adamic consciousness which enjoyed a pure and undefiled knowledge of God.[37] Hence, even now, beneath every false perspective lies an ineradicable awareness of the Creator, with which fallen man often acts in accordance despite the defective belief systems he manufactures for himself. In fact, unbelievers are restrained by common grace from thinking and acting in perfect accordance with their false beliefs, and thus, from straightaway succumbing to the pure confusion and self-destruction of sin (Prov 8:36; Jer 2:13, 19; Matt 16:25). Second, the alleged benefits of fallen man's scien-

---

non-Christian thinks he sees. For us the difference is merely that of stages of the development on the same redemptive principle." CTE, 15.

34. Recall 5.2.4.

35. In response to Gordon Clark's denial that man's knowledge is qualitatively different from that of God, John Frame lists some twelve substantial differences between the two, which include the eternal, causal (of the universe), original, and self-glorifying qualities of God's knowledge. Frame, *Doctrine of the Knowledge of God*, 22–25. Nevertheless, it will always be mystery as to how the contents of the divine intellect carry with them a distinct cadence.

36. SCE, 65. Even Christian philosophers have found this claim egregious. Plantinga, *Warranted Christian Belief*, 217.

37. CTK, 42; cf. DF4, 176, 249–51.

tific and technological beliefs are, contrary to popular opinion utterly short lived, and ultimately condemning. The aeronautical engineer may seem to be very effective, through his design of airplanes, at aiding men to arrive at their desired destinations. He lacks, however, any capacity to redirect or transport men into the heavenly abode of God (Gen 11:4; Prov 30:4–6), as opposed to the fires of hell. Additionally, insofar as the aeronautical engineer misrepresents his mastery over the physical creation as the product of chance, as opposed to a gift from God he will be guilty of generating a false worldview, and indeed of aiding others on their way to damnation should they reciprocate his perspective. The consequences of such activities will be eternally counterproductive on the Day of Judgment (Matt 18:6).[38] Third, Scripture explicitly teaches that even in this life, God will frustrate man through natural or supernatural means (Deut 28), if he should develop a sophisticated mastery over the creation and yet fail to acknowledge it as a God-given gift (Isa 10:12–14; 14:12–15; Ps 2:10–12). On the other hand, the formulation and maintenance of true, but perhaps less sophisticated beliefs (Matt 18:3) that give credence to God will generally result in natural and supernatural blessing in this life, and absolutely in the life to come (Exod 23:26; Deut 28:4–14; Job 42:10–17; Mark 10:29–31).

Finally, sin and rebellion continue to compromise the purity of one's beliefs, even after redemption.[39] Indeed, Christians capitulate to sin consciously and unconsciously, and even develop false beliefs as a result. Yet, the entirety of a believer's worldview is not rendered false by these lapses into sin/falsehood. For, the desire to be emancipated from sin by Christ is only possible and indeed intelligible from within the boundaries of a perspective that is basically true and redeemed (Rom 7:14–25).[40] At this point, it might appear as though the perpetuation of sin seriously threatens to obscure the boundaries between truth and falsity, orthodoxy and heresy, even for believers. However, the one who acknowledge the omnipotence of Christ may trust in His capacity to speak with sufficient clarity to grant believer true knowledge, even if he lacks an exhaustive, or even perfectly righteous vantage point on the truth.[41] As it stands, Christ has entrusted his people with the responsibility to prayerfully distinguish orthodoxy and orthopraxy from perversions (Matt 18:15–20; 1 Cor 5:12–13). Even when weighty disagreements arise between believers, such a phenomenon indirectly confirms the truth and clarity of the biblical teaching with respect to

38. IST, 106.

39. Ibid., 69–73, 299–301.

40. CTK, 52–56.

41. Ibid., 26

the enduring effects of sin prior to our glorification (Col 3:4).[42] And, believers ought to have every confidence that theological rifts between faithful Christians will one day be definitively overcome.

5.3 EPISTEMIC JUSTIFICATION IN CHRIST

Given his distinct theory of truth and falsity, the problem of epistemic justification does not arise for Van Til in the same way that it does for contemporary philosophers.[43] For the latter, the problem concerns how a particular true belief might be held, such that it is not haphazard or lucky, but a matter of genuine knowledge. The person who believes that a feather will fall to the ground more slowly than an anvil is correct. Yet, if the belief is based upon the false premise that it is the feather's lighter weight that makes for its slower descent (rather than its air-resistance), then the belief seems to fall short of knowledge. For, reliance on this sort of errant reasoning would contribute to detrimental conclusions in the future—e.g., that one has more time to leap out of the way of a falling 1 pound ball-bearing than 300 pound hang-glider. Presently, there are three dominant theories concerning how a belief may be justified. Internalists argue that a belief is justified when formed through a valid procedure that is translucent to the believer himself. Internalists divide into foundationalists, for whom justified beliefs are deductively or inductively derived from self-evident foundations, and coherentists for whom true beliefs are justified to the degree that they are mutually supportive of other true beliefs.[44] The third theory is that propounded by externalist foundationalists, who deny that the determining factor for justification is the performance of an internal, rational *procedure*.[45] Externalist foundationalists hold that fundamental, and self-evident beliefs about reality, reason, ethics, etc., are justified if they are formed by a healthy/reliable belief-forming *mechanism* (e.g., the human brain, as married to the various sense apparatuses). Naturally, Van Til rejects all three theories since he denies that there are self-evident foundations for knowledge. In fact, Van Til's charge that Aquinas, Barth, and Clark all succumb to a rationalist-irra-

42. Ibid., 27

43. For this reason, some have mistakenly concluded that Van Til lacked any conception of the need for epistemic justification. See Geisler, *Apologetics*, 62.

44. Because of Van Til's hefty emphasis on coherence, James N. Anderson discerns that Van Til implicitly embraced an internalist theory of epistemic justification, if he embraced any theory of epistemic justification at all. Anderson, "If Knowledge then God," 70–72. With this perspective we will have to disagree.

45. Plantinga, *Warrant the Current Debate*, 15; *Warrant and Proper Function*, 237.

tionalist dialectic, can be construed as a charge that they all oscillate between the extremes of internalist and externalist foundationalism.[46] As internalist foundationalists (rationalists), each believes he is justified in denouncing certain beliefs as false because they run into formal contradictions.[47] As externalist foundationalists (irrationalists), each admits that his faith in Christian revelation is finally justified because initiated/compelled by an external divine power, apart from sufficient, or perhaps even *any* objective evidence.[48] As a result, each of these scholars must grant that a definitive proof of Christianity is impossible, and that theological paradoxes are, in some measure, hindrances rather than catalysts to a persuasive apologetic.

At least two factors inhibit scholars from placing Van Til's view of epistemic justification among the contemporary alternatives.[49] First, because fallen man's beliefs are ubiquitously false, the problem of justification does not pertain to how individual true beliefs may be justified, but to how entirely false belief systems can be reoriented to God and reflect His mind, albeit in a finite measure. Second, contemporary epistemologists have disregarded "externalist coherentism" as a tenable position. As Laurence Bonjour explains, this option is "a view that has very little in the way of intuitive or dialectical appeal, and that, not surprisingly has rarely if ever been advocated."[50] Bonjour overlooks the fact that the Hegelian School regarded the majority of historical belief systems as "justified" on externalist

46. IST, 117; 162; CTK, 169–75; CB , 414–415; PDS, 62–72.

47. Aquinas and Clark forthrightly acknowledge this belief. Aquinas, *Summa Theologica*, 1a, 25, 4–6. Clark, *Christian View*, 26–31. But Barth also *deduces* that God's freedom is (logically) incompatible with embracing an objective and linguistic criterion (e.g., Scripture) by which to identify and dispose other alleged revelations as false—"of the Word of God, one thing is ruled out. It cannot be an entity which we can demarcate from other entities and thereby objectify." Barth, *Dogmatics*, 1.1:164. In response to this deduction, one Van Tillian critic observes, "Scripture itself never deduces from God's transcendence the inadequacy and fallibility of verbal revelation. Quite to the contrary: in Scripture, verbal revelation is to be obeyed without question, *because* of the divine transcendence." Frame, *Doctrine of the Word of God*, 437.

48. Clark and Barth are forthright about this belief. Barth, *Church Dogmatics*, 1.1:176. Aquinas, on the other hand, holds that certain truths of natural theology can be established on objective grounds, but, finally, supernatural truths must still be believed on the basis of faith supernaturally infused. Aquinas, *Summa Contra Gentiles*, 1:5–7; 4:152.

49. Van Til does not mention a theory of "epistemic justification" because such a phrase is germane to analytic philosophy, as opposed to the idealist philosophical schools with which Van Til chiefly interacted. Nevertheless, Van Til laid claim to epistemic justification in contrast to modern thinkers who, "makes assertions about the nature of the universe," even though "Without the least bit of justification he assumes that reality must answer to the nature of these laws." IST, 160.

50. Bonjour and Sosa, *Epistemic Justification*, 7 n. 4.

coherentist grounds. On the Hegelian scheme, each historical philosophical perspective is justified as relatively true by the role that it plays in the self-development of Spirit, not unlike the manner in which each note in a song is justified by the contribution that it makes to the whole. Of course, the difficulty with the Absolute Idealist scheme was that humanity itself was taken to be the highest expression of Spirit, with the result that man's failure to develop an coherent synthesis of eternity and time (internally, that is, within his own understanding) called into question the reality of an absolute system altogether.

Van Til's contention that Trinitarian Christianity procures the ends after which the Absolute Idealists groped, is best interpreted as a claim that only Christianity advances a consistently externalist coherentist theory of justification (see fig. 14).[51] For the Christian, each person of the Trinity contributes to an eternal dynamic with two other persons, and each person exhaustively comprehends that dynamic. Their knowledge is justified in a perfectly internalist coherentist fashion.[52] In turn, the self-contained Trinity granted Adam beliefs that are justified because they are in tune with, and on a course to increasingly reflect his eternal plan.[53] That is to say, Adam's initial beliefs were coherent within an as yet unrealized (and therefore external) course of development.[54] Pre-Fall Adam would have had no reason to doubt the justified status of his beliefs. Even when his premises/inferences (e.g., that a 2 pound kite would fall slower than a 1 pound apple) were challenged by experience, he would expect that those relatively imprecise premises/inferences were prerequisites to a greater discovery, and thus justified. Of course, pre-Fall man would have been kept from the inordinate suffering that follows from relatively imprecise beliefs in our fallen context. Finally, the very belief that knowledge is justified by its external coherence with God's plan is confirmed by its capacity to serve as a catalyst for greater discovery, through a process of "spiral" reasoning.[55]

51. "It is this notion of the ontological Trinity that ultimately controls a truly Christian methodology." CA, 128.

52. "We do not hesitate to emphasize therefore that God has and is complete internal coherence. As far as God's own person is concerned the subject is the object of knowledge. His knowledge of himself is therefore entirely analytic." DF4, 60.

53. IST, 14.

54. Whenever Van Til advances the claim that God is the "final reference point in all human predication" he means that every true judgment/inference is ultimately a statement, not about some individual matter, but about the divine plan which ties all things together. CTK, 12; cf. 74; IST, 37, 66, 163; DF4, 258.

55. Recall 4.4.1.

Theories of Justification	Externalism	Internalism
Coherentism	**Van Til** (Every stage of knowledge) **Hegel** (Former stages of Knowledge)	**Hegel** (Final stage of knowledge)
Foundationalism	**Aquinas, Barth, Clark** (With respect to the Word of God)	**Aquinas, Barth, Clark** (With respect to logic)

Figure 14: Theories of Epistemic Justification

After the Fall, the mode of epistemic justification becomes doubly externalist coherentist and doubly Trinitarian, since it hinges on the redemptive work of the Trinity. Because man has so mangled the image of God within Himself, and come under the wrath of his Creator, it is impossible for him to redirect his intellect toward the Truth, and justify his own beliefs. Instead, God the Son must assume human flesh and pacify the wrath toward humanity as a substitutionary sacrifice, and cleanse man's conscience by setting him on a new course to serve God (Heb 9:14; Rom 5:1–2).[56] Christ does not merely overcome man's suppression of the awareness that he is God's creature. He grants man a new self-conception as a *redeemed creature in Christ*.[57] Knowledge of this foreign status must come to man from without, through the objective Word of Christ (John 15:15).[58] In fact, only the man who has been regenerated by the Spirit and granted the mind/disposition of Christ will accept the Word of Christ (1 Cor 2:14–16; Rom 6:4). When the regenerate man is confronted by the Word of Christ, he is able, for the first time, to hear the testimony of the error of his own fallen beliefs to the truth

56. Jesus status as the "justifier" of the ungodly is married to his status as the standard of ethics and "sanctifier" of his people. CTE, 147–51.

57. PDS, 27.

58. CTK, 52; cf. PDS, 63; IST, 110–18.

of Christ's diagnosis/remedy for them. Man's self-defeating belief-system becomes, in spite of itself, and even as a witness against itself, conducive to a deeper reconnaissance of the truth, and thus, after a fashion, justified.[59] For, the many useful beliefs that the unbeliever held in spite of his presuppositions are, upon conversion, unleashed to shine forth their full significance on all of reality. Even more than pre-fall man, the redeemed enjoy assurance that their Christian belief is justified (see fig. 15 and 16) since they have seen firsthand that even falsehoods (in their self-defeat) lend their confirmation to the Faith.[60] And, since God redirected them toward truth when they were devoted to falsehood (Rom 5:8–9) redeemed men have even more reason to believe that the Spirit will drive his true but infantile beliefs unto maturity (Phil 1:6).

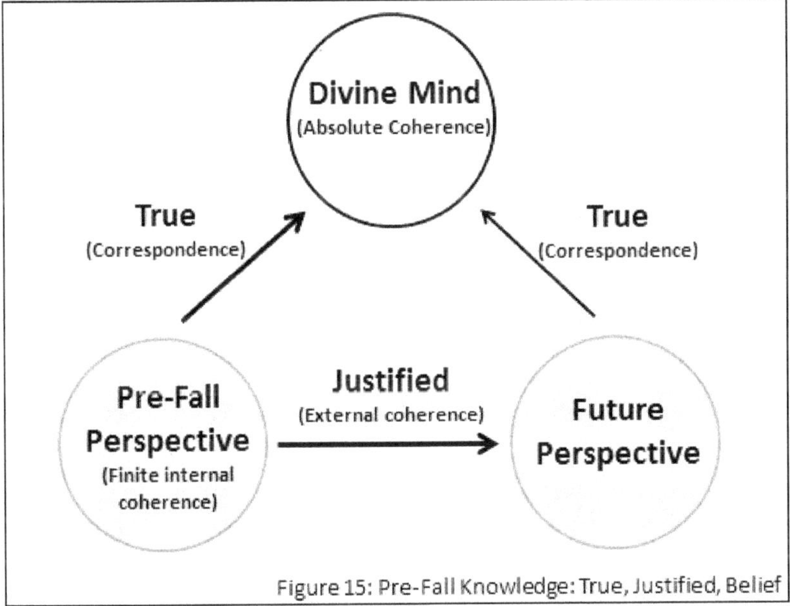

Figure 15: Pre-Fall Knowledge: True, Justified, Belief

59. Van Til explains that "Scripture constitutes the climax of the redemptive work of God. . . . The purpose of this redemptive work of Christ is that the world which has fallen into sin may be cleansed from sin and in spite of that sin reveal the glory of God." PDS, 27.

60. "As Kant felt assured of *the justice* of his position because of the fact that no knowledge was actually possible on either rationalistic or empiricistic basis, we feel assured of *the justice* of our position because no knowledge is actually obtained upon the Kantian basis." Emphasis mine. SCE, 109–10.

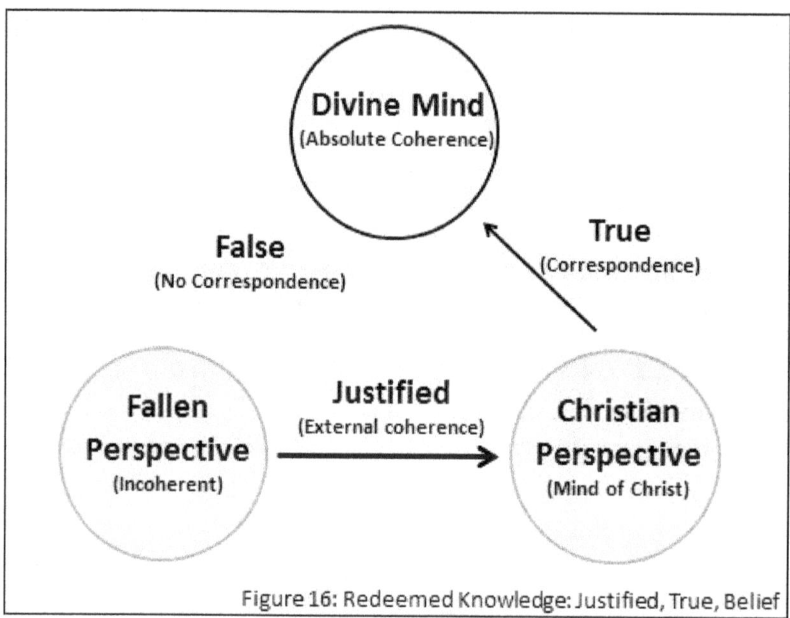

Figure 16: Redeemed Knowledge: Justified, True, Belief

An important point in Van Til's theory of epistemic justification is that Christ's Word in Scripture is self-validating[61] in the sense that all of reality testifies to it when interpreted through its lens.[62] This enables Van Til to argue that the ultimate standard for determining that Scripture is God's Word, is the system contained within it.[63] The Spirit's internal testimony involves removing opposition to, and compelling one to believe in Christ's self-attesting Word. The internal witness of the Spirit (Rom 8:16) is not an additional source of propositional revelation.[64] If it were, the Word of God would not be self-authenticating, and it would be indistinguishable from man's sinful imaginations.[65] In inspiring the Scriptures, the Spirit's duty was to guide the New Testament authors to extrapolate the meaning of the work of Christ in light of His teaching and the former Scriptures (John 15:26–27; 21:24; Luke 24:48–49; 1 John 1:2; Rev 1:1–2).[66] Even when it came to de-

61. CTK, 15, 25, 30, 33.

62. IST, 110–18.

63. Ibid., 31, 33

64. PDS, 35–37.

65. CTK, 33–34

66. Van Til espouses the "organic" theory of inspiration articulated by Warfield and Bavinck, where the Spirit's work of inspiration within the authors of Scripture is vitally linked to His external providential preparation of them. That is to say, the Spirit inspired the authors of Scripture to organize information, and to incorporate their unique personal perspectives, which they have drawn from external revelation. PDS, 25–30,

termining the parameters of the canon, the Spirit enabled the church to *recognize* the doctrines and documents that were truly divine, and by their guidance to further refine the parameters of the canon. The determination of the canon was not based on inspired pronouncements granted directly to the hearts of church leadership, as the Roman Catholics suppose.[67]

5.4 Conclusion

Although Van Til was not prone to articulating his epistemological views in the terms that have become germane to contemporary epistemology, Van Til's position will admit for translation into the now common philosophical parlance. The human experience of "knowing" is, for Van Til, thoroughly Trinitarian. After the Fall, the only way that man can actively develop "true" conceptions of God, Himself, and reality is if the Holy Spirit should change his disposition toward the revelation of Christ and allow his beliefs to be overturned and refined by divine revelation. At the moment of conversion, one's beliefs not only become true (as correspondent with the mind of God, and coherent with special revelation), they become justified (set on a trajectory to develop and to embrace ever greater depths of divine truth).

35.

67. CC, 49–50.

6

Trinitarian Logic

6.1 INTRODUCTION

Logic, for Van Til, is best defined in Bosanquet's terms, as the manner in which knowledge morphs/grows.[1] In fact, Van Til adopts Bosanquet's phrase "method of implication" to describe the consistently Christian method of reasoning.[2] That neither deduction nor induction is true to Christian reasoning, on Van Til's account, should be clear from his rejection of internalist theories of justification. As we will see, a faithful mode of reasoning must proceed through three steps that resemble those posited by Bosanquet, even though they differ from that of the Absolute Idealist in significant respects.[3] Furthermore, a Trinitarian method of reasoning demands a distinctively Christian interpretation of the laws of logic, apparent contradiction, and theological paradox.

6.2 TRINITARIAN METHOD OF IMPLICATION

First, believers ought to begin their reasoning with a concrete portrait of reality that intertwines divine revelation concerning God, man, and nature. For Absolute Idealists on the other hand, the logician begins with the

1. Bosanquet, *Logic*.
2. SCE, 2; IST, 8–9, 13–14..
3. SCE, 9–10.

unjustified intuition that reality exists as some sort of a system.[4] Practically speaking, Van Til's view demands that "in starting any investigation the general precedes the particular."[5] Before one can make a reconnaissance of "frogs" he must have a generally dependable idea of what they are (e.g., animals that are four-legged, green, created, etc.).[6] Most importantly, he must acknowledge from the beginning that his notions are generally reliable because reflective of God's intellect, through Christ and the Spirit. The Absolute Idealist, on the other hand, only becomes acquainted with the standard of truth—his pantheistic Trinity—at the apex of his dialectical intellectual efforts.

Second, the movement from an initial vision of a fundamentally coherent reality to a concentrated reflection on some individual part of said reality, births the discovery of novel qualities and characteristics, which expose the incompleteness of one's previous categories. One's entire worldview is like a logical premise, while the individual fact constructively challenges that premise. In the case of frogs, man may be led to the discovery that they begin as tadpoles, which lack the four legs necessary to his original definition. Such a discovery is analytic, because it would lack meaning except in the context of a previously known definition of a class of animals. And yet, it is synthetic because it allows new information to redefine the parameters of that class, and with that redefinition, the range of what is possible for frogs.[7] This second moment in the reasoning process, where facts challenge one's premises, need not be construed as contradicting one's earlier perspective. Indeed, if the parameters of one's categories are extended and limited in various ways by subsequent discovery, then such discoveries only serve to establish one's initial conviction that his categories are both finite and substantially true, and thus able to be refined by new revelation. On other occasions, however, fantasies (e.g., that Thor is God) may be contradicted by the already revealed system of revelation, and exposed as lies. Yet, even in this case, the redeemed man's presuppositions are not ultimately contradicted, for he anticipates that his fallen beliefs will regularly be challenged by Christ. In contrast, the Absolute Idealist admits that his highest positive vision of reality must at various points be *contradicted* by some opposing perspective/principle in order to advance

4. Recall 3.3.3.

5. SCE, 7.

6. In Van Til's words, believers know "something about everything" if only it be that it is a creature subject to the Triune Creator. IST, 83, 164–65; DF4, 282; NH, 150.

7. As Bradley explains, "analysis is the synthesis of the whole which it divides, and synthesis is the analysis of the whole which it constructs." Bradley, *Logic*, 406. Cf. DF3, 199, 205; IST, 8–9; SCE, 7–10.

toward deeper truth. This, argues Van Til, steals from man any confidence that falsity may not finally negate all truth.

Third, after allowing the facts to challenge his deductive premises, man must develop a new and more complete vision of the whole, which advances beyond the information supplied in his premise or in the facts by themselves.[8] By observing a curve segment that connects three points, man can anticipate that certain points cannot reside on the course of its trajectory.[9] By learning the rules of the game of football, man is able to formulate new strategies for winning that will surprise his opponents. For the Absolute idealists, these advances in human thought must be regarded as creative in the purest sense, and expressive of human autonomy. For Van Til, these advances are best described as re-creative.[10] For, even the most profound progressions of human thought are due to the image of God within him, and to God's gracious providence. Finally, the method of implication thus described is equally deserving of the title "transcendental" reasoning.[11] The conclusion, for example, that certain points must lie on the trajectory of a curve is appropriately stated in the disjunctive form, "either this or nothing,"[12] since the curve and the respective points so necessitate one another that reality would be reduced to a realm of confusion if the two were not true together. Likewise, the various theological conclusions established by a Christian method of implication, can be viewed as definitively proven by virtue of the impossibility of a definite set of alternative (non-Christian) perspectives.

A more complex example of this sort of reasoning is evident in Adam's act of surveying and naming the animals (Gen 2:18–20). Adam began the process with a general portrait of reality that involved distinctions between God, man, and nature. The task assigned to him demanded that he stretch his initial worldview by taking note of more complex divisions within a particular portion of nature, namely the animals. But Adam did not simply name the animals "one," "two," "three," etc., as if they were atomic units. The text implies that in analyzing each particular animal he was simultaneously synthesizing or grouping them together in classes—cattle, birds, and beasts (Gen 2:19). Not only did he develop a notion of sexual distinctions and companionship between the members of a species (analysis), but he understood that this binary division was common to each class of animals (synthesis).

8. Cf. Bradley, *Logic*, 227–28.

9. SCE, 8.

10. IST, 162; FCE, 53; CTE, 22.

11. SCE, 10–13.

12. Bosanquet, *Implication*, 92–93; cf. 3.

The grand conclusion that "for Adam there was not found a suitable helper" (Gen 2:20) clearly advances beyond any simple sort of empirical reasoning. Where did Adam get the idea that he should even have a companion? Still more, without any *a priori* definition for how "woman" ought to be, why shouldn't he have concluded that any one of the animals was an appropriate companion? Apparently, Adam ascended to the understanding that he was significantly like nature (and thus in need of a companion), and significantly unlike nature (and thus incapable of finding true companionship among the animals). Hence, Adam returned from his analytic/synthetic mission with a more profound view of himself and the world than could have been derived by mere deductive or inductive reasoning.

6.3 LAWS OF LOGIC

6.3.1 The Law of Identity

Logicians have traditionally defined the law of identity in such a way that a given reality is only properly identical with the entirety of itself (A = A). From this point of view, the law of identity cannot apply to historical realities which are constantly developing. At best, timeless forms,[13] and perhaps the human soul, may be differentiated from a multitude of moments and accidental relations, to which they are basically indifferent. The Christian, on the other hand, begins with the notion that God is identical with three distinct persons. Analogously, the created principle of identity should be viewed as stipulating that created realities are, in varying degrees, one with distinct members, moments, and relations. They are "concrete universals." In this case, David *was* the infant born to Jesse, *was* the young man who fled from Saul, and *was* the mature king who committed adultery with Bathsheba, each at different points. These three different expressions are inseparable from the concrete person, David. The obvious difference between David and the Trinity, is that the moments which differentiate David's life, when taken individually, do not exhaustively express his entire story as each of the persons of the Trinity simultaneously comprehend the divine being. Within creation, certain realities may embody more profound sorts of identity in distinction than others. A random stone will be identified as a "rock," in such a way that the object does very little to supply a unique perspective on the category, while the category itself is relatively indifferent to the specific rock. In contrast, works of art, natural systems, individual persons, political organizations, etc., manifest more profound measures of interdependence

13. CTK, 118–42.

and between themselves and their specific parts. Ultimately, the law of identity derives its own nuances of meaning from the different sorts of unity manifested throughout creation. In this case, "logic is in gear with reality, but it does not claim to control God Himself and therewith all possibility,"[14] for it "derives its meaning from the [Christian] story.[15]

6.3.2 The Law of Contradiction

As with the law of identity, the law of contradiction must not be construed in timeless terms that would render it irrelevant to concrete matters. Beginning with the insight that the Triune persons cannot be simply identified with one another without destroying their concrete unity, Christians ought to regard the law of contradiction ($A \neq \sim A$) as stipulating that concrete universals cannot encompass just any combination of members, or morph into just anything. However, neither the law of contradiction, nor objects taken in abstraction, can tell us anything specific about what is or is not possible.[16] It is only with reference to the system of reality disclosed in revelation (natural and special) that contradictories can be identified. That a square cannot be a circle is only evident from within the concrete system of two dimensional, Euclidian space.[17] However, mathematicians have hypothesized that if space were of a different nature the two could be identical,[18] and, as it stands, the two are meaningfully combined in the third dimension as a "cylinder."[19] Likewise, to claim that the Normandy invasion was the turning point of the American Civil War, is to advance a gross contradiction, but from within the story of human history (and not, for example, in historical fictition). Most importantly, the unacceptable parameters of revision and development in each system must ultimately be determined by their relationship to the Triune God, and to his redemptive historical plan. Even our notion of God, the "supreme interpretative concept"[20] of Christianity is subject to historical development *for us*. But this does not undermine man's capacity to make valid applications of the law of contradiction. For, God can and has disclosed that we may know Him *truly*, though not exhaustively, in Christ (John 14:6). As a result, whatever developments our knowledge may undergo, those developments will enhance

14. RP, 29; IST, 38.
15. DF3, 214.
16. IST, 11; CTK, 35; cf. Bradley, *Logic*, 130.
17. Cf. Hegel, *Logic*, 200–22 (§142–159).
18. Reichenbach, *Philosophy of Space and Time*, §1–11.
19. Anderson, *Paradox*, 230–31.
20. SCE, 109. Cf. CTEV, 54; CG, 64, 67, 73; CI, 31, 129; CIM, 46, 61.

rather than compromise the validity of our current perspective. Whatever surprising revisions historians may suggest, they cannot be taken seriously if they would mangle beyond recognition the organic unity of the church's historical consciousness (Matt 28:19–20), and deprive her of her God-given rule over nature and history (Gen 1:26–27; Rev 20:4). And whatever unique spatio-temporal phenomena scientists may discover at the perimeter of the universe or at the subatomic level, the Christian knows that such discoveries cannot finally obliterate the church's capacity to convene for corporate worship (Heb 10:25). For, spatial systems, physical systems, biological systems, history, etc., exist for the ends of man's communion with God according to the Scriptures.[21] Considerations such as these compel Van Til to speak of a distinctively "Christian logic,"[22] the implications of which cannot be agreed upon by the advocates of an alleged "neutral logic."

6.3.3 Contradiction

A contradictory belief refers to a sustained intellectual breach of the laws of logic. Every contradiction (a) drives a wedge between things which are combined *and* (b) confuses things which are distinct.[23] Both tendencies involve the crime of "abstracting" details of the concrete systematic reality before us with the intent to create an abstract system in opposition to divine revelation.[24] In its extreme form, the first tendency is one with those irrationalist visions of the universe which conceive of facts and particulars as basically disconnected from one another within a sphere of chance. And yet, it is at the same time rationalist because it treats individual facts and concepts as if they were comprehensible with reference to themselves. The second tendency may be identified with the rationalist vision of a single truth which supersedes every distinction (e.g., being, unity, goodness). But it too erects an irrationalist dichotomy between the "one" monistic reality, and the pluralistic world of appearance. More familiar contradictions may be understood in the same terms. The notion of a square circle (within two-dimensional

21. DF4, 50–51.

22 Ibid., 92–95; Van Til, "The Development of My Thinking," WCV, n.p.

23 "[M]an, in rejecting the covenantal requirement of God became at one and the same time both irrationalist and rationalist. These two are not, except formally, contradictory of one another. They rather imply one another. Man had to be both to be either." CTK, 49.

24. IST, 37–39, 210; CA, 32–34; CJ, 51; CTE, 200–201; CTK, 129ff. Van Til is not opposed to considering things in relative isolation from their context in order to organize them systematically. The negative and altogether self-contradictory form of abstraction involves treating any feature of the creation as if it were self-evident.

Euclidian space) confuses two distinct members of a particular system, and represents an idea that is wholly incompatible (in dichotomy) with geometry, as we know it. In every case, unbelieving contradictions attest to the Christian system by borrowing from it (see fig. 18), and failing to supply a viable alternative to it even on its own terms (see fig. 19). Finally, although Van Til refrains from defining "contradiction" directly, as we just have, his writings are nevertheless painted with demonstrations that various theological and philosophical systems are self-destructive because they combine "pure rationalism" with "pure irrationalism."[25] Such a locution is Van Til's way of saying that a particular belief system is marked by destructive self-contradiction, rather than a constructive paradox.

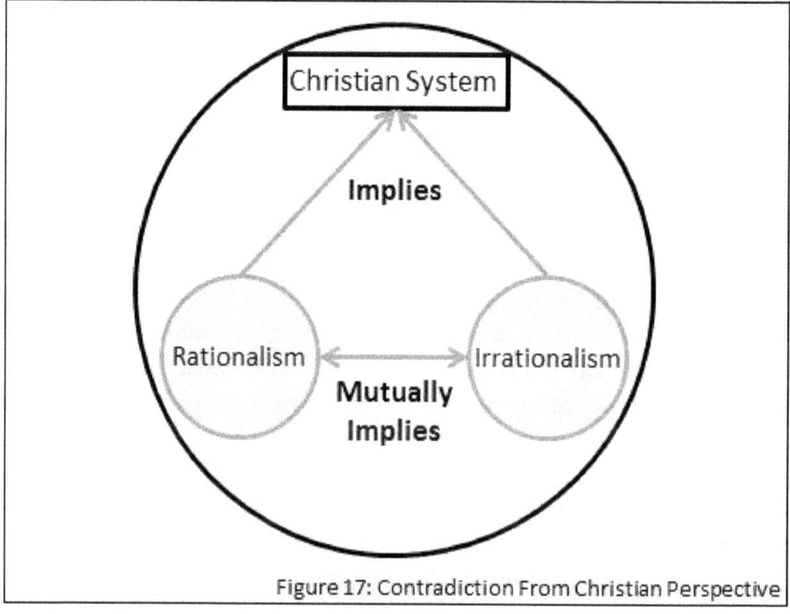

Figure 17: Contradiction From Christian Perspective

Even with formal descriptions of a proper method of implication, and of self-defeating contradictions, we must stress the fact that the one can only be distinguished from the other with reference to a concrete system. Earlier we observed that Adam's conclusion that none of the animals could serve him as a suitable companion reflects a complex understanding of the continuities and discontinuities between men and animals. But what if he had decided that he was like the animals in the sense that any one of them could function as his companion, but unlike the animals in the sense that "man" is not divisible into male and female? Adam would still be asserting a sort

25. IST, 115, 162, 174; CTK, 96; 119–35; CG, 68; RP, 141; NH, 42, 44–45; SG, 10–11; TJD, 48; JA, 101; CB, 207; *Later Heidegger and Theology*, 34.

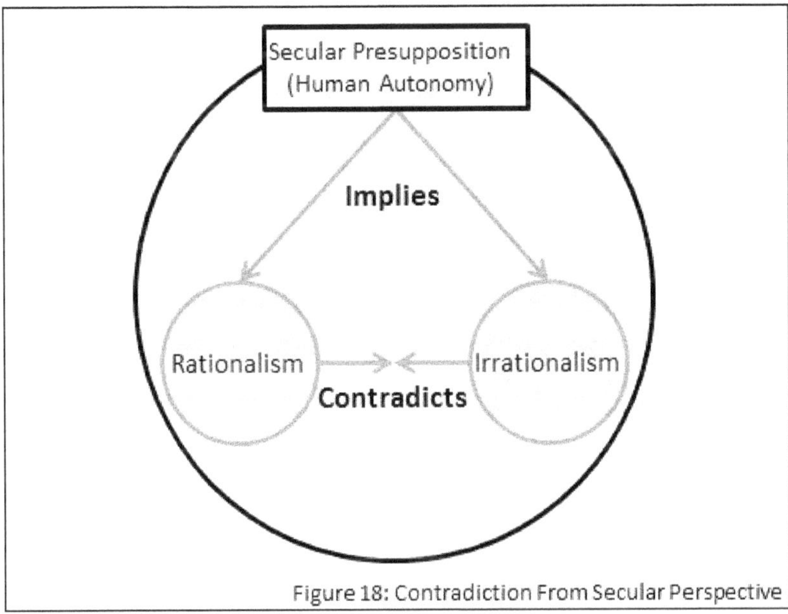

Figure 18: Contradiction From Secular Perspective

of "unity in difference" between himself and the animals. However, it would have represented a self-destructive contradiction. Adam would find himself emotionally, intellectually, sexually, and spiritually frustrated in his attempt to regard an animal as his fit companion. Still more, as he labored to live and to act in harmony with some animal, he would have to abandon the very sort of intellectual and even regal existence that enabled him to study and evaluate the animals in the first place. Hence, although Adam's actual conclusion would have left him with many mysterious questions concerning the likeness and difference between man and beast, it is clearly distinguishable from a self-defeating contradiction when considered within the context of the biblical story. The difference, then, between paradox and contradiction can be formally defined, but whether a specific concept enhances or fatally disrupts the Christian worldview can only be determined with reference to special revelation.

6.3.4 Apparent Contradiction

Van Til argues that, due to human finitude, apparent contradictions must arise at the perimeter of man's knowledge.[26] What distinguishes an apparent from a genuine contradiction is the fact that both of the apparently oppos-

26. CG, 142; cf. DF3, 44–46.

ing truths are based upon a faithful receptivity to revelation (see fig. 19). Stated another way, both contraries are implied by the Christian system, because they are based on the sorts of evidence that it sanctions as authoritative. Apparent contradictions would include apparent discrepancies within the biblical narrative (e.g., the different genealogies of Jesus in Matthew and Luke); apparent conflicts between Scriptural revelation and natural revelation (e.g., the age of the universe); and apparent divergences within natural revelation (e.g., the apparent dual nature of light as a particle and a wave, etc.).[27] When it comes to evaluating apparent contradictions, the believer has every right to expect that these can be resolved in some fashion, if all of the relevant information were available to him, since God's revelation cannot contradict itself (Deut 13:1–5; 1 Cor 14:29–33).[28] Furthermore, he may determine that the resolution must be centered on one side of the apparent conflict as opposed to the other. For example, Van Til is quite convinced that the biblical system would be destroyed if Adam were taken as anything less than a historical personage. Therefore, the conflict between the biblical doctrine of the origins of the human race and certain scientific theories with respect to the same must be resolved by a refinement of the latter, and not of the former.[29]

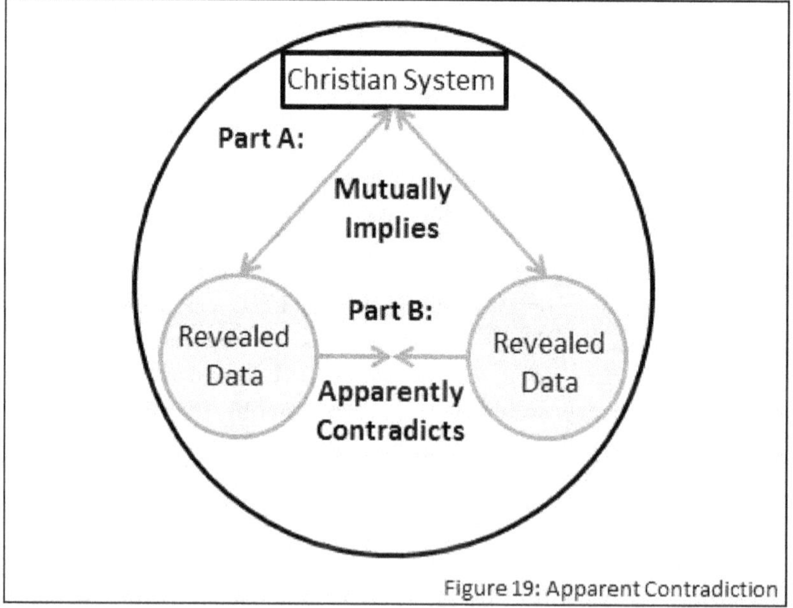

Figure 19: Apparent Contradiction

27. CTK, 34–38.

28. This point is reminiscent of the Princeton school, and particularly of William Henry Hodge. Recall 1.2.3.

29. IST, 29.

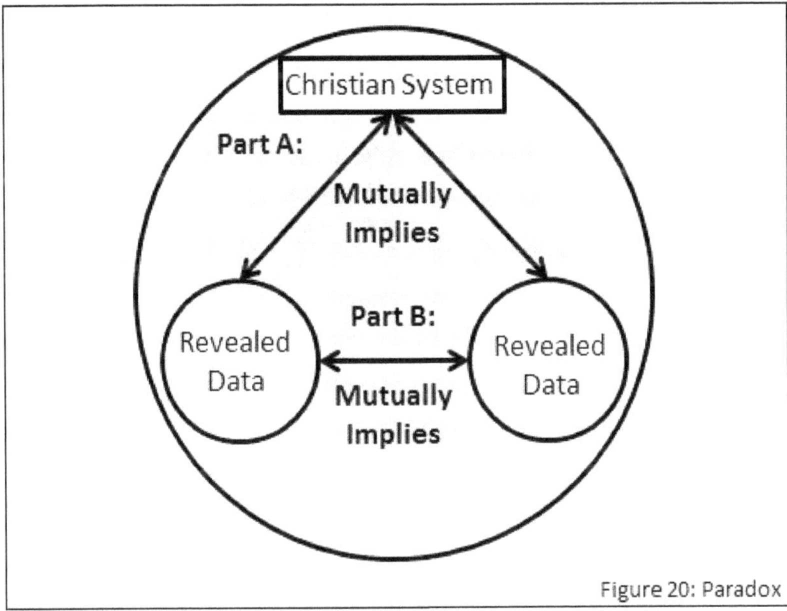

Figure 20: Paradox

6.3.5 Paradox

Although Van Til never formally distinguishes between "apparent contradictions," "mysteries," and "paradoxes," it is quite clear that he regards certain apparent contradictions to be qualitatively different from others. In the examples listed above, Van Til encourages man to seek out resolutions to the conflicting data. With respect to those apparent contradictions which we will specially designate "paradoxes," Van Til argues that pursuit of a resolution is sinfully imperceptive of their profundity. We may identify three distinguishing features of a paradox. First, a paradoxical doctrine must be based on two apparently opposing pieces of information that are required by Christian revelation,[30] and in turn prove themselves to be necessary to the very Christian system which facilitated their discovery. In other words, the poles of a paradox are discernibly essential to the Christian system, and the Christian system is essential to a right understanding of each pole. Of course, the only way for newfound truths to prove necessary/essential to the worldview through which they are discovered is if one already has a healthy appreciation for the fact that he does not fully comprehend even his basic presuppositions about reality. Furthermore, the sort of necessity of which

30. With respect to God's love for the reprobate, Van Til reasons, "How can God have an attitude of favor unto those who are according to his own ultimate will to be separated from him forever? The first and basic answer is that Scripture teaches it." CG, 140.

we speak is something quite different from formal, deductive necessity. The Christian system is not a "master concept"[31] from which one may directly deduce the opposing elements of every given paradox, and the many details of the Christian faith. However, the poles of a paradox and the Christian system to which they belong can be said to necessitate one another in the strict sense that, once they are discovered, one of them cannot be regarded as true without acknowledging the truth of the other.[32]

Second, in addition to validating and receiving validation from the Christian system, the poles of a paradox must discernibly imply one another (see fig. 20).[33] The classic Van Tillian example is the doctrine of the Trinity. Both the unity and the diversity of the Trinity require one another. For, God could not be a *self-sufficient* unity apart from an equally basic distinction of persons toward whom God might express his personality; and the three divine persons could not be meaningfully distinguished and related to one another expect in the wholly personal/rational context of the one divine Being.[34] And of course, the Christian system implies the Trinity, since it rests upon absolutely authoritative disclosures from God, and only a self-contained person who transcends the one-many problem can be such an unparalleled authority.[35] And finally, the Trinity necessitates many other essential details of the Christian system (e.g., absolute ethical standards, a covenantal theory of reality, the value of historical development, etc.). Were the paradox of the Trinity logically resolvable, and reducible to familiar categories, the entire Christian system would collapse. For, God would be comprehended by finite universals, and He would, therefore, not be the archetypal Standard/Creator of them. Notably, the same sorts of observations cannot be made about apparent contradictions. It does no service to the Christian system to take Matthew and Luke's genealogies at face value, and to conclude without further reflection that two different men—Jacob and Eli—were both at once Jesus' paternal grandfather. Indeed, the notion of a "bi-nitarian" human being would mangle a host of biblical doctrines. It is appropriate, then, to

31. CTK, 38. Cf. DF4, 206ff.

32. Variations on the phrases "mutually imply," "mutually presuppose," "mutually require," and "interdependence" are prominent in the Van Til corpus, and all have the same meaning. In the second chapter of *A Christian Theory of Knowledge* alone, Van Til identifies at least eight examples of doctrines which mutually imply one another, which one might initially suppose are at odds, or at the very least, indifferent to one another. CTK, 25–40; cf. SCE 96; CTE 21.

33. CG, 73. cf. 140; CTE, 48; DF3, 160; SCE, 49; CFC, 35.

34. DF4, 31; SCE, 97.

35. "The Bible must be true because it alone speaks of an Absolute God. And equally true is it that we believe in an absolute God because the Bible tells us of one." SCE, 12. Cf. Van Til, "God and the Absolute," 22.

theorize about possible resolutions to this particular conflict.[36] Hence, it may be said that an apparent contradiction is "vindicated" as an informative paradox only when its poles mutually imply one another and the Christian system.[37]

Third, paradoxical combinations continue to challenge men even after they have been systematically vindicated, because they stretch the boundaries of how various concepts (e.g., one, person, three, etc.) are employed in familiar contexts (e.g., when counting change, trying an individual in court, etc.). As we have seen, God's special mode of unity in diversity cannot be replicated by Jesus' paternal grandfather. If apparent contradictions establish the *quantitative* difference between man's knowledge and that of God, since man lacks sufficient information to resolve them, genuine paradoxes call attention to the *qualitative* difference between the two, since man should never expect to be able to reduce them to familiar terms. Hence, Van Til agrees with Bradley that the concept of "person" is self-contradictory, and an unworthy descriptor of the Absolute, if one embraces Bradley's "assumption that the human categories are ultimate" and self-explanatory.[38] Yet, if one begins with the assumption that human categories are analogues of God, then only the latter can confirm that they are meaningful descriptions of creatures, and truly applicable to Himself when appropriately qualified. Still more, only God can supply us with a perspective on the whole that is capable of facilitating true and dependable interpretations of ourselves, nature, and Himself. Of course, the idea of a God who is uni-personal and tri-personal is utterly challenging to us, because it is irreducible to familiar instances of unity in difference. However, if man could resolve the mystery of the Trinity by reducing His unique mode of being to an instance of something that he regularly encounters in nature or human society, then God would be degraded to a member of the universe, as opposed to that self-contained personal context upon whom all true knowledge depends.[39] Additionally, believers ought to realize that every member of reality is paradoxical (as Bradley made much headway in showing) in the sense that

36. For example, a popular explanation is that Luke's record hints at the fact that Jesus' maternal genealogy is being recorded by designating Joseph (but no other ancestor) as the "supposed" Father of Jesus (Luke 3:23).

37. Van Til alludes to both criteria in the same breath is in his short summary of the argument in *Common Grace and the Gospel*: "Such doctrines of election and freedom must be thought as limiting one another or, as supplementing and supporting one another, always with the idea that God and His revelation in Christ through Scripture gives us a theology of reality on the basis of which any human concept must be made." Van Til, "The Development of My Thinking," WCV, n.p. Cf. DF4, 207, 267; CG, 65–95.

38. SCE, 160. For a discussion of Bradley's position, recall 3.3.1.

39. Ibid. 47; cf. 49–50, 59–60, 107; CTK, 11ff.

they cannot fully illuminate their own mode of being, and must fall into contradictions when treated as self-explanatory.[40] From this perspective, the Trinity is no less paradoxical than the universe as a whole, even if our sinful suppression of the knowledge of God renders theological paradoxes less familiar (and more offensive) than those of day-to-day experience. And yet, the paradox of the Trinity is, in another respect, the most logical of all doctrines. For, He alone is capable of setting all things in their proper light, so that men may rest assured that their knowledge of reality is true even if incomplete, and in many ways, apparently contradictory.[41]

At first glance, the Van Tillian strategy for vindicating theological paradox may very well appear unnatural and impractical. However, pursuit of an appreciation for how distinct features and components (a) imply one another when viewed through the lens of a common system, and then (b) together enhance our perspective on that system is (on our account) one of the most basic characterizations of a concrete reasoning process.[42] If one became acquainted with the qualities of flesh and bones in disconnection from one another, it would initially seem as if the two sorts of material had nothing significant in common. But, viewed through the lens of the bodily system, the two clearly require one another and cannot perform their respective functions without the other. In return, a detailed understanding of the interaction between the skeletal and muscular systems makes for a more robust understanding of the human body as a whole. What this sort of example goes to show is that the method of vindicating paradox described above is a natural corollary of reasoning by implication. The chief difference between the regular process of reasoning by implication, and vindicating theological paradox is that the latter involves discerning the mutual necessity between characteristics of God, ultimate reality, human freedom, etc., which stretch the day-to-day sense of various terms.

40. SCE, 24–43; CGG, 142; DF4, 67–68.

41. CGG, 9.

42. Recall 3.3.1.

7

Coherent Trinitarian Theology

7.1 INTRODUCTION

The best way to showcase Van Til's Christian method of implication, and its capacity to vindicate paradox, is by drawing together the many theological implications of the Trinity. What follows is a short discussion of how, in Van Til's estimation, the doctrine of the Trinity undergirds, and in turn receives support from prominent, and even paradoxical, biblical doctrines.

7.2 TRINITY AND CHRISTIAN DOCTRINE

7.2.1 Creation *ex Nihilo*

Among the many implications and corollaries of the doctrine of the Trinity, perhaps the one most commonly mentioned by Van Til is that of the Creator-creature distinction.[1] The Trinity safeguards the Creator-creature distinction by demanding that the latter must have been created (a) "out of nothing,"[2] and (b) with a temporal beginning (cf. Gen 1:1; Col 1:16; Rev 4:11).[3] First, as a self-defined being, the Triune God is not reliant on a con-

1. IST, 12; cf. 114,

2. Van Til prefers the phrase "creation into nothing," as it helps to communicate the idea that creation was brought into existence where there was formerly nothing at all. DF4, 49–50.

3. IST, 114. Cf. DF4, 53, 229–32; DF3, 189; CTEV, 81; CG, 28; NM, 1–8.

trasting material universe to express Himself. In fact, it is not even possible that matter could have been a basically independent reality alongside of the Trinity. For, two relatively independent beings must rely on some third sphere to facilitate the interaction, clash, or indifference between them.[4] Hence, because the Trinity is self-contained and independent, it follows that the material reality must be other-contained and dependent. Second, for the same reason, the Trinity is incompatible with the doctrine of eternal creation,[5] according to which the creation is eternal in the sense that it has no beginning, but finite in the sense that each of its members is mutable, limited, and dependent on God as a logically prior foundation. The problem is that such a view allows "logical relations" to leap out of the created sphere as that which finally defines the relationship between God and time. Within such a static logical system, temporality would be just "as *eternal* as the idea of eternity," and the dialectical dynamic between the two would supersede both as the true synthesis of reality (see fig. 21).[6] But, the self-contained Trinity must reside above time and logic in such a way that each one began to exist at a specific point in history, and neither is allowed to take precedence over God.[7] Logical and temporal priority may serve as analogues for God's creative priority over the universe, but creation *ex nihilo* must be embraced as a paradoxical doctrine which is necessitated by the Trinity, and confirmatory of it.

4. In Van Til's words, "God would not be truly independent of the world unless the world were dependent on God. No one is absolutely independent unless he alone is independent" SCE, 16.

5. Pringle-Pattison, *Idea of God*, 300–310.

6. SCE, 43.

7. Van Til would agree with Lane Tipton's exegesis of Colossians 1:15—2:8 (over William Lane Craig's impression to the contrary) to the effect that the biblical data is unambiguous in teaching God's timelessness. Lane G. Tipton, "Paul's Christological Interpretation of Creation," 95–111. Craig, *Time and Eternity*, 14–20.

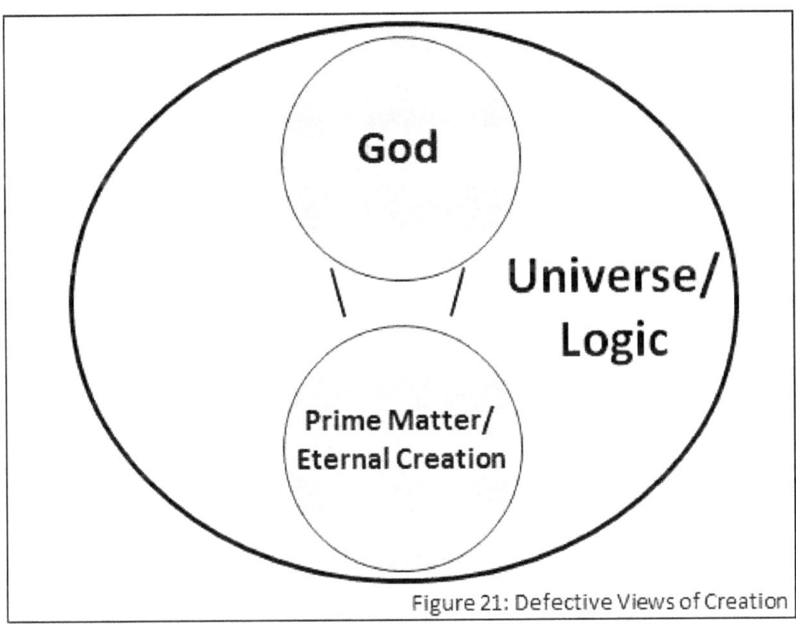

Figure 21: Defective Views of Creation

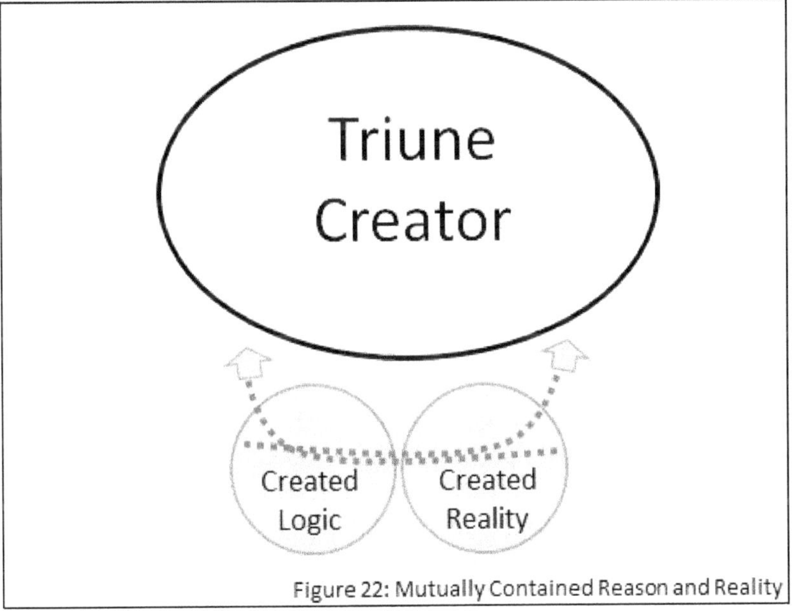

Figure 22: Mutually Contained Reason and Reality

7.2.2 Equality of Created One and Many

Having argued that time and logic are equally created, it follows for Van Til that created universals and particulars must be ontologically equal,[8] as reflections of God's eternal unity and diversity. What this means, first of all, is that neither the ideal nor the real aspect of creation is more like the Creator, such that it could reside between God and creation proper as a semi-divine mediator. Likewise, neither feature of creation is inherently evil (Gen 1:31). Quite the contrary, the created real and the created ideal must be so intertwined that they relate to God only through the mediation of the other (see fig. 22). Created universals must receive greater definition over time from the particulars to which they are married, and particulars must take on a deeper meaning when understood in terms of more complex universals. And, because ideal laws and facts mutually define one another (in the light of God), without collapsing into a static system or an irrational flux, their unity in diversity reveals their Triune Creator at every point.[9] Second, although the members of creation are ontologically on par with one another, certain created systems occupy a higher place in the economy of God's plan. "The 'mechanical laws,'" which govern physics are "lower than the 'teleological laws,'" that guide man to self-realization. This economy accounts for God's willingness to suspend physical laws to miraculously bless and facilitate, for example, man's ethical and religious ends (Exod 23:25–26; Rom 4:19).[10] It also allows us to locate the sense in which man is the preeminent *created* image of God in his concrete role as God's self-conscious assistant in ruling and organizing the cosmos (Gen 1:28; Ps. 8).[11]

7.2.3 Ubiquity of Revelation

Another corollary of a Trinitarian theology is the biblical notion of the ubiquity of revelation, such that all things must reveal their Creator in various ways (Ps 19:1–4; Rom 1:18–20). We have already seen that neither irrational chance nor a logical system of ideas guided God's free act of creation. For this reason, one might be tempted to infer that the qualities and features of created reality are purely arbitrary, but this would involve injecting an irrationalist notion into the Trinity that is completely foreign. For the God

8. DF4, 49–51; cf. IST, 23; Review of *De Noodzakelijkeheideener Christelijke Logica*, WCV, n.p.

9. CG, 64.

10. DF4, 51.

11. CTE, 36ff.

whose intellect is completely self-informed, every output of His activity must be revelatory of Him, since "there were no ideas or patterns above or distinct from the nature of God according to which God could create [them]."[12] Scripture validates such a view by seizing on a multitude of created qualities, emotions, animals, weather patterns, etc., to describe God.[13] In addition to supplying capable analogies of God, all of the members of creation must reveal the eternal plan of God, as they are exhaustively expressions of it (Rom 8:28; Eph 1:11; Matt 10:29), and indirectly color our conceptions of his eternal wisdom, goodness, grace, creativity, etc.

7.2.4 Divine Sovereignty

Understood in its fullest import, the doctrine of the Trinity, along with the doctrines of creation and natural revelation, imply a high Augustinian doctrine of divine sovereignty (Prov 16:4, 33; Ps 139:16; Matt 10:29–30; Rom 8:28; Eph 1:11).[14] Since man, his faculties, his motives and powers are exhaustively inspired by and dependent on the Absolute Creator, it follows that they must be equally subject to God's continued governance, such that they cannot deviate from His eternal plan at any point. It is equally impossible that God could elect to limit his sovereign direction or knowledge of human history at any point in order to allow for libertarian freedom on the part of man. On such a scenario, God's knowledge would be ultimately receptive, and His will ultimately reactive, to the finite creation. And if even the slightest measure of independence is injected into the creation, God must cease to be the self-sufficient source of unity and diversity, and become instead a finite member of a super-divine dialectic between Himself and mankind.[15] But of course, God is Triune. And it is impossible for His personal Will and personal Intellect to desist in exhaustively governing and comprehending all things, for if they could so negate themselves, they would have never been mutually exhaustive in the first place, but always threatened by an open future which resides beyond them.[16] So again, the doctrine of the Trinity and the doctrine of divine sovereignty mutually imply one another.

12. IST, 63; cf. 18; cf. SCE, 51.

13. Van Til encourages us to heed the advice of Herman Bavinck in being "fearlessly anthropomorphic" in our theological constructions. CG, 187.

14. CA, 128; DF4, 49–51.

15. IST, 187.

16. CFC, 110–11. SCE, 81–93.

7.2.5 Human Freedom

Among Van Til's more counterintuitive claims, is the contention that a Reformed Trinitarian theology is equally opposed to determinist and indeterminist philosophies, and thus uniquely capable of undergirding a robust ideal of human freedom. Despite the apparent opposition between determinism and indeterminism, both assert that all things are fated to act in accordance with forces—laws, desires, and/or pure chance—that are ultimately impersonal.[17] Rational determinists refer to a sort of freedom wherein one is so governed by the demands of reason that he cannot deviate from them, and is blessed with a general demeanor of tranquility. Hedonists propound an ideal freedom that is marked by the unobstructed pursuit of one's desires.[18] And indeterminists/existentialists suggest that man may be free in the sense that his choices are utterly undetermined and discontinuous with himself. Problematically, on each scenario human freedom consists of reducing oneself to impersonal principles, desires, or irrational chance. Necessarily, these ideals of freedom inhibit one from realizing greater depths of character, creativity, and self-mastery because they encourage people to becomes slaves to things which are lesser than themselves (2 Pet 2:18–19; Rom 6:16).[19] By contrast, as God is a perfect unity in diversity, human images of God should expect that free choices will be marked by a paradoxical continuity and discontinuity with the persons who birth them. That is to say, free choices are not necessitated by state of mind which precedes them (discontinuity), and yet they contribute to and enhance in a coherent way the depth of the person from whom they spring (continuity). Furthermore, man may rest assured that the supreme ideal of human freedom (creative self-development) is only realized by conforming one's will to that of an exhaustively personal Triune God (John 8:32; Gal 5:1).[20] For, the freedom of each divine person is consonant with the absolute determination of the other two.[21] In the same way, the hallmark of free choices on the part of man is not that they are uni-personal (developed by only person), but that they are multi-personal (the fruit of one person drawing out and determining a

17. CTE, 48.

18. Van Til criticizes Martin Luther and Jonathan Edwards for entertaining views that lend themselves to psychological determinism. Van Til, "The Will in its Theological Relations," WCV, n.p.; SCE, 67–69.

19. For this reason, Van Til identifies abstract ideals with the pagan idol "Moloch" who demanded human sacrifice (Acts 7:43). CI, 17, 21; CFC, 128; CC, 166.

20. SCE, 97.

21. CTE, 48; CIM, 46; GH, 170–71.

unique course of action from another).[22] Only on this scenario are personal choices inspired and driven by persons rather than impersonal deterministic forces. Not only, then, does human freedom follow from the doctrine of the Trinity, but divine sovereignty and human responsibility imply one another.[23]

7.2.6 Covenant

For Van Til, the doctrine of the Trinity implies a covenantal worldview, where man is naturally aware of and responsible to his Creator at every point from within and without, from the beginning of his existence. This point follows not only from the ubiquity of divine revelation, but from man's status as the created image of God. Each person of the Trinity is immediately self-aware as a concrete person who occupies a definite position in relationship to the other two. It follows, therefore, that man, the very *image* of God must have been created with a natural and immediate conception of himself as occupying a specific position in relationship to all subsequent men, and especially in relationship to God. In fact, Scripture continually affirms that even fallen men enjoy a definite and inextricable awareness of their responsibility to other men and to God, on the basis of which their conduct will be judged (Ps 10:3ff, Amos 1:3–2:16; Rom 2:14–15). Just as Adam was necessarily vested with a concrete conception of his place in the cosmos, it also follows that he could not have gone on living in the Garden of Eden without direct verbal communication from God regarding his existential-religious purpose through which he might please God.[24] Silence on the part of the Creator about these matters would have involved God in misrepresenting Himself as devoid of personal communication: first, because of his failure to communicate with his created image; and second, because his created image would lack any means to obediently serve his Creator, with the result that he would fail to reflect the personality of God. But, because a self-contained God cannot misrepresent Himself on any level, it follows that man needed special revelation, in addition to natural and anthropological revelation,

22. SCE, 97–98. cf. IST, 176; CG, 73,112, 121.

23. Van Til's argument, at this point, is comparable (but by no means in full agreement) to that of Donald M. Ballie, who contends that the paradoxical relationship between God's sovereign grace and human freedom as experienced by believers provides special insight in to the interpenetration of divine persons within the Trinity. Baillie, *God Was in Christ*, 106–32, 144–47.

24. "Whatever was not involved in the concept of God as the presupposition of the universe as it was when it was created had to be directly revealed to man if he was to know it at all." IST, 74.

immediately following his creation (cf. Gen 2:16ff.).[25] On the other hand, it was necessary for man to be vested with a natural knowledge of the Creator in order to recognize the Creator just as soon as He spoke.[26] Hence, natural, anthropological, and special revelation presuppose one another.[27] They call man to take mastery over the creation and to extend the kingdom of God, so that man increasingly reflects the attributes and character of God as an obedient vicegerent.[28] And yet, upon breaking the covenant with God, it follows from the same principle that man should feel himself to be condemned by God at every point in the creation. In fact, because mankind is itself a covenantal unity after the manner of the Trinity, it follows that when Adam, the head of the human race, sinned by following the Serpent, all of his offspring fell into sin with him and together lost their ability to pursue God (Rom 5:12ff.). Hence, the Trinity implies a covenantal view of man, and the happenings of a covenantal history imply a Triune Creator.[29]

7.2.7 Evangelical Soteriology

The mode of salvation through which our explicit knowledge of the Trinity is first acquired, is also implied by those intervening doctrines (of creation, revelation, man, covenant, etc.) for which the ontological Trinity is the presupposition. Clearly, if man has lost the capacity to please God upon sinning, then his salvation must come from without, in a threefold respect.[30] First, the very plan to redeem men from sin must reside in the Father's eternal election (Eph 1:4–5), since it could not have originated in the will of sinners. Second, God the Son must take on human flesh and offer Himself as a substitutionary sacrifice on behalf of sinners as God's justice requires (Eph 1:7; Rom 3:26; Prov 17:15), so that they may be reconciled to God. In His self-sacrificial obedience, Christ keeps the covenant in a manner that Adam did not,[31] and He clearly reveals that believers must follow Him in slaying their old sin nature (Gal 2:20).[32] (Notably, the doctrine of the Incarnation reinforces the earlier point that two wills—the divine and the human—may be equally operative in a single person's decision without becoming

25. CTK, 29.

26. IST, 68; CTK, 16.

27. CA, 65–66; IST, 62–109; SCE, 95.

28. CTE, 44, 47, 53, 78, 80.

29. SCE, 96ff.

30. PDS, 15, 30.

31. CTE, 37.

32. Ibid., 78–82; DF4, 87; GH, 177–79.

confused.[33]). Third, since man lacks the motivation to follow Christ as his Savior and Lord, the Holy Spirit must regenerate him from within so that he will trust in Christ (John 3:3–5).[34] The gift of the Holy Spirit is described as a seal and a down payment of a believer's future glorification, because he is the one who motivates man to increasingly emulate Christ in the present life (Eph 1:13–14; 2 Cor 1:22).

7.2.8 Common Grace

A controversial implication of the Trinity drawn by Van Til is the doctrine of common grace,[35] where God has a general disposition of compassion toward sinners in history (Ps 145:9; Matt 5:44–45), even though some have been destined to eternal punishment. As Van Til understands it, common grace can be understood as an implication of the equal ultimacy of the "one" and the "many" within creation (as it reflects the Trinity) in at least two ways. First, if humanity is both a corporate body and a multitude of individuals, then it follows that God's decision to save mankind must involve extending general blessing[36] unto each individual until and unless they have been sealed in unbelief at death (Heb 9:27), and finally severed from any possible union with the true humanity of Jesus Christ.[37] Second, although God's single disposition toward the elect and the reprobate is one of either love or disdain from eternity past (Eph 1:4–5; Jude 4),[38] it does not follow

33. IST, 124–25.

34. "The new light" of revelation provided by the Word of God, and the "new power of sight" supplied by the Holy Spirit "imply one another," for "the one is fruitless without the other." CA, 80; cf. DF4, 40; IST, 162–63.

35. The first book-length critique of Van Til alleged that his doctrine of common grace was indicative of a underlining rationalism in Van Til's thought—James Daane, *Theology of Grace*, 39, 69.

36. CG, 29–33.

37. This has led Van Til to speak of common grace as "earlier grace" which decreases through the passage of history as the true humanity in Christ is increasingly distinguished from the false humanity in Adam. In conjunction with this process of differentiation, Van Til argues that common grace not only diminishes in its extent but, that "God increases His attitude of wrath upon the reprobate as time goes on, until at the end of time, at the great consummation of history, their condition has caught up with their state." CG, 82–83. Gary North critiques Van Til's doctrine of common grace as incompatible with an optimistic eschatology. North seems to overlook the possibility that common grace may decrease in its extent because over the passage of time there will be fewer unbelievers in the world. At the same time, divine wrath may increase in the future in the specific sense that the few who remain obstinate in unbelief will be most of all frustrated by the progress of the kingdom of God.

38. CG, 64–95.

that its manifestation in time cannot be marked by multiple alterations from wrath to grace, or vice versa. God's eternal disposition of displeasure toward the reprobate is married to the fact that His gracious offer of salvation is unreciprocated by the reprobate in history.[39] Likewise, the biblical account of the Fall pictures Adam moving from a state of favor to disfavor, and Paul depicts the elect as changing from "children of wrath" to children of grace (Eph 2:3).[40]

7.3 Conclusion

The connections that have been drawn between the Trinity and several different biblical doctrines in this chapter have not involved resolving the paradox of the Trinity, or the other mysterious doctrines which follow as its correlates. Instead, they represent the development of a Trinitarian logic which is capable of vindicating paradoxes as coherent with the Christian system. Importantly, we saw nothing like an oscillating devotion to formal logic on the one hand, and irrationalism on the other, as Van Til's critics have alleged. Instead, Van Til would have us defend the faith, develop a systematic worldview, and vindicate paradox through a steadfast devotion to one and the same Christian logic.

39. Ibid., 140.

40. Ibid., 76, 78–79

PART III

Critique

8

The Looming Problem of Paradox

8.1 INTRODUCTION

Despite the sympathetic portrait of Van Til's system presented in Part II, we must reevaluate the charge that Van Til's "Christian Logic" is hampered by a hint of that rationalist-irrationalist combination that he so denigrates.[1] The root issue is not that Van Til haphazardly suspends the application of logical principles as his critics allege, but that he appears to have stopped short in the development of his own logic of implication with respect to the central Christian paradox—the doctrine of the Trinity. Stated succinctly, Van Til fails to develop any insight into why God should exist as three, and only three persons, with the result that the "three-ness" of God, as opposed to the mere "many-ness" is arbitrary, and apparently expressive of an irrationalist principle in the divine being. The unsystematic form of Van Til's treatise, and scattered presentation of some of his most impressive insights seem to confirm the conclusion that he fell short of a thoroughgoing application of his own proposed method. Furthermore, the question of how to vindicate theological paradox remains, as yet, unresolved among Van Til's most ambitious students and second generation disciples.

1. Recall 6.3.3

8.2 INCOMPLETE VINDICATION OF THE TRINITY

In chapters 4–7, we discerned that at his best, Van Til would encourage us to vindicate theological paradoxes by calling attention to how their poles mutually imply each other, as well as the Christian system. As a specific example, we saw that Van Til held that the biblical system requires a Trinitarian God Whose oneness and threeness discernibly require one another.[2] Presently, we must call attention to what may initially appear to be an inconsequential point. In fact, Van Til only demonstrated that the Absolute God, and indeed the Christian Savior must be "uni-personal" and "*multi*-personal," not "uni-personal" and "*tri*-personal." Historically, Western theologians have found it to be apparent that the Christian system is compatible only with a single supreme Creator. And Covenant theologians have discerned that a truly personal God *must* communicate with man in that direct and progressive fashion that is unique to the biblical Scriptures, if He is to sustain man in a meaningful relationship with Himself. Van Til added the insight that both the redemptive historical system and the self-sufficiency of God imply His multi-personality (see fig. 23). For, only a multi-personal deity can be a self-contained Absolute, and only an Absolute God can facilitate meaningful relationship between individuals, first in Himself, and second in redemptive history. Yet, neither Van Til nor his most ambitious disciples have advanced an insight into why God, considered in the light of the biblical system, must be three—and *only* three—persons. It may well be the case that the tri-personality of God implies the equally ultimate unity of the Godhead, as the common context within which the three divine persons mutually exhaust one another. But it does not follow that the reverse can be said, namely that the diversification and self-definition of the one Godhead implies that he should be specifically tri-personal. Likewise, it might be said that God's nature as three and only three persons is foundational to the mode of salvation and revelation found in Scripture, as it clearly sets for the work of the Father, Son, and Holy Spirit. On the other hand, it is not necessarily as clear that the Christian system is entirely incompatible with the notion that additional divine persons exist, who have yet to be revealed (see fig. 24).

2. IST, 223; SCE, 12.

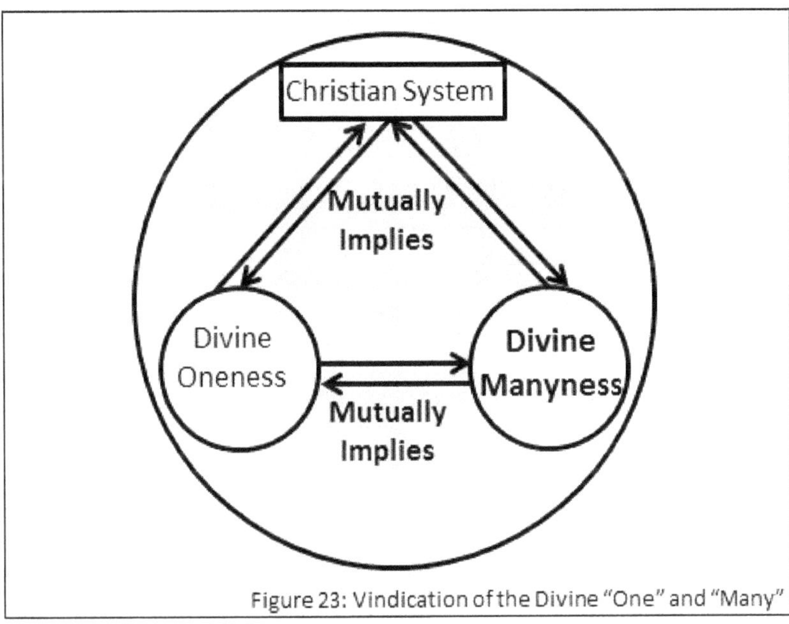

Figure 23: Vindication of the Divine "One" and "Many"

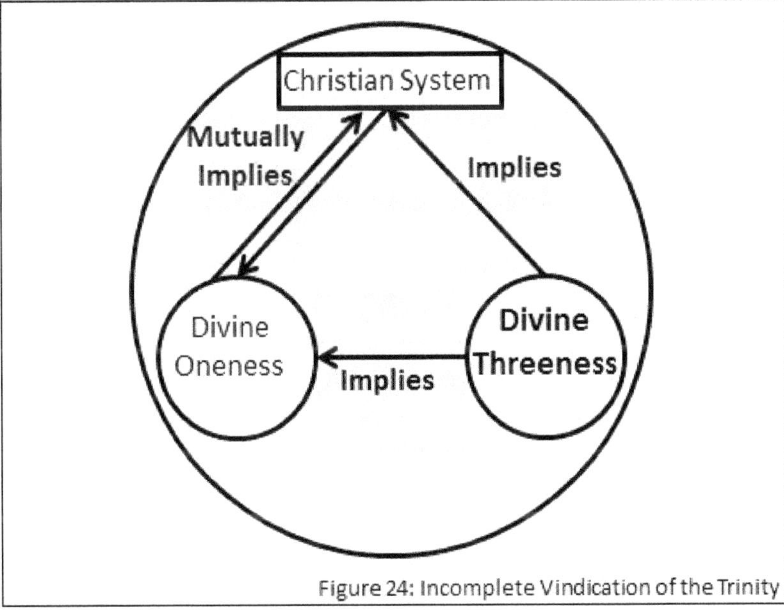

Figure 24: Incomplete Vindication of the Trinity

A comparison of two of the most important passages in the Van Til corpus reveals that Van Til's prescription to "reason by implication" cries out for some insight into why God ought to be specifically Triune; and yet, Van Til disparaged the possibility of finally advancing such an insight. Two claims from *A Survey of Christian Epistemology* and *An Introduction to*

Systematic Theology respectively reveal that Van Til sought to "implicate" his thinking more deeply into the nature of God than perhaps most theologians, and yet, he fell short of advancing a complete vindication of the Trinity.

(a) A Survey of Christian Epistemology	(b) An Introduction to Systematic Theology
"We may even say that every act of the infinite personality of God must be representational [of more than one divine person] because the only alternative to it would be that it should be impersonal. *The Trinity exists necessarily in the manner that it does. We have seen this to be so because the principles of unity and diversity must be equally original.*"[A]	"So then, *though we cannot tell why the Godhead should exist Tri-personally,* we can understand something of the fact, after we are told that God exists as a triune being, that the unity and the plurality of this world has back of it a God in whom unity and the plurality are equally ultimate."[B]

A. Emphasis mine. SCE, 97.
B. IST, 230.

In passage (a) Van Til seems to be saying that with the use of certain biblical principles we may discern that God must be Triune. In passage (b) Van Til advances the more modest claim that it is evident that God must embody unity and *plurality*, and he directly denies that we can appreciate just why God is a *Tri*-personal being. Nevertheless, a careful examination of passage (a) reveals that, in fact, Van Til is only developing the point that certain features of a covenantal worldview allow us to infer that God must exist as a multi-personal being. In this case, passages (a) and (b) do not conflict, but bear witness to a consistent position on the part of Van Til, to the effect that reasoning by implication only allows us to develop an insight into why God must exist a single, but *multi-personal* being.

Before asserting that the "Trinity exists necessarily in the manner that it does," Van Til begins chapter 8 of his *Survey of Christian Epistemology* by arguing that Calvinists have developed and maintained the "Protestant principle" in epistemology more consistently than their Lutheran and Arminian brothers. As Van Til reports, the initial expressions of Protestantism railed against the autonomy of man by insisting that one must be reconciled to God through faith in Christ, and rely on the biblical Scriptures in order to develop a true interpretation of God, man, and reality.[3] However, Calvinists explicitly held that the facts of redemption and the inspired interpretation of redemption can only be received if one has been gripped by

3. SCE, 65, 94.

the internal illuminating light of the Holy Spirit.[4] For our purposes it is important to observe that Van Til introduces the Trinity in terms of these sorts of observations about the economy of salvation, and not as a speculative inference from other biblical concepts.[5] It is from this biblicist standpoint that Van Til will turn to develop his transcendental proof for the Trinity. His argument orbits around Calvin's doctrines of the Trinity and covenant, and involves proving that each one is the precondition of intelligible human existence,[6] and that each one implies the other. Below, we will trace Van Til's argument to the effect that covenant theology implies, and even supplies some insight into why it is that God should be Triune.

According to Van Til, Calvin's covenantal position involves the view that divine revelation impresses itself upon man on all sides, since God's absolute providence is the atmosphere in which all other things exist. When faced with "any fact whatsoever" the man who dwells within a covenantal universe is "face to face with God."[7] Significantly, it is only when we view the entire universe as representational of a personal Creator that we may rest assured (on the basis of special revelation) that philosophical dilemmas exist for us and not for God, only because our minds are but finite reflections of that Infinite Being Who comprehends all things, and resolves every supposed problem.[8] Still more, it is only when we view reality as exhaustively representational of a personal Creator and His all-encompassing governance, that our own personalities and those of our interlocutors can be preserved intact. For, if the universe were itself ultimately impersonal, then every fact before us, including other human persons would ultimately be expressive of impersonal principles which do not finally comprehend themselves, cannot promise any solution to the vexing questions of existence, and cannot render reality conducive to human enterprises.[9] It is at this point that Van Til advances his insight into why the "Trinity exists necessarily in the manner that it does." Just as all human persons and relationships must be "representational" of the personal God who sustains them in order to keep from devolving into impersonal expressions, God Himself must always be representational "of the three persons who constitute" the Godhead. For,

4. Ibid., 94–95.

5. Van Til reminds us that we first "learn the trinitarian view as described from the Scripture, and accept it on the authority of Christ. But this being the case, we at the same time realize that it is this biblical position alone that offers an intelligent foundation for the existence of all of man's functions." Ibid. 97.

6. Ibid., 97.

7. Ibid.

8. Ibid., 96.

9. Ibid., 97.

the only alternative would be to conceive of God's relationships within an impersonal context, with the result that God "would be impersonal." Having grasped something of Van Til's argument, it becomes clear that Van Til is not claiming to advance an insight into why God is specifically Triune. Instead, when Van Til says that "The Trinity exists necessarily in the manner that it does," the mode of existence, or "manner," to which Van Til refers is God's "multi-personal" and "representational" nature in general, and not his Tri-personal mode of self-representation in particular. In this respect, the passages from *Survey of Christian Epistemology* and *Introduction to Systematic Theology* make the same claim, and yield the same conservative conclusion: "We cannot tell why the Godhead should exist *tri*-personally." And yet, the development of a robust rationale for why God should be multi-personal expressed in both passages, as well as his notion of a logic of implication bears witness to Van Til's expressed sense of responsibility to "implicate ourselves more deeply into a comprehension of God's plan" and, of course, into God's nature.[10]

It may seem to be of little concern that Van Til denied the possibility of vindicating the paradox involved in God's specifically threefold personality. But, taken in the most negative light, Van Til's denial threatens to upend his whole theological, epistemological, and apologetic enterprise. First, if Scripture lacks any clear indication that God is three and only three persons, and if it is not discernible by implication that God cannot be more than tri-personal, then it would seem to be possible that believers could become acquainted with additional divine persons in the future, or perhaps an infinite number of such persons, in eternity. And yet, such a concession is at odds with the intuition of Christian theologians throughout the centuries that God is specifically *Tri*-une. Even more, it undermines the finality of Christ's reconciling and revealing work, as the church still remains, as yet, unacquainted with the full number of divine persons.

Second, it is perfectly acceptable on a Van Tillian system that finite man should not be able to exhaustively discern the interdependence of every member of reality. It is quite another matter, however, to concede that any feature of the Godhead which believers herald as essential is not discernibly necessary to the preservation of all that we know of God. On a method of implication, God is the chief "interpretative concept,"[11] because each of the divine attributes revealed in redemptive history are necessary to all of the others, and (once revealed) are indispensable to a correct interpre-

10. SCE, 7.

11. CG, 9, 64, 67, 73; NM, 124; "God and the Absolute," 31; CTEV, 54; IST, 230; CTK, 12, 19.

tation of ourselves and of the world. Van Til echoes a sentiment shared by many in contending that if God were not absolutely wise, then God could not be absolutely powerful, good, beautiful, loving, or vice versa. And if God were not consonant with all of His divine attributes, then He could not function as the absolute Being that He claims to be. The same can be said for the individuality and simplicity of the divine person. However, Van Til implicitly denies that the specific tri-personality of the Godhead manifests the same indispensability to our notion of God, or to the Christian system, as do any of the above characteristics. Of course, Van Til held that God must be *multi*-personal in order to be loving, faithful, and wise in a concrete and self-contained fashion; in order for the diverse particularity of creation to be affirmed as good, right alongside of its unity; and in order to accomplish the threefold work of salvation, which man so desperately needs. But, a problem lies in the fact that if the divine nature and the Christian system can only be taken to imply an open-ended "multiplicity" of divine persons, then God *cannot* be regarded as the concrete universal or as the interpretative concept which Van Til insists that He is. For, mere multiplicity is an abstraction, which, if predicated of God apart from any numerical specification, would reduce Him to a vague, even irrational, principle of open-endedness. One might resolve to regard God as specifically tri-personal, precisely because the alternative just described is absurd and self-defeating. However, such a tack affirms rather than evades the problem just described. For, if any number of divine persons could effectively render God a concrete personal Being, then for that very reason, *only multiplicity in general*, and not any concrete number of persons, is *properly* essential to the divine being. Insofar as God happened to be any specific number of persons it would be reflective of irrational chance. One might respond that just because man cannot comprehend why God is tri-personal, it may be the case that God knows himself to be so necessarily. But, this sort of sentiment represents something quite close to a non-Christian appeal to mystery where some ultimate principle allegedly transcends the one-many problem, even though we lack any ground or capacity for appreciating why.

A final difficulty that has been taken into consideration by serious Van Tillians is that if God need not be specifically tri-personal in order to function as the final reference point of all predication, then an ambitious charlatan could mimic the claims of the Christian apologist on behalf of a "quadrinitarian" deity.[12] The heretic might assert that his quadrinity is an

12. Michael R. Butler has correctly observed that "quadrinitarian" theology could not present a viable challenge to Christianity, unless it were married to a set of Scriptures, a coherent quadrinitarian economy of redemption, a workable ethic, etc. Butler, "Transcendental Argument," 115–20. Although Butler has called attention to the

absolute person; that He has spoken in some makeshift revelation, which the heretic has recently drummed up for himself; and that he saves humanity through some four-fold personal activity. Furthermore, the quadrinitarian heretic would not even need to disprove the Christian position on its own terms. The transcendental proof for Christianity is sufficiently overturned if even one alternative position is viable on its own terms. The Christian system cannot be defended on the basis that it is the lone precondition of intelligible existence, to which the unbeliever must run after being confronted with the self-defeating character of his own beliefs. For, there is another viable precondition: a quadrinitarian deity.

To some measure, Van Til anticipates the first step to overcoming the abovementioned difficulties. By stressing the finality of Christ's revealing and redeeming work, over against Catholic and Neo-orthodox doctrines of ongoing revelation (John 14:6; Col 1:19–20; 2:9; Heb 1:2; Jude 3),[13] he implicitly holds that Scripture does provide unambiguous warrant for viewing God as three and only three persons. Even given this, however, if tri-personality is not discernibly essential to the unity of the Godhead, then the problems mentioned above persist. At least one essential characteristic of God (tri-personality) stands out from all the others (omniscience, eternality, justice, love, wisdom, etc.) as inessential. And, Van Til's claims could be countered in the name of a carefully crafted heresy. We would expect that, on the basis of that unambiguous revelation that God is specifically Father, Son, and Spirit, Van Til would encourage his students to seek a deeper understanding of how (1) tri-personality is indispensable to the unity of God; and (2) the created system of reality reflects its Creator, and is thus marked by various triadic structures. Notably, although Van Til never claims to engage in the second task, his works betray some sense of its importance. After all, the Van Til reader encounters triads in his delineation of the human faculties (intellect, will, feeling);[14] the sources of revelation (special, natural, anthropological);[15] the forms of special revelation (theophany, miracle, prophecy);[16] reasoning by implication (from whole, to member,

profound *difficulty* that would attend any project similar to constructing a full-orbed quadrinitarian worldview, the utter demonstrability of the transcendental proof would seem to require that such a project be flatly *impossible*.

13. CTK, 36; IST, 141–42. The finality of revelation in Christ does not negate the fact that man will continue to learn more about God and Himself for eternity, but only that such an exploration will always confirm and enhance the Word of Christ as it is contained in Scripture.

14. IST, 32.

15. Ibid., 64–109; cf. CA, 29.

16. IST, 122–32.

to a new whole);[17] the components of ethical activity (motive; standard; goal);[18] the chief characteristics of righteousness (spontaneous, self-determined, wide-ranging obedience to God);[19] the basic secular alternatives to Christian thought (rationalism, irrationalism, dialecticism);[20] God's activity in salvation (election, atonement, regeneration);[21] and Christ's threefold office (prophet, priest, king).[22] By developing these triadic structures and then placing them neatly alongside his robust Trinitarian theology, Van Til tickles the curiosity of his readers as to whether he is suggesting the mutual necessity of the two, or simply offering haphazard but nevertheless elegant schemes. The latter sentiment is reinforced by Van Til's refusal to develop any insight into why the archetypal triad must be specifically a unity in trinity, as opposed to any other numerical combination.

Understood more positively, Van Til's failure to pursue his method of implication thoroughly and systematically is an oddity. Why did Van Til say that we "cannot," as opposed to "have not yet," been able to "tell why the Godhead should exist *tri*-personally." After all, he advises us "to implicate ourselves more deeply" into the Christian system by continued reflection on the sources of revelation.[23] Perhaps Van Til was deterred from seeking a rationale for why God is specifically tri-personal, because, in the past, such an aim has led theologians to develop rationalist proofs for the Trinity, based on allegedly self-evident premises. Naturally, such proofs did more to call into question than to establish the truth of revelation, as they encouraged man to reason autonomously, as if he stood in a position to critique rather than to stand under it.[24] But, Van Til holds that valid theistic proofs, and at least genuine insight into why God should be a Trinity, can be formulated in a faithful fashion if one presupposes the authority of revelation. Why then, should he speak as if a vindication of God's tri-personality is beyond the pale?

The above considerations lead to a complex conclusion, which enables us to better understand how the genuine shortcomings of Van Til's labors, contribute to the practical offense of his writing style. On the one hand, Van

17. SCE, 6–10.

18. CTE, 41–153

19. Ibid., 45–46; 49–50.

20. SCE, 24–43.

21. DF4, 39–41.

22. CA, 41, 46–51.

23. SCE, 7.

24. The hallmark example of this sort of tendency is the twelfth-century school of St. Victor, with Richard of St. Victor as its leading light. Copleston, *History*, 2:178–82.

Til's position rightly calls attention to the finality of revelation in Christ (and with it, of the number of divine persons), and so makes progress in showing that the Christian system and the Trinity mutually imply one another. It might even be said that the obvious, if unstated, interdependence between the Trinity and the basic structures of an intelligible human existence raises the bar of coherence to such a high standard that, for all practical purposes, it is impossible for the advocates of a mock religion to mimic his apologetic claims. As a matter of fact, no seriously advocated belief system can mimic the claims of the Christian presuppositionalist. On the other hand, Van Til's failure to pursue a clearer and more complete vindication of the chief Christian paradoxes has supplied sufficient reason to doubt, for all but his most enthusiastic supporters, that a Trinitarian method of implication carries with it any distinctive benefits. Furthermore, it sets the bar at a rather low standard of clarity with respect to the vindication of the gamut of Christian mysteries besides the Trinity. Rarely does Van Til directly (a) identify the poles of a given paradox, (b) call attention to how they are required by one and the same Scriptural revelation/system, and (c) address how these poles prove to require each other in specific ways. At points, Van Til may note in passing or simply hint at the fact that the poles of a given paradox imply one another, or that they mutually imply one and the same system. Very rarely, however, does he give an explanation of both points in the same context. Still other paradoxes are mentioned as demanding our assent, but with no explanation as to why we ought not treat them as apparent contradictions awaiting a resolution.[25]

Van Til also neglects the task of giving a clear expression to the negative import of his vindications: that of exposing their secular, pagan, and heretical alternatives as self-defeating. Indeed, to prove that divine tri-personality and uni-personality mutually imply each other is to prove that a fivefold divine person is at odds with itself. Likewise, to demonstrate that divine sovereignty and human responsibility mutually imply each other is to show that alternative views (e.g., a partially sovereign God and a partially responsible man) are untenable, because the two poles only work together in a biblical-Reformed fashion. But again, Van Til's negative proofs are often just as difficult to parse out, as are his positive vindications of paradox.

Another defect of Van Til's treatises is that nothing like a systematic unfolding of Christian theology can be found in Van Til. Why, it might be asked, could we not (a) begin with a relatively simple portrait of the whole, (b) juxtapose it with a paradoxical piece of revelation, and then (c) observe how the two combine to make for a more robust vantage point on

25. CG, 10; DF4, 278.

the Christian system? It would seem to do wonders for clarifying the sort of reasoning that Van Til prescribes, and for drawing out the illuminating capacity of those very doctrines that many theologians have disparaged as thorns in their sides. Yet, in most of his descriptions of the Christian system, Van Til contents himself with stating the major doctrines of the Reformed Faith in succession, and then noting, here and there, several interesting, but at the same time enigmatic connections between them and a distinctively Christian metaphysic, epistemology, and ethic.[26]

8.3 SECOND GENERATION VAN TILLIANS

Although remarkable applications and advancements on Van Til's thought have been developed by his students, the basic unresolved issues with respect to the Trinity and the problem of paradox have persisted, and in some instances given rise to further difficulties. In considering the most important exponents of Van Til's thought below, the thesis is confirmed that Van Til's method of implication cries out for undergirding through a more thorough vindication of the paradox of the Trinity.

8.3.1 Greg L. Bahnsen

Undisputed among Van Tillians as the most impressive presuppositionalist debater and apologist, Greg L. Bahnsen followed Rousas J. Rushdoony in holding that an essential component of the antithesis between believing and unbelieving thought is that only the former can lay claim to immutable ethical standards. As a pioneer of the theonomy movement, Bahnsen argued for the "abiding validity of the law in exhaustive detail" (including the Mosaic civil penalties) as a necessary implication of God's immutable character.[27] But, critics of theonomy have generally argued that Bahnsen failed to give sufficient consideration to redemptive historical development, and to the role of the "many" (e.g., the successive covenants in history) in qualifying and informing the application of the "one" immutable law of God.[28]

26. DF4, 27–73; CA, 17–54.

27. Of course, Bahnsen also bases his case on biblical texts (e.g., Matt 5:17–19; Mark 10:17–19; 1 Cor 7:19; Tim 1:8–11; Heb 2:3). Bahnsen, *Theonomy*, 41–88. Cf. Rushdoony, *Institutes of Biblical Law*, 698–702.

28. Kline, "Comments on an Old-New Error," 172–89. Gordon, "Van Til and Theonomy," 271–78. In different degrees this critique has also been leveled by those who are sympathetic to theonomy. E.g., Jordan, *Through New Eyes*, 226–27; cf. 198–202. Poythress, *The Shadow of Christ*, 311–61.

In the case of Bahnsen, the tendency to emphasize the "one" somewhat over the "many," is most evident with respect to his view of logic, and his handling of theological paradox. First, despite his great success in demonstrating that atheists cannot justify their use of logic, Bahnsen had relatively little to say with respect to the indispensable role that the paradox of the Trinity plays in fostering a coherent worldview. Bahnsen may have shied away from making such an observation in his public debates in order to avoid belaboring a complex matter before uninformed audiences. But even in his seven-hundred-page analysis of Van Til's thought, Bahnsen's discussion of the Trinity as the solution to the one-many problem occupies a meager three pages.[29] Second, in executing his patented apologetic strategy of proving that only Christian theists can justify their use of logic, Bahnsen tends to treat logic as a set of static, abstract principles.[30] Here, Bahnsen's lack of emphasis on the relevance of the Trinity to apologetics is accompanied by a failure to appreciate Van Til's plea for concrete reasoning. Van Til argues that, because the created "one and many" are equal in a manner that reflects their Triune Creator, universals and logical laws *are* concrete things that grow in their depth of meaning when referred to different facts, some of which are as yet unseen (1 John 3:2).[31] For example, the revelation that logic does not prohibit God, although it does prohibit all other things from being numerically "one" and "three," represents a significant development, and qualification in our understanding of the laws of logic. Third, Bahnsen's commitment to treating logical laws as abstract principles had an adverse effect on his analysis of paradox, the chief example being Van Til's difficult notion of self-deception. By distinguishing between first and second-order beliefs, Bahnsen sought to *resolve* the Van Tillian paradox that sinners both believe, and yet deceive themselves into *dis*believing in God. Allegedly, the sinner's belief in God is an inadvertent "first order" belief *about reality*, while his disbelief represents a "second order" conviction *pertaining to himself*, in which he disbelieves *that he* believes in God. Rather than affirm and deny the same proposition (a formal contradiction), the sinner believes two logically compatible propositions that nevertheless result in great practical confusion.[32] In addition to it being questionable whether Bahnsen's ac-

29. Bahnsen, *Van Til*, 239–41.

30 Ibid., 237. Bahnsen rightly qualifies his description of logical laws and universals, noting that they are not abstract in the sense that they are self-existent, or self-evident without reference to the Creator. Ibid. 239–41. But, he fails to elaborate on how the laws of logic are uniquely qualified by the system of divine revelation.

31. Recall 6.3.1–2.

32. Bahnsen, "The Crucial Concept of Self-Deception," 25–29. Bahnsen's solution to the paradox of self-deception is remarkably similar to Bertrand Russell's solution

count comports with human experience and accurately reflects the biblical data,[33] his pursuit of a resolution ultimately involves swapping one paradox for another. For, in evading the contradiction that man affirms and denies the same proposition, Bahnsen relies on an implicit doctrine of the human will as capable of embracing two opposing courses at once—a formidable paradox in itself. Even if man believes in God reluctantly, some part of his will has a favorable disposition toward truth. And yet, man's denial of his belief in the truth represents a basic inclination toward falsehood. It matters not that man picks and chooses which "truths" he will actively suppress. The fact remains that man is quite a paradox (Ps 12:2, Rom 7:14–20; Jas 1:8), simultaneously *desiring* and *not desiring* to believe the same general thing—truth. Even granting that the will may be divided, one must finally posit the existence of a single double-minded person in whom they are united. Well-aware that rationalist labors to *resolve* theological paradox must fall short of their goal, consistent Van Tillians ought to *vindicate* the mysteries of the faith by showing how they illuminate and affirm the Christian system as a result of, and not in spite of, their challenging novelty.[34]

8.3.2 John M. Frame

Another Van Tillian school led by John M. Frame and Vern S. Poythress (see below) carries on under the designation "Perspectivalism." Drawing inspiration from the several triads developed by Van Til (with respect to epistemology, ethics, revelation, etc.),[35] John Frame contends that thoroughly Christian thinking must integrate a triad of perspectives on "God's law, the world, and oneself," because the three are ultimately "interdependent."[36] That is to say, God's authoritative pronouncements (normative perspective), the revelation inherent in the creation (situational perspective), and the revelation that shines from within the human person and his free activity (existential perspective) work together and qualify one another to produce a truly Christian vantage point on reality.

---

to that famous paradox which bears his name. Russell, *My Philosophical Development*, 76–83.

33. S. Joel Garver has listed ten noteworthy problems with Bahnsen's analysis of self-deception, and registers the general critique that Bahnsen was prone to rationalism. S. Joel Garver, "Bahnsen's Concept on Self-Deception," n.p.

34. For further discussion of this topic see Part IV.

35. Recall 8.2.

36. Frame, *Doctrine of the Knowledge of God*, 89. On other occasions, however, Poythress contends for a multi-perspectivalism as opposed to a specifically tri-perspectivalism. Poythress, *Symphonic Theology*.

Of Van Til's students, John Frame is the only one who has identified and directly labored to make sense of "The Problem of the Theological Paradox," that was left behind by Van Til. Nevertheless, Frame represents Van Til as alternating between the use of a straightforward deductive logic, and a more ambiguous method of implication.[37] In Frame's estimation, Van Til rules out some combinations as impossible on the basis of the former, and embraces others as genuine paradoxes on the basis of the latter. Thus, with respect to Van Til's denunciation of libertarian freedom as logically incompatible with the Reformed doctrine of election, Frame discerns that he "is deducing (logically! how else?) from one Scriptural truth the negation of its opposite. . . . On the other hand, [Van Til] forbids us to 'start with the idea of the sovereign control of God over all things and deduce from it the idea that there is no human responsibility.' In the one case logical deduction is permitted, even demanded. In the other case it is forbidden."[38] Van Til readers must be sympathetic with Frame's frustration that Van Til fails to directly "explain why in some cases we must rest content with such paradox while in other cases . . . we must press for an explicit logical consistency."[39] However, given our interpretation of Van Til, as embracing something similar to Bosanquet's method of implication,[40] there is no reason to suppose that Van Til is guilty of inconsistency. Although paradox is formally indistinguishable from genuine contradiction, the two are clearly distinct when considered from within the Christian system. In the case of divine sovereignty and human responsibility, we have already seen that both follow from the doctrine of the Trintiy, and the two together undergird a covenantal worldview.[41] In contrast, libertarian freedom (as married to any combination of doctrines) involves a self-contradiction because it vitiates the entire Christian system.

In articulating the positive grounds for believing a theological paradox, Frame argues that Van Til would have us begin with faithful exegesis of Scripture. Then, he would advise that we strive in our theological efforts for formal logical consistency. But, supposing "no logical consistency can be obtained without conflict with other biblical teaching, then we must remain satisfied with paradox."[42] Yet, if the account in chapter 6 is correct, a theological paradox is not what is left over after we have striven unsuccessfully for logical consistency. Nor is it sufficient to observe that apparently

37. Frame, "The Problem of Theological Paradox," 320–30.

38. Ibid., 324. Frame's quotation of Van Til is taken from CTK, 38.

39. Frame, "The Problem of Theological Paradox," 325.

40. Recall 6.1–2.

41. Recall 7.2.4–6.

42. Ibid., 325.

contradictory biblical teachings must be allowed to "limit" one another without considering how the same teachings *require* one another within the Christian system.[43] Indeed, Scripture does present us with "apparent contradictions" to which we ought to suppose that there is a resolution, even if we know not what it might be.[44] But a theological paradox represents a new and challenging category, the poles of which mutually imply one another in strict adherence to the demands of a systematic logic, based upon the Triune God and His word. Frame's account calls attention to the problems that are created by Van Til's failure to pursue his method of implication systematically, with a view to vindicating the central Christian paradox.

8.3.3 Vern Poythress

Vern Poythress supplies perhaps the most ambitious attempt to bring perspectivalist insights to bear in the reformation of logic, and the vindication of theological paradox. On the basis of John 1:1, Poythress argues that human words are analogues of the second person of the Trinity, the eternal Word of God. As the second person of the Trinity has an individual existence of His own, is the member of a common class (God) with the Father and the Spirit, and is irreducibly related to two other individuals[45] all human words must be marked by (a) instantiational; (b) classificational; and (c) associational aspects.[46] The dynamic between these three equally ultimate exigencies of language is the proper subject of the logical science.[47] Poythress observes that adoption of a perspectivalist epistemology allows believers to embrace certain theological paradoxes without shame. For example, in John 1:1 itself the same term "God" is used in two different ways. First, it is used classificationally to describe the common nature enjoyed by the persons of the Trinity ("the Word was God"). Second, it is used instantiationally to refer to a specific divine person (God the Father) to whom the eternal Logos/Son of God is related ("the Word was with God"). Furthermore, insofar as the term "God" has an associational aspect, such that it is associated with a transcendent being who exists in a unique fashion, it is to be expected that the Logos may "be God," and "be with God" in a fashion that is not reducible to

43. Frame, "The Problem of Theological Paradox," 300–305; 323–29; Frame, *Van Til*, 161–75.

44. Recall 6.3.4.

45. On Poythress' scheme, the same three attributes apply to all three persons of the Trinity. Poythress, "Reforming Ontology and Logic," 189–93.

46. Ibid., 193–95.

47. Ibid., 202.

creaturely modes of existence.[48] Hence, heretical attempts to distinguish the Logos of John 1:1 from the God (Father) alongside of whom he exists, by viewing him as a lesser, finite sort of deity, betray their reliance on a secular (as opposed to biblical) logic.[49]

Without diminishing the tremendous usefulness of Poythress' observations, his development of a Christian Logic and attendant vindication of theological paradox suffers on a couple of levels. To begin, Poythress' derivation of his triad of perspectives from John 1:1 is haphazard insofar as there is no rule by which he adduces three and only three primary perspectives on language.[50] By the same right, there is no apparent reason why Poythress' logic could not be used to vindicate a quadrinity, or any number of alleged paradoxes proposed by secular thinkers. (The pantheist may insist that "God" is an appropriate designation for the whole of reality, as well as each individual person, when used in the context theosophical discourse.) Thus, it would seem that the intuitive appeal and genuine strengths of a perspectivalist logic stand in need of a more thoroughgoing demonstration of the mutual necessity between any given triad of perspectives. And, perhaps even more fundamentally, a perspectivalist logic seems to stand in need of a demonstration that oneness and threeness of God mutually necessitate one another, in a fashion that will only allow the Trinity to occupy the position of the Absolute authority and guide of our logical reasoning.

8.3.4 K. Scott Oliphint

A group of philosophically aware Reformed exegetes has been birthed as the joint fruit of Van Til's apologetic vision, and Geerhardus Vos' biblical theological program.[51] With a self-conscious commitment to a set of (biblically-based) theological presuppositions (e.g., the Trinity, the epistemological import of time, Divine sovereignty, etc.), this school is confident, not only to advance conservative biblical exegesis, but to focus its efforts on expounding the progressive unfolding of divine revelation through Scripture.[52] In

48. Ibid. 187.

49. Ibid. 211–12.

50. The same might be said with respect to a second triad that Poythress develops with respect to what words communicate—(a) they are *expressive* of persons; (b) they communicate *information*; and (c) they *produce* certain effects. Ibid. 200–201.

51. Vos was reputedly Van Til's favorite professor during his time at Princeton Seminary. John M. Frame, *Van Til*, 19–21.

52. Moisés Silva, "The Case for Calvinistic Hermeneutics," in *Revelation and Reason*, 74–94.

return, the same school has advanced brilliant exegetical insights which undergird a presuppositional apologetic method.[53] With a clear conception of the importance of redemptive historical development, members of this school have been particularly critical of attempts to understand Van Til's project in the static term of analytic philosophy, when Van Til's position is especially married to a philosophy of history.[54]

Among those who bear the joint influence Van Til and Vos influence, K. Scott Oliphint stands out as uniquely qualified to handle theological paradox. Oliphint's most important insights appear in his concentrated study of the concept of divine condescension. In this context, Oliphint begins with an exegetical defense of the divine attribute of aseity, or self-sufficient existence, as well as several other essential divine attributes (simplicity, infinity, immutability, and impassibility).[55] On the other hand, he is equally interested in vindicating God's capacity to learn (Gen 22:12), repent (Exod 32:14), and grieve (Gen 6:6) in his condescended, covenantal relationship to humanity.[56] As a result, Oliphint is left with the task of justifying the Christian belief that the God who is immutable, omniscient, omnipresent etc. may assume an additional set of attributes (mutability, ignorance, spatial limitation, etc.) which contradict His essential nature. Oliphint employs two important strategies for handling the issue of apparent contradiction. First, he observes that the communion of God's essential and covenantal attributes follows from, and is analogous to the communion of attributes involved in the Chalcedonian definition of Christ. In this case, God's covenantal condescension in the Old Testament and the Incarnation of the Son of God in the New Testament mutually imply one another.[57] Second, Oliphint observes

53. Dennison, "The Eschatological Implications of Genesis 2:15 for Apologetics," 190–204; *Paul's Two-Age Construction in Apologetics*, 94ff. Tipton, "Resurrection, Proof, and Presuppositionalism," 41–58; "Paul's Christological Interpretation of Creation and Presuppositional Apologetics," 95–111. Oliphint, "The Irrationality of Unbelief" 59–73; *The Battle Belongs to the Lord: The Power of Scripture for Defending the Faith.* Gaffin, "Epistemological Reflections on 1 Cor 2:6–16," 103–24; Hughes, "Crucial Biblical Passages for Christian Apologetics," 131–40. Smith, *Trinity and Reality*. Although we have numbered Bahnsen among the theonomists, he too was a serious biblical exegete, who drew out the Scriptural foundation for presuppositional apologetics. Bahnsen, "Biblical Exposition of Acts 17," 235–76.

54. Dennison, "Analytic Philosophy and Van Til's Epistemology," 33–56.

55. Oliphint, *God With Us*, 51–88.

56. Oliphint cites at length B. B. Warfield's biblical study of Jesus' emotions to demonstrate that the best representatives of the Reformed tradition have embraced, rather than toned down the reality of Christ's humanity. Ibid., 148–49.

57. Building on the exegetical insights of Geerhardus Vos, Oliphint argues that John 1:1–18 teaches that the Son of God acted as the mediator between God and man even in the Old Covenant, and had assumed a condescended perspective (in sympathy) with

that when the divine mode of being is properly distinguished from a human/finite mode of being, and vice versa, each one implies its capacity to be wed to (but not confused with) the other. In light of the doctrine of divine simplicity, the divine persons are identical with and exhaustive of their being/essence. In contrast, as finite, human persons are in some sense participants in a human nature, the complex history and multitudinous variations of which no individual comprehends within himself. With these distinctions in mind, it is minimally apparent that God *is* immutable in a different fashion than He *is* mutable (upon divine condescension).[58] Likewise, the Son of God "*is* God" in a different way than He "*is* man," with the result that it need not involve a contradiction for the two predicates to define the same person. Even more, divine persons already comprehend three distinct perspectives in themselves which implies their capacity to assume an addition human perspective.[59] Finally, since human nature is something thing which all human persons assume rather than exhaust, it follows that in assuming it unto himself, the Son of God does no violence to human nature. And yet, for all of that, Oliphint is self-conscious about the fact that he hardly resolved the paradox involved in contemplating how a single person may simultaneously possess two radically different perspectives. Instead, he has reasoned by implication that such a mysterious state of affairs must be the case.[60]

In keeping with our overarching critique of Van Til, Oliphint's handling of the mystery of divine condescension/incarnation invites two critiques. First, in light of the correlation that he draws between the mutual exhaustion of multiple personal perspectives in the Trinity and the capacity for a divine person to assume a human nature/perspective, Oliphint's thesis calls us back to the question of whether Incarnation is the exclusive capacity of a *Tri*-personal God, or of a multi-personal God. In order to assert the former, a vindication of the Trinity as the lone sort of Being who can harmonize unity and diversity is in order. Second, at points Oliphint stops short of clearly and directly expounding the mutual necessity between the poles of a paradox, and at other points he suggests mutual implication cannot be discerned at all. For example, the attribute of relative ignorance which is involved in God's covenantal condescension is said to "hide," rather than to "imply" God's omniscience.[61] One wonders why the Christian thinker should not pursue a measure of understanding as to how God's essential

mankind prior to the Incarnation. Ibid., 156–79.

58. Ibid., 151–53, 204–5.

59. Ibid., 250.

60. Ibid., 208–9, 225–26, 250.

61. Ibid., 188 n. 8; 226–28.

attributes and covenantal attributes actually imply one another. Such a demonstration might begin with the observation that genuine omniscience requires the capacity to comprehend the human experience of relative ignorance. In this case, Jesus's confession of ignorance about the time of his return (Matt 24:36) confirms the utter omniscience of God, who willingly knows his creatures in the most intimate and sympathetic fashion.

8.3.5 James N. Anderson

James N. Anderson offers a unique contribution to the issue of theological paradox in particular, drawing significant inspiration from Van Til as well as contemporary philosopher Alvin Plantinga. Of course, Plantinga and Van Til differ significantly on certain fundamental matters, the former embracing a form of common sense realism, and the latter repudiating such a position. However, Anderson correctly discerns that both thinkers are agreed that belief in God ought to be regarded as "properly basic," such that one need not prove that God exists by deductive or inductive methods in order to be warranted in believing in Him.[62] On Plantinga's acutely developed theory of epistemic justification, beliefs are justified on externalist foundationalist grounds, which means that so long as beliefs are the product of a properly functioning belief-forming mechanism, which is directed to accurately conveying some aspect of reality, we have every reason to trust them without further proof.[63] Supposing that there is a God who has fashioned the human intellect with the ability to enjoy an immediate awareness of Him, the one with such an immediate awareness of deity should no more feel compelled to prove or validate his belief than the individual who relies on the information conveyed by a healthy sense of vision. It was due to an odd, epistemological sort of legalism erected by Descartes and Locke that many have been led to suppose that theistic belief must be "justified by works" (of philosophical demonstration).[64] But this supposition, Plantinga and Van Til would agree is out of accord with the genius of Calvin, who in-

62. Plantinga, "Reason and Belief in God," 73–91; cf. *Warranted Christian Belief*, 167–99. Plantinga continues, however, to affirm the validity of theistic proofs alongside of the properly basic character of theistic belief.

63. A more complete description of a warranted belief, on Plantina's terms, is a belief that has been formed by a properly functioning intellect, in a conducive environment, by a segment of that intellect's set of functions that is aimed at truth (as opposed to survival, pleasure, dream production, etc.), with high objective probability. Plantinga, *Warrant: The Current Debate*, 46–47.

64. Plantinga, *Warrant: The Current Debate*, 15; cf. *Warrant and Proper Function*, 237.

sisted that knowledge of the Creator is intertwined with the self-knowledge of His human creatures. In contrast to Van Til, Plantinga does not purport to offer a definitive proof that God exists. Plantinga's epistemology simply allows for theistic (and Christian) belief to be rational if God exists, and if He is indeed the source of the pervasive sense among men that God exists. But, it is altogether possible on Plantinga's position that theistic belief is the product of delusion, and therefore unwarranted.

Leaving aside the point that Van Til's theory of epistemic justification differs widely from that of Plantinga, Anderson's scholarly case that theological paradox can be rendered warranted on the basis of Plantinga's perspective is in many respects congenial with the position held by Van Til. With Plantinga, Anderson argues that if Christianity is true then it is perfectly reasonable that a properly functioning mind should form a basic belief in God as an unparalleled authority. And yet, Plantinga failed to give thorough consideration to whether one may be warranted in believing apparent contradictions on the basis of divine revelation.[65] It is at this point that Anderson offers his own constructive developments. He defines a theological paradox as an apparent contradiction that arises in theology, as in other fields, because of "present limitations of our cognitive apparatus."[66] The two true statements (a) "it is the 24th *day* of December" and (b) "it is Christmas *night*" may appear to be contradictory to a child for whom it is not clear that "day" may either be taken for the opposite of "night" or for the 24 hour period that encompasses day and night as its parts. The problem, as Anderson explains it, is one of "unarticulated equivocation." That is to say, the child lacks sufficient categories and semantic distinctions to resolve the apparent contradiction.[67] Nevertheless, supposing that both statements come from a source who is of greater intelligence than the child and reputable (e.g., his mom), then that child is perfectly warranted in believing both statements, if in fact they are true. All the more, Christians may be perfectly warranted in accepting the apparently contradictory revelations of an infinite God. In fact, as theological paradoxes challenge the Christian intellect, they simultaneously lend support to the Christian belief in divine incomprehensibility.[68] Practically, one may organize one's conduct so that it is consistent with paradoxes, by drawing all of the normal implications that

65. Anderson, *Paradox*, 189–92.

66. Ibid., 245; cf. 5–6

67. Ibid., 225–32

68. Ibid., 311–12.

follow from its apparently opposing propositions, with the exception of the conclusion that either proposition is false.[69]

Anderson's case in *Paradox in Christian Theology* does not advance beyond the modest claim that belief in theological paradoxes may be warranted, if they happen to be true.[70] As a result, Anderson concedes that his model for defending Christian paradox may very well be adopted by non-Christian monotheists,[71] even though it probably cannot be adopted by those who deny the existence of a transcendent personal authority. However, it is difficult to imagine why a pantheist could not justify his acceptance of certain apparent contradictions on the basis that they have been taught to him by reputable teachers (enlightened men) who possess special knowledge (via mystical experience). Even the atheist might argue that his beliefs that (a) the universe is unguided by a transcendent mind, and (b) that his mind is directed to form beliefs conducive to survival *and* truth may both be properly basic, even if he knows not how to reconcile them. He might even follow Anderson's advice to embrace every implication of both of his opposing beliefs with the exception of the conclusion that either one or both are false. Thus, despite its virtues, Anderson's account fails to do justice to the interdependence of theological paradox, a definitive apologetic, and a distinctly Christian logic as envisaged by Van Til.

8.4 Conclusion

Despite Van Til's acumen in recognizing the vast interdependence of Christian doctrines and their component parts, we have discovered that he lacked an equal ability to exposit those same implications in a lucid and systematic fashion. Even more, it has become evident that Van Til fell short of expounding the doctrine of the Trinity in such a way that the oneness of God evidently necessitates his threeness (and vice versa), and precludes the possibility that a false deity marked by additional divine persons could function equally well as the precondition of reason, science, ethics, etc. And, although the disciples of Van Til, and theologians with similar preoccupations have fruitfully developed and applied many of his insights, little

69. Ibid. 301–2

70. Anderson is equally conservative in his assessment of Van Til's transcendental proof for a specifically Triune God as "aiming high" but not necessarily entirely successful.

71. Ibid. 309. Early on, William Dennison called attention to the fact that Van Til's analytic disciples seemed overly willing to make this sort of concession. Dennison, "Analytic Philosophy," 54–55.

has been done to clarify Van Til's method of implication, or to draw out its promising capacity to vindicate Christian paradox. Unfortunately, a rigorous pursuit of this thesis has demanded that the failures, rather than the remarkable successes and fruits of each camp, receive the bulk of our attention. This negative emphasis is rectified, at least in some measure, in Part IV, where we attempt to overcome the shortcomings of Van Til's system, and to set to use the better insights of his disciples.

PART IV

Trinitarian Vindication of Christian Paradox

THE AIM OF THIS final section is to unfold the Christian system according to that sort of logic, which was implied, but insufficiently developed, by Van Til, in order to thoroughly vindicate Christian paradox. In the course of our argument and exposition, the poles of several paradoxes will be proven to imply each other and the Christian system, as well as various triadic structures which pervade that system. On the other hand, under each head, three basic alternative doctrines will be exposed as self-contradictory abstractions. Formally, the exposition begins with a basic portrait of reality, which is discernible in various forms throughout the biblical story, as a major premise. Then, an additional set of revealed information (a minor premise) is added in such a way that it both receives illumination from the major premise and challenges its completeness. Insofar as the character of the minor premise is illuminated by the earlier vantage point (the major premise), the process in view is analytic. Insofar as the major premise is set in a new light by additional information (the minor premise), the process is synthetic. The transcendental rule for determining which unique combinations of likeness and difference reflect the reality of the matter is that once both of the premises in question have been discovered, it becomes evident that neither premise could have ever been true apart from the qualification of the other (i.e., a genuine paradox). False combinations of premises, on the other hand, prove to undermine one another and to dissolve any potential bond between them, revealing that such combinations are self-contradictory abstractions (i.e., a mere contradiction).[72] After this process of reasoning by implication is complete, the resultant, more precise interpretation of Christianity becomes a new major premise, which is able to be challenged and refined by yet another novel set of revealed information.

The following systematic effort must be qualified by two points. First, the development in view is artificial in the sense that it does not represent a course that any specific, real individual has trodden in his discovery of the Christian system. But, it is authentic in the sense that it attempts to clearly convey the sort of considerations and procedures that are at work when believers organize divine revelation in that systematic fashion, which allows God to challenge our natural interpretative molds. Second, the following does not purport to represent an exclusive or even a complete exposition of the Christian system. There certainly are multiple equally valid portraits of the Christian system that may begin at different points, proceed through different connections, and end at different doctrines.

72. Taken together these rules recall dictums that lie at the base of an absolute idealist logic. Bradley tells us that, "Whatever may be [in terms of the whole], if it also must be [in terms of the same whole], assuredly is." Bradley, *Appearance*, 199; cf. Bradley, *Logic*, 425. And Bosanquet argues that we identify a "self-contradiction" by the test of "This or nothing," for if one should deny "a 'this' inherent in the general order, he would have denied that order itself, and abolished all positive basis for his own denial." Bosanquet, *Implication*, 92–93; cf. 3.

9

God (Theology)

9.1 MAJOR PREMISE

As a rudimentary major premise for our logic, we may take the somewhat generic, biblical portrait of reality as a "covenantal personalism," where men must be reconciled to God through Christ if they are to be enjoy a true perspective on reality (John 14:6). The Scriptures indicate that, from the beginning, faithful man has been aware that a single personal God (Gen 1:1; 14:19–20; Deut 4:35, 39) is the context/atmosphere within Whom all other things live and move and have their being (Acts 17:28; cf. Gen 1; Job 12:10).[1] Even from this Old Testament vantage point, it is clear that if man is to rise above the penalty of guilt and confusion that characterize his fallen life, then he is in basic need of God-given atonement for his sullied life and the fallen universe that man has affected. Additionally, the only ground of assurance that he stands in a relatively harmonious relationship to the universe, such that he might be able to interpret it correctly, is direct assurance from this Absolute God in the form of an enduring Scripture. In the New Covenant, these inferences are made even more explicit by the reconciling work of Christ, and his teaching.

1. The author is aware that many historians, biblical scholars, and theologians have detected a development from animism, to polytheism, to henotheism, to full-fledged monotheism in the development of Israel's psyche. As a presuppositionalists, however, the present author is comfortable accepting the biblical testimony that the people of God were always, at root, monotheistic.

Even in its basic expression, what we have termed "covenantal personalism" will be rejected by unredeemed men who deny that God's Word may be self-validating. Indeed, they will insist that God's existence and claims must either (a) be subject to the same methods of verification as those used elsewhere by man; (b) be incapable of verification, so that he is basically unknowable; or (c) be identical with the universe and its basic principles of verification. However, the proof that a self-verifying God does exist is transcendental, and turns on the fact that the proposed alternatives are self-defeating abstractions. The first option confuses God and man as finite members of the universe with the result that no intellect can authoritatively declare that reality is a harmony. The second position preserves God's transcendence, but in such a manner that He cannot reveal His intentions for humanity clearly or authoritatively. And the third option reduces God to that impersonal universe which is so very often frustrating and hostile to the ends of man. In each case, man cannot justify the conviction that he enjoys any true beliefs at all, much less justify any set of criteria by which he might judge the Absolute person of God.

9.2 VINDICATION OF THE ONTOLOGICAL TRINITY

A minor premise that may initially seem to conflict with the monotheistic emphasis inherent to covenantal personalism is the distinctively New Covenant revelation that God is in fact three persons as Father, Son, and Holy Spirit (Matt 3:16–17; 28:19; Luke 3:21–22; 4:17–21; 10:21; John 14:26; 15:26; 1 Cor 12:4–6; 2 Cor 13:14; Eph 1:2–13; 1 Pet 1:2; Jude 20–21). Simple deductive reasoning, where man is taken as the *measure* rather than the *image* of God, would yield the conclusion that God cannot at once be an equally uni-personal and tri-personal being. If the Father, the Son, and Spirit are the same God, then the "three" must be different titles for the same individual (as "commander," "chief," and "president" equally apply to George Washington), or the "one" must represent a generic class that sheds the distinctions of each person (as "president" applies to Washington, Jefferson and Adams alike). In contrast to this sort of reasoning, the covenantal personalist, who begins by presupposing the finitude of his concepts, ought to suppose that the revelation of the Trinity can and will expand his former notions of God and man alike, and enhance rather than compromise the consistency of the Christian system.

From the covenantal personalist position articulated earlier, it was clear that God is like man as a "person," but unlike man as that all-encompassing context within Whom man lives and moves and has his being. With the further revelation that God is Triune, it becomes clear that God differs from man in the additional respect that His being is equally identical with three co-existent divine persons. However, it also establishes a previously unappreciated likeness between God and man, by indicating that they are both related to one another (Col 1:17; cf. Luke 10:22; John 17:20–24; 1 Tim 2:5; Heb 8:16; Isa 42:6; 49:8) and to themselves (Matt 3:16; Mark 1:10; Luke 10:21; 1 Cor 2:11; Eph 4:4; 1 Cor 12:11) through the mediation of God the Son and God the Holy Spirit. Notably, neither the newfound distinction, nor the similarity, could have been gathered from one premise taken alone, or by simply combining the information supplied by each. Instead, our reasoning is analogical as it is based on the belief that our concepts are but *finite* reflections of the mind of God, with the result that the major and minor premises may shape one another in unforeseen ways. At the same time, different analogical inferences could have been draw from the same information. From the fact that the divine nature admits for multiple persons, one might conclude that deity is but a generic species. One might conclude that men are like God because they may become members of the Godhead themselves (as Jesus may be mistaken to have done), but unlike God the Father Who, alone, is originally and inherently deity. Many unitarians have been compelled to draw exactly this sort of conclusion, because it evades the apparent contradiction involved in the notion of a God who is perfectly one and three. This view has, of course, been powerfully combatted on exegetical grounds. Yet, if one begins with the presupposition that formal logical consistency places a negative restraint on what the Scriptures may teach, then rationalist non-Trinitarian exegesis must always be regarded as superior to its orthodox alternative. On the other hand, if one treats the Scriptures as a makeshift conglomeration of texts, there is no reason why the same Bible may not contain both Trinitarian and anti-Trinitarian passages. Hence, in conjunction with the task of defending central doctrines like the Trinity from the text, the systematic theologian must defend them as the only acceptable conclusions according to a distinctive sort of logic drawn, itself, from the Scriptures.[2]

The conviction that the Trinity is a central Christian doctrine can and should be met with the insight that the uni-personality and tri-personality of the Godhead necessitate one another, and are equally indispensable to that covenantal personalist worldview to which they belong. For, the three basic alternatives to Trinitarian theism—polytheism, unitarianism, and illicit numerical combinations of divine persons—deprive God of His status as the absolute personal context of creation. Polytheistic theologies expressly

2. Poythress makes a similar observation with respect Jehovah's Witness exegesis of John 1:1. Poythress, "Reforming Ontology and Logic," 212.

set the divine pantheon within an impersonal temporal sphere that is limited by nothing at all, except perhaps formal principles. Although the gods are very much like men in their fickle disputes and finite enterprises, the polytheistic schemes in which they appear reduce to outright impersonalisms, where neither gods nor men can pronounce on any matter with final certainty, because they are at the mercy of an open-ended dynamic between warring powers. In contrast, unitarians of many different stripes—Deists, Muslims, Arians, etc.—profess belief in an ultimate personal deity who governs the cosmos as its sovereign Creator. However, unitarian theology is beset with the basic problem that it must locate the relationship between God and creation in the context of an impersonal sphere. If that context is minimally defined as space-time, an empty sphere of chance then impersonalism reigns supreme and God ceases, once again, to be the master of created history. If God and man are co-members in a nexus of logically governed forms, then that most general category (undifferentiated being, perhaps), which colors and defines God and man alike, must itself evade all definition (since no more general quality may be contrasted with it or predicated of it) and, again, God and man are at the mercy of the unknown.

In contrast to the above, the doctrine of the Trinity sets all of reality and every relationship, including God's self-relationship and creature-relationship within the context of divine persons. God and man are alike in that both are defined in relationship *to* divine persons, within the context *of* divine persons. But, unlike man whose character and consciousness must develop over time, God is exhaustively defined by the three co-eternal persons and their communion.[3] The Father and the Son are related to one another within the personal context of God the Holy Spirit; the Father and the Spirit are related to one another within the personal context of God the Son; and the Son and the Spirit are related to one another within the personal context of God the Father (see fig. 25). As facilitators of the intra-divine relationships, each Triune person must not be construed as indifferent to the others whom they relate. Instead, each person in himself *is* identical with his activity of relating the other two—the Father *is* that self in whom the Son and the Spirit relate; and the Son *is* that self in whom the Father and the Spirit relate; and the Spirit *is* that self in whom the Father and the Son relate. For the same reason, each person is inseparable from his relationships to the

3. This point is implicit in the way that Van Til distinguishes God's absolute personhood from man's finite personhood—"He is perfectly self-conscious. A temporal being, on the other hand, cannot be entirely self-conscious. Man can never become pure act as God is pure act. Man's life is subject to the process of time, and this process of time, when it is an aspect of the conscious creature, involves a transition from some measure of potentiality to an ever increasing actuality." CTE, 49.

other two. By containing the Son, the Father comprehends his own relationship to the Spirit, and in containing the Spirit, the Father contains his own relationship to the Son. The same can be said for the other two divine persons. In this way, each person of the Trinity facilitates the whole dynamic of the Trinity. And for this reason, a Triune person must be defined as an individual who resides above, and is active within, a dynamic between three persons of whom he happens to be one.

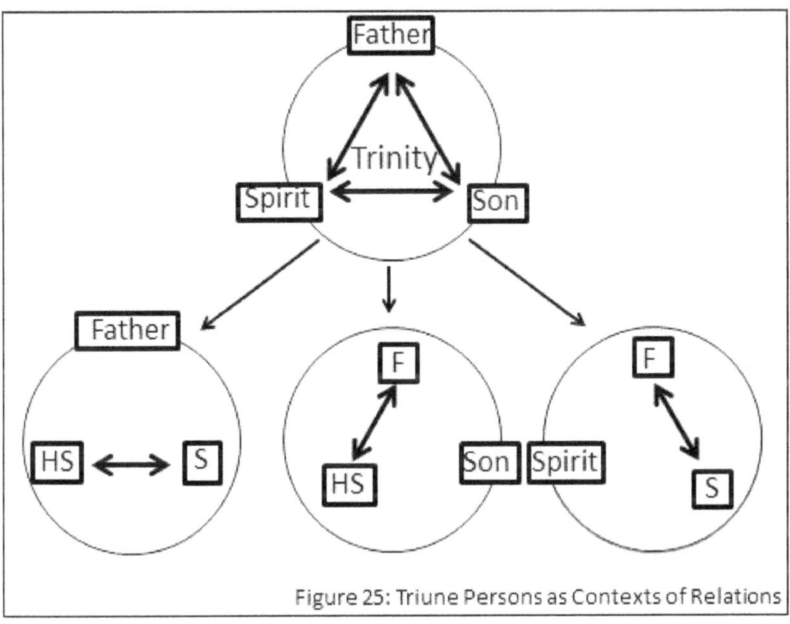

Figure 25: Triune Persons as Contexts of Relations

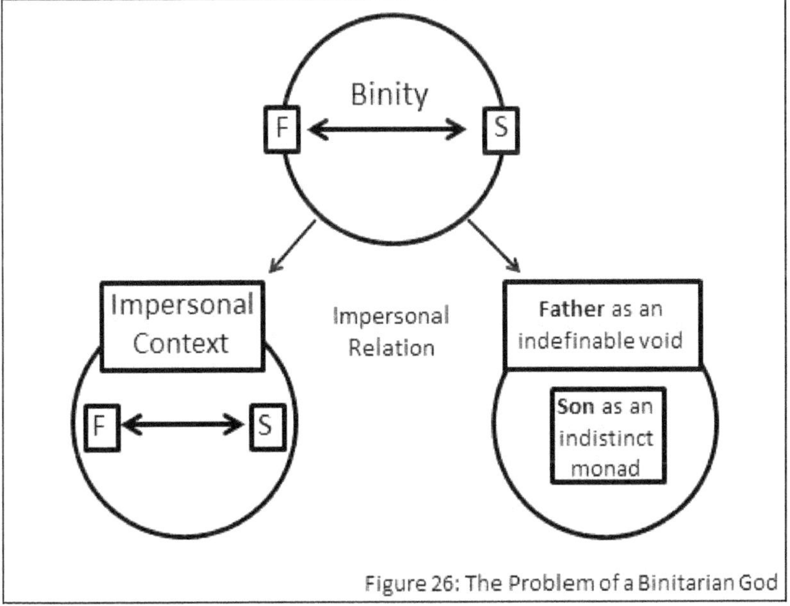

Figure 26: The Problem of a Binitarian God

Sufficient meditation on the above observations yields the conclusion that God cannot be any more or any less than three divine persons, without being reduced to a common class with those finite "impersonally-contained" deities mentioned earlier. Any other number of divine persons would create a disparity between the personal contexts and the personal relationships; between the "one" and the "many" of the Godhead. For example, if God were bi-personal—perhaps as Father and Son but excluding the Holy Spirit—one of two equally problematic conclusions would follow. Either, (a) the Father and the Son would be reliant on an impersonal context as that which could facilitate their mutual relationship and definition; or, (b) one of the two persons would have to function as an unrelated and thus undefined context, in whom the other resides as an individual monad (see fig. 26). In the former case, both divine persons are at the mercy of an impersonal universe, in the latter case, the two persons represent an indefinable context and an indefinable individual, respectively. One encounters the same sort of difficulties when the number of divine persons is haphazardly increased. For example, a quadrinity in whom the Father, Son, and Spirit are married to some forth person, "x," must subordinate the individual persons to abstract and impersonal "groups," and/or render the persons divisible into finite impersonal parts (see fig. 27). If the relationship between the Spirit and person "x" were facilitated by the Father and the Son *together*, then the actual mediator of that relationship, and that thing which comprehends the Trinity, would be an abstract and impersonal "group" formed by the Father and Son, rather than a concrete person. Neither the Father nor the Son, but that "something" between them, would be the true facilitator of the relationship between the Spirit and person "x." But the very profundity of the Trinity lies in the fact that that which unifies all things is not an unknown something, but a personal Authority Who we might come to know and trust because He is also a concrete individual. It is equally unacceptable that the Father alone might function as the context of the Spirit-"x" relationship, for then (a) the Son would be indifferent and uninvolved in some activity of the godhead, and so fail to fully express/comprehend the entire divine being in himself; and (b) the Father would cease to be an absolute person since only the relationship between Spirit-"x," and not the relationship between Himself and His Son, would fall within the sphere of His own self-activity (see fig. 27). Both the Father and the Son would be mere parts of a generic divine nature that comprehends them both. Finally, it is also to no avail to suppose that the seven possible pairs of relationships between any two persons (F-S, F-X, F-H, S-X, S-H, and X-H) could be mediated by a single third person. Such a scenario would create a disparity between the divine persons, as some would have to function as the contexts of multiple pairs of relationships, and others of only one. Again, those persons whose natures were fully expressed as the context of only one personal relationship would not comprehend the entirety of the divine nature in themselves (as several relations would fall outside of themselves). And, that one person who did comprehend all of the others and their relationships would represent an abstract unity, who depends on an irrationalist principle of individuation, since he fails to behold or to differentiate himself with respect to other co-equal persons who in turn comprehend him. Hence, to add or subtract from the number of three divine persons is to compromise an ultimately personalist view of reality, by making God identical with, or subordinate to, an impersonal context. Such a God could not speak with authority, and the servants of such a deity would lack any ground for placing their trust in Him, because He would not "know" himself solely with reference to His own person.

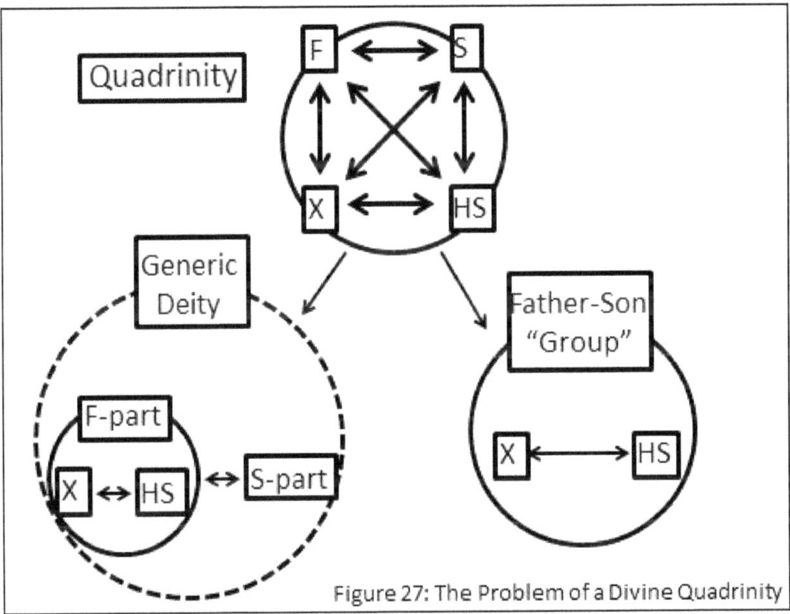

Figure 27: The Problem of a Divine Quadrinity

The upshot of our analogical reasoning is that from the vantage point of a covenantal personalist worldview, God must be three self-contained persons who are equally comprehensive of one another if God is to be a single self-contained Being, and vice versa. Notably, we have not advanced one step in resolving the paradox of the Trinity, or in explaining just how the persons of the Trinity can be mutually self-contained and thus constitute a single divine person. We have heartily accepted that the paradox of the Trinity cannot be vindicated apart from Christian presuppositions, and that those same Christian presuppositions cannot be consistently held by those who would deny the doctrine of the Trinity. In contrast to those within and without the Christian church who have judged that the paradox of the Trinity poses a serious logical "problem,"[4] we ought to judge that any such evaluation is based on a seriously problematic logic. For, on a Christian logic, the Trinity contributes to a broader analysis of the whole, and a more precise synthesis of the parts of the Christian system. Furthermore, in conjunction with same reasoning process, the basic alternatives to Trinitarianism—generic monotheism, polytheism, and haphazard combinations of divine persons—show themselves to be fictitious "abstractions," forms of impersonalism, which defeat themselves by betraying a dependence on an ideal of truth that only Trinitarian personalism will ever supply. Hence, the truth of the Trinitarian doctrine and the logical method for which it stands is vindicated transcendentally.

9.3 VINDICATION OF THE ORDER AND EQUALITY OF DIVINE PERSONS

"Trinitarian covenantalism" is an appropriate title for our revamped major premise, as it incorporates the insight that man is fundamentally related to a Triune God. And yet, this stress on the equality of the divine persons seems to clash with another pervasive biblical teaching, namely, that there is an order and economy between them (Matt 28:19; John 15:26; Eph 1:3–14).[5] First, in addition to creating the universe (Mark 13:19), and predestining believers unto salvation (1 Pet 1:2), the Father is responsible for directing the Son and the Spirit in their creative and redemptive work (Luke 11:13; John 3:16). Second, the Son is the mediator between God and creation (John 17:23; 1 Tim 2:5) and especially between the Father and believers, as the vessel through whom the Spirit is poured out (John 15:26; Luke 3:16). Third, the Spirit glorifies and completes the work of the Father and the Son by directing the creation back unto God in praise and worship (John 14:26; Gal 4:6). In fact, the Spirit is the archetypal glory of God (1 Pet 4:14; Gen 1:2 with Exod

4. Cornelius Plantinga, for example, discerns the equal ultimacy of the threeness and oneness of the Trinity poses a serious logical problem, and is compelled to embrace a social Trinitarian position that grants tri-personality a more fundamental place in the Godhead than uni-personality. Plantinga, "Oneness/Threeness Problem," 50–53.

5. Biblical theologian Lee Irons insists that Calvin, Warfield, and especially Van Til stray from the clear teaching of Scripture (e.g., John 5:26; 1 John 5:18) when the deny that the "Son's nature is derived from the Father." Irons defends Turretin's position that the Son's essence (a) *is derived* in the sense that it is communicated to Him from the Father, but (b) *is not* derived in the sense that it is an eternal nature. Lee Irons, "The Eternal Generation of the Son," n.p.

24:16–17)[6] and the chief object of the Father and the Son's affection (Isa 43:7; Matt 12:31–32). Points such as these have led theologians to discern that even before creation, the Father has eternally generated the Son (rendering him a "second" person), while the two together have eternally sent forth the Spirit (rendering him a "third" person). Furthermore, the Trinity seems to lend itself to psychological analogies where the Father is like unto an individual person/mind, the Son to an eternal expression of God's self-knowledge (John 1:1–3; 1 Cor 1:24; Ps 33:6), and the Spirit to the mutual affection and good will between the two (John 17:5). Hence, even those Reformed theologians who have stressed most of all the equal originality the divine persons (e.g., Calvin, Hodge, Warfield, Van Til, etc.) have discerned that the Father must, in some fashion "generate" the Son, and spirate the Spirit through the Son, from eternity (see fig. 28).[7] However, if our minor premise regarding economy is correct, and there is a sense in which the persons of the Son and Spirit are "from" the Father, then several undesirable results seem to follow. The Father would represent an aboriginal unrelated person for whom personal relations are secondary, and the oneness of God would seem to precede his threeness as its logical ground/source. But, as we have seen, Trinitarian covenantalism demands the absolute equality of the three divine persons in order to evade an impersonalist worldview.

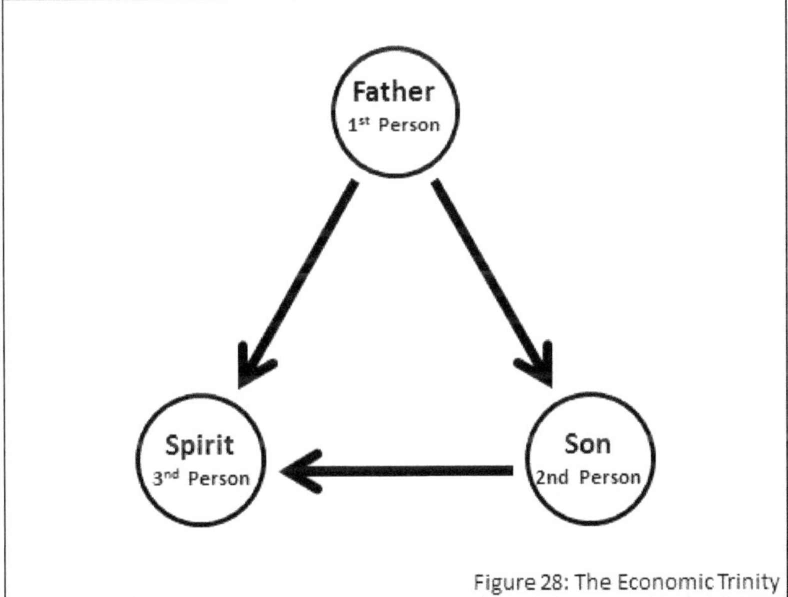

Figure 28: The Economic Trinity

7. Even Van Til is clear in teaching that there is a sense in which the sonship of the second person of the Trinity is eternal—"If we do start with Christ we are at once led back to the fact that he is the eternal Son of God, equal with the Father and the Holy Spirit. TJD, 37.

The chief obstruction to appreciating that an ontological equality implies an equally basic order between the divine persons is the failure to regard all three persons of the Trinity as self-existent (Exod 3:14; John 5:26; Acts 17:25),[8] in the sense that they are identical with their activity toward one another, as contrasting persons. Too often theologians have presumed, with Aristotle, that self-existence can only pertain to a unitary mind—"thought thinking itself"—who sheds the sorts of distinction that accompany concrete relationships. With this point of view in the background, Western theologians have often compared the Father to a unitary mind, and the Son and the Spirit to primeval acts of self-knowledge and self-will. In this case, they are eternal and at the same time owing their personal existence to an activity of the Father.[9] Insofar as the psychological analogy for God is stressed, ontological equality diminishes, and the Father alone is preserved as a self-existent ground of being, to Whom the Son and Spirit are much indebted for their secondary and tertiary existences, respectively. Once more a self-defeating unitarianism looms in the background, where, in himself, the Father is far more like an impersonal, indefinable void. Second, others, who have drawn inspiration from Calvin's emphasis on the equal originality of the divine persons, have understood the three persons' unity to be closer akin to a unity of interest or intention between three human beings, than to that sort of unity which obtains within a single mind.[10] This view runs the risk of reducing the unity of the Godhead to a synthetic product of the mutual deliberation between three wholly separate persons. Even though it may be eternal, the order between the divine persons does not enter into the very essence of the Godhead, but is more like a "group" ethos produced by the three persons. This sort of Trinitarianism veers in the direction of tri-theism, and would reduce (with polytheisms of all stripes) to impersonalism, if unrestrained. A third group has attempted to maintain the harmony between order and individuality by viewing each person as

8. In his discussion of recent scholarship with respect to the meaning of the divine name supplied in Exodus 3:14, Frame concludes that "I am that I am" is chiefly intended to express God's capacity *to be* the Savior Whom He has promised Moses that he *will be* (cf. Exod 33:19). Frame, *Doctrine of God*, 37–46. If this view is correct, then the Thomistic reading of the passage as indicating that God is "Being" pure and simple is misleading. For, Exodus 3:14 is intended to present God as acting intentionally in concrete circumstances.

9. Augustine, *Trinity*, 13–276, 14:1—15:28. Aquinas, *Summa Theologica*, 1a, 33–1a, 41.

10. This is the basic position of social Trinitarians of various stripes. Moltmann, *The Trinity and the Kingdom*, 129–50; Plantinga, "Oneness/Threeness," 50–53; Gunton, "The One, the Three and the Many," 214–19; Zizioulas, *Being as Communion*, 2ff.

a moment in the dialectic of God's self-development.[11] But this view has proven to compromise God's status as a self-complete personal context, by subjecting Him to a temporal development.

The failures of the above alternatives ought to inspire believers to pursue a refined understanding of "order" as it is applied to the Triune God. In keeping with our earlier observation that the persons of the Father, Son, and Spirit comprehend and express themselves in the whole Triune communion, it stands to reason that the order of the divine persons should itself be identified with one of the persons. And, of course, the Father is the only candidate who could occupy this position. From this identification, several interesting results follow. To begin, if the order of persons is an expression of the Father's activity toward the other two members of the Godhead, it follows that the other two members must be equally original with the Father, otherwise his organizing activity would have no object. For the same reason, although the order of the Trinity enters into the very being of God (since it is one with the personality of the Father), it is also an expression of the divine intellect and will, since the leadership of the Father is accompanied by the eternal consent of the Son and the Spirit. It is also clear that whatever the nature of the Father's leadership (which we will expound on below), he is not first within an extra-divine grid of logical or temporal priority, but first because his person is the archetype of every finite sort of order known to us. Hence, the Father is a self-existent being, not because he lacks inter-personal relationships, but because he exhaustively governs his interpersonal relationships and ensures that their modes of activity are consistent with his own. The Son is generated, and the Spirit spirated by the Father, not because they have the Father as their ontological source, but because he is the director of that divine order without which their specific roles would have no place. As we will see, the Son's role as mediator/intellect and the Spirit's role as object/will are directly related to the eternal order of persons as Father, Son, and Spirit. Finally, in light of the fact that the Father's person is one with the existential order of persons of which he is a member, it is perfectly appropriate to speak of God as "three persons" and "one person" in a fashion that even bears some analogy to human relationships.[12] Very often in human history, the charismatic personality of effective

11. On various interpretations, Hegel's onto-theology can be understood in this light. Recall 3.2.1.

12. In his survey of Trinitarian theology Robert Lethem critiques Van Til's claim—that the one divine nature is a single *person* in the same sense as the three are persons—as potentially lending itself to heresy, even if motivated by the "laudable" intention to preserve the absolute personality of God. Letham, *Trinity*, 180–81, 462. Since the three persons are personal in a specifically relational sense, Letham argues that if the one

leaders leaves an indelible mark on the social groups whom they head (e.g., Augustus's Rome; Victoria's England; Jesus' church, etc.). The same can be said with respect to the Trinity, except for the fact that the Father's person is *perfectly* and *eternally* expressed in the order of divine persons.

Given the point that the Father is identical with his ordering activity, it is appropriate to consider the nature of the Son and the Spirit's self-activity in light of the positions they occupy by the Father's direction. Just as the Son is designated a mediator between man and God, the Son is evidently a mediator between the Father and the Spirit, and between the unity of order, centered in the former, and the diversity and individuality, which, we will discover, is centered in the latter. In order to appreciate significance of the Son's role, we may begin by considering that human history has seen numerous tyrannical governments which were orderly for a time, but which squelched the individual rights and creativity of its citizens. Obviously, this cannot be the case with respect to God. Not only would such a scenario conflict with several divine attributes that we are on a trajectory to discover (justice, love, faithfulness, etc.), but it undermines the absolute personality of God, by rendering certain persons "less" active than others, because mingled with the anti-principle of potentiality/non-being. Since there must be harmony between the divine persons, and since God must be absolutely personal, it follows that the divine harmony must be centered in a personal mediator, God the Son. Notably, the Son is one with the Father in the act of sending the Spirit, and one with the Spirit in actively submitting to the Father.[13] The Son defines the entirety of the divine being by embodying the two, seemingly opposite activities, that define the Father and the Spirit. In this service, the Son is not passive. Instead, he is an intellect who defines the Godhead, only by joining the Father in sending the Spirit, and joining the Spirit in serving the Father. And in this unique work, the Son sets Himself apart as the center of divine wisdom and knowledge of God (John 1:1–3;

---

divine nature is a person, he must either be an extra-divine reality, related to the three persons and thus constitutive of a fourth, or a subject who relates to the three persons as mere attributes. Hence, Letham echoes T. F. Torrance's caution against speaking of God as a single person. Letham, *Trinity*, 181; cf. Torrance, *The Doctrine of God*, 102–3, 155–61. The root error at work in Letham and Torrance's judgments resides in their failure to glean that persons are not only defined by their status as *related*, but equally well by their status as *relators*. Insofar as the divine nature is identical with the persons as *relators* of the whole, it is necessarily uni-personal, but insofar as the divine nature is identical with all three persons as mutually related it is necessarily tri-personal.

13. The Son was uniquely fit to carry out the work of the Incarnation, possessing a fully divine nature and a fully human nature. For, in eternity the Son has always had the special role of occupying two positions—that of Leader with the Father, and that of Servant with the Spirit.

1 Cor 1:24), since by looking at the Son, the Father and the Spirit behold a perfect expression of themselves, and their distinction from each other. Finally, the Son represents a sort of equilibrium and harmony within the Godhead because he renders the work of the Father, the Spirit, and himself, complementary, so that all three may behold themselves in the same personal object.

Third, just like the principles of unity and harmony, the principle of individuation, which accounts for the distinctions between persons, must be identical with a third person of the Trinity, the Holy Spirit.[14] Meditation on human societies yields the counterintuitive conclusion that the ground of true individuality and diversity is the pervasive presence of an *identical* motive or theme that characterizes each and every will. For, in anarchical contexts, where renegades, murderers, thieves, etc., pursue mutually exclusive ends, the individual characteristics of each person are suppressed out of instability and fear. Individual giftedness, artistic ability, and style can only be manifested when a society is indirectly motivated by a common theme that manifests itself in a diversity of unique but compatible expressions of will. In a similar fashion, the individual will of each person of the Trinity is motivated by a corporate will that is centered in the Holy Spirit, to glorify God. However, the Spirit-glory of God is not an impersonal force that drives the Father and the Son to act and exist as they do. Instead, the Spirit is a person who actively serves the Father and the Son, in praise and exaltation. In this case, God's glory is not an abstract divine quality, which the Father, the Son, and the Spirit all cherish, but a specific person whose very essence is inseparable from the activity of praising God. With respect to the Father and the Son, the Spirit accompanies them in all that they do as a helper/motivator. His presence is not an indication that their individual ambitions are defective, but an indication that their ambitions are utterly perfect and thus inherently deserving of eternal praise. Therefore, the Father and the Son are unique individuals with specific activities (of ordering and harmonizing, respectively) only insofar as they actively pursue and embody the same individuating will, namely, the Spirit of glory.

The above observations yield the conclusion that the chain of Father-Son-Spirit enters into the very nature of God as organized by the Father, without rendering the Son or the Spirit unoriginal. The eternal order of individuals implies the equal originality and harmony of those individuals and vice versa. And even though the Father is the center of divine unity, all three persons contribute their own sort of unity to the Godhead. The

14. The thesis that the Holy Spirit is the archetypal individuator of the divine persons has also been articulated and defended by Colin Gunton. Gunton, *The One, The Three and the Many*, 189–90.

Father is a unity of order, the Son of harmony, and the Spirit of a common individuality (see fig. 29). Likewise, all three persons are like the Son in facilitating a harmony of relationships between persons. The Father is a personal governor, the Son a mediator, and the Spirit is a helper. And in addition to being individuals who partake of the Holy Spirit, the Trinity itself is an individual person in the Father, an individual intellect in the Son, and an individual will in the Holy Spirit. For this reason, psychological analogies that call attention to the likeness between God and an individual human being are perfectly valid. They only go awry when it is supposed that the individuality of the Godhead is logically prior to the individuality, unity, and harmony of the three ultimately original persons. Such would subordinate the Trinity to an indefinable, because unrelated, sort of unity. God can only be a self-controlled, self-defined, and self-motivated individual because all three characteristics are centered in the activity of three self-existent persons. For all of that, we must not deceive ourselves in supposing that we have advanced a single step in resolving the paradox between divine order and the equality of persons. Although there are many helpful analogies, we simply cannot conceive of how a single person can be identical with a social *order* of which he is a member, or how an individual person's faculties of intellect and will can constitute equally original and full-fledged persons. Nor is it clear how an ontological order between divine persons (as governed by the Father) can be directed to establishing their ontological equality as individuals (as centered in the Spirit), and strike a perfect harmony between the two (as centered in the Son). And yet, because we are not left without analogies, and because it is evident that the alternatives to a Trinitarian deity are impossible, it is altogether certain that God is a Trinity in exactly the fashion that the Bible describes.

Expressed in: / Person:	Divine Unity (centered in the Father)	Divine Relationship (centered in the Son)	Divine Individuality (centered in the Spirit)
Father	Order	Governor	Person
Son	Harmony	Mediator/ Definer	Intellect
Spirit	Individuality	Helper/ Motivator	Will

Figure 29: Three Trinitarian Triads

9.4 VINDICATION OF THE SIMPLICITY/MULTIPLICITY OF DIVINE ATTRIBUTES

In light of God's status as self-existent, self-defined, and self-directed, in a Trinitarian fashion, our major premise may be newly titled, "Trinitarian Absolutism." However, a fresh minor premise which may appear to undermine the details of our major premise is provided by the biblical data that assigns to God a multiplicity of attributes—eternality (Ps 90:2), infinitude (Ps 147:5), sovereignty (Dan 4:25), omniscience (Ps 139:1–12), life (Heb 10:31), truth (John 7:28), love (1 John 4:8), etc. Previously, we argued that the unity, harmony, and individuality of the Trinity must be identical with specific divine persons.[15] A consistent application of the same logic would seem to require that each of these additional attributes of God must also be identical with distinct persons (with the result that God would be more than tri-personal), if we want to avoid the conclusion that God is ultimately defined by impersonal categories. And yet, we have argued that only a Tri-personal deity can be self-contained in the fashion that is essential to human knowledge. Moreover, our emphasis on the fact that the Triune God is "simple," in the sense that He is not composed of finite parts, might be taken to require that, in reality, the manifold of divine attributes are not distinct. But this concession would seem to yield the conclusion that man's percep-

15. Recall 9.3.

tion of God (as marked by multiple attributes) is flatly equivocal with God's actual nature. Such a scenario would fatally undermine the covenantal communion and analogical knowledge that man enjoys with God.

Although they have been advocated in various manners, we may begin by rejecting three alternatives as impossible because permutations of errors that we have already dispelled. The divine attributes cannot be simple and diverse in the sense that they are: (a) unified in a hierarchy by a single attribute that contains the rest, but which evades any further definition; (b) concentrated in a single substance that cannot be defined in itself; or (c) parts of a single complex system. The first option represents something akin to Plato's ideal world, and especially Plotinus' scheme of a hierarchy of emanations from the "one." The second option presupposes something along the lines of Aristotle's matter/form and substance/attribute distinctions. And the third option represents the divine nature as an abstract "system" that cannot be identified with any one of the attributes in view. In each case, that which unifies the diversity of attributes is an indefinable nothing, which must (like any impersonal ultimate) undermine the truth and stability of man's covenantal knowledge of the Creator. In contrast to these impersonalist portraits we will discover that the divine attributes must be simple in their identity with the divine persons, and diverse in their identity with the inter-Trinitarian communion.

Within the Trinitarian theology already articulated, a set of highly relevant considerations lies dormant. The observation, that each relationship between any two divine persons must be mediated by the third, yields the insight that the persons of the Trinity infinitely contain, and interpenetrate one another. That is to say, the Father relates to the Spirit through the mediation of the Son, the Father is related to the Son through the mediation of the Spirit, and so forth, without end (see fig. 30). This infinite dynamic of the divine life has been characterized as a dance (*perichoresis*) by the Greek theologians, and has been called *circuminsession* by the Latin theologians. And yet, it is somewhat difficult to define the individual "steps" of this inter-Trinitarian dance. Not only would it undermine God's self-contained status to regard them as additional persons, but the very idea of multiple steps arises because three and only three persons generate the notion of a purely personal pirouette movement between subject, object, and context. And yet, the steps cannot be "moments" in a temporal succession, for then God would be composed of impersonal parts, and subject to time. Furthermore, the lines of personal containment extend in a multiplicity of directions quite unlike time as we know it (see fig. 31). The multiplicity cannot be one of "units" or "regions" within an expanse, for then God would once again be composite, and subject to an impersonal space. However, if the eternal "moments," or "forms"[16] of the divine life do not constitute additional persons or personal relations; and if they cannot be construed as generic "units" of time, space, or anything else that suggests a complexity of parts, then they must be qualitatively different attributes which comprehensively define the inter-Trinitarian life. In this case, they may be thought of as co-expansive regions that are qualitatively distinct.

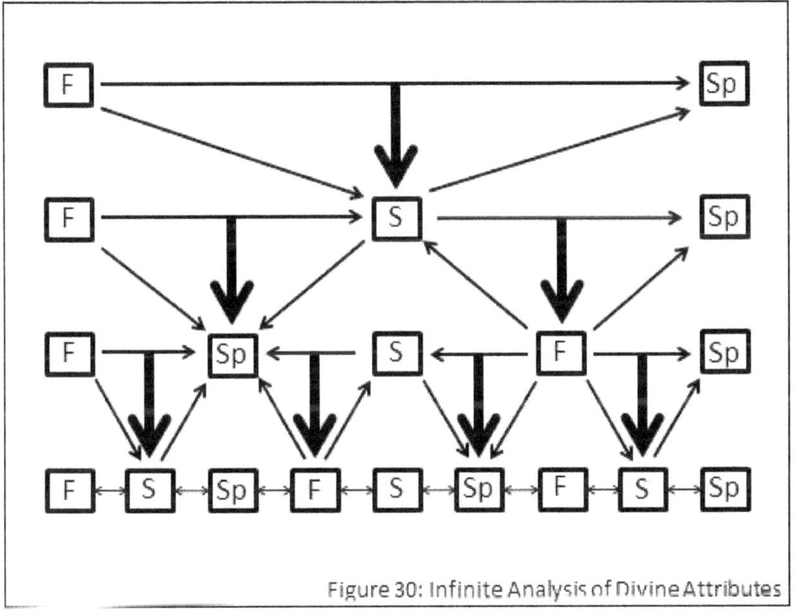

Figure 30: Infinite Analysis of Divine Attributes

16. Oliphint prefers the terms "forms" or "modes" when speaking of those attributes which define the whole of the divine nature. Oliphint, *God With Us*, 65.

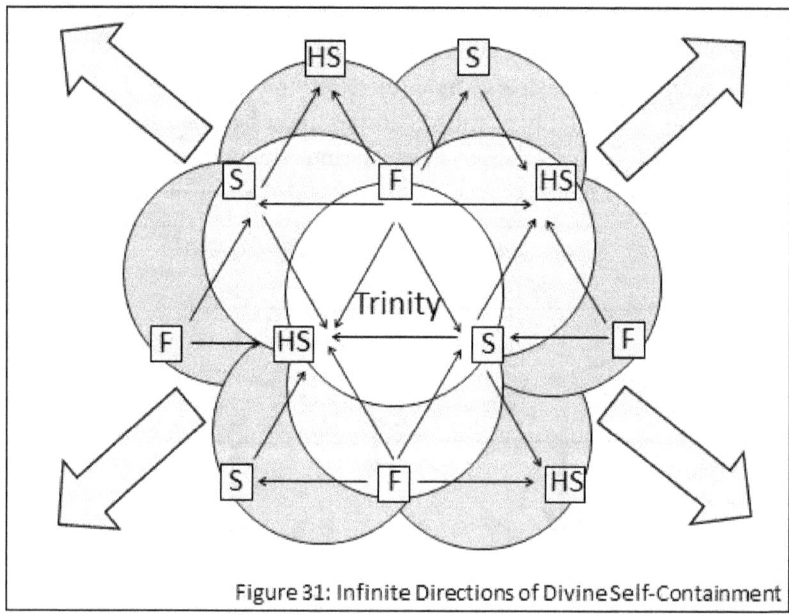

Figure 31: Infinite Directions of Divine Self-Containment

Proceeding on the view that the eternal moments are identical with the divine attributes, several conclusions naturally follow. First, the Triune God must possess an infinitude of attributes (Ps 16:11, Rom 11:33), because there can be no limit to the *circuminsession* of a deity who is self-contained in a tri-personal fashion. Each person must contain and mediate between the others without end. In fact, it is precisely because God is infinitely self-comprehensive that he is incomprehensible for finite men (Isa 55:8–9; Judg 13:18). Second, each and every attribute of God must define all of the others. This is because they are moments of the divine *perichoresis,* which, by way of analysis, must contain all of the others (see fig. 30 and fig. 31). Divine faithfulness, then, must define divine wisdom, righteousness, beauty, etc., in the sense that the latter are expressions of God's faithfulness unto Himself. Infinitude, in addition to being a distinct divine attribute, also characterizes every other attribute as possessing an infinite depth of meaning as we have just described. Third, each attribute must receive external definition without end, because each is inherently related to an infinite web of distinct moments/attributes, which must be predicated of it. In this case, faithfulness may be defined as a wise, righteous, and beautiful sort of personal existence. Fourth, our second and third points call attention to the fact that God's nature cannot be simple unless it is infinitely diverse, or vice versa. If God's nature were simple in the sense that it repelled every distinction, then "simplicity" could not even be predicated of God (for predication rests upon a real distinction between subject, object, and relation/verb); nor could "simplicity," in this radical sense, be reconciled with the notion of a Trinity.[17] God must be simple, not in the sense that His nature is consonant with a multiplicity of *finite* parts, but in the sense that His nature is identical with an infinitude of mutually exhaustive attributes. The only other option is to reduce the divine nature to a "simple"—because literally indefinable—attribute, or to a "simple"—because indefinable—substance. Of course, this bit of reasoning does not allow us to envisage exactly how the divine nature so embodies a simple unity in a diversity of attributes. But, the conclusion follows on its own (Trinitarian) terms, and is further established by the impossibility of the contrary positions, which render God, ultimate reality, and thus, all things wholly unknowable.[18] Fifth, each and every divine attribute must be equally definitive of the divine being, and must not dominate the others. God cannot be more loving than He is just, or vice versa, because both scenarios would inject finitude into the divine being.[19] Sixth, because

17. This is one of the problems with Aquinas' apologetic case for a purely simple deity, which only later, upon exposure to revelation, is known to be tri-personal. Aquinas, *Summa Contra Gentiles*, 1:13–18.

18. Alvin Plantinga's argument that divine simplicity would reduce the personal God to an impersonal property can be viewed from one of two angels, as either (a) supportive, or (b) at odds with the position articulated here. On the one hand, Plantinga's case rightly calls attention to the fact that if we suppose that the divine attributes are identical/univocal with the abstract qualities that we predicate of creatures, then assertions to the effect that God is identical with his attributes would certainly reduce God to impersonal abstractions, which are themselves united by an ultimate abstraction (being) of which nothing can be predicated. On the other hand, insofar as Plantinga would encourage us to embrace the abstract character of attributes when ascribed to creature and Creator alike, and to reject the simplicity of God, his case is at odds with the plea for analogical reasoning advanced here. On our scheme, we are forced to posit the existence of a divine class of attributes which differ from all attributes that we encounter in creation, because they are coterminous with a self-contained personal God. If such novel attributes should offend the modern mind, we must respond that the alternative view where God is subject to abstractions renders the universe expressive of an ultimately indefinable quality, which in turn would render all things beyond our capacity to know with certainty. For the argument against divine simplicity see Plantinga, "Does God Have a Nature," 225–57. Cf. Hill, *Divinity and Maximal Greatness*, 22–23. For a defense of something close to the analogical reasoning articulated in the present text, see Oliphint, *God With Us*, 63–71; *Reasons {for faith}*, 91–121.

19. John Frame discerns that the fundamental motivating factor in open theist theologies is favoritism of the divine attribute of love. Because love is supreme, open theists are willing to downplay, significantly modify, or even discard any other divine attribute (e.g., timelessness, sovereignty, justice) that seems to conflict with the supreme attribute of love. Frame, *No Other God*, 49–56. Ironically, theologians who would grant primacy to the divine attribute of love end up setting it up as a domineering principle which can tolerate no other attributes as its equal; a most unloving characteristic indeed. On our Trinitarian interpretation of God, loving mutuality is equally ultimate with a righteous respect of the order between the divine persons. Likewise, the divine attribute of love

each divine attribute contains and defines the entire stock of divine qualities, God's covenant people may rest assured that, insofar as they know God at all, they know Him in a true and dependable manner. Because God is infinite, believers know that the future will yield new and surprising expressions of the divine nature. And yet, because God is infinite in the sense that every attribute characterizes the others, believers may rest assured that future disclosures will only enhance, rather than contradict their present knowledge of God's power, goodness, truth, etc., as revealed directly in the written Scriptures.

Far from compromising God's absolute personality, the notion of multiple divine *attributes* within a simple divine *nature* is only possible for, and thus the exclusive property of, the Triune God. According to our model, the divine nature, the multiplicity of attributes, and the harmony between them, do not exist in any fashion except within the context of the Triune persons. In this case, the divine attributes are not finally united as a simple nature within any single attribute, so that, for example, "love," taken in itself, could be said to exclusively contain them all. Rather, the attributes are united as simple only within each of the divine persons, as individuated by the will of the Holy Spirit. The divine attributes are not diverse by themselves, but only as the divine persons have eternally and immutably expressed themselves in communion with one another by the orchestration of the Father. Likewise, the divine attributes are only able to mutually define one another, and constitute a single harmony, through the mediation of the Son. Hence, God is never controlled by an impersonal nature or a logical system of ideal qualities that resides above or within Him. The divine attributes are only determinative of God's activity as they are one with the person of the Father. The divine attributes only define the divine nature through the Word of the Son, for attributes cannot speak or actively impose themselves on anything. And the divine attributes are only expressed in all of their diversity and individuality by the will of the Spirit to praise and glorify every detail of the divine being. When these points are taken together, the Father, the Son, and the Spirit are consonant with three meta-attributes—control, authority/definition, and motivation/presence—which determine how every attribute (including themselves) must relate to one another.[20] Love, justice, power,

is equally definitive of the divine being as justice, eternality, and sovereignty. Van Til detects a similar subordinationist tendency in Barth's reduction of the divine attributes to freedom and love. CB, 76.

20. At this point, we are in agreement with John Frame who delineates three "lordship attributes" (control, authority, and presence) which he too allows to function as "meta-attributes" that capably organize all of the others. In keeping with Frame's work in the area, control is governing/metaphysical activity, authority is a defining/

wisdom, etc., actively control, define, and motivate each moment of the divine life, only because each attribute is expressive of a self-controlling, self-defining, and self-motivating God. God is not "self-controlled" in the sense that nothing but a voluntaristic and empty "self" determines every divine activity. He is self-controlled because the numerous moments/attributes of the divine life are just as determinative and essential to the divine person as He is of them. Likewise, God's self-definition and self-will embrace an eternal depth of definition and specification. Finally, it ought to be evident that the same cannot be said for a unitarian deity. Allah may be said to possess ninety-nine, or any other number of attributes. But the Muslim is forced to conclude that these attributes either cannot be expressed apart from his extra-divine activity (and so, implicitly, his dependence on the creation), or they must be thought of as existing potentially within Allah, as they await his interaction with creation. In either case, Allah is not the fullness of himself in himself and cannot, therefore, function as a self-contained authority. Islam's God-conception is, therefore, a contradiction.

9.5 SUMMARY

Before turning to other aspects of a Christian theology and worldview, it is worthwhile to briefly recount the transcendental argumentation thus far. First, we began with the premise of covenantal personalism and observed that its fundamental impersonalist alternatives were lacking the sort of authoritative guidance necessary for intelligible human existence. Second, we saw that, within the confines of a Christian worldview, God must be at once a unitary being and three particular persons in order to maintain His status as a self-contained, and absolute authority. This paradox was vindicated against the prominent alternatives of unitarianism, polytheism, and a dynamic pantheism, because each of the latter proved to be self-defeating, and implicitly reliant upon that lone Trinitarian worldview against which they rebel. Third, it became evident that the persons of the Trinity must be at once ordered and equally original with respect to one another. The strict monarchical, egalitarian, and dialectical views of the Trinity were ruled out, because they reduced to the bland varieties of theism rejected earlier. Fourth, the Triune God proved to embody an infinitude of attributes in the

epistemological activity, and presence is a motivating/ethical activity. Frame, *Doctrine of God*, 36–102, 398–99. However, the main difference between our two discussions is that Frame's chief interest is to convey, through exegesis, how prominent these attributes are in God's covenant relationship to man. I, on the other hand, am somewhat more interested in determining, by implication, how these attributes and the ontological Trinity mutually require one another.

divine *perichoresis* and a simple divine nature in all three persons in such a manner that the one (an infinitude of attributes) could not exist without the other (a simple divine nature in three persons). And, again, the paradox of divine multiplicity in simplicity was vindicated against its alternatives (of a formal hierarchy, substance-attribute scheme, or a complex system) on the basis that these defeat themselves and so indirectly bear witness to the orthodox Trinitarian Christian position as the true context of existence.

10

Reality (Metaphysics)

10.1 VINDICATION OF DIVINE IMMUTABILITY AND CREATION *EX NIHILO*

In light of the unsoundable depths of the divine persons and their communion, the Christian worldview may be characterized as resting upon an infinite personalism, or an infinite Trinitarianism. As a challenging minor premise, however, we may reconsider a point that we have taken for granted all along, namely that God is covenantally related to a finite universe that began to be at a specific point in time (Gen 1:1; Ps 90:2; Prov 8:23; Matt 13:35; John 1:1; 2 Tim 1:9; Rev 13:8), and has its origins *ex nihilo*, out of no prior material (Rom 4:17; Col 1:16–17; Heb 11:3; Rev 4:11). Among the many problems associated with the doctrine of creation *ex nihilo* are the facts that no examples of spontaneous creation are furnished by nature, and that the very idea of such a thing is at odds with the principle that "from nothing, nothing comes." Even more problematic for our purposes is the way that spontaneous creation seems to conflict with the doctrine of God just articulated, and thus undermine the sort of systematic logic which has been advanced as the ideal of Christian reasoning. The difficulty can be stated in any number of ways. In order to create, it would appear that the immutable God must be subject to change, as He redirects his power to the production of a finite reality. And yet, since change is a characteristic of time-bound realities, God must in fact be a finite member of the temporal universe. Stated in different terms, God's decision to create must have been motivated by some end that He has yet to realize. Yet, if God fails to realize any perfection from eternity then He must be finite and guided by ideals that exist outside of Himself.

Ironically, the offense caused by the notion of creation *ex nihilo* stems from a failure to reason about God and creation with the use of a logic that is based upon a specifically Trinitarian theology. In the previous vindication, God's infinite simplicity consisted in the fact that each moment/attribute of the divine life represents something unique and original, and is not a mere mutation or reorganization of the moments/attributes which precede or follow it. Hence, although God is immutable, since the divine *perichoresis* is ever whole and complete, He is also the archetype of spontaneity since each attribute exceeds the others as a fresh container of them. Supposing that God is immutable and novel with respect to Himself in this mysterious fashion, it follows that the only way for God to produce something "more than," in the sense of "additional" to, His infinite self, is by fashioning something that is "less than," in the sense that it does not fully comprehend, his divine self. Stated another way, in order to create something *qualitatively* different from himself (e.g., a finite *creation*) God must produce that which is *quantitatively* less than Himself (e.g., a *finite* creation). To cite a specific and most relevant example of this principle, the finite creation is less than God because it reflects the divine attribute of being "other-contained" by God (for each person of the Trinity is other-contained by two more) without at the same time echoing the divine attribute of *exhaustively* "containing" God. And yet, the severance of the former attribute from the latter makes for quite distinct qualitative differences between God and creation. Whereas God's self-contained infinity consists in the fact that each person of the Trinity is perfectly other-contained and other-containing, the creation is finite and open to indefinite development because it is other-contained but not other-containing of that Creator from Whom it receives both existence and definition.

With respect to logical reasoning, the above observations necessitate several counter-intuitive conclusions. First, finitude is not the opposite of infinitude, but its analogue. With respect to God, an analogue may be defined as that which (a) reflects a finite measure of the divine nature; and (b) is irreducibly different from the divine nature, in order that it may be compatible with the divine nature in a systematic fashion. According to this definition, an analogue is like and unlike God in different ways at every point. Insofar as the finite creation is contained by God, it is like unto God Who is also contained by Himself. But, in its incapacity to comprehend the divine nature in return, it is unlike the God Who comprehends both Himself and creation. And yet, we may just as well reason in the reverse direction. Insofar as the creation is *unlike* God in a variety of ways, it is for that very reason *like* the God Who is consonant with an utter diversity of attributes. On the other hand, insofar as the creation is *like* God, as His finite analogue, it is ubiquitously unlike God, Whose self-activity is never a partial or finite reproduction of that which has come before it. Second, in light of the above considerations, an Aristotelian logic, which exalts the laws of contradiction and identity as its chief principles, simply cannot be baptized as Christian. Nothing in creation is perfectly identical, or utterly equivocal with its Creator, or even, as we will see, with itself. Third, a contradiction is a false portrait of reality that would destroy reality's systematic unity by identifying or utterly severing realities which are at harmony, and so that it ceases to be an analogue of God. In this case, contradictions defeat themselves by undermining that lone system of reality on which they depend for their own articulation. In our current metaphysical discussion, we may identify three such contradictions. With respect to God, the creation cannot be (a) both God-contained and God-containing; (b) God-containing but not God-contained; or (c) neither God-contained nor God-containing. On the first scenario, God and creation are identical, either because the creation is a self-contained Being alongside of the Trinity, or an additional "person" in the Godhead. But, as we have seen, both of these views would subordinate God and creation to an impersonal meta-reality. On the second scenario, the relationship roles of God and the creation are reversed. The creation would comprehend God as an impersonal context, with the result that it would not in any respect be a creation, and God would not in any respect be a Creator. The third scenario renders the creation an utterly nebulous principle, which shares nothing in common with God, and cannot, therefore, be guided or even known by God. In each case, impersonalism would reign, and knowledge would be rendered impossible, because not even God would be able to function as an ultimate epistemological authority.

Armed with a logic that is consonant with a creationist metaphysic, the paradoxical relationship between God and finite reality, as well as the necessity of a specifically tri-personal creative work of God, can be vindicated. First, in keeping with the biblical designation of the Father as the divine person from whom are all things (1 Cor 8:6; Matt 23:9), as well as the Father's position as the director of the divine life, it is perfectly appropriate to speak of the Father as the primary actor in creation. However, the Father's action with respect to creation cannot involve a redirection of divine energy, or a parceling out of some measure of the divine being which he somehow transmutes into a finite existence. Such a view would render God subject to change, and destroy the Creator-creature distinction. Instead, the Father's act of creation must, as a finite exertion, be new and different from his eternal self-activity, with the result that it is itself a finite member of the creation. In fact, it must be identical with the very first moment of creation. Creation is *in time*, as the very first moment *of time*. At this point one might ask how God can be the subject of an activity that is qualitatively different from all that which came before it? To this we must confess that, although it is ultimately mysterious as to how God so acts, the doctrine of the Trinity indicates that God has infinitely realized this self-ascending capacity in Himself. Thus, we have all the more reason to believe that he is capable of spontaneously acting in a lesser fashion, and producing a finite space and time which does not, in turn, comprehend him. And, although the divine act of creation is finite and appears only within the creation itself, it is unacceptable to conclude that it is *of*, or *from* the creation, as if the universe were the author of itself. As the detractors of the doctrine point out, the event of creation represents an anomaly and even a miracle in comparison to the course of events that follow. For the believer, the event of creation unmistakably reveals God as its Author, for only He Who is eternally new with respect to Himself may elect to produce a creation that is utterly distinct from Himself. God, then, is not related to creation as if it were His natural metaphysical counterpart, like a spirit to a body. God is related to creation like a body is related to a garment or ornament that only exists to be worn by God (Ps 104:2; Exod 19:5; Mal 3:17) and to clearly accentuate His power and nature (Ps 19ff; Rom 1:19).

Second, the creative work of the Father, thus described, begs the question of how, and in what context, the Father is related to his own activity of spontaneously producing the finite universe. The answer, for the self-conscious Trinitarian, must be that the creation is sustained through, and in the context of, a second person of the Trinity: God the Son (see fig. 32). According to this model, God's relationship to creation does not suggest that He is subject to time. For the mediator between creation and God is nothing other than His own eternal Son. On the other hand, because the Son is a person, rather than a natural law or a logical relation, it does not follow that the created sphere must be eternal along with him. As the Son actively comprehends and defines the inter-Trinitarian communion, he must be viewed as defining the creation as his own, self-inspired analogue (John 1:1–3; Heb 1:2). Since the creation is but a reflection of the infinite definition inherent in the divine nature, the Son could have inspired any number of different created spheres. That he chose the one before us is an expression of his creative freedom. It is not, however, arbitrary or lacking in a rationale. In fact, it is futile to ponder whether the creation is basically an expression of the divine intellect or the divine will. Although the Father is finally related to the creation through the Son/Intellect, he is related to the Son through his

Spirit/will, and vice versa, in an irreducibly reciprocal fashion. As a result, the form of created reality can only be thought of as the product of an eternal act of deliberation in which intellect and will are utterly interfused (see fig. 33). In other words, God wills to know the creation as He does, and His intellect directs Him in what to will, in such a way that the creation is utterly like the divine nature (as an expression of the Son's intellect) and unlike the divine nature (as an expression of the Spirit's individuating will) at every point. Notably, the Son's comprehensive foreknowledge of creation excludes as impossible a Berkeleian sort of idealism, where reality is nothing more than God's knowledge of it. According to our scheme, God knows the creation in exhaustive detail. But, in its concrete existence, the creation only appears in a succession of finite moments so that the entirety of creation is never simultaneously existent. Hence, God's comprehensive, super-temporal knowledge of creation must be distinct from the creation as it actually exists at each and every point.

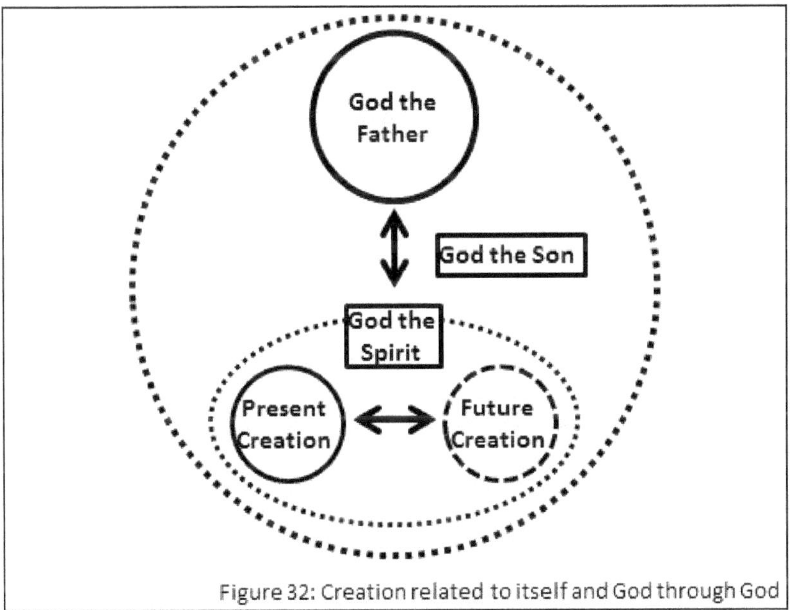

Figure 32: Creation related to itself and God through God

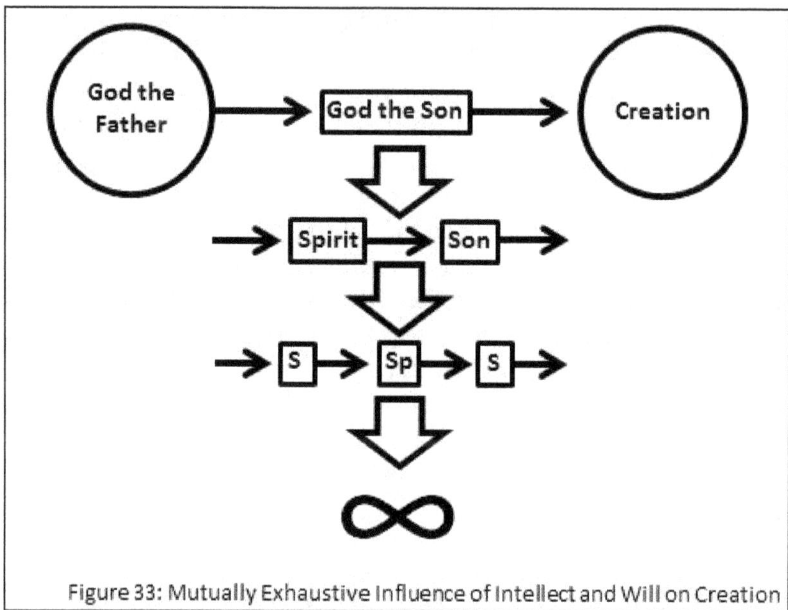

Figure 33: Mutually Exhaustive Influence of Intellect and Will on Creation

Third, although the work of the Father and the Son might appear to be sufficient for safeguarding God's infinitude alongside of his relationship to a finite creation, the Spirit performs an indispensable third function. As noted above, the moments of created reality cannot be simultaneous, as if history were a self-complete whole. In the present context we must add that the creation must be related to itself through the mediation of a third divine person, the Holy Spirit, whose activity is immanent within the creation (see fig. 32). This point hinges on the understanding that a particular member of creation is distinct from its "self," as that set of relationships that it sustains, and the historical transformations that it must undergo, through interaction with the other members of creation. If each member of creation were related to itself through other features of the creation, we would either have to posit an actual infinity of created units, or a set of privileged units/relations which were immediately self-related, and self-defined. But as we will see in the next vindication, both concepts are self-defeating, and represent perversions of divine infinity and self-sufficiency. Thus, it follows that a third divine person must be active in relating the creation to its self (cf. Gen 1:2; 2 Cor 13:14), in order that it may serve as an object to whom the Father may be related, via the mediator of the Son.[1] Finally, since the Spirit's archetypal mode of relating things to themselves is as a motivator, we must anticipate

1. "The creation proceeds from the Father through the Son in the Spirit in order that, in the Spirit and through the Son, it may return to the Father." Bavinck, *Dogmatics*, 2:426.

the point that the creation is driven to realize itself by the activity of created persons, angelic and human. This allows us to clarify that God's motive for creating is analogical to His eternal motive for being. On the one hand, God creates in order to add to His Spirit-glory a multitude of additional, but finite voices (Isa 43:7; Rev 4:8). On the other hand, these finite voices do not imply that something was lacking in God. For, man's finite glorification of God can only represent an additional reality, if it is a finite analogue of his eternally self-complete glory. The former point establishes that God's act of creation was not arbitrary, for it was aimed at a specific end. The latter point indicates that creation was not necessary, as if God were in need of it, but was an expression of His irreducible freedom.

10.2 VINDICATION OF FINITE COMPLEXITY

In light of the fact that only the Triune God can spontaneously produce a finite reality as his created analogue, it is appropriate to designate the Christian system as "Trinitarian Creationism." However, the alleged absurdities inherent in those created categories, which Scripture treats as real, may function as a minor premise which calls into question the propriety of a Creator-creature metaphysic. Space, time, physical matter, universals, free subjects, natural objects, not to mention the idea of angelic spirits, have proven to pose serious metaphysical problems. For example, whether the diverse members of reality are thought of as infinitely complex, or thought of as composed of simple parts, they seem to fall into self-contradiction.[2] That an infinite regress of complexes is impossible is evident from the fact that a complex is by definition a contingent organization of actually existing things. But if all things were contingent, nothing would be contingent because there would be no substance out of which they could be formed as secondary orders of existence. That simple units of matter cannot exist is evident from the fact that matter is spatial. But, if there were a smallest unit of matter/space which was not divisible into smaller spaces, then units which have no space would somehow combine to produce extended spaces, and that is impossible ($0 + 0 \neq 1$). Notably, time and space present their own difficulties, as they can neither be construed as having definite limits nor as being infinite. If, for example, there were a beginning to time, it would have to be preceded by an empty void (for by definition, every moment has a past). But, in order for that void to be succeeded by a particular time, it would have to be temporal (for by definition, only a prior time can precede

2. What follows is a loose reproduction of Kant's second and third antinomies. Kant, *Critique of Pure Reason*, A426/B454-A433/B461, A426/B454-A433/B461.

a future), and thus not an empty void, but another moment in time. On the other hand, an infinite succession of moments cannot elapse prior to every moment in time, for by definition an infinite series cannot be traversed or completed. Whereas some philosophers have taken these sorts of metaphysical antinomies to indicate that space and time are subjective categories, the biblical narrative commits believers to the conclusion that they are real and even precede human existence (Gen 1:1ff). And yet, an utterly irrational creation is certainly at odds with a perfectly wise and capable Creator. Thus, if the previous argument dealt with the argument against a Creator-creature metaphysic from the side of the Creator, the present vindication must dispel the companion case leveled from the side of the creature.

When set in light of the Trinitarian creationist metaphysics thus articulated, it becomes apparent that the basic features of created reality only fall into self-contradiction when they are evaluated from the perspective of an anti-Christian logic. The presumption that lies at the base of both of the above-mentioned problems is that something can only be real if it is immediately self-contained (A = A), and utterly discrete (A ≠ ~A). Whether one prefers the conclusion that a given thing is infinitely complex, or that it is composed of simple parts, it is assumed all along that what something *is* must lie strictly within the boundaries of the thing itself. With this presupposition in mind, it follows quite naturally that every member of reality must be basically complex or basically simple. It also follows that if the creation is basically complex then it must be infinitely so, and if it is to have a finite number of members, then they must be simple. And yet, to reiterate the problem in but another way, if the creation were *basically* complex it would not be *basically* anything. Indeed, all of reality would be a series of organizations that have nothing as their content. If, on the other hand, there were a simplest unit of matter which was not itself extended through smaller parts, it would deprive itself of a basic attribute of matter, namely spatial extension. The fact that such logical reasoning yields metaphysical contradictions ought to be taken as indicating that the logic, and not the reality that it labors in vein to describe, is a fiction.

In place of the logical laws of identity and contradiction as described above, the self-conscious Trinitarian ought to appreciate that a given reality is only self-identical as its existence is mediated through realities which are distinct from itself (A = A in relation to some concrete ~A's). After all, it has proven necessary to view the persons of the Trinity as identical with their eternal self-activity. On the other hand, a contradiction is a perverse and unreal vision of reality as severed from one of its concrete relations (A ≠ ~A), and/or treated as immediately self-contained (A = A). Thus, from a Christian perspective it is a contradiction to take the laws of identity and contradiction as setting limits on creation, prior to being qualified by the concrete complexes to which they apply. With this point of view in mind, the antinomies mentioned above can be replaced with a paradoxical notion of reality that at the very same time establishes rather than undermines its intelligibility. To begin, with respect to the question of whether the members of reality are "finite and simple" or "infinite and complex," the Christian logician ought to detect a false alternative marked by two equally illicit combinations. We have already argued in detail that simplicity and infinitude imply one another as equally indispensable characteristics of the divine nature. Finite simplicity is a nothing because it lacks internal distinction/ definition. Infinite complexity is a nothing because it lacks a final ground of unity, which both comprehends and defines all of its members. Neither notion is compatible with the Trinity because an utterly irrational "other" would compromise his self-contained knowledge and unchallenged power. But if the creation cannot be (a) finite and simple; (b) infinite and complex; or (c) partially both, then we may justly gather that it is (d) finite and complex (see fig. 34). That is to say, the creation must consist of a finite number of members, each one of which happens to be a complex of distinct parts. Furthermore, it is only from the vantage point of a Christian logic that these two descriptors imply rather than conflict with one another. In the event that a given reality is self-identical only as it is related to specific contrasting realities, it follows that all things are complex unities between a "self/ substance" that has relatively definite parameters, and a "self" that is manifested in external relationship. Indeed, there is a sense in which individuals which persist in mutual relationship with one another are "members" of one another. This observation certainly comports with the biblical language concerning the relationship between a husband and wife (1 Cor 7:4; Eph 4:25), between the faithful (Rom 12:5; 1 Cor 12:26; Eph 5:29), and between believers and Christ (Gal 2:20; John 17:22). Notably, if the creation consists of a finite number of members, these members must finally be marked by a finite number of parts, since there is a limited number of things to which they may relate and from which they may receive diversification. Hence, the creation and its members must be "finite and complex" in order to be either finite or to be complex, and in order to be compatible with the Triune God (see fig. 34). The multiplicity inherent in creaturely complexity is a created analogue of divine infinity, and the unity manifested in the finite members of the universe is created analogue of divine simplicity (see fig. 35).

Attributes	Simple	Complex
Infinite	Trinity (Self-Contained Reality)	Unreal Contradiction
Finite	Unreal Contradiction	Creation (Other-Contained Reality)

Figure 34: Attributes unique to the Creator and the Creation

	Divine Archetype	Created Analogue
Unity	Simplicity	Finitude
	Implies	Implies
Multiplicity	Infinity	Complexity

Figure 35: Finite Complexity the Analogue of Infinite Simplicity

The chief objections to the notion of finite complexity stem from the fact that it and several of its implications clearly evade human comprehension. The underlying assumption of such a critique is that, unless a reality can be comprehended as a discrete, self-identical something (A = A), it cannot be real. From this unquestioned conviction arise such questions as, "What is a self/substance in itself, divorced from its relations?" and "What are relations when divorced from individuals?" However, if man could perfectly comprehend finite reality in the way implicitly demanded, the notion of finite complexity and the Christian logic to which it is married would be false. Hence, it is to no avail to point out that, if things contain their relationships to external realities, then they are not really distinct from that which is "other." This is only true if the members of creation contain and fall outside of one another in the same fashion, and to the same degree. Why should it be impossible for a lion to have definite spatial parameters, while its relationship to its prey (e.g., antelope) enters into its nature, as something without which it could not exist without profound modification? The lion-antelope relationship would certainly not dissolve the two into a single self-identical organism, so long as we recognize that each animal leaves a lesser impression on the other than the form exuded by their more local selves. Again, it might be pointed out that we cannot supply things with an absolutely precise spatial definition, and even more, we cannot be certain that we have taken into account every relationship that is pertinent to the definition of a given reality. But, in the event that the creation is regarded as having been crafted by God to be accessible to man, we have every reason to believe that we may know things truly without knowing them exhaustively. Others may point out that our scheme fails to answer the question of whether there is a smallest unit of material. The notion of finite complexity neutralizes such a concern, because it denies that things are finally defined by *internal*, and largely inaccessible, units and relations. Proceeding under the guidance of the Word of God, believers may rest assured that the mutual relationships between each member of creation, which naturally impress themselves upon us, provide insight into their true nature, encouraging us to pursue ever deeper investigations of them. Finally, a creation that is marked by finite complexity supplies a definite answer to the question of whether there is a smallest metaphysical unit or an infinitely divisible creation. The Holy Spirit is the infinitesimal unity through Whom all created things are related; Who renders all things indefinitely divisible;[3] and Who compels man to increasingly realize His mastery over nature. If the

3. To contend that the Spirit renders the universe infinitely divisible is not necessarily to suggest that there is an infinite number of smaller subatomic particles. In light of the view articulated, "division" is a matter of divorcing a thing from it*self*, which is defined both by internal and external members and relations. Hence, to divorce an atom from a particular elemental construction is, in a sense to divide the atom. Notably, division of this kind is an indispensable element of creative activity according to the Scriptures (Gen 1:6–8; 15:9–11; Exod 14:21; Isa 53:5, 7).

members of creation enter into one another in various ways, and impart to one another characteristics that they would otherwise lack, it is natural to suppose that the infinite Spirit Who is active in creation has His own special effect on the universe, opening it up to unforeseeable (to us) development.

Another false alternative that appeared in Kant is between space-time as either unlimited or self-limited. Kant was correct that there could not be a beginning in time, or a limit in space, which was not preceded by another spatio-temporal moment. He was mistaken, however, to suppose that the universe may not be preceded and limited by a qualitatively different sort of space and time. Rather than leading him to deny that space and time are real, the fact that Kant's alternatives defeat themselves should have led him to the conclusion that each is an analogue which betrays its dependence on an archetypal space-time. With respect to space, we have already seen that the divine attributes co-exist and span out from one another in a fashion that resembles space as we know it. But, the distinguishing feature of divine space is that each and every attribute is (a) contiguous with all of the others, because linked by divine persons who contain them all; and (b) comprehensive of all the others. Notably, the self-contained God is exactly the sort of limit the universe needs if it is to have a real limit at all, since He is self-limited, and not a mere extension of more finite spaces which would only beg for additional limits themselves. With respect to time, we have also observed that every moment of the divine *perichoresis* is marked by a threefold personal order, which bears a similarity to the succession of past, present, and future. Far from being a bare negation of temporality, the divine attribute of "eternality" is best understood as indicating that God is simultaneously past, present, and future with respect to himself, because, in their archetypal/divine expression, the three temporal modes are but different vantage points centered in three co-existent persons.[4] With this point in mind, it is appropriate to speak of a "time" before the beginning of time which is *not* subject to an even earlier succession of finite moments, because it is an eternal where past, present, and future remain distinct even as they are coterminous. Given the failures of the alternative positions, we may say that finite space-time implies the existence of an Absolute Creator as its archetype and only possible limit. Finally, our

4. This view of divine time can be distinguished from, and compared to the views of time offered by Barth and Heidegger. Like Barth and Heidegger, the divine time which we are describing is inseparable from an *intentionality* that exists between persons. Unlike Barth and Heidegger, this intentionality *is not* expressed in temporal forms that fossilize the free creativity from which they spring. To be specific, divine time *is not* chiefly expressed in a Christ event that marries eternity to time, or in the "fallen-ness" of a free being (*sein*) that can only express itself (negatively) in finite contexts (*dasein*). Instead, it is a characteristic of the ontological Trinity as He exists in and for Himself, apart from the temporal universe.

description of God as contiguous and present unto Himself is consistent with the biblical portrait of God as equally near unto every member of his creation (Ps 139:5–12), and capable of interrupting it at any point (Acts 7:56). And, it is natural that the God, Who is past, present, and future unto Himself, should be able to maintain the same threefold perspective with respect to His creation (cf. Isa 46:10, Exod 32:9–14, Matt 24:36; Rev 4:8).

Having observed that the paradoxes of finitude, complexity, spatiality, and temporality are perfectly compatible with a Trinitarian logic, we may also observe that the creation must be marked by the same salient categories, if it is to avoid compromising the Creator-creature distinction. Genesis 1 begins by indicating that the creation was marked by (a) *spatial* distinctions between the two qualitatively different realms of heaven and earth. Without these sorts of distinctions, the creation would be a simple monad, and that is impossible. Additionally, the creation was marked by (b) *temporal* distinctions between the "beginning" and every subsequent moment in time (Gen 1:1, 5, 8, 13, 19, etc.). An atemporal creation would be a self-complete whole, thus compromising the Creator-creature distinction. On the other hand, the creation is replete with complex unities—days, plants, years, birds, beasts, etc.—that persist through time according to (c) set *laws*, and in many instances as (d) *universals* (Gen 1:11–12; 21–22; 24–25). This too is necessary, for otherwise we could not speak of the "creation" as a whole or of its members as developing through time. Indeed, each moment would exist as an unrelated, and thus self-complete, unity, and this is impossible. And although God is the ultimate source of continuity in creation, He cannot be the immediate ground of unity, for then the creation would not be distinct from its Creator as an analogical unity in difference. As a finite *expression* of God's eternal plan at every point, the unity of creation must be located within and secondarily upheld by concrete members of creation. And since only intellectual beings can actively impose and sustain a designated order on the creation in response to God's word, it is necessary to posit the reality of (e) *angelic* beings, who exercise government over the universe. In various degrees (f) living *organisms*—plants and animals—may be active in sustaining themselves as unified species along with angelic aid. In keeping with these distinctions, the Scriptures present the members of the angelic host as either good or evil, and as actively sustaining either harmony (Ps 91:11; 103:20–21; 104:4; Matt 18:10; Heb 1:7; Rev 16:5),[5] or a perverse order

5. In keeping with this conclusion, Calvin explains that the four cherubim who surround the glory-cloud in Ezekiel 1 are endowed with four heads (of a man, lion, bull, eagle) to convey the point that "no creature moves by itself, but that all motions are by the secret instinct of God, therefore each cherub has four heads, as if it were said that angels administer God's empire not in one part of the world only, but, everywhere;

within natural organisms and social structures (Dan 8:31; Matt 8:28, 31; John 12:31; 14:30; Eph 1:21; 2:2). Ideally, the angels are to serve as messengers of that harmony (through their natural and special works) which is exhaustively envisaged and ordained by *the* Word of God. Finally, the unity facilitated by angels and natural organisms cannot function as an end in itself. Messengers and their message must exist for the purpose of eliciting a response from another personal member of creation, namely (g) *man*. As the angelic message is bound up to the natural order of things, the personal response to God's Word in nature must come in the form of a re-organization of it. That is to say, the language/speech of God in nature must be met with the re-creativity of man (Gen 2:19), whose destiny it is to govern nature by imposing new structures upon it, which more deeply reflect the glory of God. As the angels sustain an order that is amiable to man in his infancy (Gal 4:1–5), man must, in his maturity, command the angels in the reorganization of nature. In this way, the creation passes with man from glory to glory (2 Cor 3:18) as the speech of God is returned unto Him by His created image bearers (Gen 1:26–27).

In addition to the systematic unity that is evident between the major features and members of creation, the portrait above distinguishes God, man, and nature as the three primary members of a Christian metaphysic. The primacy of these members does not imply that they lack internal distinctions, or in the latter two, complexity. In a manner that reflects the unity in tri-personality of God, both nature and man are marked by a spirit-matter distinction, each side of which encompasses a multiplicity of members (angels and natural structures; men and their bodies respectively). The primacy of these members consists in the fact that the dynamic of history and the manifold of unforeseen characteristics and orders that it manifests are the product of the dynamic interaction between God, man, and nature in what may be regarded as a cosmic conversation. Furthermore, it is impossible that there should be any more than three primary parties involved in this personal relationship that God sustains to his creation. Any being(s) who were active in sustaining the order of the natural context, through which God and man meet and communicate, would have to be numbered among the angels. Likewise, created responses to divine revelation may only come from man himself, or from the lower orders of creation which fall under his headship and rule (e.g., the animal kingdom). And, to posit another order of persons who are neither messengers of, nor respondents to, the speech of

---

and next, that all creatures are so impelled as if they were joined together with angels themselves." Calvin, *Commentaries*, 11:67. Others have argued that the "elementary principles" mentioned in Galatians and Colossians (Gal 4:3, 9–10, Col 2:8, 20) refer to angelic powers which are active in the natural sphere. See Peake, *Colossians*, 3:522–23.

God, is to envisage an order of persons who are not personally related to their Creator, and this is impossible. Finally, the metaphysical triad that lies at the base of the Christian portrait of reality is an *asymmetrical* vestige of the Trinity, because God Himself exists as a basic member of reality alongside of nature and man. On the other hand, it is appropriate to locate the special economic activity of each of the three divine persons in one of the major parts of reality. As the Father providentially governs the historical course of development between man and nature, he is naturally representative of God in His transcendence. As nature is a rudimentary expression of the eternal harmony that God has foreordained for the creation, it is fitting to associate nature and the angelic host with the defining and revealing activity of the Son. And, as it is incumbent upon man to respond to the direction of the Father through the Son with an obedient and creative manipulation of the natural order, it is correct to regard man as the created center of the Spirit's motivating and individuating work (see fig. 36).

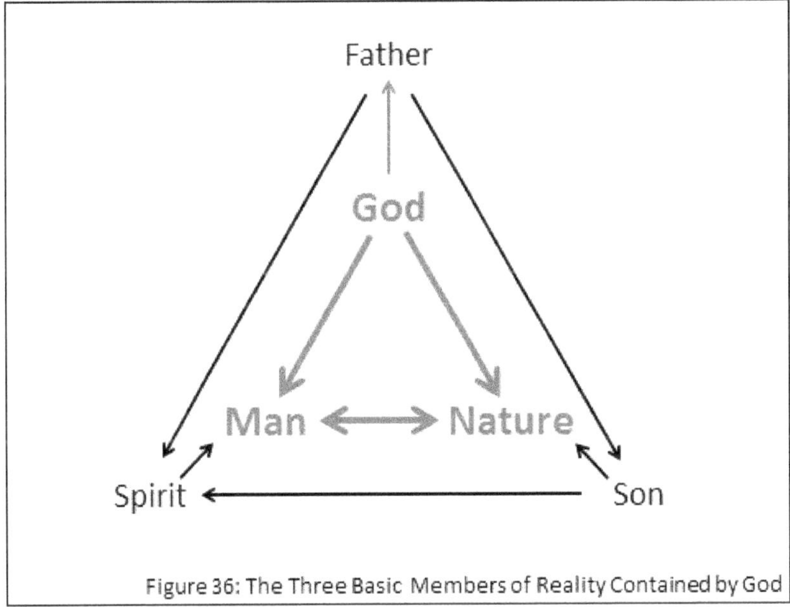

Figure 36: The Three Basic Members of Reality Contained by God

10.3 SUMMARY

At the close of this inquiry into the nature of reality, we may recount the course of our argument. First, the immutability of God proved to imply his limitless capacity to create an extra-divine reality out of nothing, and vice versa, when set within the context of the Trinitarian theology articulated previously. In conjunction with this demonstration, three prominent alternative views of creation, as independent of God, containing God, or partially governed by God, were proven to be self-contradictory because incompatible with God's immutability and infinity. Second, the finitude of creation was proven to imply its limited complexity and vice versa, as the created analogue of an infinite and simple Creator. The major alternatives to this position, that creation may be finite and simple; infinitely composite; or both, have been discredited by the brightest secular philosophers themselves, and betray faulty assumptions about the nature of being, which can only be set aright by the adoption of a Trinitarian perspective. At no point, however, have we suggested anything like a resolution to the fundamental paradoxes of a Christian metaphysic. The poles of the apparent conflicts between (a) divine immutability and creation *ex nihilo*, (b) divine completeness and created additions to his glory, (c) finitude and complexity, etc., have been proven to imply one another, and to receive validation from one and the same Christian system. But, the realities to which they refer are not reducible to simple, self-identical elements that admit for full comprehension, and neither are they finally explicable in terms of themselves. Instead, as they mutually qualify and validate one another, they invite still further qualification from the unforeseen developments of human history. Finally, although our discussion of a Creator-creature metaphysic has come on the heels of our Trinitarian theology, there is a sense in which its major teachings about the analogical relationship between God and man must temporally precede any discussion of theology. The reader will recall that it was necessary for us to cite the likeness and differences between God's Triune nature and that of his creatures from the earliest stages of this systematic exposition.

11

Nature and Man (Epistemology and Ethics)

11.1 VINDICATION OF OBJECTIVE-ANALOGICAL KNOWLEDGE

The Christian doctrine of reality articulated in the second half of the previous chapter can be titled (as a major premise), "analogical Creationism" because the finite members of creation, and the basic dynamic between them, are analogues of a transcendent Trinity. However, this vision of God as the archetypal *context* of creation (1 Kgs 8:27; 2 Chr 2:6; Isa 66:1; 1 Tim 6:16), seems to conflict with the Scriptural teaching that nature in some sense contains God and facilitates communion between him and mankind (Gen 3:8; Exod 40:34–38; 1 Kgs 8:12; John 1:14). Given the particular function of nature as the objective word of God unto mankind, the problem may be reoriented somewhat. Nature does not limit or control the divine being. But, nature, with its many categories and forms—space, time, motion, stars, seas, plants, etc.—is the medium through which divine revelation, as a kind of communication, appears, with the result that nature houses all that *man may know* about God at a given moment in time. In making this point, we are clearly working with a broader notion of "communication," as personal actions and their concrete effects, in addition to the audible/conceptual components of a language. But this qualification only raises the further question of how finite words (whether actions, productions, or speech) can facilitate true and objective knowledge of the infinite Word of God, or, even more, enable us to draw necessary conclusions with respect to how He relates to Himself and/or to the creation. Furthermore, the specification that the natural sphere contains the "knowledge" of God but not God Himself continues to conflict with those passages which indicate that God and even the "fullness of deity" has come to dwell in specific locations in heaven and on earth (1 Chr 13:6; Col 2:9).

Among those who are not prepared to concede that man is entirely ignorant of the infinite God, three positions claim many advocates. Some will grant that God cannot be known exhaustively, but will insist that a finite number of qualities, which appear in creation, may be predicated of God univocally. In this case, nature assists man in developing knowledge of God that is objectively true, but finite. Others, of a mystical persuasion, limit a pure and undefiled knowledge of God to God Himself, with the result that man must be united to God in His act of self-knowledge, if man is to know God at all. Naturally, every attempt to describe these rapturous moments with human speech must fall short of the reality they would aim at describing. Finally, dialectical theologians supply a mediating position, according to which man may only enjoy true knowledge of God when he is united with God in the act of proclaiming/knowing himself through words and acts that are flatly equivocal with God. In this case, man knows the Word of God only as he is taken up by the Word of God, in the act of adopting a fallen creation as a medium through which to express his freedom and love. Allegedly, man knows God as free only as God grants him the opportunity to join him in performing the impossible act of revealing himself. The common assumption in each of the above positions is that a true conception of a given matter must involve a univocal, and thus comprehensive conception of the same. Ironically, unquestioned devotion to this ideal of knowledge leads inevitably to the conclusion that man cannot possess any objective knowledge of God at all. On the first scenario, where man is supposed to have the capacity to possess univocal knowledge of only a few divine attributes, he is implicitly denied any knowledge of that single reality which binds them together. For, the substance of God, which lies below the few attributes and effects of God known to men, never appears in nature. On the second theory, *man* never becomes acquainted with God. Only man as he is transmuted into a member of the divine being Himself is allowed to know God. As a result, it remains impossible to communicate the Word of God unto other men via human speech, or even to prove that a given encounter with God was authentic. The third position inherits the problems of each of the above, as it asserts both, that only God can know God, and, that He, like man, knows Himself only by clothing Himself with finite forms and words that hide and obscure Him. In all three cases, the Creator-creature distinction and/or Creator-creature relation becomes compromised. Man would not know God because the latter is not manifested in the natural sphere on which human reasoning is so thoroughly dependent.

Submission to the Scriptural revelation mentioned at the beginning of this chapter demands the conclusion that God is personally present and revealed, but neither limited nor comprehended by the finite creation. The Christian logician must take this information as an invitation to refine his notion of divine "presence" so that it sheds certain elements of its spatial application, and yet draws from certain features of human experience as its most capable analogue. With respect to humanity, it is clear that to be present in and through a given medium does not always mean to be limited or superseded by the same. In fact, on occasion it means just the opposite. For example, human clothing and homes set clear spatial limitations on the persons whom they contain. And, it is obviously appropriate to speak of persons as present within them. Despite their capacity to comprehend man *spatially*, there is another respect in which man comprehends all of his synthetic contexts *ideally*. For, the latter are both produced and inspired by man, to function as analogues which accurately communicate various details of his constitution and aesthetic tastes. The furniture that man creates and with which he surrounds himself—homes, vehicles, clothing, art, etc.—are media through which his person appears, but they do not finally define him or always spatially contain him (e.g., he may be absent). In fact, the only way to fully appreciate tools' and adornments' intended significance and proper use is through man's direct verbal explanation and interpretation of them, which is a clear indication of his mastery over them. Hence, the products of human ingenuity have the capacity to reveal man, even though they are ultimately defined and limited by the scope of his intellect, and not vice versa.

The pertinent difference between man and God with respect to media of communication is that the former is, at certain points and in various ways, basically limited by an external sphere, while God is not. Quite obviously, only certain spaces in the world are directly fashioned by man, according to the rule of his constitution, while others are not (e.g., the solar system, mountain ranges, etc.). And even those synthetic spaces/constructs which have human creativity as their ideal context are marked by certain natural features which limit man's capacity to reorganize them. Imagination does not allow man to produce just anything. In fact, the human intellect, and indeed the human body have clear spatial limits precisely because man is, first of all, a finite expression of God's creativity.[1] Things are quite different in the

1. Angels, as well, are depicted in Scripture as limited in space (Matt 8:31), time (Matt 24:36), power (Dan 10:13), etc.

case of God. As the Creator of all things, God must be expressed through every member of created reality (Ps 19:1–4; Acts 14:17; Rom 1:18ff.). From this it follows that God cannot be finally located at any definite point in space-time (as if he had a body), or univocally identified with any mental/linguistic concept, because all are but analogical expressions of him. For God, the entire universe must be likened unto a garment, house, or furniture (Ps 104:2; Isa 66:1) through which He is truly present, but only because it is utterly surrounded by Him (1 Kgs 8:27) and expressive of the all-sustaining Word of His Power (Heb 1:3).[2] If God could be univocally identified with any discrete concept, He would have to be comprehended, or "housed" by some superior reality as its finite patron.

Even if an Absolute God's creation must reveal Him, for many, it seems impossible to confirm *that* the universe has a Creator, or to decipher *what* objective information about the Creator the universe supplies. We can infer the size of a man's foot from the size of his shoe because we enjoy direct knowledge of human bodies, and appreciate the manner in which shoes are fitted to human feet as their rule. But, in the case of an Absolute God where we lack any direct insight into His nature, many think that it is impossible to determine whether, and if so, the manner and measure to which any event, phenomenon, creature, virtue, etc., reflects God's mode of being. The solution to this alleged dilemma may appear overly simple: Man knows that created analogues reveal their absolute Creator truly because God utilizes them in His own self-disclosure, and confirms their capacity to reveal Him (John 1:14; 14:6). However, this solution is supported by three observations. First, if the creation relates to God as an analogue to an archetype, it follows that the mode in which divine truth inhabits finite media should not be identical with any phenomenon in man or the world. Thus, only God should be able to finally confirm that He has so revealed Himself to mankind. Second, man's (supposedly direct and univocal) knowledge of nature and himself can only be objectively true and epistemically justified if married to and qualified by an awareness of the sort of God thus described. According to the biblical scheme, the most basic and obvious attribute of created reality is its status as a means of divine communication, that cries out for further interpretation from God, and demands a worshipful response from man (Ps 104). Hence, even in the rudimentary task of measuring, the unbeliever (despite his numerical calculations) wrongly interprets his object, his measurement, and

2. Meredith G. Kline has expounded the biblical theme that God's glory cloud, as a sheath of angels (Deut 33:2), represented something akin to "clothing" that was simultaneously contained by the transcendent God. In turn, the Mosaic Tabernacle and Davidic Temple functioned as a replicas of God's heavenly clothing. Kline, *Images of the Spirit*, 35–56.

his act of measuring as self-existent and self-explanatory phenomena. The unbeliever's incorrect interpretation of his measurements is necessarily unjustifiable because he lacks divine revelation which can confirm that his mind makes genuine contact with reality, that his measurements are, or always will be sufficiently precise to accomplish his ends, etc.[3] Third, the revelation that man may know God truly through created analogues is not simply spoken by God, but implied by our Trinitarian conception of Him. The three persons of the Trinity know themselves truly and exhaustively not by way of direct self-reflection, but by beholding each of the two additional persons, through the mediation of the other. If God expresses himself exhaustively within the dynamic between divine persons from whom he is fundamentally different, it follows that he ought to be able to impart a *finite* knowledge of himself to man through created analogues that are wholly subject to his sovereign governance. Still more the doctrine of the Trinity grants us some insight into *how* created analogues may reveal the transcendent Creator, with whom they are never univocal. As God beholds himself through the dynamic of the divine persons, man must develop a true knowledge of God by (a) allowing the created analogues of God to qualify one another in surprising, and often paradoxical ways, (b) according to the verbal direction of God contained in Scripture. Hence, from a Christian vantage point is must be said that objective theological knowledge must always be analogical, and analogical knowledge of God that is formed in faithful submission to Him must always be objective.

3. This is Van Til's point when he argues that as long as ethical, natural, mathematical, and logical laws "are not based upon the self-sufficient God of Christianity" they are not "objective. For, it is then up to every man to interpret the law for himself without reference to God." CTE, 56. As offensive as this sort of claim might sound, one must, in order to appreciate its significance, engage in a thought experiment about a primal man who was met by no divine revelation whatsoever. On what basis could such an unfortunate person determine that despite his frequent observations, metals may expand and contract sporadically, so that a 1 meter iron rod regularly grows to 1.5 meters? In this case, something in the range of 1–1.5 meters would be an accurate measurement for the same iron rod, while in our (actual) practical contexts admission for such a range of accurate measurement would make for great chaos. Problematically, the man who knows nothing of his or the universe's purpose has no way of determining that the same 1 meter iron rod may not, in many practical contexts, expand to 100 meters. Unless one knows that the universe has been created for the particular purpose of facilitating human endeavors, one cannot rest assured *that* his measurements are sufficiently accurate for his ends, or even define the degree to which a given measurement must be accurate in order to be "true." Stated another way, measurements that (a) something "is x meters long" are always married to the (often unexpressed) claim, that (b) "x" is a sufficiently precise measurement for a given set of ends. It is because the unbeliever has no ground for making the second assertion, that even if his measurements would appear to be identical with that of the believer they are ultimately unjustified and false. For more on the topic of truth and falsity, recall 5.2.4.

If God and man communicate via nature, then clarification of the phenomenon of objective-analogical knowledge will require that we indicate how the three different sources of revelation—God, man, nature—contain, and furnish unique perspectives on one another (see fig. 37).[4] First, natural revelation refers to every member of the created sphere—heaven, earth, land, sea, stars, plants, animals, etc.—with the exception of man. Nature houses *the covenantal communication* between God and man as the two meet at particular locations and times, with the use of audible/written language, natural symbols (e.g., wine, bread, water), etc. As with every house and its furnishings, it is the essence of nature to serve as a medium that communicates information that transcends its mere physical form. It is by the design of God that human reasoning can be described as chewing, emotions as colors (e.g., blue = downcast), dispositions as shapes (square = disagreeable); etc. Likewise, God can speak of Himself as a fire, a bird, or a rushing wind. In fact, a biblical sacramentology rests on God's capacity to invest otherwise mundane elements with special significance, and the promise of supernatural blessing (Gen 2:9; Matt 26:26–29). Ultimately, because the God-man relationship is tied to different languages, events, places, cultures, family relations, etc., man must always develop a "situational" perspective that colors and differentiates his knowledge of reality from that of others.

4. The epistemological perspectives which we list below—situational, existential, and normative—are taken from Frame's, *Doctrine of the Knowledge of God*. In the text mentioned, Frame provides a much fuller discussion than we are able to provide here as to how the three perspectives qualify one another.

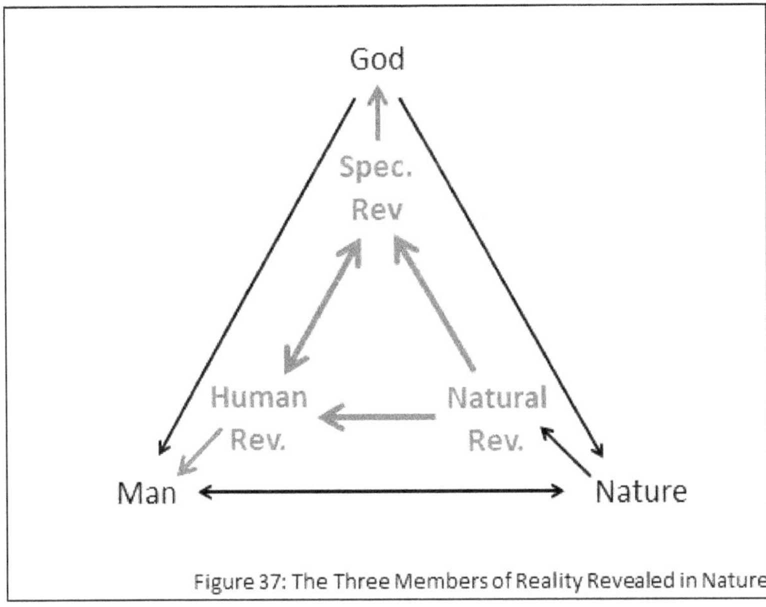

Figure 37: The Three Members of Reality Revealed in Nature

Second, if nature furnishes a real and objective stage for the God-man relationship, man functions as the ideal, purposive context of the God-nature relationship. That is to say, man's creative response to the natural universe reveals depths of meaning, potentialities, and purposes which nature cannot pronounce or realize on its own. By the same right, as man's mastery over nature enables him to enter into personal, mutually loving relationships with God and other men, he is an active participant in revealing and realizing the eternal purposes of God (Matt 22:37–39). Anthropological revelation, then, refers not primarily to the physical constitution of man, but to the synthetic forms that he freely imposes on the universe and human societies via different trades, arts, legal codes, political constitutions, worship practices, etc. Accordingly, all knowledge of reality is marked by an "existential" perspective, or subjective response that is not identical to the reality before man, but which draws out its unforeseen potentialities.

Third, special revelation supplies information that could not be discovered by natural or anthropological revelation alone, because it is supplied by the divine, archetypal context of creation. Special revelation is itself marked by a threefold form. First, it consists of miraculous interventions that suspend the normal course of events, and unmistakably reveal the transcendent governor of reality as their author. Second, special revelations are theophanies in the sense that they are accompanied by human language (and often, a glorified human form), to communicate that the divine speaker is man's archetypal Creator. And third, special revelation involves a prophetic interpretation of some feature of reality. Special revelation enables man to develop a "normative" perspective on reality that is sufficiently clear and all-encompassing (because authored by the absolute God), to function as a standard by which to judge and mediate between the opinions of men.[5]

Most important for our purposes is the fact that when any two of the sources of revelation are paired together and distinguished from the third, we can fruitfully describe the basic content of man's objective-analogical knowledge of nature, man, and God. In short, (a) God and man are alike, over against nature, in their free capacity to manipulate nature and to interpret it with linguistic clarity; (b) God and nature are similar, over against man, in their objective character and capacity to limit human freedom and subjectivity;[6] and (c) man and nature are unified, over against God, in their finitude, and thus in their capacity to be studied directly (whether empirically or introspectively). According to this scheme, each member of reality is defined by capacities that it shares with one of the other two, and by an indispensable function that it alone can perform with respect to the other two, as a result of its discontinuities with them. Man is a *free-finite* person, who, precisely because his intellect is restricted (and cannot create *ex nihilo*), must apply his energies to the natural world in a worshipful way, thereby realizing its intended purpose and bringing glory to God. Nature is a *finite-restraining* sphere, which, precisely because it cannot freely alter itself, is marked by stable and objective spheres and phenomena through which

5. Here we are echoing John Frame's insight that the normative perspective is a *human* vantage point that is based on, but never perfectly identical with the written Word of God. Recall 8.3.2.

6. At this juncture, it is appropriate to point out an important difference between our Van Tillian presentation of the Christian worldview and the similar, but different portrait supplied by Francis Schaeffer. On the one hand, because man is a *finite* being, Schaeffer represents him as residing with the rest of creation on one side of an impassible chasm opposite of the *infinite* God. On the other hand, because man is *personal*, Schaeffer represents man as residing with God on one side of a chasm opposite of the *impersonal* creation. Schaeffer, *The God Who is There*, 101–5; *Escape from Reason*, 221–24. From the Van Tillian vantage point supplied in the text, Schaeffer's representation is incomplete and as such potentially misleading. In its current form, Schaeffer's description lends itself to the scholastic view that there is something like a scale of being with God at the top, matter at the bottom, and man somewhere in between. Schaeffer ought to have understood that there is a sense in which God and the impersonal creation are alike with respect to the objective guidance and limitations that they place upon humanity. In this case, not only does man reside between God and nature, shaping the later as he worships the former, but nature resides between God and man, inspiring and instructing the latter to worship the former. In keeping with our observations, William Edgar argues that Schaeffer was overly optimistic about fallen man's capacity to reason properly about divine revelation, and under appreciative of the clarity of God's revelation from within and without. Edgar, "Two Christian Warriors," 64–70.

man may meet God, to which God may liken Himself. Finally, God is the *free-restraining* person, Who cannot be located directly in nature because He is an infinite self-contained being. Due to the universality of His personal presence, God differs fundamentally from man and nature. But, for the same reason, God is inescapably known by all men as (a) the transcendent person through Whom we enjoy harmonious contact with the universe, and (b) the ultimate object of knowledge, of whom all of reality is revelatory (see fig. 38). Hence, with respect to the positive content of our knowledge of God, we may say that it generally embraces all of the implications of both personhood (Ps 94:9) and of limiting/objective contexts as we know them (Acts 17:28), with the exception of the conclusions along the lines that God cannot be the one because he is the other.[7] Furthermore, the discontinuities between God and finite persons/contexts do not consign believers to conceiving God with the use of negative qualifications—e.g., God is a person, and yet one who is *not corporeal, not limited by time, etc.* Instead, the differences between God and creation imply a positive conception of God as the lone personal being who is capable of serving as the ultimate object and facilitator of human knowledge. Indeed, such a God is necessarily very near and even familiar unto us all.

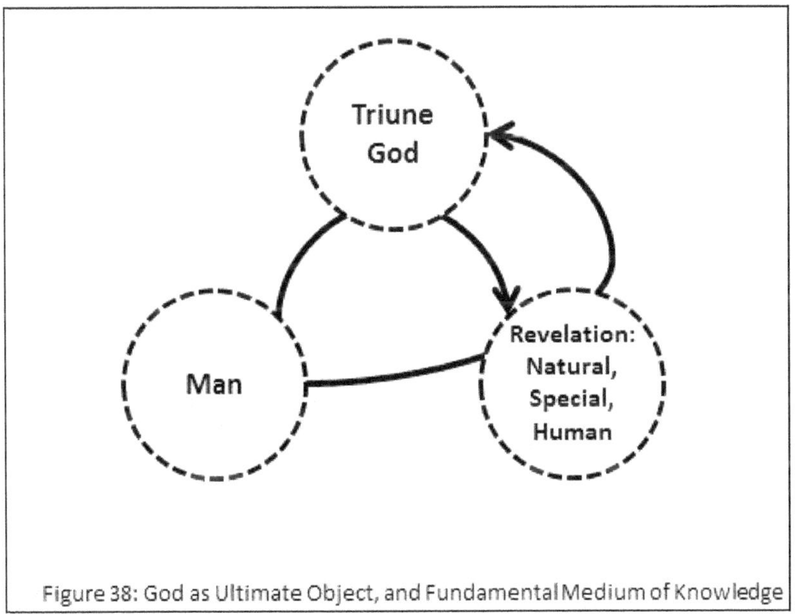

Figure 38: God as Ultimate Object, and Fundamental Medium of Knowledge

7. James Anderson takes a similar position. Recall 8.3.5.

11.2 VINDICATION OF COMPATIBILISM

The ubiquitous presence of God within the natural sphere from which he is distinct, warrants the description of the Christian worldview as "Trinitarian Sacramentalism." However, the description of man in the previous vindication, as contributing a re-creative activity to the creation, poses several challenges to the worldview articulated up to this point. In order to exert a creative effort toward the natural world of which he is a member, man must in many respects be a free, self-determinative being whose manipulations of nature cannot themselves be the products of natural processes. Indeed, freedom would seem to be one of the characteristics that distinguish man as the chief created image of God (Gen 1:26ff.), and which renders him fit to rule over the natural realm. Various scriptures warrant this conclusion, such as those where man is held ethically responsible for choosing one course of conduct over another (Deut 30:19; Isa 65:12; 66:4). Nevertheless, all of this raises the question of how man can be free like unto his Creator, without undermining our earlier observation that God is ubiquitously present in creation precisely because He controls the created sphere in exhaustive detail (cf. Gen 50:20; Ps 139:16; Prov 16:1, 33; Amos 3:6; Luke 22:22). It would seem that one must choose between the biblical portrait of man as free (because the image of God), or the biblical portrait of God as utterly sovereign. And yet, because both doctrines have been proven to be essential components of the Christian worldview, rejection of either or both would fatally undermine the whole system, and represent nothing like a feasible alternative to unbelieving thought.

Among the many responses to the predicament just described, three will occupy our attention. First, many have attempted to *resolve* the apparent conflict by defining freedom in a fashion that does not require any modification of our mechanical conceptions of determinism. Freedom, we are told, is a matter of pursuing one's deepest desires apart from any external restraint. In this case, all free choices are at once determined by the forces of nature and nurture, which are themselves determined by the supervening will of God. Problems abound with this theory. Man would not be in any respect an image of the Triune God Who spoke the worlds into existence, apart from some necessitating force within or without. On the other hand, if this doctrine of natural determinism were taken as the model for God's freedom, then it would follow that God's decision to create was necessitated by His nature, with the result that the finite creation would be granted a semi-divine status as God's necessary counterpart. Second, others attempt to *resolve* the conflict by embracing an indeterminist notion of freedom, and recasting divine sovereignty in a fashion that poses no threat to it. Freedom, first of all, is taken as a capacity to actively part ways with one's natural dispositions and desires in a thoroughly mysterious and even inexplicable fashion. God only determines the course of history in the sense that he has an intended goal for it, and is able to react accordingly to man's choices in a way that His ultimate aims are not frustrated. Ironically, the indeterminist theory makes no advance in securing human responsibility, or in rendering man the master of his own destiny. For, if human choices were basically undetermined then man would be reduced to a series of expressions that were linked together by nothing but chance. The murderer could not be held responsible for his crimes as if they were the expressions of a consistently bad character, nor would any measure of correction supply us with reason to believe that he would be any less likely to act violently in the future. Furthermore, if the same sort of freedom were ascribed to God, we would have no reason to expect that God could or would realize His intended aims for creation, for He might, in a thoroughly indeterminist fashion, choose to abandon them at some future point.[8] The third position, of which there are countless permutations, proposes a compromise, and advances a notion of bounded freedom. Apparently, free choice is limited to a definite range of options over which man has no control, while the decision for the one over the other is finally undetermined by any prior desire or disposition. This theory inherits all of the problems associated with both of the above-mentioned alternatives. Once again, human freedom does not, in any sense, reflect God's creative capacity to express Himself in a new and unforeseen light. Additionally, there is no ground for holding man responsible for choosing evil over good, since his pursuit of the one over the other is not expressive of a self-consistent character.

In each of the above positions, the chief obstruction to discerning that, in fact, human freedom implies divine determinism and vice versa, is the presumption that the sort of efficient causation between man and natural objects, or between natural objects themselves, is the only acceptable model for how God directs his human creation. In the event that this sort of determination is denied of God, it is supposed that its lone alternative is to view man as undetermined in a libertarian fashion, which cannot help but to reduce to him to a thoroughly irrational being. Two considerations supplied by the Christian worldview thus articulated are sufficient to redirect our reasoning on this matter, one with respect to humanity, and the other with respect to God. On the side of humanity, we must recall that the natural universe exists as a context which was designed for man to master as he

8. It is this sort of God to Whom the atheist critic of presuppositionalism, Michael Martin, objects. Recall 4.4.7.

worshipfully pursued his mission before God. As the special image of the Triune Creator in his ruling capacity, it must first of all be observed that the manner in which man moves himself cannot be reduced to the manner in which man moves natural objects, or the parts of a machine move one another. The sort of efficient causality evident between sunlight and plant growth, wind and the movement of a sailboat, or even man and the movement of a baseball bat, are, at best, analogues of man's mode of self-direction. Indeed, the human person is like an efficient cause of his own choices, because they proceed from him as their author. This is not to deny that the natural universe inspires man to act by exciting his senses and physical desires (e.g., his sense of hunger, beauty, desire for the opposite sex, etc.). It is only to assert that man is free in the sense that his choices, with respect to which, how, when, and why to pursue created ends, are ultimately birthed from the subject and not by his desired objects. However, unlike mechanical cause-effect relationships, the human person is both the subject and the object of his own self-determination. In a creative fashion that is foreign to natural processes, man is able to form visions for how to manipulate the world around him that advance beyond any direct instruction from nature itself, or the mere sum of the information already within him. The products of human reasoning are metaphorically described as "conceptions," which, like human offspring, are significantly like and unlike the parents who gave birth to them (Ps 7:14; Isa 59:4). Likewise, the choices which are birthed from human reasoning are free because they both proceed from, and, in turn, add greater depths of definition to, their authors.

Although it is impossible to comprehend the process at work in human volition, at least three distinct components are identifiable. First, man is able to generate visions of multiple courses of action as viable and desirable responses to his environment. Second, in addition to feeling active in envisaging different ends for themselves, people experience another sort of sovereignty in actively electing one end over the others. It is not as though a man is simply pulled toward a most desirable end as a metal is irresistibly pulled toward the strongest magnetic force, or a chariot is drawn in a direction by horses. Instead, he is able to actively advocate for any number of the ends before him in such a way that he acts as his own conversation partner (Prov 3:15; 26:12). Third, as a projected self advocates for a given alternative even as he functions as the judge which evaluates the case for one over the other, appeal is implicitly made to a third sort of self who functions as a standard which resides above them both. This third "self" is an ideal or a law whom the other two must make it their aim to realize, even if they offer distinct but equally valid interpretations of him. The result of this process is a free and self-determined choice. Supposing that one has freely chosen to marry rather than to remain a bachelor, it is common and indeed correct to gather that the pre-married man is the source or cause of the now manifest decision. But (and this is where the matter offends) the married man, as he is represented by the pre-married man in the quarters of his own deliberation, has in a certain respect elicited the choice for marriage from the bachelor (Jas 1:14). That is to say, the final effect of man's deliberation is, in mysterious fashion, the cause of the cause. Notably, the question of how the human person so relates to himself as subject, object, and ideal falls beyond his own comprehension. If, at any point in his reasoning, man stops to consider who is actively persuading, who he is trying to convince, and what sort of person he is aiming to be, he will discover that in different respects they are all one self. It has occurred to some to associate the various paths that he presents to himself with the (a) desires inspired by his senses/feelings, the judge between them with the (b) will, and the ideals to be pursued with the (c) intellect. Yet, even with these sorts of distinctions, he cannot hold at the forefront of his mind the depths and complexity of all three at once, nor even comprehend the nature of the dynamic between them. Nothing is more evident than that man is not a self-produced, or even, for that matter, a self-sustained, individual (Ps 100:3). Man knows that he is not the sole cause of his choices, that his choices are not the sole determiners of his character, and that his ideal self is not his own creation. This observation anticipates a second, equally important point, that for all of the mystery that surrounds it, human freedom necessitates divine determination as its ground.

Before turning to consider why God must determine the course of human freedom, it is pertinent to observe that individual self-determination is best represented by, and indeed inseparable from, the manner in which distinct persons compel one another to action. Before developing this point, it is important to note that we are neither offering a proof for, nor a final clarification of individual self-direction by calling attention to its likeness to the influence that persons exert upon one another. The purpose is first to presuppose and then to vindicate the "Trinitarian sacramentalist" epistemology described earlier, by observing how human freedom appears truly though not exhaustively in the house of nature. To begin, interpersonal persuasion is normally classed among the arts, rather than the sciences. That is to say, its distinct character and the processes belonging to it are recognizable, even though the persons involved in it are not subject to the sorts of quantifiable analysis or manipulation at work in the natural sciences (e.g., physics, chemistry, biology, etc.). When human persons enter into a discussion, a marriage relationship, a friendship, etc., they draw out characteristics, and inspire new perspectives from one another, which are unique and unforeseen, but at the same time consistent with persons they were beforehand. The logic of development in individual people, cultures, and world history is of a very different nature than that of, say, crystal formation, because causes at work in each do not produce obvious and anticipatable effects, as is common with simple chemical patterns. Importantly, the distinguishing feature of personal cause-effect relationships is not that they are defective and sometimes fail. It is that they are super-productive in the sense that the effects, which they inspire in their members, are often richer than one could even begin to anticipate. At other times, the graciousness of one individual provokes an unanticipated, negative response from others. In the same way, when we speak of human freedom, we have in mind the creative capacity to exceed the boundaries of the information and impulses that one has within, by birthing choices that are at once like and unlike the subject from whom they proceed.

In addition to serving as a capable analogue of individual freedom, it is equally true that interpersonal relationships are indispensable to individual freedom. In fact, individual persons cannot be self-directing except as they exist in a threefold interpersonal relationship, consisting of an authority, a subordinate, and a companion (see fig. 39), which inform his own consciousness as an ideal, a subject, and an object within himself. First, the ideal self, which enables man to adjudicate between various courses of action, must be modeled after a concrete person who is originally distinct from and external to each individual. The reason for this is simple: man cannot be the Creator of his own ideal self (Ps 100:3). For, the possession of an ideal self is the prerequisite to the threefold self-movement which we call freedom. If man were originally a simple, faceless individual whose ideal self is but a projection from his original emptiness, or modeled after impersonal nature, he would never be able to engage in the internal conversation from which free creativity flows. The only sort of person who might function as an archetypal "self," who imparts to man a vision of an ideal "self" to be pursued, is the self-contained Trinity, whose life is directed by, through, and to persons, and never by impersonal principles. Initially, the ideal self with whom man identifies must come to him in the form of a law to be obeyed.[9] However, that man was to embody the law and in turn present a vision of the ideal for humanity unto others, is evident from man's responsibility to impart his God-given sense of self-identity and purpose to children (Gen 18:19) made in his image (Gen 5:1–3).

9. Hodge makes a congenial point when he considers the question, "What is the law which prescribes to man what he ought to be and to do?" His answer is that "Law, as it reveals itself in the conscience, implies a law-giver, a being of whose will it is the expression, and who has the power and the purpose to enforce all its demands." In Hodge's estimation, if the law were our own subjective creation, then we might feel "ashamed" for breaking it, but we could not feel anything like moral "guilt." Hodge, *Systematic*, 2:182.

Throughout redemptive history, prophets especially serve as the mouthpiece of God in communicating through word and deed new information concerning God's purposes for humanity (Exod 4:16; 7:1; 2 Kgs 6:21; Luke 10:22; John 1:18). Second, although any number of objects can and do excite man to creative action, the chief created object of his affection must be a human companion in the form of brothers, friends, and, initially, a female spouse (Gen. 2:22–23). This is not to deny that human freedom ought to be directed to pleasures such as the consumption of food, exploration, manipulation of nature, sex, etc. (Deut 14:26). But, if man were to mistake his chief end as interaction with impersonal material he would be reduced to a slave rather than a master of nature. This is most evident in addictions of various kinds (Prov 23:29–35), but it is the essence of every from of idolatry (Ps 135:15–18). In relation to nature, man could never be self-sacrificial (Mark 10:45) in the fullest sense of giving all the depths that his person has to offer unto a significant other. Nor could he enter into an interpersonal order that reflected the Trinity (Lev 19:2). Hence, human freedom consists, not only in the fact that each individual is able to envisage and advocate multiple courses for himself, but in the exercise of that freedom by and toward other persons. It is no surprise then that the entirety of the law should be bound up in utilizing one's creativity in the loving service of one's brother and of God (Mark 12:29) as represented by the human authorities whom God has set in place (John 17:3; Prov 24:21; Exod 20:12). Nor is it odd that God's law is presented as the impetus to free self-development and creativity (John 8:28, 32; Jas 1:25).

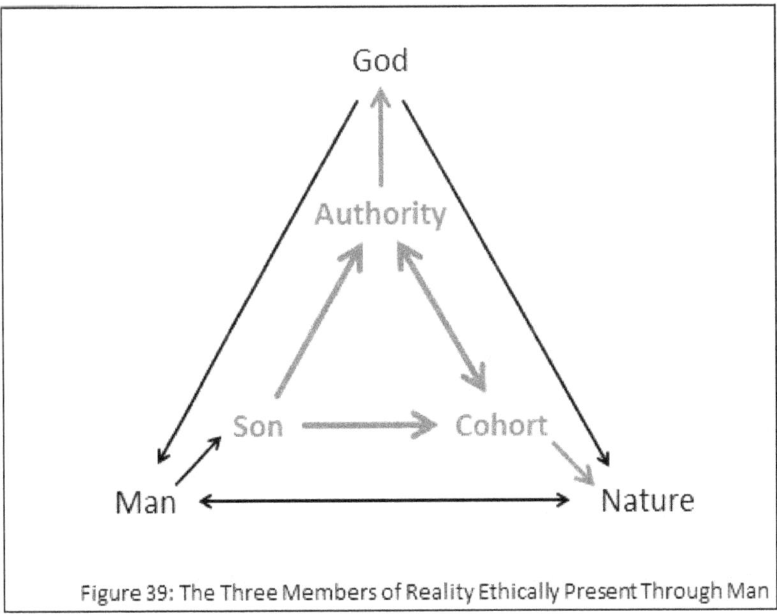

Figure 39: The Three Members of Reality Ethically Present Through Man

Having observed that persons determine themselves and influence one another in a manner quite different from how they shape and direct impersonal objects, many have supposed that it represents a regressive tendency among the Reformed to describe God as predestining, rather than personally persuading, men unto salvation. For, such language harkens back to those impersonal relationships which man sustains to the natural sphere, rather the different sorts of persuasion and inspiration at work between men.[10] Ironically, this pervasive sentiment represents a retreat rather than an advance on analogical and personalist thinking. For, it makes the mistakes of (a) *identifying* God's sovereign governance of man with one sort of human relationship to the exclusion of other equally relevant ones, and (b) rendering it unclear how God's determination of man is at once like and unlike (an analogue to) the cause-effect relationships that appear in creation. First, as God and man are both *persons* it is perfectly appropriate to infer that as men act on one another in manner that draws out their individuality and freedom, so also God moves men in a manner that establishes and seals their personal freedom. But, there is another relevant likeness between God and man. Both are *craftsmen*. In this case, the manner in which man effectively controls the products of his creativity must be allowed to inform us as to how God controls his human creatures. In the case of man-made structures (houses, vehicles, machines, political states), the initial form imparted by man determines their subsequent outworking to the degree that its material component *did not* possess a prior teleology of its own. In other words, a clockmaker controls the mechanism of his clock to a greater degree than a statesman controls the course of his political organization, because the former deals with relatively simple metals, and the latter deals with relatively complex persons. With this point in mind, we must conclude that God's control over human history is exhaustive, because man and indeed every detail of the universe has been fashioned by him *ex nihilo*. Second, when both of these points are taken together, two inferences must be rejected as erroneous and out of accord with analogical reasoning. One cannot conclude on the basis of the first comparison, that God's determination of human freedom is in some measure uncertain and insubordinate to his control, because these are characteristics of inter-human determination. On the basis of the second comparison, we must conclude that God-man determination differs from man-man determination in the specific respect

10. To state the argument in Martin Buber's terms, a position like that represented in the Westminster Standards with respect to divine sovereignty and predestination reduces the Creator-creature bond to an "I-it" relationship as opposed to an "I-thou" relationship. Buber, *I and Thou*, 51ff. At its roots, this position is deeply Kantian and is characteristic of too many neo-orthodox and Barthian theologians to be listed.

that the former is efficient in a manner comparable to man-nature determination. It is equally invalid to conclude from the second comparison that God must be guilty for the evil actions of his human creatures, since human engineers are held responsible for the accidental, and especially intentional, harms produced by his structures and machines (e.g., when human engineers construct unstable bridges, produce computer viruses, etc.). On the basis of the first comparison, we must conclude that God-man determination differs from man-nature determination in the specific respect that, in a manner comparable to interpersonal determination, man is free and thus responsible for his other-inspired choices.

Should one object to this bit of analogical reasoning on the basis that it yields the self-contradictory notion of God-determined freedom, we must respond that just the opposite is true. Human freedom and divine sovereignty imply one another. Human freedom implies the governance of a foreign power, who is at once person-affirming and yet perfectly efficient in sustaining man as a mysterious unity whose choices follow from, and at the same time realize, a single complex self. On the other hand, God's transcendent determination of creation implies the existence of a free analogue, for only then can the creation reveal something of the inter-personal determination at work in the Triune Godhead. Furthermore, the doctrine of the Trinity is emblematic of the fact that personal choices which are sovereignly determined by the divine person are nevertheless free. For, each person of the Trinity exhaustively determines the choices of the other two, but in such a way that the freedom and individuality of each is confirmed rather than compromised. Hence, God's sovereign governance of human decisions implies the freedom and significance of the latter. Should one reject this notion of God-determined freedom, and the analogical logic on which it is based, he must be confronted with the fact that he must at the same time forfeit any standard for distinguishing freedom from determination, truth from error, and right from wrong. In this case, he cannot intelligibly proffer his views, or critique the Christian position, without at the very same time proving those views to be false.

11.3 SUMMARY

At this point, we may recap the transcendentally vindicated conclusions reached in the previous two proofs, and consider how they present created reality as developing through a reciprocal historical relationship between man and nature under the auspices of God. In our discussion of nature, we argued that human knowledge can only be objective if it is mediated through a natural sphere in which the personal nature of God is truly and really present, even though not exhaustively. There, it became clear that the essence of analogy is to convey objective information about the Creator, while verbal interpretation of analogical reality, supplied by God, is indispensable to forming an objective understanding of analogy itself. Confidence that God, much less any finite person, can communicate information via symbols and language can only be maintained if God has revealed Himself verbally, and through natural and anthropological analogues which cry out for and confirm His verbal interpretations of them. Following this discussion of nature, we observed that man is free precisely because he is self-determinative in a manner that is foreign to the natural creation, and yet determined by the Triune God as his archetype. As man and God appear in nature as objects of revelation, God and nature are represented by the human roles of leader and companion, respectively. In this case, as nature facilitates deeper communion between God and man, man actively realizes God's ends for human relationship, and so enhances the depth of the revelation that appears in the natural sphere. All of nature is represented by man's personal companion (bride), and all of humanity must be contained by nature as its proper abode. As nature colors all the revelation of God to humanity, so man determines (either positively or negatively) God's disposition (of pleasure or wrath) toward nature (Num 35:34; Rom 8:20–21). In Scripture, the advance toward deeper relationship between man and nature, man and man, and man and God appears in a covenantal history that extends from Adam to Christ, and unto the last day. Finally, although we have not given direct attention to epistemological or ethical matters until the chapter at hand, it should be evident that all of our reasoning has, from the beginning, heeded the covenantal responsibility to submit to the revelation of God at every point.

12

Fall and Salvation (Hamartiology and Soteriology)

12.1 VINDICATION OF GOOD-INSPIRED EVIL

As the universe is driven unto its end by both the free creativity of man, and the overarching determination of God, the Christian worldview can be characterized as "Trinitarian compatibilism." Perhaps the most daunting challenge to this position, when taken as a major premise, is the pervasive reality of sin and evil, to which natural and special revelation give ample testimony (Gen 6:5; Eccl 8:11; Jer 17:9; Rom 3:9–18). God can and does determine all of the free acts of men in such a way that men remain responsible for their choices. And even if God ordains the wicked choices of men for purposes which are thoroughly good (Gen 50:20; Acts 2:22–24), man's original pursuit of sin poses a unique problem. For, according to the Christian worldview, as it has been expounded thus far, and according to the testimony of Scripture, the universe was created thoroughly good, without any natural evil or disharmony in it (Gen 1:31; 1 Tim 4:4), and no inclination toward evil in the hearts of men (Eccl 7:29). If the proverb is true that a "good tree cannot bear bad fruit" (Matt 7:18; cf. 12:33) it would seem that the personal members of creation—human and angelic—cannot be the authors of sin and evil. Because evil certainly does exist, it would seem necessary to conclude that God is the primary cause of evil, either in the form of a natural disorder that would frustrate man and compel him to sin, or an original lust within his personal creations that militated against their higher interests. But, if God is the author of evil[1] in this immediate and culpable sense, then he cannot be trusted, the biblical testimony about him is false (Hab 1:13; Jas 1:13; 1 John 1:4), and thus, the Christian worldview has no advantage over its non-Christian alternatives.

Three basic theodicies have appeared regularly among philosophers and Christian theologians alike. First, some have argued that evil is an uncreated anti-divine principle which God has the power to limit and restrain but not to finally expunge from reality. This view cannot be reconciled with the Christian system thus articulated, because it deprives God of His status as a self-contained Creator to whom all other things relate as creations. Practically speaking, this view calls into question the very distinction between good and evil, as both are equally original, and neither has a metaphysical advantage over the other, casting doubt on every divine promise since God's nemesis may successfully frustrate and pervert his administration of them. Second, others grant that God is the primary cause of what appears to us as "evil," but exonerate Him from guilt on the hypothesis that, in truth, every created evil is a natural and necessary part of a good order of things. Of course, it is only from a divine perspective that the most dastardly crimes of humanity are transmuted into components of an all-encompassing "good." If the first position was guilty of granting God and evil an identical metaphysical status, as opposite but equally eternal principles, this second position is guilty of creating such a vast dichotomy between divine goodness as we know it and goodness as known to God, that it effectively renders the latter unknowable. In contrast to an analogical theory where God and man are similar and dissimilar at every point, this theory asserts that God and man are incomparable from the side of man, but flatly identical from the vantage point of God. A third group has taken the position that God can be regarded as the cause of evil, but absolved of any guilt associated with it, so long as evil is construed as a "negation" of that order which He originally bestowed on creation. In this case, God may cause evil to exist indirectly, by withdrawing his restraining grace from His personal creatures, with the result that their lower desires and lusts are allowed to revolt against their better knowledge with respect to how to serve God. God, it is thought, may be the *deficient* cause of sin (by withdrawing his restraint), while man is the *efficient* cause of his sin, and alone worthy of condemnation. Nevertheless, this theory inherits all of the problems of the previous two. Implicitly,

1. John Frame is correct to observe that the phrase "author of evil" is ambiguous, and need not necessarily suggest that God is responsible or guilty for its existence. But, as Frame also notes, the phrase has traditionally been taken to carry with it the negative connotation of culpability for sin. It is in this latter, traditional sense that we use it here. Frame, *Doctrine of God*, 174–75.

God is guilty for creating man with a natural inclination to sin. And, an anti-divine principle alongside of God disallowed Him from producing free creatures with no inclination to sin.

Meditation on the commitments involved in our position up until this point requires the conclusion that sin was self-inspired by personal members of creation that were thoroughly good, in such a way that man is the author of evil and not God, even though God foreordained for evil to come to pass. In fact, it must be argued that a flawless creation, which is set on a historical course to realize greater depths of goodness, implies the capacity to sin on the part of man, and the reality of sin implies the concrete historical character of man. The acceptability of this proposed thesis, however, can only be appreciated when good and evil are not misunderstood as simple, self-identical qualities. Prior to the Fall, Adam's character was righteous, but only in such a manner that it was set on a course to realize greater depths of righteousness, and finally to attain the reward of ethical maturity. The individual stages, the whole course of his development, and the reward of human righteousness, are all good in their own distinct fashion, but only as they are related to one another. In all of this, man is the image of the Triune God, Whose goodness bursts forth eternally from, through, and to Himself, in the personal order and mutual respect between the Father, the Son, and the Holy Spirit. Nevertheless, man differs from God in that the beginning, the course, and the end of His righteous character appear at different times in history, with qualities that can only appear in a temporal succession. At the beginning, man was created pure and righteous in such a way that he was without sin, but was able to sin. Throughout the course of his life it was man's mission to pursue a sinless character that was ever more responsive to God's covenantal demands. At the end of his ethical life, man's obedience was to finally be sealed with an ethical character that could not sin (Matt 25:46; Rom 8:29). If man were simply endowed with a righteous character that *was not* sinful, but was under no obligation to actively pursue greater depths of righteousness, then his goodness would not transcend that of a plant. Man would never be able to reflect the Triune God's intentionality in possessing the moral attributes that belong to Him. But, if man were under an obligation to pursue righteousness and to resist sin, apart from the endowment of an originally righteous character, then the fulfillment of his obligation would be the product of chance (rather than indicative of a good character). And if man's ethical obligations carried with them no promise of final vindication, pursuit of good would differ not at all from the pursuit of evil, since both would be marked by a perpetual sort of dissatisfaction and restlessness that is uncharacteristic of God. Finally, if righteousness consisted solely in the reward of eternal life that was conferred upon men without regard for their character, or subsequent conduct, it would be grossly arbitrary, and fail to reflect the Glory of the Spirit, which follows from and accompanies the Holy order and acts of the Father and the Son.

In light of the complex and historical character of human righteousness, it is not difficult to discern that ethical maturity implies a prior ability to sin, and that man's initial ability to pursue good or evil and to triumph in resisting the latter is consequential for the consummation of his righteousness. This does not mean that man was imperfect in his infancy. Quite the contrary, his ability to actively resist an evil of which he was capable rendered him perfectly fit for the ethical task before him. Indeed, an initial creation that was fully rewarded with all of the benefits belonging to a persistently righteous life and character would be most imperfect for the reasons mentioned above. Significantly, the complex and historical character of human righteousness also sheds light on how man in his infancy, although predisposed to obedience, could form a notion of evil and culpably pursue it as if it were good. First, man would have formed an idea of evil as a negative counterpart to his knowledge of the good course prescribed to him in the law. From God's positive command to reproduce, Adam would have possessed some concept of sins of omission delineating a failure to pursue his God-given ends. From the negative command to refrain from touching the forbidden tree, Adam would have developed an idea of sins of commission, or active transgressions of God-given boundaries. Second, man's capacity to culpably deceive himself that these sins were good is inseparable from his capacity to think abstractly, which, in this context, involves treating parts of God's law and stages of personal development as good in and of themselves. Specifically with reference to the Tree of Good and Evil, it is evident that at some future point Adam would have been granted access to the tree. God implies just as much by expressly declaring that all of the trees of the garden were good for food and to be at Adam's disposal (Gen 1:29; 2:9). And later Scripture affirms that the ability to discern the difference between good and evil is a positive characteristic of mature wisdom (Deut 1:39; Isa 7:16; 2 Sam 14:17; 1 Kgs 3:7–9). The important point about these observations is that the application, and even the very form, of the law must grow and change as man matures through obedience to it. What this means is that a character which was good and appropriate at one time may not be for another, and a commandment that is good and true in one context may very well be obsolete in another. This does not mean that God's law is arbitrary at any point. The law of God is consistent in a historical fashion, so that the earlier parts anticipate the latter as their goal, while the latter always look back to the former as their foundation. Nevertheless, at the root of all sinful thought lies a tendency to treat some portion of God's law as self-complete, and, thus, as in conflict with the other details of God's law. This allows man to appeal to something good (a part of God's law) in order to justify sinning (breaking God's law). Looked at from another angle, man justifies shirking his explicit duties (refraining from the tree) on the basis that he is pursuing an end that is good in and of itself, regardless of how it is obtained (the reward of mature wisdom). Third, on this account, sin does not consist solely in forming abstract ideas. Man' imaginative ability allows him to divorce images and attributes from their natural contexts and to combine them in fictional forms (e.g., the form of a man and the form of a horse are combined in a centaur) that are perfectly appropriate for producing creative stories. Sin consists not only in developing abstract ideas, but in allowing them to guide one's reasoning as if they were self-complete perspectives on reality.[2] It involves negating certain details of God's revelation in favor of others. Insofar as undesirable revelation continues to present itself in a natural and special form, it must be perverted so that man may evade its clear demands. Sinful thinking manifests itself in a self-destructive course of history, and a sinful society that is a mockery of the one intended for mankind by God (cf. Gen 4:1–24).[3]

Although it remains mysterious as to how man moved from treating the whole of the law as his standard, to pitting parts of God's truth against itself, the biblical account of the Fall is abundantly clear that it was not accidental. Instead, it indicates that, on a corporate level, sin originated from created persons who had all of the information they needed to resist it. Reserving the question of how sin originated in the Serpent/Satan for later, it is clear from the Genesis account that he not only persuaded man to sin by setting forth a lie, but by drawing him down a course of abstract reasoning that allowed the same lie to function as a rule of thought. Satan begins by assuming the form of a serpent whom Adam and Eve would have had no reason to fear, given their God-given position over the animals. Rather than address Adam directly, who had been charged with the responsibility of guarding the garden (Gen 2:15), Satan confronts his helpmate, Eve. His carefully worded question for Eve was whether God had set forth a blanket prohibition from eating from the trees of the garden (Gen 3:1). Of course, God had not. God had explicitly said that all fruit was good for food (Gen 1:29; 2:9), and Eve recalls that only one tree carried with it the penalty of death for touching it. Satan responds with a direct contradiction of God's

2. Frame draws similar distinctions with respect to abstract reasoning. Frame, *Doctrine of the Knowledge of God*, 169–91.

3. Evaluation of this sinful life and history, in contrast to that which has been graciously bestowed on believers by God, is the chief interest of the second book of Augustine's *City of God*. Augustine, *City of God*, 429–1091.

claim, and the reasoning at work behind it is a rudimentary example of abstract thinking. If fruit is really good for food, then every particular piece of fruit may be enjoyed as food, and that is that. Any additional claim that it is also good, or perhaps better for the time being as an educational device, to be peered at, but not eaten, represents an obvious contradiction of the earlier, and of course, complete interpretation of the goodness of fruit. In fact, it can easily be discarded as a lie. Satan appealed to something good—the law of God—as a ground for disobeying the law of God (cf. Matt 4:1–11). But, in order to support his argument, Satan had to reinterpret God in light of it, casting Him as forbidding the tree out of a selfish desire to prevent Eve from attaining the sort of wisdom and maturity necessary for governing the creation. As dominion was a good that man was slated to possess, Satan appealed to something good as the attainment for something evil. The description of Eve as observing that the tree "was good for food," "delightful to the eyes," and "desirable to make one wise," indicates that she had taken in the heart of Satan's argument, and was prepared to test it (Gen 3:6). As sin calls into question the propriety of the law of God itself, by offering a false alternative to it, it might seem that some neutral standard (e.g., an experiment) must be allowed to establish one law as true over another. Cunningly, however, the Serpent seems to have been aware that the willingness to test God and his law already represents a decision in favor of oneself and of one's experience, as divorced from God, as the ultimate standard of truth. Nevertheless, God does not immediately descend in judgment on the Serpent after his lie, or even on Eve for her active transgression of the prohibition. It is not until Adam judged Eve's act as good, by repeating it himself, that sin was consummated. The point in this seems to be that sin conceived, and even sin executed, are not the same thing as the mature adoption of sin as one's true ideal.[4] Hence, although Satan is subsequently called the Father of lies (John 8:44), and Eve is described as having been deceived (2 Cor 11:3; 1 Tim 2:14), Adam is held responsible as the one through whom sin entered the world (Rom 5:12, 15, 16–17; 1 Cor 15:22; Hos 6:7.)

Many able commentators have found the Genesis account of the Fall to be strangely silent with respect to the origins of the devil's sin, and even

4. Seizing on distinctions developed later in the Pentateuch, James Jordan proposes that Adam's sin should be regarded as "high-handed" (cf. Num 15:30–31; Exod 21:14; Heb 10:26–28) whereas, "Eve's sin was one of being led astray, a 'sin of ignorance'" (cf. Lev 4:2, 22, 27; 5:15, 18). In light of Jordan's argument that high-handed sin, if confessed reverts to the status of a redeemable offense (Lev 6:1–7), there would seem to have been the possibility that Adam and Eve could have averted something of the penalty for sin if Adam would have responded to God's judgment-inquiry (Gen 3:8–13) by humbly taking responsibility for his trespass, rather than by proudly blaming God for creating Eve. James B. Jordan, "Liturgical Man, Liturgical Woman," n.p.

unclear as to how Adam and Eve found the devil's lie compelling. However, the correlativity between individuals as ideal, objective, and subjective selves, and communities as authorities, sons, and companions, should lead us to appreciate that the account supplies us with an objective portrait of how each individual culpably succumbed to sin. The basic point is that if Satan is the first false authority, Eve the first sinful companion, and Adam the first son of God to judge sin as good, then the interaction between the three must be expressive of the internal course of capitulation to sin in each individual. Application of this perspective to the devil's fall into sin is sufficient to shed some light on the lure of sin in individual persons, despite its finally nebulous character.

Although the devil was the first to utter a word of deception unto mankind, he was also the first to actively pursue his own *self*-deception. Indeed, the scriptural details about Satan's sin enable us to appreciate that his self-deception was only consummated in his deception of others. To begin, it is evident that the angelic host was created before man, perhaps with the highest heaven itself (which apparently was not empty like the earth—Gen 1:1–2), as they praised God when He formed the earth (Job 38:7). This means that, prior to the production of man, Satan and the angels had a self-conception as the most dignified governors of creation, under the leadership of God. Furthermore, that the angels were created with a natural inclination to accept their duty is evident from God's declaration on the sixth day, that all things were "very good" (Gen 1:31). Yet, with the disclosure that man was destined to have priority over the angels as the highest created image of God, it would be incumbent on the angels to allow God's plan to refine their earlier self-conception. Undoubtedly, the angels always apprehended an idea of sin as disobedience. But, with the challenge to grow by taking on a new task as servants to mankind, an opportunity to reason sinfully arose. The angels could recast disobedience (to their new obligations) as a lawful pursuit of their former obligations/status, so long as the latter were taken to be perfectly good in and of itself rather than as a stage on a God-given trajectory. In addition to a handful of Scriptures that imply that Satan's fall was motivated out of envy of his former position, and hostility to the man who would commandeer it (1 Tim 3:6; Rev 12:4), the fact that Satan casts God as forbidding Eve to touch the tree out of a selfishness is perhaps an even stronger indicator of his envy. After all, where would Satan have gotten the idea of selfishness if not from his own corrupt heart? Likewise, the best indicator of how Satan became enmeshed in his own false perspective is supplied by his deception of Adam through Eve. After all, what confidence could Satan have had that his method of deceiving man would be effective, if he were not already smitten by it firsthand? How then did Satan deceive man? As we have seen, in addition to confronting him with a lie, he invited Adam's helpmate to test its validity. In the same way, Satan's act of deception must have been preceded by a mental reconnaissance, a premeditation on sin in which he became a voyeur of himself as he carried out his own murderous experiment on mankind (cf. Jas 1:14). However, just as the sin of Eve was not consummated until it was judged good and reciprocated by Adam, neither Satan's vision of a false ideal, nor his premeditation on how to realize it, was complete, until he judged his schemes good by carrying them out (cf. Jas 1:15). As both Eve and Adam could have and should have resisted Satan's lie at its very core, before it birthed sin and death in the human race, so Satan should have slayed his first notion of sin by standing upon his better knowledge of God's Word (as Jesus later would—Matt 4:1–11). Eve's impressionability, and especially Adam's silence and passivity, depict the disposition that every individual sinner takes toward himself, prior to advancing into new depths of sin. It matters not that sin has, from the beginning, been proposed to men from without, and that all of Adam's posterity are born with sinful ideals (Ps 50:5; 58:3–4). The fact is that they follow the devil's lead by inventing new kinds of evil (Rom 1:30).

Satan's capitulation to a course of sin in and through himself rendered him a sinner. But, only by successfully leading humanity down the same path, could the full effect of sin, namely, death (Jas 1:15), work its way through the entire creation. Prior to Eve's disobedience, both she and her husband should have served as witnesses, along with the Holy Spirit, against the Deceiver (Deut 17:6; 19:15; Matt 18:16). Had they resisted the devil, they would have advanced toward maturity, whereby the revelational testimony of nature and the depths of personal communion between man and man, man and nature, and man and God, would have only been enhanced. But, with the Fall of Adam and Eve, Satan became not only a sinner, but the Father of lies, with a perverse son (fallen man), and an adulterous bride (fallen woman) to reflect his own fallen self (2 Tim 2:26), as a sinful law, subject, and object. This trio appears throughout the remainder of the biblical story (Rev 19:20—20:2, the dragon, the beast, and the false prophet/the harlot) as a chord of three strands, which is not easily broken (Eccl 4:12). To the perverse mind, nature testifies to itself as a hostile beast, governed by an equally hellacious god. Ethically, the roles normally occupied by men (authority, son, cohort) are replaced by roles expressive of strife and enmity. Godly leaders are replaced by tyrants who rebel against God's law, brothers and companions are replaced by murderers (Gen 4:1–24), and the sons of men testify to themselves that they are deeply perverted (see fig. 40). Nevertheless, the creation continues to bear witness to the existence and longsuffering of God, because man's frustration with his broken state, not to mention the relative normalcy of the world that allows him to meditate on that frustration, shines forth the revelation of the true

God (Ps 19:1–4; Rom 1:18ff.). Although man suppresses the truth wherever he encounters it, his capacity to so react to divine revelation in accord with his sinful aims, and to persist in that rebellion for a time, is a persistent witness of the image of God within and the goodness and wisdom of God from without. And yet, the image of God is so tarnished that man cannot of himself elect to pursue God once again. Prior to the Fall, man could isolate a part of himself in such a way that it inspired a deviation from his true self. After the Fall, man is hostile to God at the core of his being, and nature manifests the wrath of God at every point. Hence, although he continues to possess a creative freedom (to do greater wickedness) there is no unblemished part of his character which might inspire him to pursue God (Jer 13:23).

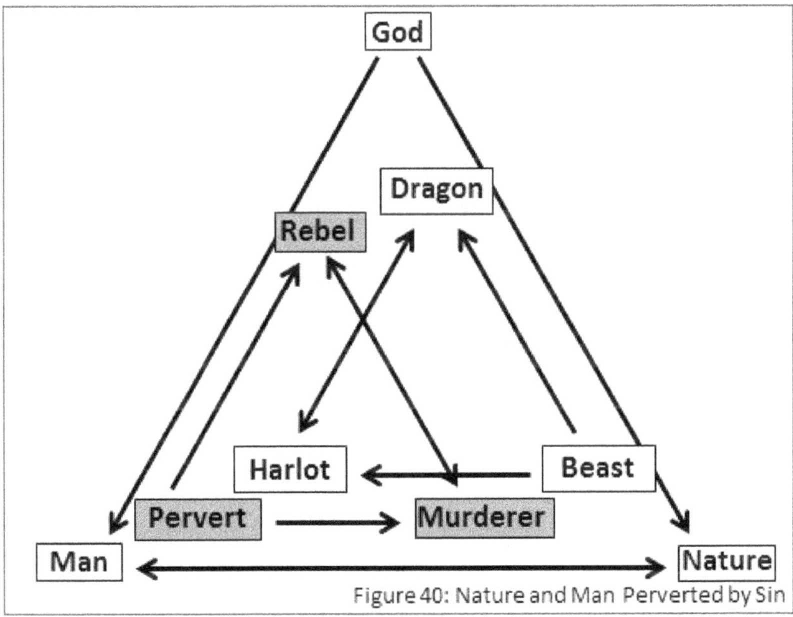

Figure 40: Nature and Man Perverted by Sin

According to our account, historical goodness implies the ability to sin as a prerequisite to the pursuit of an eternal reward, and vice versa. In fact, those who are finally glorified are impervious to sin, because they have completed a historical development where their "selves" are challenged to develop into something new, and during which, they might pit the law of God against itself. And yet, objections persist. Some will remind us of the proverb that a good character cannot bear evil fruit (Matt 7:18). However, this truth spoken by Christ may be affirmed as altogether true with respect to mankind at the time when Christ was speaking. It is of the essence of the position articulated that man, and with him the very nature of his freedom, should take on new characteristics over time. After the Fall, the wicked are established in their sin in such a way that they cannot bear good fruit, and the redeemed are made slaves of righteousness in such a way that any persistence of sin must be accredited to an old and foreign nature (Rom 7:17–20). Others might argue that if the ability to sin is characteristic of goodness, then God himself must be subject to temptation. The exact opposite conclusion, however, is demanded by the position supplied above. Man's original ability to sin is directly related to his capacity for growth and passivity in relation to himself. The Trinity, on the other hand, is eternally grown (complete), and utterly active in relation to himself through the Father, the Son, and the Spirit, with the result that he is impervious to temptation and sin (Jas 1:13; 2 Tim 2:13; Heb 6:18). Nevertheless, for all of this, many will maintain the conviction that there is something basically mysterious, and indeed unbelievable, about the idea that thoroughly good creatures could willfully sin. To this sentiment we can have no objection at all, except that to take it as grounds for denying the biblical account is itself exactly the sort of sinful thinking prescribed to man by the devil. Satan advises that if a matter as described by God is not perfectly lucid to you, then proceed on the points of information that are clear, and receive ample testimony from your own experience. In other words proceed on sight, not on faith. The problem with this sort of thinking is that when taken as self-referential, the world of sight and our basic axioms defeat themselves. For example, the axiom that good creatures cannot have birthed wicked choices will drive one to one of three conclusions. Evil is either (a) an uncreated anti-divine force; (b) directly created by God; or (c) somehow both. And yet, we have seen that on each of these scenarios the distinction between good and evil is either so magnified that the former cannot claim mastery or superiority over the latter, or, it is effectively dissolved so that the two cannot be distinguished from one another. In either case, one forfeits the right to speak of good or evil, to insist that one *ought* to draw any conclusion from a set of evidence, and/or to detract from the biblical message on the basis that its teaching is faulty. Ironically, then, objections to the biblical account of the Fall indirectly testify to its truth. For, they are the fruits of man-made worldviews of which the advocates, no matter how brilliant, refuse to accept the most basic implications. Sinfully motivated objections to divine revelation are every bit as unbelievable and irrational as the self-defeating vantage point adopted by man at the Fall. In one respect, all of our reasoning up until this point has confirmed this same basic insight, as the Christian position has repeatedly been set against three sorts of self-defeating abstractions: (a) those that created unwarranted dichotomies; (b) those that erase meaningful distinctions; or (c) those that do both.

12.2 VINDICATION OF THE SINLESS HUMANITY OF JESUS CHRIST

In this final vindication, we return to the gospel message with which our inquiry began. Through the stages of reflection represented above, the Christian worldview might be described as one marked by "Creator-creature hostility," as the latter has fallen and incurred the judgment of the former by his own willful disobedience. And yet, for the servants of Jesus Christ, nothing could be more certain than that such hostility does not define the final condition of mankind before God. The gospel is that God the Son took on human flesh so that as one person with two distinct natures, he might atone for his people's sins with a death of superabundant worth, and then empower them to usher in the kingdom of God through the Holy Spirit. This climactic solution to man's plight, however, poses its own problems for several of the other established conclusions, which we have reached thus far. Even if the previous doctrines of nature and compatibilism validate the idea that God could be locally present in a human body, and that the human and the divine natures could be distinct and yet in perfect harmony in the same person, other problems remain. Perhaps most daunting, is the idea that a Holy God could unite Himself with a corrupt human race, and that race could, in turn benefit from the righteous obedience of a foreign power. It would seem that if Jesus' humanity were genuine, then the Son's humanity must be sinful and repulsive to a Holy God. And, if Jesus' deity is genuine, then His obedience unto death cannot aid man in realizing his God-given ideal, and His temptation and suffering must have been a mere show (Jas 1:13). What renders this sort of argument significant is that it appeals to Scriptural premises that have performed an indispensable function in the logic thus described. God cannot look upon sin with pleasure much less become a sinner (Ps 5:4–5; 11:5; 45:7). Men are ubiquitously sinful (Rom 3:23; Ps 14; 53), and from their very birth (Ps 51:5; 58:3). And, man's ethical realization is reached through his own active pursuit of God (Ps 15; 24:3–5; Jas 1:12). Taken together, the premises seem to demand that Jesus cannot be man if He is truly God, and He cannot be God if He is truly man.

The basic alternatives to the traditional doctrine of Christ are known well. First, some argue that Jesus was strictly a human teacher, whose mission was to persuade men to pursue a sort of righteousness and salvation on their own, and who was only recast as a sinless God several generations after his death. Second, others argue that Jesus was God, and that His sublime perfection was incompatible with a sullied human race, and conclude that He merely appeared to be human. And third, many others, in their attempts to retain something of Jesus' humanity and deity, have developed positions that confuse the two natures in such a way that He is neither true man nor true God. Whether one begins with a Jesus Who was God and then forfeited many divine attributes in the Incarnation, or with a Jesus Who was human but somehow attained a semi-divine status, the basic problem is the same. Such heresies confuse the Creator-creature distinction and undermine the entirety of the Christian worldview. If God can shed any attribute that belongs to Him as God, then He is not the immutable and trustworthy Authority Whom men need in order to navigate their lives. And, if man can, in any measure, acquire the ontological attributes of deity then, once again, "God" must be viewed as a time-bound substance, which is subject to change. The first two positions may be able to retain a Creator-creature distinction, but they too are self-destructive abstractions. For, on their terms, man and God have not, and/or need not, be reconciled in a faithful covenant relationship. So long as they have not be reunited thus, God can only be known as a cold and distant force (Acts 17:23). And man will only think of himself in autonomous, self-sufficient, and indeed self-righteous terms (Isa 64:6). Such men will suffer as much frustration trying to justify their beliefs as they will trying to justify themselves.

When set against the backdrop of the doctrines of nature, man, and sin articulated thus far, the apparently conflicting elements of an orthodox Christology prove to imply one another. In order to appreciate this point, we must begin with a brief digression concerning universals, and particularly "human nature." A universal is not simply an abstract set of qualities that are shared by multiple particulars. It is a definite history and trajectory, as well as the concrete interaction between particulars that are marked by similar and congenial attributes. Living creatures are particularly concrete because they are active in producing the different particulars that will aid in the realization of the species as a whole. But man is unique in that he both generates the diverse members of the human race, and does so in a self-conscious fashion. (Angels are self-conscious, but they do not reproduce.) Although both universals and particulars are concrete and subject to development, the two differ in that the former are more stable and consistent, and the latter are more novel and diverse. With this general understanding of universals in mind, a problem with the idea of a fallen and self-destructive humanity immediately presents itself. A race of perverted individuals, rebellious leaders, and murderous brothers has no future when left to itself (Prov 8:36; Matt 16:25; Rom 1:24–32), and therefore cannot be a universal in the sense described. Hence, before the objection can be raised as to how Jesus could have assumed a nature that was continuous with that of fallen man, one must come to an understanding of how fallen humanity was at all able to persist as a universal. In fact, to answer the latter question is to effectively answer the first. The first man, Adam, who succumbed to sin, was only able to persist after the Fall for one moment without incurring the depths of God's righteous wrath, because he was succored by the common grace of the second, new Adam to come. For, the only way that fallen humanity could have a concrete kingdom and history of its own, is through the restraining power of a true humanity, and a true future to whom it was destined to give way. For this reason, the old man/nature is, in many respects, a false and self-conflicted universal, as it is but a parasite on a foreign history, which is Christ. Therefore, the only sort of humanity that the Son of God could assume if he were to possess continuity with the race of men before him, would be a pure and undefiled humanity that defined a new future for man, and allowed the fallen race to be continuous with itself. In saying this, we must not be misunderstood as holding to the pre-existence of Christ's humanity. For, it is as an unmerited, and by many, unreciprocated "future," that Christ holds all things together (Col 1:18).

The conclusion demanded by our prior commitments was that Christ must have redefined the human nature that he assumed so that he was a member of the human race, and yet free from its degradation and guilt. Further reflection yields the conclusion that, insofar as Jesus was able to redefine and restore humanity, he must have been fully God, and insofar as that restorative work was not simply effected immediately (via the Incarnation), but only through his life, death, resurrection, and ascension, he must have been fully human. In taking up the first point, it is necessary to recall the scope of Adam's original duty before God. It was incumbent on Adam to obey the law as defined by God's image within him, and as defined by special revelation. His mission was not simply to obey, but to mature by expending his spirit in the task of sharing the creation with his bride (and vice versa), and returning it to God in a more glorious form. Man would be a finite conduit through which the eternal Spirit of God increasingly glorified the Father and the Son. Nature (which includes man as an object of revelation) would increasingly reflect the divine harmony between the Father and the Spirit, centered in the Son. In this way, man and creation would pass from earlier stages of glory, through self-sacrifice, to higher stages of empowerment by the Spirit and revelation from the Logos. If there is to be any future for man, there must be a *restoration* of a God-glorifying image in man through the intervention of a power that is utterly foreign to man. Notably, this foreign power cannot have come in the form of a natural son of Adam, who was kept from sin merely by God's sovereign decree. For, in this case, God would have to grant new life to at least one human person apart from any atoning sacrifice, and so deny the righteous stipulations that follow from His own character (Prov 17:15). Furthermore, were God in the business of saving men by fiat, such would not only call into question the need for atonement, it would conflict with a biblical ethic of self-realization. It is equally impossible that the Savior could be a sinless man who lacked any natural connection to the human race. Rather than function as humanity's redeemer, he would, at best, be its replacement. He might be charged with the responsibility to guard a new bride from the onslaughts of sin, but he would be powerless to adopt the children of Adam as his bride and purge her wicked heart from sin. He could not offer himself for her as a substitutionary sacrifice. It is man's natural duty to pursue God self-sacrificially, with the result that he would have nothing to offer in her stead (Ps 49:7–9). In contrast, the orthodox position preserves God's righteous self-consistency, and establishes Christ's capacity to save. Instead of simply ordaining that an exceptional son of Adam should be free from sin, God the Son assumes human flesh in such a way that His *prior* holiness and imperviousness to sin renders His humanity spotless and pure. In turn, the death of this same Jesus is able to cover an immeasurable multitude of sins, because it was not simply an act of human obedience, but of the eternal God Who was under no natural obligation to take up the plight of man (John 10:18). Whatever guilt and displeasure the Father had with mankind, it was finally taken away, because outweighed by the unsearchable glory of God the eternal Son, Who bore it on behalf of His people.

The ethical perfection of Christ, although originating in his eternal deity, was equally dependent on his own active pursuit of the will of God in the flesh. As Jesus was righteous from conception, it was incumbent on him to pursue more mature obedience, and he would finally have to be sanctified through death, before being rewarded with a resurrected life at the right hand of the Father. As an inherently holy God, Jesus could be, and as a true man Jesus needed to be, vivified by the Spirit at His conception. But, he was also rewarded with greater Spirit-empowerment at various stages in his ministry (e.g., at his baptism, before/after his temptation, the transfiguration, the resurrection, the ascension) for faithfully and patiently pursuing his God-given ends. In this way, Christ fulfilled the whole duty of mankind, and took on three different sorts of ministries with respect to it. First, in his adult ministry, Christ appears as a prophet announcing, and in his ministry exercising the power of, a new humanity that has been reconciled to God and vested with authority to rule under Him. Jesus is the new, and indeed ultimate, special revelation, through Whom men must re-interpret themselves and all of reality. Second, in his death, especially, Christ functions as a priest Who sanctifies His bride, the church, by dying in her stead at the culmination of a life of perfect obedience. In the cross, Jesus offers up His human spirit (Matt 27:50), and with it the Holy Spirit (Heb 7:16; 9:14) by

Whom His spirit was empowered, only to receive Him back again in the resurrection with a newfound authority to pour Him out on all flesh. Post-Pentecost history then provides men with an objective picture of the sort of power and worth that characterized the life Jesus offered up to God in His atoning death. Third, Jesus is resurrected in the power of the Spirit as the Victor over death and as the human Son of God, who is alone worthy to sit at the right hand of God, and to exercise authority in the earth. In contrast to the rebel, murderer, and pervert that humanity had become, Jesus became a holy Prophet, Priest, and King.

A presumption that must be turned on its head in the present context is that, because Jesus' divine nature was impervious to sin, the progress in righteousness just mentioned, not to mention His temptation and suffering, must have been fictitious. In truth, the very opposite conclusion is required. Precisely because Jesus was God, His temptation by the devil, and His agony at the cross were, in their gravity, beyond comparison to that of all other men. For, at Adam's fall the devil appealed to a barely developed sense of worthiness to partake of a blessing that had been put off by God for a time, and to a sense of justice that it was unfair for God to keep him from it. How much more, then, was there opportunity for Satan to appeal to the God-man's sense of value and self-worth, in suggesting that He make for Himself some food, or test the Father's devotion to Him, or to grasp hold of the kingdoms of the world to which no being in heaven or earth was ever more rightfully entitled than Himself? And who could look at the task of bearing the guilt of all sin and experiencing the Father's wrath with a more nauseating horror then the man who loved God's eternal holiness above all other things (since He was one with God) and shared his opinion more than any other, concerning just how dark, detestable, and damnable sin must be? Jesus' human awareness, that divine victory was certain, could itself have been torturous in certain ways, since it had been delayed for many years, and because He would have been most of all aware of the suffering through which it would have to be accomplished. At this point, the impious will object that this answer presupposes both the distinction between, and communion of, the two natures of Christ in the very manner that the objection was slated to undermine. But, the point is that doctrines which must be true, and which can be true *according to the demands of the Christian system*, certainly are true. Should the unbeliever set down as a principle that a personal union between the divine and human natures is impossible, we must respond that any such claim is a self-defeating farce. For, man can have no certainty about any principle whatsoever apart from reconciliation to the omniscient Creator in a manner that is alone achieved by the Christ of Scripture, and can only be so achieved, if Christ is so defined.

An important feature of Christ's redemption of the *human race*, is that it cannot be a holistic redemption unless some individuals are excepted from it. Too many, supposing that they are securing the dignity of Christ's work as a *redeemer* have flirted with, or capitulated to, the universalist position, and in spite of their better intentions, reduced him to a mere *reformer*. Such a view can only retrogress on the point already established, that sin is not a mere negation, or a vaporous aura, or an unwanted disposition to which men occasionally succumb. It is not the sort of thing that Jesus can help us to overcome or avoid as a mere counselor. Sin is a concrete history, community, and "man," who are bent on destroying themselves and others. And this enemy is not merely an external devil. The human race would have had an external enemy and that alone, only if Adam and Eve had resisted the Serpent, and slayed him not more than one breath after his first lie. In the actual course of events, men themselves became children of the devil and enemies to the purposes of God (John 8:41, 44; 1 John 3:8, 10). As a result, humanity is enslaved, not simply to the devil (John 12:31; 2 Cor 4:4), but to a sinful man/community who dwells within them individually and corporately (Rom 6:6; Gal 5:24; Eph 4:22; Col 3:9; 2 Thess 2:3). As a result, the fractured and self-conflicted human race must be saved from a real enemy within itself. Just as sinful aberrations from man's Christ-defined character must be purged by the fire of the Spirit (1 Cor 3:12–15), so some individuals are divided from the true humanity by the preaching of the Word (2 Cor 2:15–16).[5] In fact, the latter comprise that reprobate community from which God's people are not fully free until the rebellious are definitively judged and separated from the people of God (Matt 25:41–46). This is why texts which describe Christ's salvation *of the world*, often speak of it in the very same breath as a salvation *from the world* (Isa 66:23–24; Rev 5:9–10; 1 John 4:14, 5:4). And yet, the efficacy of Christ's saving work does supply believers with confidence in a progressive, "eschatological universalism"[6]

5. Kuyper likewise argued, "how wrong it is to suppose that the real stem of humanity shall be lost, and that merely an aggregate of elect individuals shall be saved. On the contrary, it should be confessed that in hell there is only an aggregate of lost individuals, who were cut off from the stem of humanity, while humanity as an *organic whole* is saved, and as such form the body of Christ." Kuyper, *Encyclopedia*, 113.

6. B. B. Warfield coined the phrase, "eschatological universalist" in his explanation of several Johannine texts (1 John 2:2; John 3:16) that speak of the universal effect of Christ's salvific work. Warfield explains that Jesus, "came into the world because of love to save the world, in order that he might save the world, and he actually saves the world. Where the expositors have gone astray is in not perceiving that this salvation of the world was not conceived by John—any more than salvation of the individual—as accomplishing itself all at once. Jesus came to save the world, and the world will through him be saved; at the end of the day he will have a saved world to present to his father." And yet, Warfield is quite clear that from his doctrine of an eschatologically saved

where humanity at large is redeemed, just before it is finally glorified and returned by Christ unto the Father (1 Cor 15:23–28; Matt 13:31–32; Dan 2:44; Rev 20:4).

A final consideration is that Christ's redeeming work does not deprive man of the opportunity to actively participate in the pursuit of holiness unto the glory of God. The work of Christ certainly does usher in an alteration to the original paradigm for the progression of man, according to which he: (a) is not sinful, (b) will not sin, and (c) cannot sin. Christ does not simply restore believers to a status where they are (a) not sinful. Instead, Christ is the first fruits and head of that eschatological, righteous, and resurrected humanity that cannot sin. The gospel is that the future has burst into the present with a saving power and authority in which believers may partake, via union with Christ. On the basis of the fact that Christ is fully victorious over sin, and believers share in the victory, they are set free from bondage to sin in order that they may pursue righteousness (Eph 2:10; Phil 2:12; Titus 2:14; 1 John 5:2–3), and through preaching and discipleship, usher in that eschatological order promised by God. For, as king, Christ does not simply issue a new law, but pours out His life giving Spirit, so that men may be governed by the mind of Christ in this life, even though not with final perfection. Hence, the gracious salvation bestowed by Christ is not simply compatible with the ethic of self-realization that we have described, but is the only guarantee for a fallen race that they will not fall short of their goal. For, they know that "he who began a good work in you will perfect it" (Phil 1:6). On the basis of this same assurance, generations of believers may rest assured that they will be able to advance in their mastery and understanding of every facet of nature and revelation. In fact, such motivation and confidence has been at work in the present study from its inception.

12.3 SUMMARY

The course of our argumentation with respect to evil and salvation can be recounted briefly here. Evil, we have argued, must be the self-inspired product of an originally good creature. If evil were created by God, uncreated, or a pure negation then either the distinction between good and evil, or the primacy of the former over the latter would be lost altogether. In order to exist as the really problematic thing that it is, and yet remain under the sovereign control of God, evil must be the product of retrogressive and abstract

world, "it does not follow that . . . no single man of all who ever lived in the world omitted [from salvation]." Warfield, "Jesus Christ the Propitiation for the Whole World," *Shorter Works*, 2:176, 174. Cf. Kuiper, *For Whom Did Christ Die?* 95–100.

thinking on the part of men and angels, which births a perverted order and history within the created sphere. In fact, the capacity for sin and evil on the part of men and angels is implied by their historical duty to realize a mature ethical consciousness (analogous to that of the Trinity), which in turn implies the capacity to sin against God's command to refrain from it. After having fallen, man's only hope for redemption lies in a God-given Savior. Christologies which present the Savior as strictly human, strictly divine, or a hybrid of both undermine the notion of reconciliation between man and God by (a) confusing the Creator-creature distinction, and/or (b) failing to account for how the Christ achieves a re-union between the two. On our account, the genuine humanity of the Savior implies that he should be sinless, in a manner that thoroughly reflects his divine nature. For, the continuity and prolonged history of the fallen human race has always presupposed the renewed humanity of Christ (as a future reality) as a parasite presupposes a host. By the same right, the pure deity of Jesus Christ implies the genuine frailty of his humanity, and renders infinitely painful the prospect of bearing the guilt of human sin. Hence, both the paradoxes of evil and of the dual nature of the Christian Savior are vindicated by virtue of the fact that their poles mutually imply one another, and are equally indispensable to the Christian system of truth. In fact, the renewed consciousness bestowed by Christ which we explicitly identify at the end of our argument has, at the same time, been clearly presupposed by every step throughout.

12.4 CONCLUSION TO PART IV

The foregoing argument may be construed as the unfolding of a single transcendental proof for a particular interpretation of biblical Christianity. At its modest beginnings, the Christian system was construed in "covenantal personalist" terms, and vindicated on the basis that man must persist in vital relationship to an omniscient Creator/Redeemer in order to know anything at all. Every subsequent step in the argument involved grasping how those features of the Christian system which seem to conflict with each other from a fallen vantage point actually imply one another, and function together as paradoxical truths that both confirm and enhance the less mature (but still true and faithful) perspective with which we began. In short, we have engaged in a sustained exercise of reasoning by implication in the manner bequeathed to us by Van Til. As for the unbelieving logic which caused us to fret at the veracity of theological paradox in the first place, it has been turned on its head as the handmaiden of an impersonalist metaphysic that fatally undermines itself at every turn. Whether dealing with questions of God, reality, knowledge, ethics, sin, or salvation, unbelieving thought cannot rise above the three self-defeating alternatives of an empty unity, a chaotic diversity, or an unhappy marriage of the two.

Conclusion

The path toward the vindication of Christian paradox has been neither short nor simple. Drawing primary inspiration from Cornelius Van Til, it was necessary to locate his perspective historically, as arising from different emphases prevalent at Old Princeton and the Free University of Amsterdam, and among absolute idealist philosophers. The upshot of this threefold source of inspiration was an appreciation for objectively valid apologetics; antithesis between Christian and non-Christian worldviews; and the exaltation of central Christian paradoxes as illuminative of reality. To be specific, Van Til held that the Trinity represents the perfect ideal of truth and harmony, because no quality or activity of the three members falls outside of the auspices of the single "whole," and no feature of the one Deity fails to be perfectly reflected in each of the three persons. Such a God is exhaustively *self-contained*. Supposing that this specially revealed Creator exists, it follows that he must enjoy perfect comprehension and control of his own robust life and existence, as well as of all other things. Furthermore, if we take God's diagnosis of sin seriously, it becomes clear that the only reason why people do not immediately acknowledge God as the transcendent ground of harmony in the universe, and as the immanent source of assurance that they are intelligibly related to reality, is because they are guilty of suppressing God's voice in all things. Naturally, fallen men will vehemently deny that they know God in any culpable way, and may even denounce the Trinity as a contradiction. Nevertheless, Van Til believes that Christianity can be definitively proven (with its paradoxes left fully intact) by virtue of the fact that the unbeliever cannot justify his own confidence that his reasoning about these matters (or any matter) penetrates the actual nature of reality without appealing to the very sort of God Whom he opposes. On the other hand, the paradoxes of the Christian faith can be vindicated as true, on their own terms, by a method of implication that involves discerning how the supposedly conflicting elements of a given paradox actually necessitate one another, and together perform an indispensable function within the Christian system.

Although persuaded that Van Til's perspective is fundamentally correct, we discovered that both he and his disciples failed to go the distance in employing a method of implication systematically and completely to the paradoxes of the Christian Faith. For example, it was not clear that specifically three divine persons (as opposed to more or less) are essential to maintaining a self-contained divine unity. As a result, it was equally unclear that a specifically *Trinitarian* Deity is alone capable of enabling man to have true and dependable knowledge. In the hope of refining a Van Tillian position in this area, the present author has argued that God can only be an Absolute person if He is Tri-personal, in such a manner that each pair of persons are related to one another through none other than the third. Were the divine being exhausted by any more than three persons, the relationship between any pair would either have to be facilitated by but one of the several remaining persons (so that one person is not fully expressed in some part of God's self-activity), or by all of the remaining persons together, as a "group" (which is an abstraction, and not a concrete *person*). Hence, only a specifically *Tri*une God can exist as a perfectly self-contained person, and it is exactly this sort of God upon Whom the Christian system, and indeed all rational discourse, depends. Utilizing the same methodology, and allowing insights from each vindicated paradox to guide our inquiries into the others, we went on to vindicate eight additional paradoxes pertaining to the: (a) order and equality of divine persons; (b) simplicity and multiplicity of divine attributes; (c) divine immutability and temporal creation; (d) finitude and simplicity of creation; (e) analogical and objective character of human knowledge; (f) sovereignty of God and freedom of man; (g) original goodness of man and his capacity for sin; and (h) sinlessness and genuine humanity of Christ.

At the close of our own systematic endeavor, one could ask, just as we have of Van Til, whether we have sufficiently implicated ourselves into the Christian system to convey the force of a Christian logic, and to stave off heretical perversions of it, that might be hailed as capable of mimicking our transcendental claims. At this point, it is helpful to recall that one implication of a Christian vantage point is that one need not enjoy exhaustive knowledge in order to enjoy true knowledge. Practically speaking, this means that our beliefs are true and justified when they have been vindicated to an overwhelming *degree*, rather than vindicated *absolutely*. Presently, it is difficult to imagine how the unbeliever could feasibly maintain the distinctness of his heretical alternative to Christianity, while acknowledging his need for an ontological Trinity, creation *ex nihilo*, divine sovereignty, human responsibility, the Incarnation, etc. For, our account has shown that transcendental argumentation, reasoning by implication, and a long list of distinctively Christian doctrines must stand or fall together. Nevertheless, with healthy appreciations for our own finitude and the relentless cunning of unbelief, we must be fully convinced that the solvency of the position articulated will be challenged both on its own grounds and by ever more subtle permutations of the non-Christian perspective. As it stands, our account falls short in its failure to vindicate a gamut of remaining Christian paradoxes. Indeed, we have hardly touched on the details of the *ordo salutis*, the ministry of the Holy Spirit, eschatology, etc. However, if the position defended is at all correct, then it must, for that very reason, cry out for greater depths of refinement, and even invite the onslaughts of unbelief. Death is the prerequisite to resurrection. And, our lengthy engagement with Van Til and refinement of his views are intended to testify to a consciousness that would sooner put to death its natural convictions on account of Christ than regard even the most staggering paradox of His message as anything but unadulterated wisdom. If the position expounded is capable of conveying this Spirit, then it is surely set on a course to inspire believers to reason ever more self-consciously as men who are unashamed of the gospel (Rom 1:16).

Bibliography

Allison, Henry E. *Kant's Transcendental Idealism: An Interpretation and Defense*. Rev. and enl. ed. New Haven: Yale University Press, 2004.

Anderson, James N. "If Knowledge then God: The Epistemological Theistic Arguments of Alvin Plantinga and Cornelius Van Til." *Calvin Theological Journal* 40 (2005) 49–75.

———. *Paradox in Christian Theology: An Analysis of its Presence, Character, and Epistemological Status*. Paternoster Theological Monographs. Milton Keynes, UK: Paternoster, 2007.

Ameriks, Karl. *Kant and the Fate of Autonomy: Problems in the Appropriation of the Critical Philosophy*. Cambridge: Cambridge University Press, 2000.

Aquinas, Thomas. *Summa Contra Gentiles*. Vol. 1–4. Translated by Anton C. Pegis, James F. Anderson, Vernon J. Bourke, and Charles J. O'Neil. South Bend, IN: University of Notre Dame Press, 1975.

———. *Summa Theologica*. Translated by The Fathers of English Dominican Providence. 1948. Reprint. Allen, TX: Thomas More, 1981.

Augustine. *The City of God*. Translated John. O'Meara. London: Penguin, 1972.

———. *On The Holy Trinity*. Translated by Arthur West Hadden. In *Ante-Nicene Fathers*, vol. 3, edited by Philip Schaff, 13–276. 1887. Reprint. Peabody, MA: Hendrickson, 2004.

Bahnsen, Greg L. *By This Standard: The Authority of God's Law Today*. Tyler, TX: Institute for Christian Economics, 1985.

———. "The Crucial Concept of Self-Deception." *Westminster Theological Journal* 57.1 (1995) 1–31.

———. "The Encounter of Jerusalem with Athens." In *Always Ready: Directions for Defending the Faith*, edited by Randy R. Booth, 235–76. Nacogdoches, TX: Covenant Media, 2006.

———. *No Other Standard: Theonomy and Its Critics*. Tyler, TX: Institute for Christian Economics, 1991.

———. *Theonomy in Christian Ethics*. 3rd ed. Nacogodoches, TX: Covenant Media, 2002.

———. *Van Til's Apologetic: Readings & Analysis*. Philipsburg, NJ: Presbyterian & Reformed, 1998.

Baillie, Donald M. *God Was in Christ*. New York: Schribner's Sons, 1948.

Barth, Karl. *Church Dogmatics*. Edited by G. W. Bromily and T. F. Torrance. Translated by G. W. Bromily. 14 vols. 1937. Reprint. Peabody, MA: Hendrickson, 2010.

Bavinck, Herman. *The Certainty of Faith*. Translated by Harry der Nederlanden. 1980. Reprint. Scarsdale, NY: Westminster Discount Books, n.d.

———. *The Philosophy of Revelation*. 1907. Reprint. Scarsdale, NY: Westminster Discount Books, n.d.

———. *Reformed Dogmatics*. Edited by John Bolt. Translated by John Vriend. 4 vols. Grand Rapids: Baker Academic, 2003–8.

Beiser, Frederick C. "Introduction: Hegel and the Problem of Metaphysics." In *The Cambridge Companion to Hegel*, edited by Frederick C. Beiser, 1–24. Cambridge: Cambridge University Press, 1993.

Bonjour, Laurence, and Erenst Sosa. *Epistemic Justification: Internalism vs. Externalism, Foundations vs. Virtue*. Malden, MA: Blackwell, 2003.

Bosanquet, Bernard. *The Essentials of Logic: Being Ten Lectures on Judgment and Inference*. London: Macmillan, 1903.

———. *Implication and Linear Inference*. London: Macmillan, 1920.

———. *Knowledge and Reality: A Criticism of Mr. F. H. Bradley's Principles of Logic*. London: Kegan Paul, Trench and Co. 1885.

———. *Logic or the Morphology of Knowledge*. Oxford: Clarendon, 1911.

———. *The Principle of Individuality and Value: The Gifford Lectures for 1911, Delivered in Edinburgh University*. London: Macmillan, 1912.

———. *The Value and Destiny of the Individual: The Gifford Lectures for 1912, Delivered in Edinburgh University*. London: Macmillan, 1913.

Bouma, Clarence. "Christianity's Finality and New Testament Teaching." *The Princeton Theological Review* 26.3 (1928) 337–54.

———. "Hegelianism and Theism." *The Princeton Theological Review* 25.2 (1927) 201–14.

Bradley, Francis Herbert. *Appearance and Reality*. Edited by J. H. Muirhead. New York: Swan Sonnenschein & Co., 1893.

———. *The Principles of Logic*. London: Kegan Paul, Trench, and Co., 1883.

Brown, Colin. *Philosophy and Christian Faith*. Downers Grove, IL: InterVarsity, 1968.

Buber, Martin. *I and Thou*. New York: Charles Schribner and Sons, 1958.

Burbidge, John W. "Hegel's Conception of Logic." In *The Cambridge Companion to Hegel*, edited by Frederick C. Beiser, 86–101. Cambridge: Cambridge University Press, 1993.

Butler, Joseph. *The Analogy of Religion Natural and Revealed*. New York: Phillips and Hunt, 1906.

Butler, Michael R. "The Great Debate Gets Personal." http://members.ozemail.com.au/~seccomn/phil/martin refute2.htm (accessed January 27, 2011).

———. "The Transcendental Argument for God's Existence." In *The Standard Bearer: A Festschrift for Greg L. Bahnsen*, edited by Steven M. Schlissel, 65–124. Nacogdoches, TX: Covenant Media, 2002.

Calvin, John. *Commentaries*. Translated Thomas Myers. 22 vols. Grand Rapids: Baker 2003.

———. *Institutes of the Christian Religion*. Edited by John T. McNeil. Translated by Ford Lewis Battles. Louisville, KY: Westminster John Knox, 1960.

Cannata, Raymond. "History of Apologetics at Princeton Seminary." In *Unapologetic Apologetics: Meeting the Challenges of Theological Studies*, edited by William A. Dembski and Jay Wesley Richards, 57–76. Downers Grove, IL: InterVarsity, 2001.

Caird, Edward. *Hegel*. Edinburgh: Blackwood and Sons, 1883.

Carnell, Edward J. *Christian Apologetics*. Grand Rapids: Eerdmans, 1956.

Clark, Gordon H. *A Christian View of Men and Things: An Introduction to Philosophy*. Grand Rapids: Eerdmans, 1952.

———. *Karl Barth's Theological Method*. Philadelphia: Presbyterian & Reformed, 1963.

———. *The Trinity*. Jefferson, MD: The Trinity Foundation, 1990.

———. "The Wheaton Lectures" delivered at Wheaton College, Illinois 1965. In *The Works of Gordon Clark*, vol. 7, edited by Laura K. Juodaitis, 27–99. Unicoi, TN: Trinity Foundation, 2009.

Collett, Don. "Van Til and Transcendental Argument." *Westminster Theological Journal* 65 (2003) 289–306.

Copleston, Frederick. *A History of Philosophy*. 8 vols. New York: Doubleday, 1962–67.

Craig, William Lane. *Time and Eternity: Exploring God's Relationship to Time*. Wheaton, IL: Crossway, 2001.

Daane, James. *A Theology of Grace: An Inquiry into and Evaluation of Dr. C. Van Til's Doctrine of Common Grace*. Grand Rapids: Eerdmans, 1954.

Dennison, William D. "Analytic Philosophy and Van Til's Epistemology." *Westminster Theological Journal* 57.1 (1995) 33–56.

———. "The Eschatological Implications of Genesis 2:15 for Apologetics." In *Reason and Revelation*, edited by K. Scott Oliphint and Lane G. Tipton, 190–204. Philipsburg, NJ: Presbyterian & Reformed, 2007.

———. *Paul's Two-Age Construction in Apologetics*. 1985. Reprint. Eugene, OR: Wipf & Stock, 2000.

de Vries, John Hendrik. "Biographical Note: Abraham Kuyper 1837–1920." Preface to, *Lectures on Calvinism*, by Abraham Kuyper, i–vii. Grand Rapids: Eerdmans, 1931.

Dooyeweerd, Herman. "Cornelius Van Til and the Transcendental Critique of Theoretical Thought." In *Jerusalem and Athens: Critical Discussions on the Philosophy and Apologetics of Cornelius Van Til*, edited by E. R. Geehan, 74–89. Philipsburg, NJ: Presbyterian & Reformed, 1980.

———. *In the Twilight of Western Thought*. Philadelphia: Presbyterian & Reformed, 1960.

Edgar, William. "Two Christian Warriors: Cornelius Van Til and Francis Schaeffer Compared." *Westminster Theological Journal* 95.1 (1995) 57–80.

Forester, Michael N. *Hegel and Skepticism*. Cambridge: Harvard University Press, 1989.

———. "Hegel's Dialectical Method." In *The Cambridge Companion to Hegel*, edited by Frederick C. Beiser, 130–70. Cambridge: Cambridge University Press, 1993.

Frame, John M. *Apologetics to the Glory of God: An Introduction*. Philipsburg, NJ: Presbyterian & Reformed, 1994.

———. *Cornelius Van Til: An Analysis of His Thought*. Philipsburg, NJ: Presbyterian & Reformed, 1995.

———. "Divine Aseity and Apologetics." In *Revelation and Reason: New Essays in Reformed Apologetics*, edited by K. Scott Oliphint and Lane G. Tipton, 115–30. Philipsburg, NJ: Presbyterian & Reformed, 2007.

———. *The Doctrine of the Christian Life*. Philipsburg, NJ: Presbyterian and Reformed, 2008.

———. *The Doctrine of God*. Philipsburg, NJ: Presbyterian & Reformed, 2002.

———. *The Doctrine of the Knowledge of God*. Philipsburg, NJ: Presbyterian & Reformed, 1987.

———. *The Doctrine of the Word of God*. Philipsburg, NJ: Presbyterian and Reformed, 2010.

———. *No Other God: A Response to Open Theism*. Philipsburg, NJ: Zondervan, 2001.

———. "The Problem of Theological Paradox." In *Foundations of Christian Scholarship: Essays in the Van Til Perspective*, edited by Gary North, 295–330. Vallecito, CA: Ross Hose, 1979.

———. "Reply to Don Collet on Transcendental Argument." *Westminster Theological Journal* 65 (2003) 307–9.

———. *Salvation Belongs to the LORD: An Introduction to Systematic Theology*. Philipsburg, NJ: Presbyterian & Reformed, 2006.

Fuller, Daniel P. "Benjamin B. Warfield's view of Faith and History: A Critique in the Light of the New Testament." In *Bulletin of the Evangelical Theological Society* 11.2 (1968) 75–83.

Gaffin, Richard B. "Epistemological Reflections on 1 Cor 2:6–16." *Westminster Theological Journal* 57.1 (1995) 103–24.

———. "Geerhardus Vos and the Interpretation of Paul." In *Jerusalem and Athens: Critical Discussions on the Theology and Apologetics of Cornelius Van Til*, edited by E. R. Geehan, 228–37. Philipsburg, NJ: Presbyterian & Reformed, 1980.

Garver, Steven Joel. "Bahnsen's Concept on Self-Deception." In *Christendom Essays*, edited by James B. Jordan. Niceville, FL: Transfiguration, 1997. Online: http://joelgarver.com/writ/phil/bahnsen.htm (accessed August 25, 2011).

Geisler, Norman L. *Christian Apologetics*. Grand Rapids: Baker, 1987.

Geisler, Norman L., and Paul D. Feinberg. *Introduction to Philosophy: A Christian Perspective*. Grand Rapids: Baker, 1980.

Gentry, Kenneth L. *Covenantal Theonomy: A Response to T. David Gordon and Klinean Covenantalism*. Nacogdoches, TX: Covenant Media, 2005.

Gilson, Etienne. "The Spirit of Thomism." In *Philosophy in the 20th Century: An Anthology*, edited by William Barrett and Henry D. Aiken, 4:629–51. New York: Random House, 1962.

Gordon, T. David. "Van Til and Theonomy." In *Creator, Redeemer, Consummator: A Festschrift for Meredith G. Kline*, edited by Howard Griffith and John R. Meuther, 271–78. Reprint. Eugene, OR: Wipf & Stock, 2000.

Green, William Brenton. "The Function of Reason in Christianity." *Presbyterian and Reformed Review* 6.23 (1895) 481–501.

———. "The Metaphysics of Apologetics: Parts I–VI." *Presbyterian and Reformed Review* 9 (1898) 60–82, 261–288, 472–499, 559–694; 10 (1899) 25–57, 237–266.

———. "Yet Another Criticism of the Theory of Evolution." *Princeton Theological Review* 20.4 (1922) 537–61.

Griffin, Edward H. "The Epistemological Argument for Theism." *Presbyterian and Reformed Review* 13.51 (1902) 341–63.

———. "Personality the Supreme Category of Philosophy." *Presbyterian and Reformed Review* 13.52 (1902) 507–23.

Gunton, Colin E. *The One, The Three and the Many: God, Creation, and the Culture of Modernity: The Bampton Lectures 1992*. Cambridge: Cambridge University Press, 1993.

Guyer, Paul. "Thought and Being: Hegel's Critique of Kant." In *The Cambridge Companion to Hegel*, edited by Frederick C. Beiser, 171–210. Cambridge: Cambridge University Press, 1993.

Hart, Trevor. *Regarding Karl Barth: Essays Toward a Reading of His Theology*. Carlisle, UK: Paternoster, 1999.

———. "Revelation." In *The Cambridge Companion to Barth*, edited by John Webster, 37–56. Cambridge: Cambridge University Press, 2000.

Hegel, G. W. F. *Logic: Being Part One of The Encyclopedia of the Philosophical Sciences (1830)*. Translated by William Wallace. Oxford: Oxford University Press, 1975.

———. *Phenomenology of Spirit*. Edited by J. N. Findlay. Translated by A. V. Miller. Oxford: Oxford University Press, 1977.

———. *The Philosophy of History*. Translated by S. Sibree. New York: Dover, 1956.

Hepp, Valentine. *Calvinism and the Philosophy of Nature: The Stone Lectures Delivered at Princeton in 1930*. Grand Rapids: Eerdmans, 1930.

Hill, Daniel J. *Divinity and Maximal Greatness*. New York: Routledge, 2010.

Hodge, Charles. *Systematic Theology*. 3 vols. Peabody, MA: Hendrickson, 2003.

Hodge, C. Wistar. "Some Aspects of Recent German Philosophy." *Presbyterian and Reformed Review* 7.26 (1896) 211–27.

Hodge, William Henry. *Intuitive Perception; Presented by a New Philosophy of Natural Realism, in Accord with Universally Accepted Truths*. Danvers, MA: General, 2010.

———. "The Infinite, Contradictory, and Faith." *Princeton Theological Review* 2.4 (1904) 592–98.

Hoeksema, Herman. *The Clark-Van Til Controversy*. Unicoi, TN: The Trinity Foundation, 1995.

Hume, David. *A Treatise of Human Nature*. Sligo, Ireland: Hard, 2006.

Hughes, Philip Edgcumbe. "Crucial Biblical Passages for Christian Apologetics." In *Jerusalem and Athens: Critical Discussions on the Philosophy and Apologetics of Cornelius Van Til*, edited by E. R. Geehan, 131–40. Philipsburg, NJ: Presbyterian & Reformed, 1980.

Irons, Lee. "The Eternal Generation of the Son." The Upper Register. http://www.upper-register.com/papers/monogenes.html (accessed August 25, 2011).

Johnson, John J. "Is Cornelius Van Til's Apologetic Method Christian, or Merely Theistic?" *Evangelical Quarterly* 75.3 (2003) 275–68.

Jones, W. T. *Hobbes to Hume*. Vol. 3 of *A History of Western Philosophy*. 2nd ed. San Diego: Harcourt Brace Jovanovich, 1980.

Jordan, James B. "Liturgical Man, Liturgical Woman—Part 1." *Rite Reasons News Letter* no. 86 (May 2004) n.p.

———. "Patriarchal Dominion." *Biblical Horizons Newsletter* no. 108 (August, 1998) n.p.

———. *Through New Eyes: Developing a Biblical View of the World*. Reprint. Eugene, OR: Wipf & Stock, 1999.

Jue, Jeffery K. "Theology Naturalis: A Reformed Tradition." In *Revelation and Reason: Essays in Reformed Apologetics*, edited by K. Scott Oliphint and Lane G. Tipton, 168–89. Philipsburg, NJ: Presbyterian & Reformed, 2007.

Kant, Immanuel. *Critique of Practical Reason*. Translated and edited by Marry Gregor. Cambridge: Cambridge University Press, 1997.

———. *Critique of Pure Reason*. Edited and translated by Paul Guyer and Allen W. Wood. Cambridge: Cambridge University Press, 1998.

Kline, Meredith G. "Comments on an Old-New Error: A Review Article." *Westminster Theological Journal* 41.1 (1990) 172–89.

———. *Images of the Spirit*. Reprint. Eugene, OR: Wipf and Stock, 1999

———. *Treaty of the Great King: The Covenant Structure of Deuteronomy; Studies and Commentary*. Grand Rapids: Eerdmans, 1963.

Knudson, Robert D. "Progressive and Regressive Tendencies in Apologetics." In *Jerusalem and Athens: Critical Discussions on the Philosophy and Apologetics of Cornelius Van Til*, edited by E. R. Geehan, 275–98. Philipsburg, NJ: Presbyterian & Reformed, 1980.

Krabbendam, Henry. "Cornelius Van Til: The Methodological Objective of a Biblical Apologetics." *Westminster Theological Journal* 57.1 (1995) 125–44.

Kuiper, R. B. *For Whom Did Christ Die? A Study of the Design of the Atonement*. Wipf & Stock, 2003.

Kuyper, Abraham. *Encyclopedia of Sacred Theology*. Translated by Jay P. Green Sr. Lafayette, IN: Sovereign Grace, 2001.

———. *Lectures on Calvinism*. Edited by John Hendrick de Vries. Grand Rapids: Eerdmans, 1931.

Letham, Robert. *The Holy Trinity in Scripture, History, Theology, and Worship*. Philipsburg, NJ: Presbyterian & Reformed, 2004.

Levering, Matthew. *Scripture and Metaphysics: Aquinas and the Renewal of Trinitarian Theology*. Malden, MA: Blackwell, 2004.

Martin, Michael. "Does Induction Presume the Existence of God." *Skeptic* 5.2 (1997) 71–75. Online: http://www.infidels.org/library/modern/michael_martin/induction.html (accessed August 25, 2011).

———. "Does Logic Presuppose the Existence of God." Online: http://www.infidels.org/library/modern/michael_martin/logic.html (accessed August 25, 2011).

———. "The Martin-Frame Debate: The Transcendental Argument for the Non-Existence of God." Online: http://www.infidels.org/library/modern/michael_martin/martin -frame/ (accessed August 25, 2011).

MacLeod, Donald. "Amsterdam, Old Princeton, and Cornelius Van Til." *Westminster Theological Journal* 68.2 (2006) 261–82.

Magee, Glenn Alexander. *Hegel and the Hermetic Tradition*. Ithaca, NY: Cornell University Press, 2001.

McConnel, Timothy I. "The Influence of Idealism on the Apologetics of Van Til." *Journal of Evangelical Theological Society* 48.3 (2005) 557–88.

McCormack, Bruce. "Grace and Being." In *The Cambridge Companion to Karl Barth*, edited by John Webster, 92–110. Cambridge: Cambridge University Press, 2000.

McGrath, Alister E. *Intellectuals Don't Need God and Other Modern Myths*. Grand Rapids: Zondervan, 1993.

McTaggart, John. *The Nature of Existence*. 2 vols. Cambridge: Cambridge University Press, 1921.

———. *Studies in the Hegelian Dialectic*. Cambridge: Cambridge University Press, 1896.

Meuther, John R. *Cornelius Van Til: Reformed Apologist and Churchman*. Philipsburg, PA: Presbyterian & Reformed, 2008.

Miller, E. D. "Professor Royce's Idealism." *Princeton Theological Review* 3.2 (1905) 258–98.

Minton, Henry Colin. Review of *Intuitive Perception; Presented by a New Philosophy of Natural Realism, in Accord with Universally Accepted Truths*, by William Henry Hodge. *Princeton Theological Review* 2.2 (1904) 317–24

Moltmann, Jürgen. *The Trinity and the Kingdom*. Translated by Margaret Kohl. Minneapolis: Augsburg Fortress, 1980.

Montgomery, John Warwick. "Once Upon an A Priori." In *Jerusalem and Athens*, edited by E. R. Geehan, 380–92. Philipsburg, NJ: Presbyterian & Reformed, 1980.

Moore, George E. "The Refutation of Idealism." In *Twentieth-Century Philosophy: The Analytic Tradition*, edited by Morris Weitz, 1:15–34. New York: Free, 1966.

Mourad, Ronney. *Transcendental Arguments and Justified Christian Beliefs*. Lanham, MD: University Press of America, 2005.

Muller, Richard A. *Post-Reformation Reformed Dogmatics: The Rise and Development of Reformed Orthodoxy, ca. 1520 to ca. 1725*. 4 vols. Grand Rapids: Baker Academic, 2003.

Nash, Ronald. "Attack on Human Autonomy: Review of *A Christian Theory of Knowledge*," by Cornelius Van Til. *Christianity Today* 14, Jan. 16, 1970, 349–50.

———. "Gordon Clark's Theory of Knowledge." In *The Works of Gordon Haddon Clark*, edited by Laura K. Juodaitis, 7:105–42. Unicoi, TN: Trinity Foundation, 2009.

———. *The Word of God and the Mind of Man*. Philipsburg, NJ: Presbyterian & Reformed, 1982.

Noll, Mark A, ed. *The Princeton Theology 1812–1924: Scripture, Science and Theological Method from Archibald Alexander to Benjamin Breckinridge Warfield*. Grand Rapids: Baker Academic, 2001.

North, Gary. *Dominion and Common Grace: The Biblical Basis of Progress*. Tyler, TX: Institute for Christian Economics, 1987.

Notaro, Thom. *Van Til and the Use of Evidence*. Philipsburg, NJ: Presbyterian & Reformed, 1985.

Oliphint, Scott. *The Battle Belongs to the Lord: The Power of Scripture for Defending the Faith*. Philipsburg, NJ: Presbyterian & Reformed, 2003.

———. *The Consistency of Van Til's Methodology*. Scarsdale, NY: Westminster Discount Book Service, n.d.

———. *Cornelius Van Til and the Reformation of Christian Apologetics*. Scarsdale, NY: Westminster Discount Book Service, n.d.

———. *God with Us: Divine Condescension and the Attributes of God*. Wheaton, IL: Crossway, 2012.

———. "The Irrationality of Unbelief: An Exegetical Study." In *Revelation and Reason*, edited by K. Scott Oliphint and Lane G. Tipton, 59–73. Philipsburg, NJ: Presbyterian & Reformed, 2007.

———. *Reasons {for faith}: Philosophy in the Service of Theology*. Philipsburg, NJ: Presbyterian & Reformed, 2006.

Orr, James. *The Christian View of God and the World: As Centering in the Incarnation; Being the First Series of the Kerr Lectures*. 1893. Reprint. Vancouver: Regent, 2002.

———. "A Thoroughgoing Realist." Review of *Intuitive Perception; Presented by a New Philosophy of Natural Realism, in Accord with Universally Accepted Truths*, by William Henry Hodge. *Expository Times* 15 (1903–4) 409–10.

Peake, A. S. *The Epistle to the Colossians*. In *The Expositor's Greek New Testament*, edited by W. Robertson Nicoll, vol. 3. Grand Rapids: Eerdmans, 1970.

Pinnock, Clark H. "Philosophy of Christian Evidences." In *Jerusalem and Athens: Critical Discussions on the Philosophy and Apologetics of Cornelius Van Til*, edited by E. R. Geehan, 420–26. Philipsburg, NJ: Presbyterian & Reformed, 1980.

Plantinga, Alvin. "Does God Have a Nature." In *The Analytic Theist: An Alvin Plantinga Reader*, edited by James F. Sennet, 225–57. Grand Rapid: Eerdmans, 1998.

———. "Reason and Belief in God." In *Faith and Rationality: Reason and Belief in God*, edited by Alvin Plantinga and Nicholas Wolterstorf, 16–93. Notre Dame, IN: University of Notre Dame Press, 1983.

———. *Warrant: The Current Debate*. Oxford: Oxford University Press, 1993.

———. *Warrant and Proper Function*. Oxford: Oxford University Press, 1993.

———. *Warranted Christian Belief*. Oxford: Oxford University Press, 2000.

Plantinga, Cornelius, Jr. "The Threeness/Oneness Problem of the Trinity." *Calvin Theological Journal* 23.1 (1998) 37–53.

Pringle-Pattison, Andrew Seth. *Hegelianism and Personalism*. Danvers, MA: General, 2009.

———. *The Idea of God in the Light of Recent Philosophy*. 2nd ed., rev. Oxford: Oxford University Press, 1920.

———. *Scottish Philosophy: A Comparison of the Scottish and German Answers to Hume*. Edinburgh: Blackwood and Sons, 1885.

Poythress, Vern S. "Reforming Ontology and Logic in the Light of the Trinity: An Application of Van Til's Idea of Analogy." *Westminster Theological Journal* 57.1 (1995) 187–219.

———. *The Shadow of Christ in the Law of Moses*. Philipsburg, NJ: Presbyterian & Reformed, 1991.

———. *Symphonic Theology: The Validity of Multiple Perspectives in Theology*. Philipsburg, NJ: Presbyterian & Reformed, 1991.

Quine, Willard Van Orman. *From a Logical Point of View: 9 Logico-Philosophical Essays*. Cambridge: Harvard University Press, 1980.

Ratzsch, Delvin Lee. "Abraham Kuyper's Philosophy of Science." *Calvin Theological Journal* 27 (1992) 277–303.

Reid, Thomas. *An Inquiry into the Human Mind: On the Principles of Common Sense*. Edinburgh: Bell and Bradfute, 1801.

Reichenbach, Hans. *Philosophy of Space and Time*. Translated by Maria Reichenbach and John Freund. New York: Dover, 1958.

Richardson, Kurt Anders. *Reading Karl Barth: New Directions for North American Theology*. Grand Rapids: Baker Academic, 2004.

Rorty, Richard. "Wittgenstein, Heidegger, and the Reification of Language." In *The Cambridge Companion to Heidegger*, edited by Charles Guignon, 337–57. Cambridge: Cambridge University Press, 1993.

Rushdoony, Rousas. *By What Standard? An Analysis of the Philosophy of Cornelius Van Til*. Vallecito, CA: Ross House, 1995.

———. *The Institutes of Biblical Law*. Nutley, NJ: Presbyterian & Reformed, 1973.

———. "The One and Many Problem—The Contribution of Van Til." In *Jerusalem and Athens: Critical Discussions on the Philosophy and Apologetic of Cornelius Van Til*, edited by E. R. Geehan, 339–48. Philipsburg, NJ: Presbyterian & Reformed, 1980.

———. *The One and the Many: Studies in the Philosophy of Order and Ultimacy*. Fairfax, VA: Thoburn, 1971.

Russell, Bertrand. *My Philosophical Development*. New York: Simon and Schuster, 1959.

———. *The Problems of Philosophy*. Oxford: Oxford University Press, 1912.

Schaeffer, Francis A. *Escape from Reason*. In *The Complete Works of Francis Schaefer*, 1:206–70. Wheaton, IL: Crossway, 1993.

———. *The God Who is There*. In *The Complete Works of Francis A. Schaeffer*, 1:5–202. Wheaton, IL: Crossway, 1993.

Silva, Moisés. "The Case for Calvinistic Hermeneutics." In *Revelation and Reason*, edited by K. Scott Oliphint and Lane G. Tipton, 74–94. Philipsburg, NJ: Presbyterian & Reformed, 2007.

———. "Dialectic." In *The Cambridge Companion to Philosophy*, edited by Robert Audi, 232–33. 2nd ed. Cambridge: Cambridge University Press, 2001.

Smith, Ralph A. *Eternal Covenant: How the Trinity Reshapes Covenant Theology*. Moscow, ID: Canon, 2003.

———. *Paradox and Truth: Rethinking Van Til on the Trinity*. Moscow, ID: Canon, 2002.

———. *Trinity and Reality: An Introduction to the Christian Faith*. Moscow, ID: Canon, 2004.

Solomon, Robert C. *From Hegel to Existentialism*. Oxford: Oxford University Press, 1986.

———. *In the Spirit of Hegel: A Study of G. W. F. Hegel's Phenomenology of Spirit*. Oxford: Oxford University Press, 1983.

Sproul, R. C., John Gerstner, and Arthur Lindsley. *Classical Apologetics: A Rational Defense of the Christian Faith and a Critique of Presuppositional Apologetics*. Grand Rapids: Zondervan, 1984.

Stoker, Hendrik G. "Reconnoitering the Theory of Knowledge of Prof. Dr. Cornelius Van Til." In *Jerusalem and Athens: Critical Discussions on the Philosophy and Apologetics of Cornelius Van Til*, edited by E. R. Geehan, 25–71. Philipsburg, NJ: Presbyterian & Reformed, 1980.

Taylor, A. E. *The Faith of a Moralist: The Gifford Lectures Delivered in the University of St. Andrews, 1926–1928*. 2 vols. London: Macmillan, 1930.

Turretin, Francis. *Institutes of Elenctic Theology*. Edited by James T. Dennison Jr. Translated by George Musgrave Giger. Philipsburg, NJ: Presbyterian & Reformed, 1992.

Tipton, Lane G. "The Function of Perichoresis and the Divine Incomprehensibility." *Westminster Theological Journal* 64 (2002) 289–306.

———. "Paul's Christological Interpretation of Creation and Presuppositional Apologetics." In *Revelation and Reason: New Essays in Reformed Apologetics*, edited by K. Scott Oliphint and Lane G. Tipton, 95–111. Philipsburg, NJ: Presbyterian & Reformed, 2007.

———. "Resurrection, Proof, and Presuppositionalism: Acts 17:30–31." In *Revelation and Reason: New Essays in Reformed Apologetics*, edited by K. Scott Oliphint and Lane G. Tipton, 41–58. Philipsburg, NJ: Presbyterian & Reformed, 2007.

Torrance, Thomas F. *The Doctrine of God, One Being Three Persons*. Edinburgh: T. & T. Clark, 1996.

Van Til, Cornelius. "Calvin as Controversialist." In *Soli Deo Gloria: Essays in Reformed Theology: Festschrift for John H. Gerstner*, edited by R. C. Sproul. 1971. In *The Works of Cornelius Van Til*, CD-ROM, version 1.0, n.p., edited by Eric H. Sigwald. New York: Labels Army Company, 1997.

———. *The Case for Calvinism*. Nutley, NJ: Presbyterian & Reformed, 1964.

———. *Christ and the Jews*. Philadelphia: Presbyterian & Reformed, 1968.

———. *Christian Apologetics*. Edited by William Edgar. 2nd ed. Philipsburg, NJ: Presbyterian & Reformed, 2003.

———. *Christian Theistic Ethics*. Philipsburg, NJ: Presbyterian & Reformed, 1974.

———. *Christian Theistic Evidences*. Philipsburg, NJ: Presbyterian & Reformed, 1976.

———. *A Christian Theory of Knowledge*. Philipsburg, NJ: Presbyterian & Reformed, 1974.

———. *Christianity and Barthianism*. Philadelphia: Presbyterian & Reformed, 1962.

———. *Christianity in Conflict*. Edited by Steven J. Vander Hill. Glenside, PA: Westminster Seminary, 1995.

———. *Common Grace and the Gospel*. Nutley, NJ: Presbyterian & Reformed, 1972.

———. *The Defense of the Faith*. 3rd ed. Philipsburg, NJ: Presbyterian & Reformed, 1967.

———. *The Defense of the Faith*. Edited by K. Scott Oliphint. 4th ed. Philipsburg, NJ: Presbyterian & Reformed, 2008.

———. "The Development of My Thinking." A personal letter written to John Vander Stelt in 1969. Reprinted in *The Works of Cornelius Van Til*, CD-ROM, version 1.0, n.p., edited by Eric H. Sigwald. New York: Labels Army Company, 1997.

———. "God and the Absolute." *Evangelical Quarterly* 2 (1930). In *Christianity and Idealism*, 7–35. Philadelphia: Presbyterian & Reformed, 1955.

———. *The God of Hope: Sermons and Addresses*. Philipsburg, NJ: Presbyterian & Reformed, 1978.

———. *The Great Debate Today*. Nutley, NJ: Presbyterian & Reformed, 1971.

———. *An Introduction to Systematic Theology*. Philipsburg, NJ: Presbyterian & Reformed, 1974.

———. *The Later Heidegger and Theology*. Philadelphia: Presbyterian & Reformed, 1964.

———. *The New Modernism*. Philadelphia: Presbyterian & Reformed, 1947.

———. *Paul at Athens*. Philadelphia: Presbyterian & Reformed, 1954.

———. *The Protestant Doctrine of Scripture*. Nutley, NJ: Presbyterian & Reformed, 1967.

———. "Reformed Epistemology," Th.M. thesis, 1927. Reprinted in *The Works of Cornelius Van Til*, CD-ROM, version 1.0, n.p., edited by Eric H. Sigwald. New York: Labels Army Company, 1997.

———. *The Reformed Pastor and Modern Thought*. Philipsburg, NJ: Presbyterian & Reformed, 1971.

———. "Response to Rushdoony." In *Jerusalem and Athens: Critical Discussions on the Philosophy and Apologetic of Cornelius Van Til*, edited by E. R. Geehan, 348. Philipsburg, NJ: Presbyterian & Reformed, 1980.

———. Review of *De Noodzakelijkeheideener Christelijke Logica*, by D. H. Th. Vollenhoven. *Calvin Forum* 1.6 (1936) 142–43. Reprinted in *The Works of Cornelius Van Til*, CD-ROM, version 1.0, n.p., edited by Eric H. Sigwald. New York: Labels Army Company, 1997.

———. *The Sovereignty of Grace: An Appraisal of G. C. Berkouwer's View of Dort*. Nutley, NJ: Presbyterian & Reformed, 1969.

———. *A Survey of Christian Epistemology*. Philipsburg, NJ: Presbyterian & Reformed, 1951.

———. "The Theism of A. E. Taylor." *Westminster Theological Journal* 1.2 (1939). Reprinted in *Christianity and Idealism*, 57–75. Philadelphia: Presbyterian & Reformed, 1955.

———. *The Theology of James Daane*. Philadelphia: Presbyterian & Reformed, 1959.

———. *Why I Believe in God*. Philadelphia: Committee on Christian Education of the Orthodox Presbyterian Church, 1948. Reprinted in *The Works of Cornelius Van Til*, CD-ROM, version 1.0, n.p., edited by Eric H. Sigwald. New York: Labels Army Company, 1997.

———. "The Will in Its Theological Relations." Handwritten paper presented to C. W. Hodge, at Princeton Seminary in 1924. Reprinted in *The Works of Cornelius Van Til*, CD-ROM, version 1.0, n.p., edited by Eric H. Sigwald. New York: Labels Army Company, 1997.

Vos, Geerhardus. *Biblical Theology*. Carlisle, PA: Banner of Truth, 1948.

———. *The Pauline Eschatology*. Philipsburg, NJ: Presbyterian & Reformed, 1994.

Walker, Ralph C. S. "Kant and Transcendental Arguments." In *The Cambridge Companion to Kant*, edited by Paul Guyer, 238–68. Cambridge: Cambridge University Press, 2006.

Warfield, Benjamin Breckinridge. "Apologetics." In *The New Schaff-Herzog Encyclopedia of Religious Knowledge*, edited by Samuel Macauley Jackson. 1908. Reprinted in *The Works of Benjamin B. Warfield*, 9:3–21. Grand Rapids: Baker, 2003.

———. "Augustine and the Pelagian Controversy." Reprinted in *The Works of Benjamin B. Warfield*, vol. 4, 289–412. Grand Rapids: Baker, 2003.

———. "Calvinism." In *The New Schaff-Herzog Encyclopedia of Religious Knowledge*, edited by Samuel Macauley Jackson, 2:359–64. 1908. Reprinted in *The Works of Benjamin B. Warfield*, 5:353–69. Grand Rapids: Baker, 2003.

———. "Calvin's Doctrine of the Knowledge of God." *Princeton Theological Review* 7 (1909) 219–325. Reprinted in *The Works of Benjamin B. Warfield*, 5:29–130. Grand Rapids: Baker, 2003.

———. "Calvin's Doctrine of the Trinity." *Princeton Theological Review* 7 (1909) 553–562. Reprinted in *The Works of Benjamin B. Warfield*, vol. 5, 189–284. Grand Rapids: Baker Books, 2003.

———. "Darwin's Argument against Christianity and against Religion." *Homiletic Review* (January 1889) 9–16. Reprinted in *Benjamin B. Warfield: Selected Shorter Writings*, edited by John E. Meeter, 2:132–41. Philipsburg, NJ: Presbyterian & Reformed, 2005.

———. "The Idea of Systematic Theology." *Presbyterian and Reformed Review* 7 (1896) 243–71. Reprinted in *The Works of Benjamin B. Warfield*, 9:49–87. Grand Rapids: Baker, 2003.

———. Introduction to *Apologetics: The Rational Vindication of the Reformed Faith*, by Francis R. Beattie, 19–32. 1903. Reprinted in *Benjamin B. Warfield: Selected Shorter Writings*, edited by John E. Meeter, 2:93–105. Philipsburg, NJ: Presbyterian & Reformed, 2005.

———. Introductory Note to *The Encyclopedia of Sacred Theology*, by Abaham Kuyper, 1898. Reprinted in *Benjamin B. Warfield: Selected Shorter Writings*, edited by John E. Meeter, 1:447–54. Philipsburg, NJ: Presbyterian & Reformed, 2005.

———. "Jesus Christ the Propitiation for the Whole World." In *The Expositor* 21 (1921) 241–53. Reprinted in *Benjamin B. Warfield: Selected Shorter Writings*, edited by John E. Meeter, 2:167–77.

———. "The Latest Phase of Historical Rationalism." *Presbyterian Quarterly* 9 (1895) 36–67, 185–210. Reprinted in *The Works of Benjamin B. Warfield*, 9:585–618. Grand Rapids: Baker, 2003.

———. "The Person of Christ." In *The International Standard Bible Encyclopedia*, edited by James Orr, 4:2338–48. 1915. Reprinted in *The Works of Benjamin B. Warfield*, 2:175–209. Grand Rapids: Baker, 2003.

———. *The Plan of Salvation*. Grand Rapids: Eerdmans, 1980.

———. "The Real Problem of Inspiration." *Presbyterian and Reformed Review* 4 (1893) 177–221. Reprinted in *The Works of Benjamin B. Warfield*, 1:169–226. Grand Rapids: Baker, 2003.

———. Review of *Some Dogmas of Religion*, by John McTaggart. *Princeton Theological Review* 5 (1907) 288–94. Reprinted in *The Works of Benjamin B. Warfield*, 10:146–54. Grand Rapids: Baker, 2003.

———. *Revelation and Inspiration*. Vol. 1 of *The Works of B. B. Warfield*. Grand Rapids: Baker, 2003.

———. "Ritschl the Rationalist." *Princeton Theological Review* 17 (1919) 533–84. Reprinted in *The Works of Benjamin B. Warfield*, 7:3–52. Grand Rapids: Baker, 2003.

———. "St. Paul's Use of the Argument from Experience." *Expositor* (March 1895) 226–36. Reprinted in *Benjamin B. Warfield: Selected Shorter Writings*, edited by John E. Meeter, 2:142–51. Philipsburg, NJ: Presbyterian & Reformed, 2005.

———. "Tertullian and the Beginnings of the Doctrine of the Trinity." *Princeton Theological Review* 3 (1905) 529–57; 4 (1906) 1–36, 145–67. Reprinted in *The Works of Benjamin B. Warfield*, 4:3–109. Grand Rapids: Baker, 2003.

———. "Trinity." In *The International Standard Bible Encyclopedia*, edited by James Orr, 5:3012–22. 1915. Reprinted in *The Works of Benjamin B. Warfield*, 2:133–172. Grand Rapids: Baker, 2003.

Wartenberg Thomas E. "Hegel's Idealism: The Logic of Conceptuality." In *The Cambridge Companion to Hegel*, edited by Frederick C. Beiser, 102–29. Cambridge: Cambridge University Press, 1993.

Weaver, Gilbert B. "Man the Analogue of God." In *Jerusalem and Athens: Critical Discussions on the Philosophy and Apologetic of Cornelius Van Til*, edited by E. R. Geehan, 321–27. Philipsburg, NJ: Presbyterian & Reformed, 1980.

White, James Emery. *What is Truth? A Comparative Study of the Positions of Cornelius Van Til, Francis Schaeffer, Carl F. H. Henry, Donald Bloesch, Millard Erickson*. Nashville, TN: Broadman and Holman, 1994.

White, William. *Van Til Defender of the Faith: An Authorized Biography*. Nashville, TN: Thomas Nelson, 1979.

Wippel, John F. "Metaphysics." In *The Cambridge Companion to Aquinas*, edited by Norman Kretzmann and Eleonore Stump, 85–127. Cambridge: Cambridge University Press, 1999.

Zachman, Randall C. *John Calvin as Teacher, Pastor, and Theologian*, 209–29. Grand Rapids: Baker Academic, 2006.

Zizioulas, John D. *Being as Communion: Studies in Personhood and the Church*. Crestwood, NY: St. Vladimir's Seminary, 2002.

Subject Index

www.ingramcontent.com/pod-product-compliance
Lightning Source LLC
LaVergne TN
LVHW010942100826
845153LV00002B/122
* 9 7 8 1 4 9 8 2 2 6 5 0 9 *